TERRORIZING WOMEN

ROSA-LINDA FREGOSO

AND CYNTHIA BEJARANO, EDITORS

TERRORIZING WOMEN

Feminicide in the Américas

WITH A PREFACE BY MARCELA LAGARDE Y DE LOS RÍOS

 DUKE UNIVERSITY PRESS   DURHAM AND LONDON   2010

© 2010 Duke University Press
All rights reserved
Printed in the United States of
America on acid-free paper ∞
Typeset in Carter and Cone Galliard
with Gill Sans display
by Keystone Typesetting, Inc.
Library of Congress Cataloging-in-
Publication Data appear on the last
printed page of this book.

IN MEMORY OF
THE WOMEN AND GIRLS
WHO HAVE BEEN MURDERED
AND DISAPPEARED.

Contents

MARCELA LAGARDE Y DE LOS RÍOS
Translated by Charlie Roberts

Preface:
Feminist Keys for
Understanding Feminicide

THEORETICAL, POLITICAL, AND
LEGAL CONSTRUCTION

It all began over the alarm sounded to bring attention to the crimes against girls and women in Ciudad Juárez more than fifteen years ago.

From the horror and dismay came protests and demands for justice. Nonetheless, time passed, and there was no satisfactory response from the authorities. Organizations were established to provide support to the victims' relatives and to struggle against violence against women, and groups cropped up to provide services to victims that spoke out forcefully as part of social movements in defense of human rights and of women's and feminist movements. Despite such initiatives, the homicides have continued. Voices of protest spoke out first locally and then nationally; since then, Ciudad Juárez has become known worldwide for crimes committed against girls and women through intense campaigns to dismantle the impunity that has accompanied these killings.

The concept of feminicide has transcended the borders of Mexico—and rightfully so—because the organizations engaged in the process of seeking justice, and in the more general social movement, have had recourse to international organizations, both civil and intergovernmental. Statements and reports have been issued by Amnesty International; the Inter-American Court of Human Rights; the European Parliament; legislatures of European countries, such as the Congreso de los Diputados of Spain; the U.S. Congress; local governments in several countries; nongovernmental organizations (NGOs); and women's networks, among many others. In her most recent visit to Mexico, United

Nations High Commissioner for Human Rights Louise Arbour made very strong statements about feminicide to the government.

Mexico has received more than fifty recommendations from international human rights agencies and rapporteurs of several United Nations mechanisms. They include demands that the government determine the facts in all of the cases, ensure access to justice for the victims' family members, and increasingly implement policies with a gender perspective to confront the crimes and their causes and to eradicate violence against women and impunity (Comisión Especial para Conocer 2006c).

The civic organizations and families have received expressions of direct solidarity and have taken joint action to pressure the authorities and to raise awareness of violence against women. They have toured other countries; participated in forums, conferences, and press conferences; and told the stories, time and again, of what happened to daughters, sisters, students, or tourists and have found great sympathy. Yet they have been treated unjustly, with contempt, paternalism, lack of professionalism, negligence, and violence, by the widest array of authorities, from the police, public ministries, prosecutors, female attorneys (*procuradoras*), and directors of mechanisms put in place to serve women to governors and presidents of the republic. Family members and activists have knocked on institutional doors and helped organize hearings, speeches, and rituals of governmental exaltation and artistic festivals of solidarity, such as the annual International Day for the Elimination of Violence against Women on November 25; the sixteen days of activism; and International Women's Day on March 8. Although they face intimidation and violence, as well as all types of efforts to manipulate the situation, they continue to fight for justice.

Ideologies and Other Practices

A particular culture has emerged around the crimes of Ciudad Juárez and Chihuahua constituted by how what has happened is addressed, and also by literary and poetic, pictorial, sculptural, musical, photographic, theatrical, filmic, and other artistic creations. The communications media — including the print media, radio, and, especially, television, as well as national and international news programs — have gone to the scene and covered the issue from various perspectives, ranging from yellow journalism to serious journalistic analysis in pursuit of the truth. Academics have also approached the issue, and long-term research projects have been undertaken, as well as theses, essays, courses, seminars, and short courses (*diplomados*), all motivated by a profound commitment to contribute, through scientific inquiry, to the analysis of the situation to take action and eradicate crimes against girls and women.

Besides originating out of indignation and a commitment to justice, NGOs have taken action to provide legal, psychological, and economic services and support to the victims while also constituting a forum for critical discussion, information, lobbying, and pressuring the authorities. They have also created observatories to monitor the process. They have maintained the voice of protest, demanded justice, and mobilized solidarity. They began by asking how many had been killed and set out to count them. They have forcefully demanded, time and again, "*Ni una muerta más* (Not one more dead woman)!"

The movement has given rise to the most varied political expressions: demonstrations, rallies, religious rituals, protest encampments, exhibitions, and installations. It has also engaged in broad creativity and skill building and capacity building with groups, organizations, and individuals to become informed of the situation, acquire certain knowledge, and even get academic training and dealt with all kinds of individuals and philanthropic, financial, and solidarity institutions, in Mexico and elsewhere, with whom it should engage.

APPROACHES

Explanations that reflect different ideologies and different degrees and levels of knowledge and information — journalistic, academic, and political — circulate in the media and among the organizations.

There has been speculation based on criminology in which hypotheses are put forth as to whether the assailants are serial killers. Psychiatric profiles are suggested that consider them mentally ill or psychotic. Psychoanalytic and semiotic approaches see the crimes and the criminals as part of a system of communication and power based on belonging to fraternities and forms of totalitarian control over bodies and territories (Segato 2003c, 2006).

There are also sociological and anthropological analyses that examine the crimes in the context of the reality of the border zone and that consider the economic status, class, and power of the female victims and of the perpetrators, as well as the impact of the North American Free Trade Agreement and the *maquilas* (cross-border assembly plants) on uneven and disorganized development, marginalization, and poverty (Washington Valdez 2005). There are also studies on the links between the rise of the so-called Juárez Cartel and the first gender-based crimes.

Finally, there are culturalist perspectives that, in combination with prior explanations, emphasize the *machista* and misogynist culture that is supposedly a core trait of Mexican identity.

Some points of view are simplistic and traditional, and others are more evolved, documented, and complex. The simplistic and traditional points of view have helped generate fantastic myths; the more evolved views have made very important contributions to profound and complex scientific knowledge not only of the violence but also of its relationship to patriarchal social organization and patriarchal power.[1] Some reproduce an "otherness" in their perspective: It is others who engage in this conduct. There are some who note the exceptional nature of certain prevailing characteristics in the area, a border region with many migrants and a high incidence of crime.

The predominant trend depicts the crimes as a phenomenon, as an unusual, exceptional occurrence that only happens there and only in that way. Several hypotheses circulate, with great credibility, that tie the homicides of girls and women to other criminal activities and groups, such as the selection of the victims and the use of their damaged bodies as coded languages among powerful men, businessmen, or among criminals and their gangs. It is presumed that there are ties between the homicides of girls and women and organized crime and drug trafficking (González Rodríguez 2002). The killings have also been said to be related to the direct production and marketing of hardcore pornography and other perverse forms of the violent reification of women.

For several years, the authorities have failed to disclose any information on their inquiries or have done so only in a partial, incomplete, and confused manner. They have acted inefficiently in prosecuting crimes; they have even had to release a person allegedly responsible who was tortured and have fostered widespread distrust of law enforcement and its institutions. There has been a full-fledged confrontation among NGOs, press, and public officials. How many girls and women have been killed? The authorities contradict themselves almost all the time. There is no certainty in many cases that the victims correspond to the bodies or remains handed over to loved ones, and it is not known whether some girls and women who have disappeared correspond to unidentified corpses. In more recent cases, an arduous effort has been made to ensure better investigations in technical terms and to secure the involvement of forensic anthropologists to identify remains in unresolved cases. For fifteen years, disinformation, uncertainty, and anxiety have held sway, fostering the exaggeration or downplaying of the facts with a sensationalist tone.

Most notable is the omission of the key fact — key because it is consistent and apparent: The vast majority of the crimes are committed against girls and women. The victims' gender is taken into account only as one more item of information, as if it were merely a question of classifying the victims as "male" or "female" without any social context or consideration of oppressive power relations. In the extreme, the victim's gender is treated with bias and, if gender is taken into consideration, it is to point to the victim's evident culpability.

In this way, there is no recognition or investigation of the gender status of the girls and women who have been the victims and of the assailants who, in the immense majority of cases, are men. There is no analysis of the overall conditions in analyzing a multi-determinate event. The scientific perspective in general that one finds in academics, politics, and in the defense of human rights — in particular, women's human rights — is set aside. Androcentrism envelops most of the information and most of the investigation into the problem and gives rise to partial speculation, failing to address the core of the problem.

In an early effort to become familiar with the situation, and basing my opinions on available knowledge, I recall repeating — as so many continue to repeat — that the women murdered in Ciudad Juárez were poor and young; that many of them worked in the maquilas; that they were dark-skinned and had long hair; and that they had been kidnapped, humiliated, tortured, mutilated, and raped before they were killed in cold blood and their bodies were left in the street, in the desert, or in open spaces.

The stereotype was cast and persists, despite other evidence.

As a feminist anthropologist, I was asked by feminist colleagues who were involved in the investigation of the cases to contribute to an explanation of the events in Ciudad Juárez. I proposed to analyze the crimes against women and girls through a feminist lens and to define them as feminicide. The category and theory of feminicide emerge from feminist theory through the works of Diana Russell and Jill Radford. I based my own analysis on their theoretical and empirical work as elaborated in their volume *Femicide: The Politics of Woman Killing* (1992). The translation for femicide is *femicidio*. However, I translated femicide as *feminicidio*, and this is how it has circulated. In Spanish, *femicidio* is homologous to homicide and solely means the homicide of women. For this reason, I preferred *feminicidio* in order to differentiate from *femicidio* and to name the ensemble of violations of women's human rights, which contain the crimes against and the disappearances of women. I proposed that all these be considered as "crimes against humanity." *Femini-*

cide is genocide against women, and it occurs when the historical conditions generate social practices that allow for violent attempts against the integrity, health, liberties, and lives of girls and women.

From Feminicide to Feminicidal Violence

In 2003, I agreed to run as a candidate for the lower house of the Mexican federal legislature, the Chamber of Deputies. I was elected and became a member of that legislative body with the firm purpose of taking action to address feminicide and to legislate on the matter and with a view to adopting legislation that spelled out the crime of feminicide.

The previous legislature had formed an entity known as the Special Commission to Monitor the Investigations into the Homicides of Girls and Women in Ciudad Juárez. It was our hope that another such entity would be formed by the 59th Legislature. I already had incipient information about and reports of crimes against girls and women in other parts of Mexico. For this reason, the group of legislators from the Partido de la Revolución Democrática (Revolutionary Democratic Party; PRD), of which I was part, proposed — and the Chamber of Deputies approved — the creation of a Special Commission to Make Known and Monitor Feminicides in Mexico and Efforts to Secure Justice in Such Cases (Comisión Especial para Conocor y Dar Seguimiento a las Investigaciones Relacionadas con los Feminicidios en la República Mexicana y a la Procuración de Justicia Vinculada).

This represented enormous conceptual and political progress, because the inquiry was not limited to the events in Juárez. Instead, it encompassed the whole country, and the subject was no longer *homicides* of girls and women but *feminicides*. For the first time, a legislative commission included the term *feminicide* in its name and sought from a feminist gender perspective to gain familiarity with the problem, take action, and help eradicate it.

The name of the Special Commission did not, as I would have liked, contain the words "on feminicide in Mexico." Instead, the Junta de Coordinación Política (Board of Political Coordination) chose to use the words "on feminicides." This created confusion about whether each homicide should be called a feminicide — the version that has come into popular use through the media and the movement — or whether a set of homicides in a given territory should be called "feminicide."

Before long, the Special Commission developed several lines of work, including denouncing such homicides when they happened and demanding justice; shifting the focus of investigation from feminicide or feminicides to feminicidal violence to produce more knowledge about the violation of women's human rights in Ciudad Juárez and throughout Mexico; and producing legislation on feminicide. In this context, I made a proposal to typify feminicide; over time, other legislators introduced other initiatives. Another line of work was approving a budget to do this work and to confront violence against women.

The Diagnostic Research

To learn more about the problem, the Speical Commission performed an assessment of feminicidal violence throughout the country (Comisión Especial para Conocer 2006b, 2006c). For the first time, research was done based on official information about what had happened from 1999 to 2006, only in relation to intentional and unintentional homicides (*homicidios dolosos* and *homicidios culposos*, or murder and manslaughter). We wanted to learn the scale of the problem in Ciudad Juárez and in the rest of the country.

Crimes against girls and women were examined in the framework of gender violence and in relation to all forms of violence against girls and women on which we found official information. The results of the research were surprising: One thousand two hundred and five girls and women were murdered in all of Mexico in 2004, which means that an average of four girls and women were murdered per day.[2] More than six thousand girls and women were murdered in the six years from 1999 to 2005. Accordingly, one can deduce that more than one thousand girls and women are murdered every year in Mexico, and the situation has not changed.

The following figures and rates are for 2004, the only year for which we had official information from twenty-nine states and Mexico City, which allows for a comparison. Different data came from different sources, and not all used the same methodology. The figure for girls and women murdered is from the offices of the Attorney General (Procuradurías Generales de Justicia) of each state and the Mexico City; some include intentional and unintentional homicides, but most include only intentional homicides, excluding unintentional homicides from the count. The analysis must consider that the missing part of these data means that the figures are lower. And lacking more information, they allow for only a cautious approximation. The state rates of female homicides are based on the same criteria; only the number of intentional homicides per 100,000 women is calculated, and such figures do not include unintentional homicides. Therefore, they are not comparable, either, and are merely indicative. See, for example, the case of Veracruz, whose rate of 1.144 per 100,000 people is low, in relative terms, and the number of homicides of girls and women is very high, at 264, when adding up the intentional and unintentional homicides, yet the rate is calculated based only on the intentional homicides, leaving out the unintentional ones, of which there were 188, many more than the seventy-six intentional ones. The state of Mexico, with eighty-six homicides of girls and women, has a very high rate of 4.136 per 100,000, even though they did not include unintentional homicides. How high would the rate be if they were to include them?[3]

The Servicio Médico Forense (Forensic Medical Service) reported that 743 girls and women were murdered in Mexico City, the country's capital, in the five years from 1999 to 2005. The Procuraduría General de la República (Office of the Attorney-General) reported that in the twelve years from 1993 to 2005, a total of 379 girls and women were killed by intentional homicide in Ciudad Juárez, Chihuahua.

Who Were They?

The girls and women murdered in Mexico had different ages, and included girls, elderly women, young women, older women, and adolescents. They belonged to all social classes and socioeconomic strata; some were rich women, from the upper class and the elite, though the majority were poor or marginal. The full array included illiterate women, with little schooling (as was the case for most of the victims), though there were also students in vocational schools and universities, and graduate students with excellent academic records. To their assailants, these women, either single or married, were spouses, former spouses, coinhabitants, girlfriends, former girlfriends, daughters, step-daughters, daughters-in-law, mothers, mothers-in-law, cousins, close friends, neighbors, employees, bosses, subordinates, or unknown. Their occupations varied: the victims were service providers, dancers, peasants, teachers, vendors, waitresses, researchers, models, actresses, and bureaucrats. Most were hard-working girls and women; some were on vacation, others were unemployed students and transients. Also killed were women associated with criminals, and upstanding citizens, activists, politicians, and women in government. Almost all were Mexican, and among them, some were Tzotzil, (such as the Lunas of Acteal), Rarámuris, and Nahua. Others were foreigners, including those from Canada, the Netherlands, the United States, El Salvador, Korea, Brazil, and Guatemala. Most were killed in their homes, though some bodies were found in the street, in a vacant lot, along a roadside, in a ravine, in a store, at a construction site, in a car, in a cave, in an upland area, along a highway, in the desert, in a river, or in a house for holding kidnap victims, and it is not known where they were killed. Some had marks of sexual violence, though in most cases there is no trace of sexual violence. Some were pregnant, others were disabled; some were locked up, others kidnapped. All were tortured, mistreated, and intimidated, and they experienced fear and humiliation before being killed. Some were beaten to death, others were strangled, decapitated, hung, stabbed, and shot; some were mutilated and bound. For some, their remains were placed in a sack, a suitcase, or a box, put in concrete, dismembered, burnt, or stretched. All were held in captivity; all were isolated and unprotected. Terrified, they experienced the most extreme impotence in their defenselessness. All were assaulted and subjected to violence until death. Some of their bodies were mistreated even after they had been murdered.

Most of the crimes remain in impunity.

Feminicidal Violence

Research on feminicide arose from the acknowledgment that in Mexico, and worldwide to different degrees, all women experience forms of gender violence in the course of their lives, and many also experience class, racial, religious, judicial, legal, and political or cultural violence. There is an evident simultaneity and cross-fertilization of various forms of violence linked to various forms of social oppression. All women experience violations of their human rights stemming from the subaltern social status and political subordination of gender that affects them. It is in that framework that feminicide must be explained.

Accordingly, violence against girls and women was recognized in its specificity, framed in the political gender relationships between women and men and in the relationships of class, ethnicity, and age, and it was associated with the complexity of social status, life situation, and position of women. Research was done on institutions' interventions to address gender violence against women, as well as government policies to learn of their content in terms of gender equality and equity and the budgets earmarked to that end. An analysis was done of the legislation, and misogynistic content, or content that was identified as being at odds with gender equality, gender equity, and the advancement of girls and women.

Due to the enormous differences and the inequality characteristic of Mexico, regional geographic criteria were used with the categories center, north, or south; capital city and province, city, and town; southern or northern border; and regions with a presence of indigenous peoples, as well as regions with high, medium, and low levels of human development. A feminist analysis was done of gender and human rights. We also relied on the human-development paradigm and methodology. The human-development indicators used by the United Nations Development Program were used as guidance for research, including the Human Development Index, the Gender Development Index, and the Gender Empowerment Index.[4] The Human Security Index had yet to be published (Lagarde y de los Ríos 1996).

I am certain that no one knew, until then, that Nayarit should be a matter of concern for us, as it was the leading state for feminicide in Mexico, with a rate of homicides for girls and women estimated at 4.485 per 100,000 people.[5]

Working with these results, we made progress in theorizing about feminicide, which had been limited to homicides, and the category of feminicidal violence, which implies the violent deaths of girls and women such as those that result from accidents, suicides, neglect of health, and violence. Of course, the whole set of determining factors that cause them came to have an empirical grounding. This definition takes as the point of departure the assumption that such deaths are caused in the framework of gender oppression and other forms of oppression and therefore are avoidable. Because of this, they are violent deaths.

A Few Findings

The results of the diagnostic research make it possible to verify several theoretical theses, including that violence against women is serious and complex and results from multiple factors. It results from the synergistic articulation of a set of determinations based on domination and sex.

Gender-based violence articulated with the violence inherent in classism, racism, and age and ethnic discrimination, as well as any sectarianism, is a constant reality for women of all ages, social classes, socioeconomic groups, regions, and parts of Mexico.

The prevailing violence is worse where there is less social development of women; it affects mostly women with little or no schooling, but women with higher education have not been exempt from it. Violence is aggravated under permanent or temporary conditions of social exclusion and situations of dependence or of minimal or nonexistent citizenship for women. Under patriarchal normality, the existence of any woman placed in isolation or under total domination is at risk, for she may be subjected to harm, independent of her wishes and conscience.

Feminicidal violence is the extreme, the culmination of many forms of gender violence against women that represent an attack on their human rights and that lead them to various forms of violent death. In many cases, these forms of gender violence are tolerated by society and the state; at other times, citizens live feminicidal violence with powerlessness, for there are few channels available for the enforcement of rights.

Feminicidal violence is produced by the patriarchal, hierarchical, and social organization of gender, based on supremacy and inferiority, that creates gender inequality between women and men. It is also due to the women's exclusion from power structures or their exposure to oppressive powers, be they personal, social, or institutional. And it results from the acceptance and tolerance that are demonstrated by the multiple complicities among supremacist, macho, and misogynist men — indeed, from the social silences that prevail about those who commit crimes and are not punished.

The impunity that stems from the inaction, insufficiency, or complicity of state institutions with gender inequality contributes to feminicidal violence — and, therefore, to violence against girls and women. This constitutes institutional gender violence by omission, negligence, or complicity of the authorities with the assailants when it is a question of violence inflicted on women by persons or groups. Institutional violence also results from the acceptance of inequalities, discrimination, and violence as normal, which reinforces the permanence of state structures that perpetuate gender inequality and do not recognize or guarantee the rights of women. To the contrary, they act in defense of patriarchalism in both society and the state.

Feminicidal violence flourishes under the hegemony of a patriarchal culture that legitimates despotism, authoritarianism, and the cruel, sexist — macho, misogynist, homophobic, and lesbophobic — treatment reinforced by classism, racism, xenophobia, and other forms of discrimination.

The failure to consider what crime is constituted by the whole set of harmful acts that put women's lives at risk helps reproduce feminicidal violence. Even though many forms of violence against women are criminal offenses, to violate women is not considered a crime. That is the opinion of even those whose duty it is to prosecute and sit in judgment of the perpetrators of such violence and who should provide protection and ensure women's right to live in safety and free from violence. Violent men therefore enjoy an ideological and political complicity between authorities and assailants.[6] In such a climate, there is a clear absence of democratic rule of law in relation to women.

The structural conditions of the social organization of genders are the foundation for feminicidal violence. Even though there has been progress, the state continues to foster the conditions in which gender oppression finds expression.

To varying degrees, the failure or omission on the part of the state, in terms of not promoting or advancing equality between women and men or gender equity, contributes actively to feminicidal violence. Women are not considered people with rights; nor are they treated as citizens. Therefore, the authorities who should be seeking justice in many cases act as accomplices of the assailants in attacking women's security, dignity, and interests. It is also apparent that women are not deemed to have full rights in the areas of education, health, the economy, and politics. Women's advancement should be a priority for the state.

In summary, in Mexico there are two levels at which the rule of law has broken down in relation to women: first, in the concept of legality, which does not apply to women; and second, in the everyday gender violence perpetrated by men in social life, further violating the human rights of persons and legality. The institutions are overtaken because they are obsolete or because the law and the procedures for its enforcement are obsolete. In social life, illegality prevails across multiple spheres and activities, and women, who are already disadvantaged by their gender, find themselves at even greater risk.

Addendum: Some Anthropological and Legal Categories

After arduous processes of analysis, going back and forth between theory, empirical results, and the legislative possibilities, that is, what can be legislated, I gradually refined my own categories.[7] They are as follows:

GENDER VIOLENCE

Gender violence is misogynist violence against women for being women situated in relationships marked by gender inequality: oppression, exclusion, subordination, discrimination, exploitation, and marginalization. Women are victims of threats, assaults, mistreatment, injuries, and misogynist harm. The violence may be physical, psychological, sexual, economic, and property-related, and the modalities of gender violence may be in the family, workplace, or school; in the community; in institutions; and via feminicide.

FEMINICIDE

Feminicide is one of the extreme forms of gender violence; it is constituted by the whole set of violent misogynist acts against women that involve a violation of their human rights, represent an attack on their safety, and endanger their lives. It culminates in the murder of girls and women. Feminicide is able to occur because the authorities who are omissive, negligent, or acting in collusion with the assailants perpetrate institutional violence against women by blocking their access to justice and thereby contributing to impunity. Feminicide entails a partial breakdown of the rule of law because the state is incapable of guaranteeing respect for women's lives or human rights and because it is incapable of acting in keeping with the law and to uphold the law, to prosecute and administer justice, and to prevent and eradicate the violence that causes it. Feminicide is a state crime.

FEMINICIDE AS A LEGAL CATEGORY

The political construct defining feminicide as a crime was approved by the Chamber of Deputies but was subsequently rejected by the Senate, where a report is to be issued.[8] A draft decree has been proposed that amends several definitions of the Federal Code of Criminal Procedure. For example, article 1 proposes that the third chapter on feminicide is added to the second title of the second book, and Article 149 reads as follows:

> One who, for the purpose of totally or partially destroying one or more groups of women on grounds of their gender status, perpetrates, by any means, crimes against the lives of the women belonging to the group or groups. This offense shall be punished by a prison term of 20 to 40 years, and a fine of 4,000 to 10,000 pesos. For the purposes of this article, gender status is understood to be the social construction that determines stereotyped sociocultural behaviors, in which women are at a disadvantage, face discrimination, and are at high risk as a result of an unequal power relationship. When the offense is committed by a public servant, the penalty shall be increased by up to one-half.

THE LAW AND THE CATEGORIES

In the cause to eradicate violence against women and girls and to construct their human rights, legislating is part of an all-encompassing process that involves social movements, activism, study, and awareness-building, as well as the possibility of theoretically naming, from a feminist gender perspective, those facts that are made invisible, irrelevant, or considered normal; of making them visible; of creating knowledge; and then of having the capacity to introduce into law guidelines, mechanisms, and policies configured as a binding legal framework. One will have to build the capacities that make it possible to go forward along the arduous path for the law to become a matter of state policy, and to become a way of life and of coexistence.

Therefore, having contributed to this law has been significant, as it contains a feminist perspective and is the only law in the Mexican legal framework in which women are recognized as juridical subjects and in which the legal interest protected is the life of women. It is also important to have placed in the body of the General Law of Women's Access to a Life Free from Violence concepts and categories that are fundamental to this philosophical, theoretical, and political approach.[9] As legal categories, their enunciation contains the hypotheses of their transformation. Let us conclude with some definitions that in Mexico are now law.

FEMINICIDAL VIOLENCE, GENDER VIOLENCE ALERT, AND GENDER VIOLENCE

Chapter V on feminicidal violence and the gender violence alert Article 21.

> Feminicidal violence is the extreme form of gender violence against women, the result of the violation of their human rights in the public and private spheres; it is made up of the whole set of misogynistic forms of conduct — mistreatment and physical, psychological, sexual, educational, economic, property-related, family, community, institutional violence — that entail social impunity and impunity by the state, and, on placing women at risk and in a defenseless position, may culminate in homicide or attempted homicide — that is, in feminicide and in other forms of violent death of girls and women, specifically death due to accidents and suicide and preventable deaths stemming from lack of security, neglect, and exclusion from development and democracy.

Article 22 of Chapter V states: "Gender violence alert is the whole set of emergency government actions to confront and eradicate feminicidal violence in a given local or regional area, whether by individuals or the community itself." And Article 23 of Chapter V states: "The gender violence alert on violence against women shall have as its fundamental objective to ensure women's safety and the end of violence against them, and eliminate the inequalities produced by legislation that harms their human rights."

Notes

A preliminary version of this chapter was requested by the State Secretariat for International Cooperation to be published in the book *Nuevas líneas de investigación y mecanismos de conocimiento*, University, Gender, and Development Series (Universidad Autónoma de Madrid, in press).

1. Part of the research by Patricia Ravelo was used as the basis for the text "Violencia feminicida en Chihuahua" (Ravelo 2005b). Also relevant are Monárrez Fragoso 2000, 2001, 2005a; Monárrez Fragoso and Fuentes 2004.

2. This figure and the preceding one come from the Instituto Nacional de Estadística, Geografía e Informática (National Institute for Statistical and Geographic Information; INEGI) and Secretaría de Salud (Ministry of Health; SSA). See Cámara de Diputados del H. Congreso de la Unión 2006.

3. Ibid.

4. United Nations Development Program, "Human Development Report," Centro de Comunicación Investigación y Documentación entre Europa, España y América Latina, Madrid, 1993; idem, "Human Development Report," Fondo de Cultura Económica, Mexico City, 1994; idem, "Human Development Report," Harla, Mexico City, 1995; idem, "Human Development Report," Mundi-Prensa, Madrid, 1996.

5. This rate is four times greater than the lowest, which is for Yucatán, with .560 homicides per 100,000 people.

6. Celia Amorós (1990) analyzes the patriarchal politics stemming from identification among men and their serial patriarchal pacts — among others, the exclusion of women that it implies, which is itself a form of violence and which is the basis for other forms of violence against women.

7. The categories cited here were the basis for creating the legal categories found in the Ley General de Acceso de las Mujeres a una Vida Libre de Violencia (General Law of Women's Access to a Life Free from Violence), which entered into force in Mexico on February 2, 2007.

8. This legislative definition of feminicide as criminal conduct is found in the General Law of Women's Access to a Life Free from Violence and definition of feminicide as a crime against humanity, initiatives approved by the Honorable Chamber of Deputies (Comisión Especial para Conocer 2006e).

9. This law was a major step forward in taking on violence against women. The legislative report issued on its adoption notes that it is "the first law in the Ibero-American countries which develop[s] the different forms of violence from a gender and women's human rights perspective: violence in the family, violence in the community, violence in the workplace, violence in schools, institutional violence, and feminicidal violence, in addition to establishing the mechanisms for eradicating each of these forms of violence" (Comisión Especial para Conocer 2006e).

Acknowledgments

My appreciation and thanks go to Waded Cruzado, past provost and interim president of New Mexico State University (NMSU); Pam Jansma, former dean of the College of Arts and Sciences; and Jim Maupin, head of the Criminal Justice Department, for their support for this project. I also recognize Craig B. Schroer, the Benson Latin American Collection's Electronic Information Services librarian at the University of Texas, Austin, and Molly Molloy, Latin American and Border Studies librarian at New Mexico State University, for their research expertise.

Numerous people helped bring this anthology to fruition. Sonia Flynn helped translate and edit the *testimonios*; my colleagues and friends Victor Muñoz, Dana Greene, Andrea Trimarco, Cristina Morales, and Dulcinea Lara accompanied me to countless protests. To Sally Meisenhelder, *mi comadre en la lucha*: thanks for your loyalty and fierce commitment to fighting for women through Amigos de las Mujeres de Juárez. To Jeff Shepherd, thank you for reading sections of this manuscript, participating in advocacy work at the border, and accompanying me through this journey; you are my rock. To my family, your patience, prayers, and endurance are invaluable to me. And finally, to the families of the murdered and disappeared women and girls of Ciudad Juárez and Chihuahua City, Chihuahua, Mexico, and their advocates, *muchas gracias* for your tremendous bravery in the search for justice. Your example and histories will remain with me, always. *No nos olvidaremos de ustedes, ni de ellas*. We honor your courageous efforts through this collection.

CYNTHIA BEJARANO

I received financial support for this project from the Social Science division and the Chicano/Latino Research Center at the University of California, Santa Cruz (UCSC), and the Office of the Provost at the University of Southern California (USC). My thanks to the staff in the Social Sciences division at UCSC and School of Cinematic Arts at USC for expediting these funds. In the course of working on this book I have benefited from lively and spirited discussions with graduate students in my seminars on human rights and feminism at UCSC and on human rights in the Americas at USC. I am indebted to the filmmaker Lourdes Portillo for introducing me to the issue of feminicide. Special thanks to my colleague Jonathan Fox (Latin American and Latino studies, UCSC) for his generous comments. I am especially grateful to my sister Angela Fregoso for permission to publish her photographs and for traveling with me to monthly protests in Ciudad Juárez. To my partner, Herman Gray, and my family, thank you for your support and encouragement. My deepest appreciation and respect goes to *familias* and activists on the front line of the struggle to end injustices. It is from their courageous and determined acts, their persistence, perseverance, and unyielding insistence that we learn how to forge a better future for our children and a more humane and just world.

ROSA-LINDA FREGOSO

We are both indebted to research assistants at our respective institutions. Cynthia thanks the graduate assistants who helped compile data for this project: Emilia Bernal, Mario Cano, Lydia Guerrero, Praveen Kanumala, and Amith Patel, all from NMSU. Rosa-Linda thanks her UCSC graduate assistant Sandra Alvarez for coordinating the initial soliciting of manuscripts and Evelyn Parada and Irene Sánchez at UCSC and Noelia Saenz at USC for invaluable assistance.

We also thank John Cheney at USC and D. Travers Scott, also at USC, for his assistance in the preparation of this manuscript for final submission to Duke University Press. At Duke, we are especially indebted to Ken Wissoker for his advice, wisdom, and support for this project. We thank the three anonymous readers whose hard questions, probing comments, and suggestions have made this a much better work.

We also acknowledge the feminist activist Esther Chávez Cano for her women's rights advocacy and tireless work to end gender violence in Ciudad Juárez. She died on December 25, 2009, after a long battle with cancer. Finally, we express our heartfelt appreciation and gratitude to the activists, attorneys, journalists, academics, filmmakers, and community members who have committed themselves to this journey and to the contributors to *Terrorizing Women: Feminicide in the Américas*, who risk their lives to tell these stories. *Ni una más.*

ROSA-LINDA FREGOSO
AND CYNTHIA BEJARANO

Introduction:
A Cartography of Feminicide
in the Américas

> I insist on being shocked. I am never going to become immune. I think
> that's a kind of failure, to see so much [human atrocity] that you die
> inside. I want to be surprised and shocked every time.
> —Toni Morrison, *Toni Morrison Uncensored*

We are driven to write this book by our shock and outrage at the ongoing atrocities whose fissures and replication imperil our human communities. As Toni Morrison asserts, we insist on being shocked, refuse to
become immune to the large-scale violence that began in the 1990s and
that, as Arjun Appadurai (2006, 10) reminds us, "appear[s] to be typically accompanied by a surplus of rage and excess of hatred." Our focus
in this book is on the low-intensity warfare waged on women's bodies
that is now routine in many Latin American countries.

Prior to the brutality committed against women's bodies during the
ethnic conflicts in Bosnia-Herzegovina and Rwanda, the international
community had been slow in recognizing the historical reality of wartime violence against women, the fact that gender-based violence "is an
integral and pervasive component of warfare" (Moshan 1998, 1).[1]

We are never going to become immune, so we name gender-based
violence as a weapon of terror. Since World War Two alone, the incidents of rape during armed conflicts are shocking, from the German
Nazi soldiers' raping Jewish and Soviet women to the raping of Viet-
namese women by U.S. soldiers and the sexual atrocities committed
against women during civil wars in Liberia and Sierra Leone.[2]

There have been even more cases of horrendous, terrifying assaults
committed against women during counterinsurgency wars in Latin

America: the use of rape as a tool of terror by security forces in El Salvador, Perú, and Haiti; in death camps and torture chambers during Argentina's and Chile's Dirty Wars. In Honduras, the notorious Battalion 3–16 sexually tortured and raped women prisoners; during the thirty-six-year war, Guatemalan security forces raped indigenous women and girls.

Even as mass raping of women in recent armed conflicts continues,[3] the international community no longer disavows sexual violence of this magnitude. Due in large measure to the presence of female journalists covering the war in the former Yugoslavia, immense media and political attention focused on gender-based violence as an integral and pervasive weapon of war. But it has taken years of feminist advocacy in law and international forums to shift public discourse and understanding of gender-based persecution in wartime. "The development of international laws addressing gender-based violence during the twentieth century," according to Nicole Eva Erb (1998, 407), "demonstrates a clear progression from an atmosphere of unspoken tolerance, in which rape and sexual assault were considered inevitable byproducts of war, to a climate approaching zero-tolerance, in which gender-based violence is gradually understood as a discrete criminal category requiring special recognition under international humanitarian law."

Largely at the behest of the Women's Caucus for Gender Justice, rape and other forms of sexual violence are defined within the newly constituted International Criminal Court (ICC) at the Hague as "war crimes" and "crimes against humanity" if they occur as "systematic and widespread attacks against civilians." One of the major feats of the Women's Caucus is the extension of these criteria to enumerate persecution based on gender as constituting a "crime against humanity." As the Women's Caucus successfully argued in 1997, "Gender crimes are incidents of violence targeting or affecting women exclusively or disproportionately, not because the victims of such crimes are of a particular religion or race, but *because* they are women" (Moshan 1998, 155; emphasis added).

Yet gender-based violence of a widespread and systematic nature does not occur just during war or armed conflicts; large-scale violence against women often continues in "post-conflict" situations. Nor are all "gender crimes" widespread and systematic; many occur in everyday life and involve private individuals, acting alone or in groups, targeting civilians.[4] As members of the Women's Caucus asserted, gender violations do not have to be systematically or prevalently enacted to be "brutal" and "extreme,"[5] and they often occur outside the "existence of some type of hostilities" (Charlesworth 1999, 389). The effects of violence do not necessarily end when hostilities are over. Alongside "direct violence" there is "indirect violence," or "the long term effects of armed conflict, which often disproportionately affect women" (Brems 2003, 119). Large-scale violence may involve a combination of everyday, arbitrary interpersonal (private) *and* widespread and systematic (public) gender-based atrocities occurring both in "peacetime" *and* in times of war (see Lagarde y de los Ríos, this volume).[6]

During the last decade of the twentieth century, we witnessed unspeakable forms of degradation and violation of women's bodies and their being: disappearances, murders, mangled, burned and tortured bodies, raped girls and women, both in the context of wartime and so-called "peacetime."[7] Women's rights advocates, researchers, and feminist legal scholars are using the terms *femicide* and *feminicide* to refer to this phenomenon.

This volume examines the growing incidents of feminicide as it has been elaborated in the writings of feminist researchers, witness–survivors, women's rights and human rights advocates, and legal theorists working on and from regions in Latin America. We aim to stage a trans-disciplinary dialogue between academics, legal theorists, and practitioners of human rights, from the global South and North, whose cumulative expertise and knowledge offer a new discursive framing and critical grounding for understanding the phenomenon of what is now widely recognized as feminicide.[8]

The concepts of feminicide and femicide are used interchangeably in the literature on gender-based violence and among the contributors to this volume. These are evolving concepts that, as noted in Bueno-Hansen's chapter, are "still under construction." However, we will make a case for *feminicide* and, in the process, contribute some analytic tools for thinking about the concept in historical, theoretical, and political terms. In arguing for the use of the term *feminicide* over *femicide*, we draw from a feminist analytical perspective that interrupts essentialist notions of female identity that equate gender and biological sex and looks instead to the gendered nature of practices and behaviors, along with the performance of gender norms. As feminist thinkers have long contended, gender is a socially constructed category in which the performance of gender norms (rather than a natural biological essence) is what gives meaning to categories of the "feminine" and "masculine." Instead of a scenario in which gender and sex necessarily concur, the concept of feminicide allows us to map the power dynamics and relations of gender, sexuality, race, and class underlying violence and, in so doing, shift the analytic focus to how gender norms, inequities, and power relationships increase women's vulnerability to violence.

Our elaboration of feminicide is based on the knowledge and expertise of feminist and legal scholars, researchers, and activists working in the fields of human rights and gender justice throughout Latin America. In preferring the concept feminicide over femicide, we aim to register the shift in meanings as the concept traveled from its usage in the English-language (North) to a Spanish-speaking (South) context. In other words, we are using *feminicide* to mark our discursive and material contributions and perspectives as transborder feminist thinkers from the global South (the Américas) in its redefinition—one that exceeds the merely derivative. Although we have translated *feminicide* literally from the Spanish word *feminicidio*, which, in turn, derives from the English *femicide*—a concept developed by, among others, the U.S.-based feminist sociologist Diana Russell—the translation we are speaking of is also discursive. From a linguistic angle *feminicidio* (rather than *femicidio*) is a more accurate translation for *femicide*, given the particularities of the Spanish language, which requires the use of "i" to create compound words from two terms with etymological roots in Latin (*femina* for "female"; *caedo, caesum* for "to kill").[9] Even so, these interpretations ignore the cultural elements of translation. In other words, a probe into "cultural" (and not just "linguistic") translation yields different understandings about how concepts, theories, and knowledges are transformed in their travels to other geographic contexts, and in this particular case, to the ways in which a concept such as *feminicide* is reappropriated in response to local circumstances (Gunew 2002).

Years ago, the Cuban anthropologist Fernando Ortiz (1975 [1940]) developed a theory of transculturation as a model for mapping the changing dynamics of culture resulting from the mutual and multidirectional exchanges across one cultural system to the other. We draw from his insight to elaborate a cartography of feminicide that takes into consideration its transcultural elements; the dynamic, fluid, and mutual influences resulting from cultural interactions between scholars and gender-justice advocates in the global South and North. Our preference for *feminicide* over *femicide* in this anthology is both political, in that we aim to advance a critical transborder perspective, and theoretical, in that we aspire to center the relevance of theories originating in the global South for the formation of an alternative paradigm (knowledge, logics, subjectivities, traditions). In taking this approach, our desire is to dismantle the colonialist formulation of Latin America as "a field of study rather than a place where theory is produced" (Mignolo 2000, 193).

As editors of this volume, our translation of *feminicidio* into *feminicide* rather than *femicide* is designed to reverse the hierarchies of knowledge and challenge claims about unidirectional (North-to-South) flows of traveling theory. Based on a decade of working on the issue, both of us have witnessed the back and forth of theory making and political practices that inform our current understanding of feminicide and the ways in which the concept has changed and evolved as its thinking traveled South, where other circumstances shape the experience of gender-based violence against women. Our cartography of feminicide proposes a reconfiguration of knowledge hierarchies that contests the notion of seamless translation — that is, the idea that Latin American feminists have merely appropriated theories from feminists of the global North without modifying or advancing new meanings in response to local contexts. Rather, in the process of borrowing the concept and adapting it to local circumstances, we have generated new understandings about feminicide. The concept of feminicide thus highlights the "local histories" of theoretical reflection on the part of Latin American, Latina, and U.S.-based researchers; human rights and gender-justice advocates, witness–survivors, and legal scholars as we came into contact with bodies of knowledge elaborated elsewhere.

Building on the generic definition of *femicide* as "the murder of women and girls *because* they are female" (Russell 2001a, 15), we define *feminicide* as the murders of women and girls founded on a gender power structure. Second, feminicide is gender-based violence that is both public and private, implicating both the state (directly or indirectly) and individual perpetrators (private or state actors); it thus encompasses systematic, widespread, and everyday interpersonal violence. Third, feminicide is systemic violence rooted in social, political, economic, and cultural inequalities. In this sense, the focus of our analysis is not just on gender but also on the intersection of gender dynamics with the cruelties of racism and economic injustices in local as well as global contexts.[10] Finally, our framing of the concept follows Lagarde's critical human rights formulation of feminicide as a "crime against humanity" (see Lagarde y de los Ríos, this volume).

In the Latin American setting, the first documented use of the concept *feminicidio* is in the Dominican Republic, where during the 1980s feminist activists and women's groups used the term in their campaigns to end violence against women in the region (see Comitê Latino-americano do Caribe para a Defesa dos Direitos da Mulher 2007). As noted in the preface to this volume, Marcela Lagarde first introduced the term into academe in 1987 (see Monárrez Fragoso 2002). Around the same time, the sociologist Julia Monárrez Fragoso used the term *feminicidio* to describe the sexual murders of women and girls first observed and documented in 1993 in the Mexico–U.S. border region of Ciudad Juárez by Ester Chávez Cano, the women's rights activist and founder of the city's first rape crisis center.[11] Others, such as the scholars Ana Carcedo Cabañas and Montserrat Sagot of Costa Rica and Hilda Morales of Guatemala, prefer the concept *femicidio* to describe the misogynist murder of women. These feminist theoretical and political thinkers from Latin America used *feminicidio/femicidio* to represent murders in non-war settings, whereas in a similar time frame Asja Armanda of the Karita women's group in Croatia deployed the concept of femicide to depict large-scale and systematic sexual violence committed against Croatian women during the civil war in Bosnia-Herzegovina.[12]

As a result of tenacious activism on the part of women's rights advocates, the concept since then has been adopted by nongovernmental and intergovernmental organizations and by grassroots groups, as well as in major regional *encuentros* (meetings) and academic conferences, to make visible inhumane forms of violence against women and girls, particularly in the context of so-called peacetime.[13] In 2007, the Inter-American Court of Human Rights agreed to hear arguments for three cases of feminicide (the "cotton field" cases) that will serve as legal precedent for cases of gender violence in a non-war context and for enumerating feminicide in international law.[14] In December 2009 the IACHR issued a historic ruling in the "cotton field" murders. In an 167-page opinion, the court found Mexico in violation of human rights conventions for its failure to prevent and investigate the murders of Claudia Ivette González, Esmeralda Herrera, and Laura Berenice Ramos. This ruling represents the first time that the term *feminicide* is used and enumerated in international courts.

Since 1993, more than five hundred women and girls have been murdered and more than one thousand have disappeared in the state of Chihuahua, Mexico, alone.[15] Of the five hundred murders, approximately one-third were killed under similar circumstances: They were held in captivity, raped, sexually tortured, and mutilated, and their bodies were discarded in remote, sparsely populated areas of the city.[16] Women's rights groups have documented similar violence in other regions of Mexico, where between 1999 and 2005 more than six thousand women and girls were victims of gender-based murder.[17] In Guatemala since the year 2000, more than thirty-five hundred women and girls have experienced similarly brutal forms of violence in the post-conflict period. As these figures make evident, the level and extreme nature of violence against women requires a new concept such as *feminicide*, which can work as a conceptual tool not only for antiviolence advocacy but to further a feminist analytics on gender-based violence. It is thus crucial that we build on the definition of *feminicide* with sufficient conceptual precision and clarify what can and should be considered feminicide.[18]

As a descriptive term for the rise in gender-based murders, *feminicide* begs the question about the crime context in the region. Studies on violence in Latin America suggest that feminicide finds fertile ground in areas where the murder rates of men are also high (Lagarde y de los Ríos 2006, 23), so feminicide could be seen as part of an overall increase in the rate of homicide in Latin America, a region with high levels of violence (Koonings and Kruijt 1999). In 2004, the World Health Organization considered Latin America "the most 'crime ridden region' in the world, with 27.5 homicides for every 100,000 people . . . compared to twenty-two in Africa and fifteen in Eastern Europe." The homicide rate is even more alarming in Guatemala, which registered 45 homicides per 100,000 people in 2005 (Unga 2006, 171). Yet as the case study in Costa Rica by Sagot and Carcedo reveals, increased levels of overall violence is not necessarily an indication of higher rates of feminicide.

Further research is needed to determine whether more women are being murdered as part of an overall increase in the homicide rates or whether the female-to-male ratio has remained constant over time. Although analyzing crime rates through a gender analysis may partly account for the increase in the female share of the murders, this alone does not account for the gender dynamics at work. As feminist researchers and activists argue, what makes feminicide so distinctive is that it makes visible forms of violence that are rooted in a gender power structure.

The scale and range of the violence in general and the specific brutality and severity of rape, sexual torture, and mutilation suggest high levels of misogyny and dehumanization of women. Treating feminicide as the gendered form of homicide is thus misleading, given that it obscures the power differentials that feminist theorists have long contended increase women's vulnerability to violence. As Lagarde (2005, 25) explains, "Violence in general is a major component in the majority of crimes against men; however in the case of women, *submission* to masculine violence is central to their experiences." In other words, unlike most cases of women's murders, men are not killed *because* they are men or as a result of their vulnerability as members of a subordinate gender; nor are men subjected to gender-specific forms of degradation and violation, such as rape and sexual torture, prior to their murder. Such gender differences in the experience of violence suggest the need for an alternative analytic concept, such as feminicide, for mapping the hierarchies embedded in gender-based violence.

In thinking about feminicide in theoretical and political terms, it is important to underscore the spirited and dynamic debate in the field of gender-based violence about the use of *feminicidio* over *femicidio*. There is currently no unanimity among Latin American feminist researchers and activists for one term over the other. Those who prefer *feminicidio* follow Lagarde's formulation, which emphasizes the element of impunity and implicates the state as a responsible party (*feminicidio* as state crime). Other researchers in Central America, such as Carcedo, Sagot, and Morales, find Lagarde's formulation limiting and insist instead on *femicidio* because it more accurately describes "the misogynist murder of women, independent of the element of impunity or the participation of the state." For Sagot, "Whether or not there is impunity or state compliance (or lack thereof) with its responsibility to guarantee security and justice for women, the assassination of women *because* they are female constitutes a universal problem transcending borders and forms of governance."[19]

One of the primary aims of this collection of essays is to contribute to the political and legal process of defining and advancing a human rights framing of feminicide. Lagarde's (2006, 20) definition of *feminicide* is a starting point for thinking about the concept in historical, analytic, and legal terms: "El conjunto de delitos de lesa humanidad que contienen los crímenes, los secuestros y las desapariciones de niñas y mujeres en un cuadro de colapso institucional. Se trata de una fractura del Estado de derecho que favorece la impunidad. El feminicidio es un crimen de Estado (The entirety of crimes against humanity, including the murders, the kidnappings, and the disappearances of girls and women within the frame of institutional breakdown. It involves a breach in the rule of law, which favors impunity. *Feminicide* is a state crime)." As a member of the Mexican Congress, Lagarde drew from an evolving body of international law and defined *feminicide* within a human rights framework that considered both the public and private dimensions of gender-based violence. This human rights framing implicates the state for its failure to act with due diligence—that is, to take reasonable steps to prevent, investigate, and penalize gender-based violence.[20] The concept of feminicide bridges the "private" and "public" distinction by incorporating into its definition *both* systematic and systemic or structural violence sanctioned (or commissioned) by state actors (public) and violence committed by individuals or groups (private), since most of the violence suffered by women happens at the hands of private actors.

Public and Private

In defining *feminicide* as the murder and disappearance of women and girls because they are female, the authors of this collection, along with other Latin American scholars and women's rights advocates, have drawn from Russell's (2001a) definition of *femicide*.[21] Prior to Russell's formulation, feminist legal scholars had defined the crime of "rape" as a form of torture predicated on the impulse to "degrade and destroy a woman based on her identity as woman"—or *because* she is female (Copelon 1995). This inclusion of rape as "elements of torture, slavery, genocide," is considered to be a "reliance on a progressive reading into existing human rights provisions" (quoted in Saiz 2004, 62), or what the legal scholar Patricia Sellers (2002, 301) refers to as "a form of legal piggybacking," as rape is not considered a violation of human rights on its own terms. This progressive reading of rape as a form of torture has been an important advance given that "torture is the most widely outlawed human rights violation" (Lutz and Sikkink 2000, 634).[22]

The distinction of rape as a form of torture resulted in part from the strenuous activism by women's rights advocates denouncing "rape as a tool of war and torture by state officials in El Salvador, Perú, and Haiti" (Medina 1985; Meyer 1999, 65).[23] As we noted earlier, this legal redefinition of rape as a form of torture also informed the enumeration by the Women's Caucus of "gender crimes" as "incidents of violence targeting or affecting women . . . *because* they are women." Thus, the naming of murder and disappearance of women as "feminicide" can be seen as part of a wide-ranging effort in feminist jurisprudence and human rights law to make visible gender persecution targeting women per se for who they are.

In coming to this political understanding of gender-based violence, feminist theorists first had to place women's subjectivity and experience of violence at the center of a feminist analytic. Feminist analysis is a lens for representing violence from the perspective of gender, and in this regard "gender" is an element not of explanation but, rather, of interpretation that provides an angle (rather than a model) for understanding the power dynamics and relations of gender, sex, race, and class underlying violence (Young 2005). One of the principal obstacles feminist researchers of violence have confronted is the hierarchical division between "public" and "private" forms of violence.[24]

The distinction between the public and the private realms encumbers women in essential ways. Until very recently, violations of women's rights were considered a "private" or "cultural" matter best left to the discretion of the family. This consideration of women's rights as "private" or "cultural" rather than public or political reinforces gender hierarchies because it "renders women subject to the control of patriarchal familial authorities — father, brothers, and husbands — with the understanding that familial matters are 'private' and therefore beyond the scope of governmental authority and intervention" (Binion 1995, 516–17). Calling for the extension of "governmental authority and intervention" into the private sphere may be just as problematic from a gender-justice perspective; however, so, too, is consigning violence to the "private" sphere, for this mechanism has rendered violence against women invisible from public scrutiny and concern.

Feminist approaches to violence studies — the violence-against-women paradigm — sought to disassemble the private and public divide by framing violence against women as embedded within a patriarchal system of regulation and control over women's bodies. Early elaborations of "femicide" characterized the practice as a "phallic crime" that, by terrorizing women whenever they challenged patriarchy, was designed to maintain a regime of "male supremacy and entitlement."[25] In the pioneering anthology *Femicide: Sexist Terrorism against Women*, the authors considered femicide to be the most extreme expression of "sexist terrorism" (Radford 1992), perpetrated by misogynist men whenever they feel threatened by women acting collectively to claim their rights or challenge male authority (Caputi and Russell 1992, 16–17).[26]

In attributing the roots of femicide to the historically unequal power relations between men and women, Jane Caputi and Diana Russell redefined the killing of women as "politically motivated violence," similar to racial violence that is historically rooted in unequal power relations between racial groups and aimed at maintaining a regime of racial hierarchy.[27] This shift in the framing of the murder of women as "political" (public) followed a similar impulse in feminist redefinitions of the meaning of violence against women to encompass not just private forms (i.e., "men's violence against their partners in the form of rape, assault and murder"), but also systematic and large-scale acts of violence committed by state actors against civilians. However, the emphasis on gender-based violence as "political" or "public" does not necessarily do away with the public–private boundaries; it often has the unintended consequence of subordinating the less "spectacular" forms of gender-based violence. The efforts to frame sexual violence as "political" (public) within a changing body of international law, as "war crimes" and "crimes against humanity," is limiting in its representation of gender-based violence in either–or terms, since, as Hillary Charlesworth (1999,

388) explains, "The consequences of defining certain rapes as public in international law is to make private rapes seem somehow less serious."

The emphasis had also shifted from gender-based violence (rape, assault) in intimate relations to that enacted by states in warfare, as we noted earlier. Yet the private and public distinction "between the acts of state and nonstate actors" remained in place (Charlesworth 1999, 387). More recent elaborations build on an understanding of the private sphere as "an even wider area, extending to all relations among private persons, in contrast to their relations with public authorities" thereby moving the focus beyond the domestic sphere of familial and intimate partner relations. "Contemporary doctrine and case law," according to Eva Brems (2003, 112), "increasingly accept the responsibility of states to prevent and remedy human rights violations among private individuals."

This understanding is what makes the redefinition of *feminicide* from a human rights perspective so transformative in that it extends beyond the private–public divide. The concept of feminicide addresses and responds in part to this shortcoming, acknowledging the limits of the dichotomy between public (systematic and state) and private (interpersonal, individual and non-state) violence for understanding violence in the particularities of each individual country or regional situation.[28]

Following feminist human rights thinkers who contend that the distinction between systematic and widespread or state-sanctioned (public) and arbitrary or individual (private) forms of gender-based violence is a problematic one, our use of feminicide moves beyond a model of inclusion. That is, instead of adding private to public violations, we aim to question the either–or formulation to account for the ways in which all such breaches are interconnected, both private *and* public. In Mexico, recent formulations shift the definition from a notion of violence as an attack on women's honor or the sanctity of motherhood to an understanding of gender-based violence as linked to systematic discrimination and an assault on women's personhood and rights to life, liberty, security, and dignity. This connection to systematic and systemic discrimination is crucial for "applying the concept of human rights within international law to gender-based violence" (European Commission 2008, 20).

As Systemic Violence

There are no survivors of feminicide. All we have are the voices of witness–survivors (families) who speak for them. As the most extreme expression of crimes against women's life and liberty, feminicide names the absolute degradation and dehumanization of female bodies. Yet we would also like to shift the focus from women as "victims" to an understanding of how gender norms, inequities, and power relationships increase women's vulnerability to violence, as Carcedo and Sagot explain in their chapter. Feminicide is rooted in political, economic, cultural, and social inequalities, including the equally significant power relations based on class, race, sexual, and racial hierarchies. As an extreme form of gender-based violence, feminicide does not just function as a "tool of patriarchal control but also serves as a tool of racism, economic oppression, and colonialism" (Smith 2006, 417). In this sense, egregious violations of a woman's bodily integrity cannot be simply "physical" or restricted to a model of "personal injury." Rather, such violations involve systemic and structural forces, a multiplicity of factors and intersecting logics.

Feminicidal violence finds fertile ground in social asymmetries and is most acute under conditions of "extreme marginalization and social, judicial and political exclusion . . . and forms of gender oppression, including mechanisms of devalorization, gender exclusion, discrimination, and exploitation" (Lagarde y de los Ríos 2006, 22).[29] In Ciudad Juárez, whenever a corpse is found, according to Julia Monárrez Fragoso (2005b), there is an 80 percent probability that she comes from the "western zone," which has the highest concentration of immigrant population and the least infrastructure. It is women and girls living under "high levels of insecurity, vulnerability, an absence of social and political protection, and in zones of social devastation, where insecurity and crime prevail, along with coexistence marked by illegality . . . the disintegration of institutions, and the rupture of the State of Law" who, according to Lagarde (2006, 23), are most threatened by feminicidal violence. Crucial in this regard are devastating, neoliberalist-driven structural changes — economic, political, and social — that have precipitated extreme forms of violence in the region.[30]

A consideration of feminicide as systemic violence roots large-scale gender-based violence as part of the scenario of extreme inequality, poverty, unemployment, and social marginalization. Yet even as these egregious violations can be considered the most extreme effects of structural adjustment, the neoliberal agenda alone is not a sufficient explanation for the emergence of feminicide. The pervasive specter of civil wars and Latin America's Dirty Wars must also be factored into the architecture of feminicide, for the sexual degradation and dehumanization of feminicidal violence echo the repressed history of regimes of punishment designed for women under military regimes (Monárrez Fragoso 2005b, 62).

The militarization of daily life stemming from "the legacy of repressive dictatorships and civil wars . . . form the backdrop to new and disturbing forms of violence [such as feminicide] that seem to be on the rise in post authoritarian Latin America" (Koonings and Kruijt 1999, 3). Decades of civil war and military reign resulted in two hundred thousand dead and forty thousand disappeared in Guatemala; more than thirty thousand dead and disappeared in Argentina; and nearly seventy thousand, most of them indigenous peoples, slaughtered in Perú.[31] The brutality of feminicidal violence harks back to this era of state terrorism, when security forces and death squads resorted to brutal repression as a common practice to terrorize the populace by subjecting them to torture, arbitrary detention in death camps, extrajudicial execution, and disappearance. Most of the victims of state terrorism were "vulnerable civilian participants in movements or sectors which challenged the military's political goal or doctrines" (Brysk 1999, 243), especially populists, labor unions, students, teachers, and indigenous groups. While state security forces administered violence across the social spectrum, when it came to women, the terror inflicted by state-sponsored torturers took gender-specific forms (Hollander 1996, 46).

Similar to the practices of dehumanization evident in feminicidal violence, the torture of women under sadistic military regimes in Latin America involved degrading, inhumane, and cruel methods "systematically directed at [women's] female sexual identity and female anatomy" (Bunster-Burotto 1993, 257). Gang rape, sexual slavery, mutilation, torture, and forced pregnancy were part of the ongoing and insidious forms of terrorizing imprisoned women during the military dictatorships of Southern Cone countries such as Chile, Argentina, Paraguay, and Uruguay and in countries such as El Salvador, Nicaragua, Honduras, and Guatemala, where the state waged counterinsurgency wars against mostly unarmed civilians.[32] While in Guatemala, members of the military and civil patrols raped and terrorized indigenous women; in Argentina, "at the height of the military dictatorship's 'Dirty War,' bored junior officers who were members of torture squads would cruise the streets in the infamous Ford Falcons looking for pretty girls to sequester and take back to the camp to rape, torture, and then kill" (Hollander 1996, 63).

The unbridled misogynist practices of military regimes illuminate the intersections of "political repression" and "patriarchal culture" as mutually constituting forces. By "strengthen[ing] male-dominated institutions and intensify[ing] misogynist ideology," terrorist states reinforced a "violent patriarchy" that normalized violence against women (Hollander 1996, 46). It is precisely this relationship between machismo and violence and the mutually constituting forces of militarized, misogynist institutions; emphatic masculinism; and random, arbitrary violence that have helped to fuel contemporary expressions of feminicide (Domínguez-Ruvalcaba 2007).

Decades of military rule and civil wars have had both long-term structural and psychic impacts (what Ignacio Martin-Baró calls "the militarization of social life"; quoted in Hollander 1996, 57) that have persisted beyond the reign of the terrorist state in the "destructive behavior of members or ex-members of the military" (quoted in Hollander 1996, 57). Just as significant is the "historic structure of impunity" resulting from amnesty laws that have failed to hold state officials and former members of the security forces accountable for egregious crimes. This is the case in Guatemala, for example, where "genocidaires have never been brought to justice and impunity reigns more than a decade after the signing of peace accords" (Sanford 2008, 105). The chapter by Hilda Morales thus connects the rise of newer forms of violence such as feminicide to the historical structure of impunity in which, as Kees Koonings and Dirk Kruijt (1999, 11) explain in a different context, "at the level of daily law enforcement . . . random and arbitrary violence persists despite the demise of authoritarian rule."

Indeed, the end of military rule and counterinsurgency wars did not necessarily eliminate state terror, for it has persisted in what these authors refer to as "the proliferation of arbitrary repression with systemic logic" (quoted in Koonings and Kruijt 1999, 11). To this day, arbitrary and random forms of violence perfected during the Dirty Wars pervade the entire security apparatus, in police and law enforcement, in paramilitary bands involved in vigilantism and current "social cleansing" campaigns,[33] in the militarization of policing functions — all repressive practices that contribute to the untold forms of violence and degradation on the rise in post-authoritarian Latin America. Judith Galarza, head of the Federación Latinoamericana de Asociaciones de Familiares de Detenidos-Desaparecidos (Latin American Federation of Associations of Families of the Detained-Disappeared) in Caracas, an association of relatives of political prisoners and disappeared in Latin America, teased out the connection between feminicide and Mexico's Dirty War of the 1970s, noting that "several high ranking Chihuahua state officials implicated in organized crime began their careers as policemen active in the Dirty War" (quoted in Paterson 2008, 7).

Today, state-sanctioned terror practices and the unrestrained and tyrannical use of force, persist in a barely disguised and subcontracted form of repression and coercion (Fregoso 2006). State terror has been out-sourced to other "corporatist" sectors, as explained in the chapter by Rita Segato, to paramilitary bands involved in the recent emergence of vig-ilantism ("which may be state tolerated but is not wholly state spon-sored" [Brysk 1999, 240], to private armies and privatized security forces (former and current members of law enforcement) working for the globalized networks of the drug-, weapons-, and human-trafficking in-dustries, to the private armies of the ruling elite — all claiming the right to exercise sovereignty. In the era of neoliberal capital, the greater mobility and availability of weapons and private armies for hire means that mili-tary operations are no longer the sole monopoly of states (Fregoso 2006).[34] As the chapter by Héctor Domínguez-Ruvalcaba and Patricia Ravelo Blancas shows, the widespread impunity for atrocities com-mitted against women and the unfettered continuation and spread of feminicide can be seen as part of this militaristic scenario: the con-vergence of various coercive forces, the complicity of public officials and the organized-crime industry, in alliance with the ruling economic and political elite, all underwritten by the towering specter of state terrorism.

A Critical Human Rights Perspective

As we noted earlier, the international community now recognizes gender-based violence as a human rights violation. This means that as an extreme practice of violence embedded in gender power dynamics, feminicide is linked to a pattern of systematic discrimination; it breaches a woman's right to life, liberty, security, and dignity. In Latin American societies where strict gender norms of feminine and masculine identities prevail, there is also a historical pattern of deadly violence aimed at non-gender-conforming women, which further violates their right "to live out their sexuality in ways other than heterosexuality" (Radhika Coomoraswamy, quoted in Saiz 2004, 55).

As the former Special Rapporteur on Violence against Women, Radhika Coomoraswamy was the first United Nations expert to "explicitly articu-late a concept of sexual rights" and conceptually connect gender violence and discrimination with sexual orientation. According to Ignacio Saiz, Coomoraswamy considered violence against non-gender-conforming women to be "part of a broader spectrum of violence inflicted on women for exercising their sexual autonomy in ways disapproved by the commu-nity" (Coomoraswamy, quoted in Saiz 2004, 55).[35]

In many Latin American societies, widespread discrimination on the grounds of sexual orientation remains largely invisible despite a historical pattern of state and structural violence against queer people, which can also result in feminicide. Although strict gender norms and the social stigma attached to homosexuality partially account for the social indifference and silences around violence against transgender women, it is the state and judicial forces that are ultimately responsible for institutionalizing homophobic violence. In speaking about violations of the sexual rights activists in Latin America, Natasha Jiménez of Mulabi (Espacio Latinoamericano de Sexualidades y Derechos, or Latin American Space for Sexualities and Rights) remarks, "The 'official history' of humankind, as we know it, is a history in which 'travestis,' trans and intersex women are invisible. . . . Most of us are forced to live in the margins of society after being rejected by our families and the community as a whole. When we organize ourselves to defend our rights, usually we face police abuse and extortion. The price we pay for becoming leaders and encouraging our peers to resist is often murder, torture, arbitrary arrest, or forced displacement" (Human Rights Watch 2008).[36]

Former Special Rapporteur Cumaraswamy once called "sexual rights . . . 'the final frontier' for women's human rights" (quoted in Saiz 2004, 55). Although the essays gathered in this collection do not explicitly address the conceptual link between sexual and gender rights, attempts are currently under way to locate sexuality within a more comprehensive framing of feminicide.[37] The invisibility of transgender women and the silences around sexuality rights in Latin America demand that we make a concerted effort to highlight the extent to which violence against non-gender-conforming people is an egregious human rights violation that needs to be addressed in any framing of and politics surrounding feminicide.

As president of the Comisión Nacional de Feminicidio (National Commission on Feminicide in Mexico), Lagarde played a key role in advancing a human rights perspective on gender-based violence in Mexico. The Ley General de Acceso de las Mujeres a una Vida Libre de Violencia (General Law of Women's Access to a Life Free from Violence) formulated by the commission is not just a "law against violence" (negative right) but a law that guarantees women the right to live free from violence (positive right).[38] Lagarde also played a key role in focusing on the element of "impunity," the role of the state, and the inclusion of "disappearance" in the conceptual elaboration of feminicide.

Yet Lagarde's inclusion of "disappearance" under the rubric of feminicide could be seen as problematic, for it begs the question of why "disappearance" would be characterized with the same finality as murder, given that some of the women may or may not be dead — that is, they may later reappear.[39] In some respects, conceptualizing disappearance as a component of feminicide forecloses the possibility (and the relatives' hope) that many of the women may still be alive, perhaps trafficked or held in captivity in sexual or labor slavery. However, there is also a compelling reason for placing disappearance within the ensemble of crimes against humanity.

As we noted above, the feminist reformulation of rape as torture represents what Sellers calls a form of "legal piggybacking," or progressive reading into existing international human rights provisions. A similar strategy is at work with the coupling of murder and disappearance. In international law, "disappearance" as a crime against humanity has no statute of limitations, and a progressive reading into international human rights provisions could eliminate the statute of limitations for murders of a feminicidal kind.[40] For example, in Mexico the statute of limitations for murder is fifteen years, whereas "disappearance" is "not subject to statute of limitations under customary international law" (Roht-Arriaza 2005, 121). As the chapter by Adriana Carmona, Alma Gómez, and Lucha Castro suggests for the case of Silvia Arce, missing since 1998, a legal precedent could be made for disappearance in the context of feminicide as a crime against humanity by drawing on the case example of Chile. In that instance, "murder and disappearances" committed during Chile's military regime, according to Naomi Roht-Arriaza (2005, 121), are considered "imprescriptable — they can have no statute of limitation due to the heinous nature of the crimes and the continuing international interest in its suppression."[41] Besides, this characterization of feminicide as crimes against humanity could also "give rise to an obligation on the part of the primary state, as well as of the international community," which as Juan Méndez and Javier Mariez-currena (1999, 88) indicate, "may be satisfied by creating an international criminal court, or by allowing courts of other nations to exercise the principle of international jurisdiction."

For Carmona, Gómez, and Castro, Lagarde's proposition of feminicide as a "state crime" in effect shifts the understanding of violence to consider "institutional forms" (state and judicial structures) as well as both public and private forms of gender-based violence, as well as murder and disappearance, as a social mechanism that "serves to reinforce a systematic pattern of subordination and exclusion from codified rights" (quoted in European Commission 2008, 24).[42] Although international law still favor "holding states accountable . . . for violations perpetrated by public authorities, rather than committed by private actors" (Brems

2003, 113), this conceptual framing of feminicide is part of a vigorous movement to establish women's rights as human rights and to name gender-based violence as a violation of human rights.

The Comisión Interamericana de Mujeres (Inter-American Commission of Women; CIM) was the first international body to define gender-based violence as a violation of women's human rights and to specify "the duties of states to address this endemic social problem" (Meyer 1999, 58). Established in the 1920s, the CIM has had a decades-long tradition of pressuring governments in the Americas "to bring national laws into compliance with international norms in the area of women's rights" (Meyer 1999, 66). In 1988, it drafted the Inter-American Convention on the Prevention, Punishment and Eradication of Violence against Women (Convention Belém do Pará) in which it expanded the violations suffered by women from "domestic violence" to include "institutionalized violence perpetrated or tolerated by the state" and redefined "rape and sexual abuses as forms of repression or torture" (Meyer 1999, 67). Although rape is not listed as a "human rights violation in the [Universal Declaration of Human Rights], CEDAW [Convention on the Elimination of All Forms of Discrimination against Women], [or] the International Covenant for Economic and Social Rights," in 1994,[43] the Convention of Belém do Pará, "became the first of its kind to frame rape as a human rights violation in both private and public spheres" (see CEDAW 2005, Article 2; Sellers 2002, 296–301).

Situated in the nexus between gender-based violence, systematic discrimination, and exclusion from codified fundamental rights, feminicide as we have defined the concept is part of feminist efforts to categorize violence rooted in a gender power structure as a human rights violation. The emphasis on human rights provided by the concept of feminicide triggers the obligations of the international community to pressure and hold the state accountable, as the chapter by William Simmons and Rachel Coplan observes.[44] Similar to the term *genocide*, first coined by the Polish international lawyer Raphael Lemkin to describe what the Turks did to the Armenians in Turkey, *feminicide* provides an analytic and legal framework for locating state accountability around "crimes against women's life and liberty."[45]

Lagarde's discussion of feminicide as "state crime (*crimen de Estado*)" is crucial in this regard, for it reiterates the state's role and responsibility (by commission, toleration, omission) for egregious breaches of women's human rights. This human rights framing implicates the state for its failure to act with due diligence[46] — that is, to take reasonable steps to prevent, investigate, and prosecute gender-based violence — and it incriminates the state and judicial bodies that institutionalize misogyny. It also underscores the state's responsibility for (or failure in) *prohibiting* violations of women's human rights. Here it is important to underscore that we prefer the language of *prohibition* to that of *protection* because we do not advocate a "protective approach to human rights of women" or the use of "protective instruments which see women as especially vulnerable and in need of protection" (see Brems 2003, 108). A reliance on the logic of protection, according to Iris Young (2003), extends patriarchal ownership and control and further disempowers women. For Charlesworth (1999, 386), "the proprietary image of women . . . [is] underlined by the language of protection rather than prohibition of violence."

Most violence against women is committed by individuals rather than the state; however, several authors in this book will argue that a state's failure to guarantee women's rights to live a life free from violence is itself a human rights violation. In emphasizing a human rights approach, the concept of feminicide implicates both governments that violate human rights and private actors who perpetrate violations of human rights. In framing feminicide as a "state crime," several contributors in this volume point to the state's role in fomenting a climate of impunity for the most heinous violations of women's rights: murder, torture, sexual violence, and forced disappearance. Women's rights groups in Latin America have long maintained that the government's failure to investigate human rights violations thoroughly or to follow through in prosecution, often "because of lack of will to do so by officials in charge of institutions with specific duties in that regard", creates a climate of impunity that in turn propels more violations (Méndez and Mariezcurrena 1999, 85).[47]

This link between histories of sexual violence during armed conflicts and the current surge of feminicide was recently stressed by Special Rapporteur on Violence against Women Yakin Ertürk. In addressing the problem of impunity, Ertürk called for the prosecution of perpetrators of "sexual violence used as a weapon of war during armed conflicts in Central America" as a deterrent for "future acts " (Ertürk and Commission on Human Rights 2005, 2). Angélica Chazarro, Jennifer Casey, and Katherine Ruhl take up this question in their study of how a government such as Guatemala's (as well as El Salvador's and Honduras's) practiced impunity by changing domestic laws or passing amnesty laws for human rights violations during periods of armed conflict, which in effect "preclude investigations or punishment" of security forces and former military commanders (Méndez and Mariezcurena 1999, 85).[48]

Rights for Living

The focus of this volume is on feminicide and disappearance. However, by emphasizing structural and systemic forms of violence, we aim to advance a more comprehensive framing of human rights harms that goes beyond the liberal humanist emphasis on violence as "personal injury" limited to physical violence. Rather, we advocate broadening the agenda of gendered human rights violations through a feminist understanding of rights as "substantive and indivisible," a notion of human rights as not just *of* the living but *for* living.

In discussing the philosophical, practical, and political questions underpinning human rights discourse, Wendy Brown (2004, 463) finds human rights approaches to justice limiting, especially if the "moral discourse on pain and suffering" is uncoupled from a "political discourse of comprehensive justice." Brown (2004, 461) entertains the limits of a moral definition of human rights violations in which the "global problem facing human-kind" is conceived of or framed as "terrible human suffering consequent to limited individual rights against abusive state power." It is less about what is wrong, given that these practices aim to "right" human wrongs, than about the limits of this kind of framing of human rights for a progressive agenda insofar as it ignores "the conditions by which people can or cannot exercise their rights," and in so doing elides social and economic rights (Wilson 2002, 260).

The human rights *for* living approach we are advocating bases its comprehensive justice project on the "principle of indivisibility," or the idea that civil and political rights are indivisible and inseparable from economic rights to food, health care, and shelter. It is a perspective that calls for deep changes in social structures. This notion of human rights *for* living, as "substantive and indivisible" — the right to work, food, health care, and housing, along with the right to a life free from violence and torture — opens up new possibilities for treating feminicide as part of a broader set of human rights violations that affect women and for framing remedies within a comprehensive justice model that considers peoples in local communities as agents of social change.

In this volume, we have gathered the writings, insights, reflections, and interventions of multiple actors in the struggle to end feminicide in the Americas. From the beginning, our concern has been to highlight an array of empowering voices and ways to create long-lasting social change. In bridging diverse genres of knowledge — the voices of the mother/relative/survivor/activist, the voices of the lawyers litigating on their behalf, the voices of the grassroots activists, the voices of scholars and legal theorists, and the haunting voices of the female victims of feminicide and disappearance — our aim is to probe the collective actions required to end the large-scale violence and atrocities affecting our communities. It is out of the multiplicity of intersecting perspectives that human rights *for* living are best articulated in the following matrix of justice, human security, and local remedies.

Remedies for the injuries and suffering caused by feminicide and disappearances are complex and varied. They range from legal, juridical, and state-centered methods to human security and community-based approaches to justice. Even as we recognize the importance of the legal and judicial realm for remedying injustices, we harbor deep suspicion about legalistic remedies and "rule-of-law" approaches centered on the state. Yes, "law" has an expressive function in that it "formally restores social values and norms." However, the production of human rights law that is state-centered can lead to the "reempowerment of the state" (Baxi 2006, 211) and the further disempowerment of everyday people. It is for this reason that we consider it crucial to go beyond the state, as well as beyond instruments and accords such as the Universal Declaration of Human Rights.

Human rights activism aimed at reducing human suffering in Latin America often advocates for the applicability, institution, and enforcement of international law within the nation-state. However, as feminists we have strong reservations about state-centered (criminal) approaches to justice and propose instead alternative forms for responding to human rights atrocities. Unlike the "'true believers' in the promise of international law," we join those Vasuki Nesiah calls "skeptics or agnostics" who view legal interventions "as merely a strategy towards certain political goals" (2006, 805).[49] In the following pages, we examine several models of justice that frame human rights violations less as offenses against the state than as a violation of human relationships. We also consider alternative community-based approaches for responding to human rights harms, especially ones that empower and involve those affected by feminicide and disappearances "to participate in deciding what to do about the wrongdoing" (quoted in Law Commission of Canada 1999, 28).[50]

A comprehensive justice approach to human rights *for* living, as "substantive and indivisible" — the right to food, shelter, and work, along with the right to a life free from violence and torture — opens new possibilities for thinking about people's safety and security that go beyond the rhetoric of "physical protection" and "threats to the body politics" as framed within a "national-security" model and for treating gender-based atrocities as more than sexual violence against women.

For as Franke (2006, 819) indicates "to see the 'gender issue' surface only in the case of sexual violence is to elide the gendered dimensions of war, violence, and the investment in killing over caring."

In treating security for women as more than physical protection, the notion of rights *for* living affirms women's need for personal and social safety in tandem with or inseparable from their need to live healthy and productive lives. Security also means embracing women's sexual diversity, along with an "emancipatory vision of sexuality," as a "social good to be respected, protected, and fulfilled" (Saiz 2004, 64). This idea of "security" differs substantially from state-centered understandings of security, drawing instead from a notion recently advanced under the auspices of the United Nations Development Program (UNDP), which defines "human security . . . as freedom from fear and freedom from want" in the realms of "the economy, food production, health, the environment, the personal and community level and politics" (Truong et al. 2006, ix).[51]

This people-centered approach to human security focuses on gendered forms of human rights violations and sufferings that are often overlooked — poverty, hunger, illness, homelessness, and displacement — and that, as noted earlier, are rooted in structural and institutional inequities. Marginalized women whose gendered forms of exclusion intersect with other social categories such as class and ethnicity are the ones most vulnerable to financial, personal, and community insecurities, aggressive policing practices, and other forms of gendered violations. In drawing from the principle of indivisibility, this security model is crucial to a comprehensive justice framework that focuses on the empowerment, human rights, and dignity of women.[52] It positions women as active agents of cultural, economic, and social change as they work to end the silence around gender-based violence and raise awareness about its devastating effects on their communities.

A number of the community-generated approaches we describe below go beyond a national security model of justice and instead reimagine safety and security "based on a collective commitment to guaranteeing the survival and care of all peoples" (Communities against Rape and Abuse 2006, 250). We also consider an approach to justice that, although centered on international human rights law and the state, can be a useful tool for empowering communities in democratic processes of justice making: the transitional justice model developed at the end of military dictatorships and authoritarian governments in Latin America during the 1980s.

Transitional Justice

The transitional justice approach centers the "rights and needs of victims and their families" and relies on "international and humanitarian law in demanding that states halt, investigate, punish, repair, and prevent abuses" (International Center for Transitional Justice).[53] Transitional justice aims to reveal the multilayered causes of violence, heal the wounds caused by this violence, and create systems to stop future human rights abuses. The recognition first and foremost of the human suffering and injuries committed against relatives and victims of feminicide and disappearance, transitional justice is a useful model for revealing truths about feminicide cases through truth-telling mechanisms and offers accountability and prosecution of offenders, including the implicated or negligent state actors. Transitional justice also involves "public access to police, military, and other governmental records; public apology; public memorials; reburial of victims; compensation or reparations to victims and/or their families (in the form of money, land, or other resources" (Franke 206, 813). This justice approach also offers a space for healing and reconciliatory processes and for creating the structural changes necessary for sustainable peace and comprehensive justice.[54] Although it requires a dose of state power,[55] the version of transitional justice developed through the International Center for Transitional Justice (ICTJ) is also unique in its exploration of the effects that gender and sexualized violence have on countries affected by violence.

No human rights approach to justice can be applied universally, and, as Katherine Franke (2006, 813) notes "transitional justice will always be incomplete and messy." Transitional justice projects have a specific history in addressing human rights abuses in post-conflict societies, and yet they have been limited in their ability to create a process of change that is systemic rather than time-sensitive, that involves the community in the peace-building process, and that creates a strong foundation for "public confidence" and "authentic public engagement" (John Paul Lederback, quoted in Borer 2006, 7). There are also limits to a transitional justice focus on "reconciliation." As President Michelle Bachelet of Chile has remarked: "In my view, [reconciliation] does a disservice to the memories of thousands of victims of the Pinochet regime, to the many thousands more who were tortured and to their families — many of whom still do not know what actually happened to their relatives, spouses, friends" (quoted in Rieff 2007, 1).

Even though transitional justice is a model developed for transitional moments or post-conflict situations "after a repressive regime [has been] toppled or a civil war [has] ended and before new, more democratic institutions are consolidated," (Méndez and Mariezcurrena 1999, 88) its principles have emphasized and enabled a notion of justice as a lived experience. Juan Méndez (2006, 120) writes, "The most significant aspect of Latin American experiences, however, is that the process of truth and justice has outlived the transitional periods (however measured) and that these demands are now widely accepted as applying to nontransitional situations as well. Moreover, each society has found ways of keeping alive the demands for truth and justice beyond the neat 'stages' in which those policy decisions were supposed to be made."

Marta Vedio of La Plata's Human Rights Association has also stated (Roht-Arriaza 2005, 104–105), "The truth is a right belonging to the whole society." In this collection, as Eva Arce, Julia Huamañahui, Rosa Franco, and Norma Ledezma Ortega declare in their *testimonios*, the relatives of the disappeared and of feminicide victims have been denied the right to truth and a right to know what happened to their loved ones. The right to truth is an obligation that the state owes to the relatives and to the entire society: "To disclose . . . all that can be known about the circumstances of the crime, including the identity of the perpetrators and instigators" (quoted in Méndez and Mariezcurrena 1999, 88). Besides the right to truth, the relatives of the disappeared women invoke the right to mourn their dead, for bereavement is "one of the most deep-seated fundamental needs in all human cultures"; it "require[s] that the location of the loved one's remains be known and that the mourners have a body to mourn" (Roht-Arriaza 2005, 101). For the relatives of the murdered and disappeared women, the right to truth and right to mourn are foundations for long-lasting justice.

One of the unique features of transitional justice is the stress on an empathic form of listening that privileges the significance of "the narrative, subjectivity, and the experiential dimensions of truth telling" (Borer 2006, 22) as expressed by family members as victims or survivors of human rights abuses. Transitional justice projects are considered to be victim-centered because they validate the truths derived from witness–survivors' own *testimonios*, and provide a forum for contesting official state narratives that often misrepresent and obfuscate the truth behind human rights atrocities. Moreover, in transitional justice projects, the narrative truth produced by family members in the form of *testimonios* of human rights violations they have experienced at the hands of state officials, who harass and intimidate and mislead relatives about investigations, is given just as much weight as forensic or legal evidence.[56]

Yet, engendering transitional justice has not been a smooth process. Early truth commissions in Argentina and Chile overlooked "testimony from women" and "assumed a gender-neutral approach" that according to Theidon (2007, 457), "privileges men and their experiences." Subsequent commissions in Guatemala, South Africa, and Perú have incorporated a gendered perspective with varying degree of success, actively encouraging, facilitating and seeking to include women's voices in truth-seeking processes.[57] These more recent transitional justice projects place an emphasis on women's agency in peace, justice, accountability, truth, and reconciliation as essential for coming to terms with past human rights atrocities and incorporate a gender analysis into the truth-telling mechanisms. In prioritizing "sex-specific and gender-based violence in their mandates rather than treating such violence as secondary," these transitional justice projects "support private hearings within truth commissions to discuss sex- and gender-based violence instead of during public hearings, and they provide women the space for anonymous testimonies when discussing sexualized violence" (Hayner 2001, 77–79, as cited in DeLaet 2006, 168–69nn).

Yet despite the efforts to actively seek out women's voices and experiences of violence, more work needs to be done to advance gendered justice in transitional justice projects. Feminist interventions into the field have pointed to a number of issues that undermine the interests of women, including transitional justice's narrow definition of sexual violence as "rape," its treatment of gender-based atrocities as exclusively "sexual," and the elision of the gendered dimensions of war (see Nesiah 2006; Franke 2006; Theidon 2007; Ní Aoláin and Rooney 2007).[58] Prioritizing rape and sexual violence over other "human rights harms that affect women," according to Franke (2006, 821) "has had the effect of sexualizing women in ways that fail to capture both the array of manners in which women suffer gross injustices, as well as the ways in which men suffer gendered violence as well." While transitional justice taps the legal system in its approach to human security, there are other meaningful community-generated projects aimed at addressing and making visible feminicidal violence.

OBSERVATORIOS COMUNITARIOS (CITIZENS OBSERVATORIES)

Observatorios Comunitarios have a long history in Latin America, serving as a mechanism for collective action that involves communities in witnessing, observing, and monitoring state agencies and ensuring that they exercise due process. Observatorios Comunitarios are similar to citizens' watch groups in terms of their independence and autonomy from government authority or power and in the provision of local, community-based solutions for citizens' participation in democratic processes.

Established in 2006 the Observatorio Ciudadano del Feminicidio (Citizens' Observatory on Feminicide) is the largest *observatorio* dealing with feminicide throughout Mexico. It represents roughly forty-two civil society organizations from seventeen Mexican states, including women's groups, human rights groups, indigenous women's organizations, legal-defense groups, and academic and religious organizations. While the membership includes both men and women, the leadership in the observatorio, like that of most women's rights projects, is primarily female.

Representatives provide monthly updates on feminicidal violence in their home states, including information on feminicides reported monthly in local newspapers. Widely recognized by national and international governments, the Observatorio Ciudadano del Feminicidio currently networks with other Latin American countries that face increases in feminicide, such as Guatemala and Nicaragua, collaborating across state and national borders to monitor governments and to end feminicide and other forms of gender-based violence (Red de Salud de las Mujeres 2008). The observatorio is part of an effort to typify (or enumerate) feminicide within national law, advocating for the full implementation of the federal Ley General de Acceso de las Mujeres a una Vida Libre de Violencia (2007) and for the establishment of a new system of prevention, sanction, and elimination of violence (known as Sistema Nacional sobre la Violencia contra las Mujeres y el Programa Nacional Integral de Prevención, Atención, Sanción y Erradicación de la Violencia; Olivares and Villalpando 2007).

Another observatorio based in Mexico City, the Observatorio Ciudadano de los Derechos de las Mujeres (Citizens Observatory on Women's Rights), draws its membership from twelve organizations, including Nuestras Hijas de Regreso a Casa (May Our Daughters Come Home), Justicia para Nuestras Hijas (Justice for Our Daughters), and the Centro de Derechos Humanos de la Mujer (Center for Women's Human Rights) of Chihuahua. Its primary goal is to ensure the implementation of human rights standards, norms, and principles as articulated in international law and treaties such as CEDAW. The main objectives of the Observatorio Ciudadano de los Derechos de las Mujeres include (1) strengthening the inclusion of women in the national agenda; (2) fortifying the use of international recommendations in Mexico; (3) combining the terms of human rights and women and girls' rights; (4) sensitizing and informing the public about the phenomenon of feminicide; and (5) positioning international recommendations more squarely in the elaboration and implementation of public policies.[59] Both observatorios work to strengthen community-based accountability strategies by involving a coalition of grassroots activists, NGOs, academic researchers, and human rights activists in implementing women's human rights and holding governments accountable. Like other community-based justice models, the observatorios have made a concerted effort to empower communities in witnessing, observing, and monitoring government entities and ensuring that they follow through with due process and procedures for justice.

GRASSROOTS NGOS

Nuestras Hijas de Regreso a Casa and Justicia para Nuestras Hijas are local, family-activist organizations working across national borders. Based in the State of Chihuahua, Mexico, these grassroots NGOs are part of an expanding transnational network of alliances aimed at building the capacity of mostly poor communities "to be direct architects of their local political worlds" (Appadurai 2006, 135). Partnering with local and cross-border activists, both NGOs have focused on building the capabilities of families to investigate the murders and disappearances of their loved ones, and, more generally, to work collectively in the area of women's human rights.

Nuestras Hijas de Regreso a Casa, based in Ciudad Juárez, involves family members directly in advocating on their own behalf in the area of judicial and social justice. In addition to demanding accountability from federal, state, and local authorities in solving the crimes of feminicide and disappearances, Nuestras Hijas helps to build capacity by educating families on judicial and legal processes and in the area of psychological and physical well-being. For example, the group has developed educational workshops and support groups to help the families of recent victims deal with and transform their anger, suffering, and pain into political action. It has also filed complaints against the government for corruption and negligence and worked with national and international NGOs to apply pressure on the Mexican government to resolve the cases of feminicide.

Nuestras Hijas de Regreso a Casa has extended its advocacy to a wider arena through RadioFem, a radio link and radio station broadcasting out of their offices. Along with reports about the ongoing feminicide and disappearances, RadioFem covers topics ranging from gender empowerment, women's rights, and safety to children's understanding of gender violence. Although the group has experienced difficulties in accessing radio waves, Nuestras Hijas continues to post links to Radio-Fem on its website (http://www.mujeresdejuarez.org), defying the government's efforts to remove its "on air" programs.

As Carmona, Gómez, and Castro explain in greater detail, Justicia para Nuestras Hijas was established in 2002 by families of murdered and disappeared women in Ciudad Juárez and Chihuahua City and includes a small group of lawyers and legal advocates involved in the investigation of feminicide and the disappearances. Like those of Nuestras Hijas de Regreso a Casa, the members of Justicia para Nuestras Hijas are mostly poor families with limited formal education and resources. The group also builds capacity among the mothers of murdered girls and women, training them to be paralegals and advocates within the judicial processes, especially since family members have proved to be the best record keepers and investigators into the murders and disappearance of loved ones.

The work of Justicia para Nuestras Hijas has catalyzed another NGO in Chihuahua City, the Centro de Derechos Humanos de las Mujeres (Center for Women's Human Rights), which was established in 2005 to support survivors of domestic violence and human rights atrocities at every stage of the judicial process. Unlike many women's centers, the Centro de Derechos Humanos de las Mujeres is organized on the principle of indivisibility that we spoke of earlier, taking a comprehensive view of gender-based violence that links interpersonal (physical) violence in intimate and familial relations with social, cultural, and economic forms of violence that affects poor as well as indigenous (Tarahumara-Rarámuri) women.

Although Justicia para Nuestras Hijas, Nuestras Hijas de Regreso a Casa, and the Centro de Derechos Humanos de las Mujeres are homespun organizations operating with limited funding, all three have taken leading roles in the international campaign to end feminicide. They have created alliances with other grassroots, national, and international women's rights groups in a campaign to end gender-based violence and feminicide; they are also leaders in forging international solidarity campaigns throughout Europe, the United States, and Latin America, and in carrying out public political acts, protest marches, demonstrations, public forums, and caravans for justice. While the groups grew out of struggles to end feminicide in the region, other community-centered approaches to justice focus on empowering women and eradicating domestic violence.

DEFENSORAS COMUNITARIAS (COMMUNITY DEFENDERS)

Although the Peruvian Truth and Reconciliation Commission (TRC) was instituted to enable the country's transition to democracy by revealing truths and implementing accountability for human rights atrocities during the armed conflict, a question among women and human rights groups in Perú lingers: "¿Porque no se hace justicia (Why isn't justice achieved)?" To respond to what some groups consider the failures of the TRC process, a community-generated strategy has taken shape among local indigenous community members from villages and cities. The Defensoras Comunitarias (Community Defenders) are primarily indigenous women trained as the first line of legal defense to hear a variety of cases of human rights violations against women and children in their regions.

Developed in partnership with foundations such as the Legal Defense Institute and the United Nations Children's Fund (UNICEF), the Defensoras Comunitarias have developed a community-based justice model for building the capabilities of poor, mostly indigenous people to serve as human rights monitors, observers, and local interpreters of human rights in the community. The Defensoras Comunitarias also serve as community watch groups and as legal-aid and social-welfare offices. Based on a collective commitment to guaranteeing the survival and care of all peoples, the Defensoras Comunitarias monitor and work to settle conflicts within their own communities, thereby circumventing the criminal justice system of the state, which has been particularly hostile to indigenous communities. In working with women in their communities, the Defensoras Comunitarias intervene in troubling situations and provide guidance throughout the justice system, accompanying survivors of violence in their visits to the police, district attorney, and judicial offices. The Defensoras Comunitarias also intervene in cases of police brutality and domestic violence and make frequent visits to homes, sending a strong message to the violent offender that they are watching and monitoring him.

The Coordinadora Departamental de Defensorias Comunitarias del Cusco (CODECC) started in 2000; two years later, the Defensorias Comunitarias del Cusco had grown to forty people. By 2005, five hundred community members, mostly women from urban and rural communities, had joined the organization as volunteers in their communities. The Defensorias Comunitarias are officially recognized by the Ministerio de la Mujer y el Desarrollo Social (Ministry of Women and Social Development; MIMDES) and across Peruvian civil society as advocates in decision-making processes involving the implementation of laws, the rendering of justice, and the improvement of the lives of survivors of gender-based violence (Coordinadora Departamental 2005).

The witness–survivors (families of murdered and disappeared women) and grassroots activists working on behalf of human rights, demanding justice and accountability from their governments and calling for an end to violence against women, are the direct architects of change in their local political worlds. Survival is a feature embedded in the everydayness of poor communities. As witnesses to and survivors of untold forms of degradation, relatives and their advocates stand at the epicenter of survivability, facing intimidation and harassment from state authorities and violence from an economy, a criminal justice system, and political institutions that typically leave them out of any decision making. Even as they continue to wrestle with terrible hardships, witness–survivors have managed to transform their pain and suffering into a resource for empowerment and agency (Bejarano 2002).

Women who have survived human rights atrocities throughout Latin America are key players in creating an alternative approach to human security. These are women who strive to live without fear and without want and who are vital in the prevention of future violence because more than anyone else they understand the intimacies of violent societies and the everydayness of violence in women's lives. More often than not, societies tend to further marginalize survivors of violence by encouraging the erasure of violent histories as a mechanism of reconciliation and moving on. For many, reconciliation "implies turning a page," as Chile's President Bachelet recently remarked (as quoted in Rieff 2007, 1). Yet, as Edith Wyschogrod reminds us, "Survivors of atrocity become deeply uncomfortable signifiers for the post-atrocity societies within which they live, excessive to structures of normality that privilege forgetting, getting over and getting on with things through the denial of the terror of death, especially the possibility of mass death" (quoted in Cubilié 2005, xii).

Those who survive gender violence may be viewed as uncomfortable reminders of a society's violent history. However, witness–survivors and their families also have the moral authority and ethical power to instill public confidence and create the public engagement required for deep, long-lasting peace and democracy. Female survivors are working (often invisibly) to take greater control of decision making in their communities, to achieve a more equal status with men, and to influence peace, justice, and democratic movements (Valenzuela 1999). As they struggle on the ground in urban and rural communities throughout Latin America, witness–survivors and women's rights activists possess the "survival capital" that offers a multilayered framework for strategies to combat "wars against women." They model for all of us the aspirations and utopian dreams necessary to create new pathways, to build "deep democracy," and to enable new protagonists in campaigns for justice and human equality across borders.

Part 1, "Localizing Feminicide," maps the locations of feminicide. The contributors offer feminist analytics of feminicide and a robust set of arguments on the structural patterns of violence within each society. In "Localizing Feminicide," we point to the shared cross-border links for confronting and understanding the phenomenon to end this form of violence. Part 2, "Transnationalizing Justice," tracks legal routes for remedying injustices and alternative remedies that are more accessible to communities. Part 3, "New Citizenship Practices," probes strategies for confronting feminicide, the shaping of new subjectivites, and models of justice for creating long-lasting change. As principal catalysts of the social movement to end feminicide, the four *testimonios* included in the book offer personal reflections of witness–survivors and activists who confront terror daily.

"Localizing Feminicide" begins with an essay by Mercedes Olivera, who provides a framework for positioning the impact of structural and social violence on women. Olivera's contribution reflects on the relationship between neoliberal capitalism and the rise of feminicidal violence, which together produce a social ecology in which marginalization and political exclusions, inequalities, poverty, authoritarianism, and rigid gender norms flourish. Whereas Olivera locates feminicide structurally, Julia Estela Monárrez Fragoso's essay alerts us to the corporal effects of neoliberal capitalism, in this case unpacking the ways in which patriarchy and capitalism intersect to produce women's bodies as "sexually fetishized commodities." For Monárrez, the location of feminicide on women's bodies illustrates how masculine domination expresses its entitlement through the possession, consumption, and disposal of women's bodies.

Similarly, Rita Laura Segato's contribution probes women's bodies as the terrain through which sovereign and discretionary power expresses its reign and territorial control. Segato begins her analysis by considering how feminicide is a signature and communication system through which the powerful sector relays its dominion and superiority across the social order. Segato alerts us to the insidious function of feminicide as a system of communication for announcing the omnipotence and invisibility of what she terms the "shadow state."

Several chapters move from the female body to the concrete manifestation of feminicide in regional locales. Angélica Chazarro, Jennifer Casey, and Katherine Ruhl turn their lens to Guatemala. Focusing on the asylum case of Rodi Alvarado, they address the intersection of domestic and mass-scale forms of violence, as well as the Guatemalan government's failure to respond to the extreme brutality Rodi Alvarado experienced at the hands of her husband. The authors contextualize the underlying conditions that give rise to feminicide in Guatemala, including the legacy of military violence, the failure of the legal system, and a historical structure of impunity and systemic discrimination.

Two chapters in particular discuss the complicity of state actors with organized criminal networks. In her essay on the murder and disappearance of prostitutes in Mar del Plata Argentina, Marta Fontenla points to the direct involvement of police authorities in networks of prostitution and the human-trafficking industry and the corruption of the criminal justice system in investigating and prosecuting the crimes. Similar to Fontenla, Hilda Morales Trujillo roots violence against women in the historical structure of impunity, legacy of armed conflict, and militarization of social life. Drawing from her expertise as an attorney and human rights activist, Morales begins her discussion on the limits of legal categories for murder in Guatemala and offers a perspective on how the concept of femicide is employed in legal and political discourses.

Montserrat Sagot's and Ana Carcedo Cabañas's empirical study of the incidents of femicide during a nine-year time frame provides a comparative gender analysis of murder rates in Costa Rica. Pointing to the limits and discrepancies in the categorization of women's murders, Sagot and Carcedo flesh out the properties of femicides through a detailed demographic and contextual analysis of explicit violence within gender socialization. Similar to Sagot and Carcedo, Adriana Carmona López, Alma Gómez Caballero, and Lucha Castro Rodriguez draw from a typology of feminicide to demonstrate the range and rate of its occurrence. Like Morales, their involvement in legal and human rights activism has shaped their understanding of feminicide from a critical human rights perspective as "crimes against humanity." This chapter in particular offers case examples of scapegoats who were falsely accused and tortured into confessing to feminicide, as well as the failure of judicial systems to ensure the rights of the accused. The authors explicitly raise the significance of the disappeared in advocacy around gender violence, and like other contributors they address the failure of government institutions to remedy these atrocities and underscore the need for interventions beyond the nation-state.

"Transnationalizing Justice" starts with the need to think about and devise remedies beyond the nation-state. Héctor Domínguez-Ruval-caba and Patricia Ravelo Bueno Blancas explicitly discuss the influence and power of the new corporatist sector at every level of society, including the state. They call for a reformulation of human rights law beyond its nation-state framework to accommodate not just human rights violations by state actors but also the just as prevalent violations committed by private (corporate) actors in what they term "extra-governmental" space.

William Paul Simmons and Rebecca Coplan pursue a comprehensive set of remedies that address both feminicide and the structural factors that have exacerbated the crimes. They highlight legal remedies that transcend the nation-state, such as litigation before the Inter-American Court of Human Rights and civil suits in U.S. courts under the Alien Tort Statute, as well as economic-development approaches primarily through international financial institutions. Deborah Weissman focuses her discussion on transnational remedies by attending to "economic liberalization," the roles of transnational actors, and U.S. economic policy through the North American Free Trade Agreement (NAFTA). For Weissman, the increase in the murders of women can be traced to economic globalization and the exclusion of women from the social contract in places where "market-value predominates."

Christina Iturralde offers a creative framework of justice that speaks to the failure of conventional models of accountability. Drawing from Rama Mani's approach to justice in post-conflict situations, Iturralde discusses the limits of a rights paradigm and presents an imaginative framework for addressing massive violations of human rights in places where unequal distribution of resources are major factors impeding social justice. Like Simmons and Coplan, Iturralde calls for interventions that address the root cause of violence and build the capacity of communities in legal-empowerment approaches.

We argue that transnational justice is not limited to the interstate system or legal-juridical top-down approaches. In the final section of the book, "New Citizenship Practices," Alicia Schmidt Camacho, Pascha Bueno-Hansen, and Melissa W. Wright probe the gendering of public space through their deft studies of the new political voices, alliances, and forms of solidarity emerging across regional boundaries.

Schmidt Camacho begins her study of new emergent forms of citizenship in Chihuahua by looking at how state practices at the national and local level conspire to exclude the most marginalized women from "the sphere of rights." She alerts us to the contradictory nature of "border spaces" as sites for the production of denationalized subjectivity — whose most extreme expression is feminicide — and for the making and gendering of new political subjects. It is the vitality of the justice movements and the assertion of new forms of agency on the part of the family activists that are engendering and transforming Mexican women's citizenship.

In a comparative study of women's rights NGOs in Perú and Guatemala, Bueno-Hansen traces the strategic use of the term *feminicidio* in networking and building cross-border alliances. Even as the term has served feminist activists well in their demands for recognition of women's legitimacy in the public sphere, *feminicidio* is more limited in its utility for codifying violence against women in the penal code of Perú.

Mindful of the difficulties feminist activists face in Mexico, Wright explores how leaders of Mujeres de Negro (Women Wearing Black) in Chihuahua assert the rights of women to exist in the public sphere, despite long-standing prohibitions around women's access to the public sphere of politics in the region. Wright's case study of Mujeres de Negro alerts us to the challenges of navigating the dangerous political terrain of Chihuahua but also teases out some of the inventive moves crafted by women's rights activists as they build fluid and mobile networks and alliances across national boundaries.

Finally, we include four *testimonios* by relatives of murdered and disappeared women and girls. Eva Arce, Julia Humañahui, Rosa Franco, and Norma Ledezma Ortega document their firsthand experiences as witness–survivors of the atrocities we discuss throughout this book. The *testimonios* speak most directly and publicly for the women and girls who cannot voice their resistance to terror or express their own claims to human rights and justice. As witness–survivors, the relatives claim their rights *for* living and comprehensive justice, for a model of justice that is at once transformative and healing, empowering and re-humanizing, that affirms the dignity and ethical response-ability of all members of human communities in righting human wrongs. The *testimonios* and activism of the relatives of the murdered and disappeared women teach us how to be ethical and response-able human beings. "[Their] resistance to terror," as Carolyn Forché (1993, 46) reminds us, "is what makes the world habitable: the protest against violence will not be forgotten and this insistent memory renders life possible in communal situations."

Notes

1. Gender-based violence makes visible violence rooted in a gender power structure, as defined in European Commission (2008, 24): "To the extent that violence is founded on a gender power structure and serves to reinforce that structure, its exercise systematically undermines the victim's access to a

wide range of fundamental rights anchored in international law, for example, repeated domestic abuse of women, rape (as a means of war, the ICC recognizes it as a crime against humanity), and child maltreatment." In 1992, the CEDAW Committee defined gender-based violence as "violence that is directed against a woman because she is a woman or that affects women disproportionately. It includes acts that inflict physical, mental, or sexual harm or suffering, threats of such acts, coercion, and any other deprivation of liberty" (Recommendation 19, see European Commission 2008, 24). As Brook Sari Moshan (1998, 2) adds, "Rape has always been a fundamental and accepted military tactic. Historically, soldiers considered rape to be one of the spoils of war, associated with success in battle and serving as evidence of complete victory. Rape has functioned as a military tactic, a way to terrorize populations during warfare and to assert control over war enemies."

2. As Nicole Erb (1998, 402) writes, "Nazi soldiers raped Jewish and Soviet women; and Japanese soldiers forced Korean women into sexual servitude and raped Chinese women during the Japanese invasion of Nanking China; during the Iraqi invasion of Kuwait, Iraqi soldiers raped Kuwaiti women; during the military coup in Haiti, armed forces raped female supporters of the overthrown President Jean-Bertrand Aristide; during the civil war in Rwanda, Hutu militiamen raped Tutsi women and Tutsi men raped Hutu refugees; during the ethnic conflict in the former Yugoslavia, military officers from all sides raped women from targeted groups."

3. During the civil war in Ivory Coast, fighters "gang raped" women and forced them into sexual slavery; during the Liberian civil war, armed militias raped three out of four women; in Sierra Leone, militias from all sides committed countless sexual atrocities.

4. For a discussion of the debates about the definition of "gender" and the enumeration of gender crimes during the Preparatory Committee sessions leading up to the Rome Conference, which established the ICC, see Moshan 1998; Oosterveld 2005.

5. Moshan uses the terms *savage* and *brutal*. However, given the colonialist history of the term *savage* as applied to indigenous and Third World communities, we have substituted the term *extreme* for *savage*.

6. In an analysis of political violence, *arbitrary* can mean either depending on individual discretion or marked by or resulting from the unrestrained and often tyrannical use of power (see Koonings and Kruijt 1999).

7. According to Ellen Lutz and Kathryn Sikkink (2000, 640), "Latin America helped introduce the term 'disappearance' (*desaparición*) into the international human rights vocabulary due to the widespread and systematic basis of disappearances in the 1970s." The Inter-American Convention on Forced Disappearance of Persons, adopted by the Organization of American States in 1994, "defines 'disappearance' as 'the act of depriving a person or persons of his or their freedom, in whatever way, perpetrated by agents of the state or by persons or groups of persons acting with the authorization, support, or acquiescence of the state, followed by the absence of information or refusal to

acknowledge that deprivation of freedom or to give information on the whereabouts of that person, thereby impeding his or her recourse to the applicable legal remedies and procedural guarantees'" (Lutz and Sikkink, 635fn9).

8. Feminicidal violence in the Americas is not restricted to Latin America. See Amnesty International 2007, which focuses on sexual violence against indigenous women in the United States.

9. Julia Monárrez Fragoso (2005a) cites the linguist Martín González de la Vara of the Colegio de la Frontera Norte, who explains the etymology and proper translation of *feminicidio* in this way. Also, the Spanish *femicidio*, according to Marcela Lagarde (2006, 20), is insufficient because it is a synonym for homicide and in this sense "literally means the murder of women."

10. Although in the book we do not explicitly examine the structures of homophobia, it is important to make the conceptual link between gender-based violence and violence targeting women because of their sexual orientation and identity.

11. Based on an interview conducted by Julia Monárrez Fragoso. The year 1993 is an arbitrary starting point, according to Monárrez, given that there is evidence of killings before the signing of NAFTA in 1994. In the local academic context, Monárrez first used the term in a talk titled, "Feminicidio," delivered at the Universidad Autonoma de Ciudad Juárez in 1998. She drew from Lagarde y de los Ríos (Monárrez Fragoso 2002).

12. See Russell 2001b, 9, where she also notes that Catherine MacKinnon used the concept of *feminicidal* practices along with *genocidal* practices in a lawsuit against war crimes that she filed on behalf of survivors of mass femicide in Bosnia-Herzegovina's civil war.

13. Femicide was central to Amnesty International's global campaign in 2003 against violence toward women. The report Feminicidio en América Latina 2006), prepared for the Inter-American Commission on Human Rights of the Organization of American States by a consortium of women's rights activists, exemplifies the productive use of feminicide as a concept for documenting the alarming increases in the rates of murders and disappearance of women and girls throughout the region.

14. As of this writing, three cases have been presented before the Inter-American Court of Human Rights: Laura Berenice Ramos, Claudia Ivete González, and Esmeralda Brenda Herrera, all found brutally murdered in the infamous "cotton field" case in Ciudad Juárez, where eight women's bodies were found. The cases that have been submitted to the Inter-American Human Rights Commission are those of Sylvia Arce (for disappearance), Paloma Ledezma, and Minerva Torres.

15. Ciudad Juárez is a case in point. Between 1985 and 1992, thirty-seven women had been violently murdered, whereas in the same seven-year time frame (1993–2001), women's rights groups documented an increase of 700 percent, or 269 violent murders.

16. Monárrez Fragoso (2005b) has developed the term *feminicidio sexual sistematico* for these types of murders.

17. The National Institute of Statistics, Geography and Information Technology (INEGI) in Mexico notes that in 2004 alone, eight hundred women were killed in Mexico City (Cámara de Diputados del H. Congreso de la Unión 2006).

18. See Jonathan Fox (2005), who makes a similar argument for the concept *transnational citizenship*.

19. E-mail communication with the editors, June 2, 2008.

20. In international law, the state's breaching of its obligation to prevent, protect against, investigate, and punish human rights violations is referred to as *failure to exercise due diligence*. In elaborating this human rights framework, Lagarde draws from the Convention of Belém do Pará.

21. While the English-language use of *femicide* dates back two centuries, Russell (1977, 2) first used the concept in testimony before the first International Tribunal on Crimes against Women in Brussels in 1976, where she drew from the Oxford English Dictionary's definition of *femicide* as "the murder of women and girls by men."

22. According to Lutz and Sikkink (2000, 634), "Nearly all Latin American nations have long prohibited torture as a matter of domestic law. . . . Torture is one of a handful of rights in the International Covenant on Civil and Political Rights for which no derogation is permissible. The customary international law prohibition similarly has a jus cogens, or non derogable character. Thus, under no circumstances may states take measures to annul the prohibition against torture." Also, "Formulations that explicitly deal with violence refer only to torture and cruel and unusual punishments; [these are] specifications which led some feminists to analyze domestic violence, for instance as torture" (European Commission 2008, 22).

23. In the case of *Raquel Martí de Mejía v. Peru*, the Inter-American Court of Human Rights found sexual violence inflicted by security forces (public authorities to "satisfy elements of torture" and thus a violation of "Mejía's human rights" (Sellers 2002, 301). Rape is thus "recognized as a component of jus cogens obligations" for which no derogation is possible.

24. The division of society into spheres of "public" and "private" life has long been a vexed concern for feminists, since such a demarcation is based on a hierarchy that reinforces gender inequalities. In many societies, the realm of the public is privileged as the sphere of production, governance, and politics; the private is devalued as the realm of reproduction, the family, and child rearing. Even though the delineation of these two domains can vary across national and cultural settings, "across classes, among different racial and ethnic groups, among different regions within the country, between urban and rural environments," as Donna Sullivan (1995, 128) explains, "The shared feature of the public/private distinction in different contexts is the attribution of lesser economic, social, or political values to the activities of women within what is defined as private life."

25. In describing femicide as a "phallic crime" tolerated by the state and other hegemonic groups, Jill Radford and Jane Caputi and Diana Russell

aimed to eliminate "the obscuring veil of non-gendered terms such as homicide and murder," as evident in the case of the serial murderer Jack Lepine, who in the 1980s had confessed "he hated women, particularly feminists," yet U.S. media and criminologists continually referred to the pathological rather than the "political nature of Lepine's crimes." For Caputi and Russell, Lepine's crimes had little to do with pathology and dementia, given that his stated hatred "of women, particularly feminists" contradicted this simple assumption and suggested instead that his murders of women could be considered in the political language of "hate crimes" as a form of "sexist terrorism, motivated by hatred, contempt, pleasure or sense of ownership over women" (Radford 1992; Caputi and Russell 1992, 14–15).

26. To develop this "male backlash" thesis, Caputi and Russell established a correlation between rates of increase in lethal acts of violence against women, on the one hand, and rising levels of women's activism and challenges to "male supremacy and entitlement," on the other. Insofar as the "dramatic escalation" in murders of women and girls coincided with the emergence of feminist activism in the United States during the 1960s, femicide could be interpreted as a form of "male backlash against women" (Caputi and Russell 1992, 16–17). This "male backlash" thesis would inform subsequent studies of feminicide in Latin America.

27. As Caputi and Russell (1992, 13) add, "Most people today understand that lynchings and pogroms are forms of politically motivated violence, the objective of which are to preserve white and gentile supremacy."

28. In some regions of Mexico (e.g., Chihuahua), sexual violence is aimed at the destruction of a community; however, it does not result from war, armed conflict, or a direct attack by state actors. Feminicide in other instances is large-scale and occurs in "post-conflict" situation, as the examples of Guatemala, Argentina, El Salvador, and Perú make evident, and involves non-state or corporate actors targeting individual women as well as women as a group. There are also examples of feminicide (e.g., in Costa Rica) that, similar to most gender violence, take place in the context of intimate relationships and everyday life but that, cumulatively and because of the impunity involved, are also of a large-scale nature.

29. The concept of *feminicidal violence* applies to those misogynist actions aimed against women's security and that place women's physical and mental integrity at risk: see Ley General de Acceso de las Mujeres a una Vida Libre de Violencia 2007.

30. The deteriorating economic situation in Latin America can be traced to the international debt crisis of the 1980s (1983–88), when many developing countries approached the International Monetary Fund and the World Bank seeking emergency loans and debt relief. In exchange for financial bailouts, economists from the world's financial institutions mandated structural-adjustment policies (SAPs) that they alleged would create economic stability and prevent future crises. These structural-adjustment measures included deregulating trade (free trade) and eliminating barriers to foreign investment,

privatizing state enterprises, and implementing drastic cutbacks in govern-ment spending. With SAPs mandated during the 1980s and 1990s — what came to be known in Latin America as *neoliberalism* — unemployment soared, and real wages plummeted. The social and economic infrastructure of middle-class, but especially of poor, communities throughout the region was devas-tated by rising unemployment rates and forced wage cuts, the elimination of price controls on food and fuel, and an escalating cost of living, coupled with sharp cuts in public expenditures that had benefited poorer groups. Without a minimal social safety net, much less "universal forms of social security or a system of social protection," the poor and low-income groups suffered the most. The neoliberal agenda failed to deliver the promised economic growth. Instead of creating "economic stability and preventing future economic crises," the SAPs engendered massive social instability and insecurity (see Elson 2002, 99).

31. In international law, *genocide* is defined as the "intent to wipe out a group simply because of who it is (or perceived as), to erase a group of people as such. . . . It targets not just the individual but the whole social fabric." Spain has the most expansive definition of genocide: "as a crime against groups, whatever their nature" (Roht-Arriaza 2005, 47–48).

32. Even among the leftist revolutionary army, there was complicity among men, according to Norma Vásquez (1997, 143), who writes that "violence against women and rape were not uncommon in the ranks of the FMLN [Farabundo Martí National Liberation Front]," adding that there was a lack of response from the leadership.

33. Victoria Sanford (2008, 110) defines social cleansing as " a mechanism of selective or arbitrary repression that is systematically produced by either armed actors with ties to the state or by private actors who carry out repres-sion with the acquiescence, complicity, support or toleration (whether delib-erate or involuntary) of the state."

34. Alison Brysk (1999, 241) refers to "death squad activity as a form of 'subcontracting state coercion.' " According to Brysk, "States subcontract with the informal sector when they face unusual threats or seek to engineer a fundamental policy transformation, but for some reason require 'plausible deniability.' "

35. Hector Domínguez-Ruvalcaba has more recently examined this con-ceptual link between gender-based violence and systematic discrimination against people because of their sexual orientation or gender identity. Writing about cultural production in Mexico, Domínguez-Ruvalcaba (2007, 6) ex-plores the fatal relation between patriarchal law and violence in turn-of-the-century Mexico, in what he calls "the recent compulsion for immolating women and homosexuals."

36. A nationwide study conducted in Argentina in 2006 concluded that state agents were responsible for more than 80 percent of the violence in-flicted on transgender and transsexual people (Berkins 2007, 127–28). That same year, Human Rights Watch (2006) issued a report that implicated Gua-

temala's state police in the murder with impunity of transgender women and gay men in Guatemala City. Transgender rights defenders from Argentina, Guatemala, Mexico, Colombia, Perú, and Jamaica face deadly threats often from state authorities, as evident during the recent militarization of northern Mexico's border region. Since the arrival of military forces in Ciudad Juárez in early 2008, as part of President Felipe Calderón's war against the Cartel Juárez, violence against transgender women has increased. LGBT activists in the border region regularly face deadly threats, "arbitrary detentions, physical assaults and threats of disappearance by agents of the Milipol [military police]" (Comunicación e Información de la Mujer or CIMAC, 2008. In Juárez, an LGBT human rights center is named after "Fany," a transgender women's rights activist who was killed by police while she was video recording police violence against transgender people on the streets" (see "Agudizan abusos contra mujeres transgénero en Ciudad Juárez" 2008). The editors acknowledge input from Dana Greene, a criminologist at New Mexico State University, and from the attorney Adela Loyoza, who spoke persuasively about activism and violence against LGBT people.

37. In an e-mail conversation with the editors, one of our contributors, Héctor Domínguez-Ruvalcaba communicated the work he and other colleagues in Mexico are currently undertaking that explores the conceptual link between gender-based and sexuality-based murders within a feminicide framework.

38. Chihuahua became the first state in Mexico to approve the Ley General de Acceso de las Mujeres a una Vida Libre de Violencia in January 2007.

39. Article 7 of the Rome Statute of the ICC defines "crime against humanity" as "any of the following acts when committed as part of a widespread or systematic attack directed against any civilian population, with knowledge of the attack," including, but not limited, to murder; extermination; enslavement; deportation or forcible transfer of population; imprisonment or other severe deprivation of physical liberty in violation of fundamental rules of international law; torture; rape, sexual slavery, enforced prostitution, forced pregnancy, enforced sterilization, or any other form of sexual violence of comparable gravity; enforced disappearance of persons; crimes of apartheid; and other inhumane acts of similar character causing great suffering or serious injury to body or to mental or physical health.

40. In the Inter-American Convention on Forced Disappearances, "forced disappearances constitute a crime against humanity" (Roht-Arriaza 2005, 95). According to the Naomi Roht-Arriaza (2005, 74, 113), "Disappearances, as a species of crimes against humanity, were not subject to statute of limitations under customary international law," in part because "disappearance is a continuing crime, so neither amnesty law nor the statute of limitations could apply until the body was found."

41. As Roht-Arriaza (2005, 161) explains, "Nuremberg Tribunals, the [Universal Declaration of Human Rights], the Covenant on the Non-Applicability of Statutes of Limitations, and the more recent jurisprudence of the [International

Criminal Tribunal for the Former Yugoslavia] and the [International Criminal Tribunal for Rwanda] to conclude that crimes against humanity had a special status in customary international law, which made them imprescriptable."

42. See Convention of Belém do Pará, Article 1: "For the purposes of this Convention, violence against women shall be understood as any act or conduct, based on gender, which causes death or physical, sexual or psychological harm or suffering to women, whether in the public or the private sphere" (available online at http://www.summit-americas.org/Belemdopara .htm, accessed November 3, 2008).

43. In fact, "patriarchy" is not even mentioned in the Universal Declaration of Human Rights as a "violent structure" (Cubilié 2005).

44. According to Méndez and Mariezcurrena (1999, 88), if the human rights violation is of the magnitude of "genocide, war crimes, and crimes against humanity," then the obligations of the international community "may be satisfied by creating an international criminal court, or allowing other courts of other nations to exercise the *principle of international jurisdiction.*"

45. Under international law, the state has three types of obligations: to respect human rights, to protect human rights, and to fulfill human rights (Hamilton 2004, 4).

46. This *failure to exercise due diligence* is outlined in Convention of Belém do Pará, Article 1.

47. Méndez and Mariezcurrena refer to this as "de facto impunity."

48. According to Méndez and Mariezcurrena (1999, 85), the state is in violation of international law when it allows "impunity for the most egregious human rights crimes such as extrajudicial execution, torture and disappearance, when committed systemically or on a wide scale."

49. Nesiah makes this comment in the context of a feminist critique of the transitional justice model as discussed below (See Nesiah 206).

50. Our approach draws from the "restorative justice" model that redefines crime "not so much as offending against the state . . . but as an injury or wrong done to another person or persons" (Law Commission of Canada 1999, 28).

51. The concept of security that is developed here is analogous to the United Nations' construct of human security. The term *human security* was first introduced in the UNDP's Human Development Report for 1994 (United Nations Development Program 2005).

52. As Patricia Mohammed (2006, 295) adds, "Human security rel[ies] on the fundamental characteristic inherent in the concept of gender . . . its adaptability, convenience, responsiveness, capacity for molding and remodeling, respectful of different histories and climates and taking on as many colors, nuances, and shapes as there are peoples and societies."

53. International Center for Transitional Justice, http://www.ictj.org/en/tj/?printer_friendly=1 (accessed March 10, 2008).

54. The ICTJ lists the following mechanisms as available in the transitional justice approach: "domestic, hybrid, and international prosecutions of perpetrators of human rights abuses; determining the full extent and nature of

past abuses through truth-telling initiatives, including national and international commissions; providing reparations to victims: compensatory, restitutionary, rehabilitative, and symbolic reparations; providing institutional reform including the vetting of abusive, corrupt, or incompetent officials from the police and security services, the military and other public institutions including the judiciary; promoting reconciliation with divided communities, including working with victims on traditional justice mechanisms and forging social reconstruction; constructing memorials and museums to preserve the memory of the past, and [finally and perhaps most importantly for this book], taking into account gendered patterns of abuse to enhance justice for female victims": ICTJ website, available online at http://www.ictj.org/entj ?printer_friendly=1 (accessed March 10, 2008).

55. We thank Jonathan Fox for this observation.

56. In his discussion of the TRC process, Richard Wilson argues that there are four types of truth narrowed into two basic "truth paradigms." These paradigms are the forensic truth and the narrative truth. "The forensic truth is a legal and scientific notion of uncovered facts and corroborating evidence, including investigations of the causes and patterns of violence as well as individual incidents of gross violations of human rights. The narrative truth included the three categories of personal, social and healing or restorative truth and emphasized narrative, subjectivity, and the experiential dimensions of truth telling" (as cited in Borer 2006, 22).

57. For a detailed account of the limited success of the Peruvian Truth and Reconciliation Commission's incorporation of a gendered perspective, see the dissertation by Pascha Bueno-Hansen (2009).

58. Another aspect of the gender dimension of transitional justice, such as the differential effects of enforcement of legal norms, is beyond the scope of this chapter. For an excellent overview, see Ní Aoláin and Rooney 2007.

59. See the Academia Mexicana de Derechos Humanos website, available online at http://www.amdh.com.mx (accessed July 7, 2009).

PART I

Localizing Feminicide

Translated by Sara Koopman

Testimonio

EVA ARCE, MOTHER OF SILVIA ARCE,

DISAPPEARED ON MARCH 11, 1998

On March 11, 1998, Silvia went to collect the money she made selling jewelry on credit to female dancers and never came home. I was told about it four days later, when Octavio [Sylvia's husband] and Ángel, my grandson, came to my house to tell me that Silvia hadn't come home to sleep. My granddaughter, Esmeralda, told me that on that day her mom had asked her to put an avocado, an onion, and a tomato in a little backpack for her, and that she would eat them while she collected the money from the girls, and to tell Octavio to go pick her up. Esmeralda said that when Octavio came home, she told him to go pick up her mom, but he said that first he was going to sleep for a bit, and then he would go for her. He told me, however, that he woke up late and didn't go for her.

Later, he changed his story and said, "I went for her, and she wasn't there," and added that the parking lot attendant had told him that the dancers had been fighting outside the place and that they had called the police. The attendant explained that Silvia had been waiting for the truck when a white Cavalier car pulled up. A man got out and put her in the car and took her with him. When the car pulled away, the police arrived, and by then there were no dancers outside, so the police left. That day when they came to tell me all this, I got very nervous and we went looking for her.

My son and Octavio said, "Where are you going to go now if everything's closed?" But I went anyway hoping to find someone who had some information. We went back to the house, and the next night we went to the place where Silvia went to collect the money from the dancers. It was so dark that you couldn't see anything in the parking lot.

I kept looking but couldn't see anything. I came back and went to the place where the girls danced, and Octavio was there at the bar, drinking. When he saw me, he said, "You can't come in here." I went out, and just then a man and a young woman went in; then the young woman came out again. I asked her about Silvia, and she told me, "She hasn't come since Wednesday." I said to her, "What do you know?" and she told me, "Ma'am I can't say anything, because if I say anything, they'll kill me, and if they take me to make a declaration, I'm not going to say anything in her favor." She went back into the bar, and I stayed there where the cars were parked.

When I saw a man, I went and asked him about Silvia, and he told me she hadn't come back since Wednesday. Then another man came up and said, "This guy and I have the place now, and we're still settling accounts. I'm a *licenciado*,[1] and he's the nephew of *XYZ*, and on Wednesday he left the place to him and I'm going to help him." I said to him, "What do you know about Silvia?" and he said, "She hasn't come back since Wednesday when she was eating at a table here. She's a good girl, but I haven't seen her since." At that point I decided to go to the district attorney's office around midnight or 1:00 a.m., to file a criminal complaint. I was told to come back on Monday to the Sexual Crimes Unit. I kept asking for my daughter, but no one knew anything. On Sunday I went to the DA's office, and the officers told me, "We don't know anything, come back in the evening." Then the agents assigned to the case told me, "Ma'am, when your daughter comes back, you will have to take her to a place for her to recover," and they told Octavio, "You'd better go to sleep because you're always drunk." At that point, we went back to the house.

On Monday I went back and spoke directly to the special prosecutor to investigate crimes against women. She sent me to the *judicial* (state police officer) to ask him what he had investigated. The police officer said, "Why are you looking for her? She's happy having fun. You go back to your house; she's going to come back." That made me suspicious, and I responded, "Is it that you know where she is, or do you have her in that place where she's having fun?" He burst out laughing and got up and left me there.

I walked out with my girlfriends Judith and Mari, and we agreed to set up an encampment in front of the DA's office. A lot of people joined us and brought photos of young women, which they placed there for people to see, because the women were also disappeared. I went out every afternoon to look for Sylvia, yet no one would tell me anything. We kept protesting in front of the DA's office, but they never gave us any credible response — just pure lies and mistreatment. The *judiciales* would laugh and say, "Let's see who lasts the longest," and others told me, "We're just waiting for the order to go get her," and they never did anything. It was all a lie; all of them knew where she was being held, and they never rescued her. I have heard there is a cassette where they recorded that they had killed her and that they buried her where she couldn't be found. I keep going to the DA's office with the hope of finding her alive or dead, but none of the officials there care. It's been eleven years, and there is still no response. They have several lines of investigation, but they don't investigate. There continues to be impunity. . . .

I know they are kidnappers, the commander of the PGR [Procuraduría General de la Repúblic, or Attorney General's Office].[2] . . . I've investigated a lot, but it hasn't done me any good, because I tell them everything, and they don't do anything. Neither the *prosecutor* nor the federal Attorney General's Office — it's the same thing: They don't do anything. I keep asking what have they done, and it's the same story. The years go by, and prosecutors come and go, and the only thing they do is tell us nothing, and they refuse to meet with us when we ask for appointments to see the DA. They never give us appointments, so it's all stuck — Silvia's case as well as Ángel's.[3] I don't know what they have against me, because always wherever I go they have me totally under surveillance.

In 2003, they beat me and surrounded my house. They have followed me and called me on the phone to threaten me. They've tried to pick me up, too. Once they left me a message to go to the Hotel Lucerna to identify the body of my daughter, Silvia, but I didn't go. They wanted to put one over on me, and I thought: I'm not going; they'll disappear me, just like they did my daughter, Silvia. I went to ask for help with the investigations to a news reporter from the United States who ended up making fun of me. I still keep getting threats: "We're calling you from the court, we're calling you from the Fourth Criminal Court." And they told me, "We're giving you three days," and hung up on me. At the airport in Juárez, two people followed me. I had to ask for help and have someone come for me. Downtown, too, an Asian man in a black suit was following me, and a woman helped me escape.

I have been harassed and threatened instead of getting news about my daughter. What I want is to find her and not get so many threats and for them to stop harassing me. I want justice and for them to find my daughter. I'm not going to stop. I'm going to keep going, with God's help. Since my daughter disappeared, I've been living in hell. I'm a nervous wreck now, because that's all that's left to us. We don't live in peace for fear that something is going to happen to us, and we don't have any trust, because here in Juárez, respect, values, everything's been lost. It's ended up being a corrupt government, where impunity rules. There is no more justice, for as much as we ask for the punishment of the guilty and for them to give me back my daughter, they don't hear me, and they don't pay attention. I want to live in peace, but we don't have that.

Notes

1. *Editors' note:* A *licenciado* is a person with a bachelor of arts or bachelor of sciences degree.

2. *Editors' note:* All three persons mentioned are police officers.

3. *Editors' note:* Gang members mysteriously killed Ángel, her grandson, when he was seventeen.

MERCEDES OLIVERA

Translated by Victoria J. Furio

Violencia Feminicida

VIOLENCE AGAINST WOMEN AND

MEXICO'S STRUCTURAL CRISIS

> The World Bank and IMF, two grindstones of the same mill, imposed
> the violence of the free market on us. . . . In such a "democracy,"
> who's really in charge?—Eduardo Galeano

Women are being murdered in Mexico at an alarming rate. Since the
1990s, this rate has increased so dramatically — in direct relation to the
expansion of neoliberalism — that, under pressure from feminists, the
government has finally had to recognize it as a national problem. It can
be viewed as an expression of the country's current crises of governability, internal security, and respect for human rights.

Although there have been episodes of multiple murders of women, feminicides — which once were linked to particular regions, such as Ciudad
Juárez — have become a pathology that has spread throughout Mexico. In
2002, there were more than five thousand cases nationally (Lagarde y de
los Ríos 2005). For the most part, the victims are women of childbearing
age murdered with guns or knives, but many are also beaten, burned, or
poisoned. The fact that the perpetrators are so rarely punished and that
the number and viciousness of crimes against women continue to increase reveals the government's political incapacity to deal with this kind
of crime.

Many of these killings are carried out by unknown assailants. Others
occur in public security actions. In the majority of cases, however,
women are murdered by someone known to them or related through
work, family, or romantic involvement. According to the World Health
Organization, 70 percent of the women murdered throughout the world

in 2002 were victims of their husbands or lovers (Urias 2005). Their bodies, often found on the street, show the brutality carried out against them: A large percentage are beaten and tortured before their deaths.

With Mexican Congresswoman Marcela Lagarde y de los Ríos, I view feminicide as but the extreme end of a range of violations of women's human rights — a direct and extreme expression of economic, political, social, and gender violence that is structural in nature.[1] Much of this generalized violence is exerted against women for being women — that is, it is misogynous.

Violence against women, an expression of men's power, is present in various forms and degrees throughout women's lives. As a naturalized part of the culture, symbols, institutional functioning, and cultural prescriptions, it shapes identities and internalizes subjectivities. In all societies, the cultural models for being a woman assign positions to women that subordinate them to the personal and institutionalized power of men, creating real and symbolic inequalities. These inequalities are expressed in direct and hidden messages, discriminatory actions and excluding omissions, lack of resources, limits on freedom and coercion, objectification, exploitation, self-depreciation, feelings of guilt and shame, deception, and false justifications. In all of these situations, violence against women progressively develops from insinuations, offensive comparisons, harassment, threats, verbal intimidation, abuse, irresponsibility, betrayal, and abandonment to beatings, forced sex, rape, and persecution. It even appears in other realms, such as counterinsurgency and war.

From this perspective, feminicide and feminicidal violence can be identified as specific forms of gender violence, which is defined by the United Nations as a mechanism of domination, control, oppression, and power over women (United Nations 1979). Although gender violence does not always result in murder, it does increase the possibility of it. Gender violence is a constant violation of the human rights of women and girls. Its presence in the home, on the street, in the community, in the workplace, in government, in church, in organizations, and within couples allows tension and hatred to build up and reaffirms and reproduces gender relations of domination and subordination. In this chapter, I analyze briefly some of the structural causes of recent violence against women in Mexico. Taken together, they demonstrate the failure of the neoliberal system to provide either development or a model of democracy in our country (Mexico).

Having defined feminicide and feminicidal violence as a direct expression of the structural violence of the neoliberal social system, we could pursue its causes in the political realm or in the ways in which individuals have been divided and battered by the violent dynamics of social transformation. Putting the neoliberal mandates into practice through institutionalized patriarchal power, Mexico's so-called political class and its business and financial sectors have undermined and violated both society's and individuals' rights, interests, and needs. In the case of women, one outcome of the processes on both levels has been murder.

At the same time that we consider the increase in violence against women, we must also take into account the increase of violence within families and of personal violence in general. These are the other side of the systemic violence of the neoliberal social structure, which creates a social ecology in which men are driven to hypermasculinity, exaggerating the violent, authoritarian, aggressive aspects of male identity in an attempt to preserve that identity. The counterpart of these attitudes is found in the subordinate positions of women in relation both to men and to institutionalized masculine power. In the face of neoliberalism's increasing demands, the dysfunction and obsolescence of these stereotypes is ever more evident. The disturbances they have always produced in personal relations are inflamed by the current social violence. Conflicts within couples and families as masculine domination is brought into question and delegitimized steadily increase the levels of violence and, of course, the risk of murder. These conflicts are multiplied under the pressure produced by unemployment, poverty, social polarization, alcoholism, and insecurity, among the many other problems that fill daily life with tension.

Neoliberal Dynamic, Economic-Political Crisis, and Violence against Women

The United Nations committee that recently investigated the murders and disappearances of women in Ciudad Juárez and Chihuahua concluded that they had to be seen not as isolated cases but as a product of a "situation of violence in a structurally violent society" (United Nations 2003a). It therefore recommended "combating criminality concurrently with the structural causes of gender violence, including domestic, intrafamilial and public incidents such as sexual abuse, homicides, kidnapping, and disappearances." Its report associates these cases with the high density of the cities bordering the United States and with the establishment of *maquilas* and the predominance in them of poorly paid female workers. The lack of job opportunities for men, according to a subsequent report, "has changed the traditional dynamics of relations between the sexes . . . creating a situation of conflict towards women because [the changes in employment patterns] have not been accompanied by a change in either traditional patriarchal attitudes and mentalities or the stereotyped vision of the social roles of men and women" (Committee on the Elimination of Discrimination against Women 2005, 7–11).

Indeed, poverty, unemployment, the disintegration of the peasant economy, and migration — all more acute since the government of President Carlos Salinas de Gortari (1988–94) accelerated neoliberal policies — are, along with the national crisis of governability, the most important structural causes of the increase in violence against women. Julio Boltvinik (2000) and Hernandez Laos (2000) maintain that in 2000, more than 75 percent of the country's population was poor or extremely poor. According to a recent survey, this figure now exceeds eighty percent (Boltvinik 2005). Although official sources recognize only between 45 percent and 52 percent as poor, a survey by the Organization of American States (OAS) concludes that Mexico, Brazil, and Colombia form a "triangle of extreme poverty" in Latin America because, in addition to high rates of poverty, they demonstrate insufficient progress with regard to the lowering of levels of maternal mortality and unemployment, to providing health services and comprehensive primary education, and to maintaining environmental sustainability. This situation is the result of the intense social polarization brought about by neoliberalism, which has deepened historical inequality and fostered corruption and inefficiency in governments that maintain oligarchic, authoritarian, and patriarchal social structures even though they are now disguised as democracies (Organization of American States 2005).

In Mexico, where neoliberal policies are applied dogmatically, favoring national and transnational companies and financial institutions at all costs, President Vicente Fox (2000–2006) adopted a discourse that systematically denied the exasperating social realities experienced by the population, among them marginalization; social, legal, and political exclusion in urban and rural areas; and a critical absence of human rights. The government reported that the economy had grown by 3.4 percent a year and that poverty had been reduced in a six-year period by 6.1 percent. This is something of an illusion, however, because in fact by 2006 we had barely returned to the levels of poverty that existed before the crash of 1995. Moreover, the growth described refers only to the macroeconomic level. What poverty reduction there has been in rural areas was actually due to the transfer of resources by government assistance programs and to remittances from the United States, both of which are used more for consumption than for investment.[2] Consequently, Mexico is among the countries in Latin America with the least improvement in human development in recent years, with barely 1.3 percent growth in per capita income between 1990 and 2003 (United Nations Development Program 2005). During this same period, real salaries remained stagnant, while unemployment increased from 600,000 in 2000 to 1.027 million in 2005, and inequality increased to the point that "five percent of the income from the richest households would be enough to pull twelve million Mexicans out of poverty, reducing the national poverty rate from sixteen percent to four percent" (González and Vargas 2005, 1).[3] And, of course, as bad as inequality and marginalization are in central and northern Mexico, they are much more severe in the south, where there is a high percentage of indigenous people and peasants.

Growth in industrial production and exports is also somewhat fictitious, since most of it comes from the maquiladoras, with little value added, minimal technology transfer, and volatile capital investment. Meanwhile, petroleum production is on the point of collapsing, both because of the rapid exhaustion of reserves accelerated by demand from the United States and because of the use of the profits to cover the country's current expenditures rather than for reinvestment (González and Vargas 2005).

The widespread poverty that results from these conditions has forced women to join the labor market under conditions of great inequality and vulnerability, basically because of their lack of training and freedom of movement and because the jobs to which they have access are in services and the informal economy, with low and unreliable incomes.[4] Many women work ten- to twelve-hour days in domestic service, restaurants, and small factories without any guarantees or benefits. The "flexibilization" of labor — the growth of temporary, informal work — throughout the economy has facilitated an increase in the exploitation of women, in the process feminizing poverty, access to jobs, and exploitation. According to a national survey, in 2005 95.38 percent of women considered economically active were employed in informal jobs in services and sales or some combination of the two. One-fourth of those in sales were self-employed in small establishments, and the rest worked for others, although not all received salaries (INEGI 2005). Poverty and marginalization have also forced women into prostitution or criminal gangs.

The massive integration of women into the labor force in search of a wage has effectively destroyed the traditional model of a sexual division of labor without changing the collective imaginary that women are dependent on men and that their obligations are in the home. In addition to working for wages, women continue to bear the responsibility of domestic chores, child care, and the organization of daily life, forcing them into double and triple shifts. But women are also questioned and made to feel guilty at the neighborhood and community levels and through the discourse of the right-wing government, which, for example, holds them responsible for juvenile delinquency. Supposedly, by "opting" to work outside the home, women are "neglecting their maternal obligations." Beyond ignoring men's responsibilities, this discourse deflects attention from the fact that violence and unemployment are a failure of government.[5]

The contradictions between the vision and the reality of being a woman not only affect the situation and subjectivity of women but cause a crisis in the images men have of themselves. The reason for this is that the changes in women's situations often lead them both to become fuller citizens and to develop gender consciousness. The fact that women acquire and manage their own resources troubles many men, especially in cases in which a woman's income is greater than that of her partner or in which the woman has decided on separation. For many men, the stereotypical self-image of the *macho* makes it difficult to accept roles that are inferior either objectively or symbolically to those of their mates. It is not uncommon in this situation for men to direct their aggression against their wives and children. Men's insecurity under these circumstances is often the cause of abandonment, divorce, and murder.

One symptom of the breakdown in traditional families and the increase in women's responsibilities and work outside the home is the large and growing percentage of households headed by women — almost 40 percent in Mexico in 2005. This one figure brings together the employment crisis, the absence of fathers in the lives of children, and the redefinition of feminine roles. At the same time, changes in women's economic situation, while they may increase individual women's possibilities of self-determination, do not thereby lead to the elimination of subordinate gender and class status. The reason for this is that the cultural and economic contexts in which these changes are occurring are not yet themselves changing. These contexts are deeply embedded in Mexico's individual and social ways of being (what Pierre Bourdieu [1999] calls "habitus"), and altering them will involve a more profound transformation.

Meanwhile, in addition to the economic distress of the middle class and the poor, there is the fact that the peasant model of production is breaking down, forcing a wave of rural workers to migrate to the United States. Several factors have contributed to this, almost all of them related to the implementation of neoliberal policies. The privatization of communal lands (*propiedad social*), which became possible only with the changes to Article 27 of the Constitution in 1992, has been promoted in recent years through the Programa de Certificación Agraria (Agrarian

Certification Program; PROCEDE), particularly in the north and central regions of the country, where large tracts of arable land have been urbanized or rented for agro-industrial production. In addition to defining boundaries and dividing the land of each *ejido*, or community, PROCEDE has permitted placing individual titles for plots in the names of family heads, mostly men. Women have in general been excluded, despite the fact that most of them work the land and that under the ejido regimen the plots were considered family property.

Nationally, women with personal rights to land constituted only 16.31 percent of holders of ejido and communal land in 2001 (INEGI 2001). Most were widows who were holding the land until their eldest sons, heirs to the title, came of age. The women recognized by PROCEDE, however, are even fewer. According to the Registro Agrario Nacional (2005), for example, between January 1993 and May 2005, women in Chiapas held land rights in only 14.25 percent of the communal units and 11.74 percent of the ejidos. In all, barely .7 percent of communal landowners and 3.4 percent of ejido owners are women.

Despite the fact that they have no rights as title holders, in general women manage family plots when their husbands migrate. This, of course, adds to their burdens, because even though they may hire others to help work the land, they remain responsible for cultivating and harvesting it. Even worse, many migrants sell their family plots to pay for their travel and the services of a "coyote" to get them to the United States. Women and children in these cases are even more dependent on men's remittances, which, of course, are always at risk as men are captured and expelled from the United States, lose their lives in the attempt to cross the border, or after months or years of absence start new families in the States. With migrants now tending to stay two years or more in the United States, wives left behind essentially become single mothers, which places great stress on them and their children (Bartra 2005).[6]

Finally, privatization has extended to public services. Reduction in health services is felt in the quality of life of most Mexicans and is statistically detectable in, for instance, the relative increase in maternal and infant mortality (United Nations Development Program 2005). Given the lack of resources and of prenatal care, population growth, which continues to be high in rural sectors (3.6 percent), occurs at the expense of women's health, demonstrated by their rapid aging and high morbidity rates. Public education has also suffered, and even public higher education has ever fewer resources for scientific and technological development.

Violence and Ungovernability

The economic crisis has given rise to various types of social violence. One of these arises from the existence of guerrillas whose movements repeatedly have been violently repressed. The massacre that most tragically illustrates this official violence occurred in 1997 in Acteal, Chiapas, where a paramilitary force trained by the army attacked a group of more than fifty people, most of them women and children, suspected of supporting the Zapatistas. Refugees from surrounding hamlets, the victims were trapped and murdered in a Catholic chapel. After the slaughter, the assassins mocked the symbols of maternity by hacking the women's breasts with machetes and extracting the fetuses from those who were pregnant (Olivera and Cárdenas 1998).

Beyond Chiapas, terror is also the objective of the army's permanent militarization of Guerrero and Oaxaca, typically in close coordination with state police. The destruction of villages, cornfields, and harvests, as well as harassment, the threat of sexual violence, jailing, disappearances, and the killing of men and women — all almost always unpunished — have served to generate and perpetuate a climate of fear. In the face of such terror, thousands of *campesinos* have fled their land; poverty, illness, and intrafamilial violence have increased; and women have seen their freedom of movement curtailed (Servicio Internacional para la Paz 2005). But surprisingly, official violence has stimulated women as well as men to defend their villages, even blocking the army's entrance to their communities with their bodies on occasion, as recently happened in Xo'yep, Chiapas (Speed 2000). Counterinsurgency strategies have also taken the form of development programs competing for adherents with the organized resistance groups, predictably leading to internal divisions and confrontations within communities.

Meanwhile, so-called organized social violence has become a crisis for the government, despite the significant expenditures to combat it. Much is spent, for instance, in fighting the drug cartels, which in recent years have been at war among themselves over distribution zones and control of points of entry into the United States. Thousands of deaths have resulted. Narco-corruption is so great that official security structures have had to be continually replaced as gang members penetrate or bribe the police. In September 2005, several top police officials, including the federal director of public security, died in a suspicious helicopter crash that many in the media and the public believe was caused by drug gangs. Some researchers and journalists now believe that Mexico has become like Colombia in the sense that the *narcos* have practically become a parallel power. President Fox and the government tried to conceal the extent of the violence, but it surpassed all of their efforts. Indeed, the murders of women that first attracted attention to feminicide as a national problem were those of Ciudad Juárez, which many journalists and activists believe may be related to the powerful drug cartels along the U.S.–Mexican border.

The proliferation of violent youth gangs is also associated with poverty, unemployment, drug trafficking, and the lack of prospects for young people. Such gangs have become a permanent threat to young women in particular, especially on the borders and in the larger urban centers. The increase in rapes, robberies, and kidnappings puts young women at constant risk, with very little institutional protection. Misogyny is a recurrent trait of the gangs' violations of women's human rights. In Chiapas, the state with the second-highest rate of murders of women after Chihuahua, for example, many of the bodies found show the marking "MST" or just "s" carved somewhere on the body as a terrifying insignia of the border gang Mara Salvatrucha.

In recent years, one of the pretexts for direct U.S. intervention in Mexico has been the struggle against insecurity and violence, which always employs violent means in return. President Fox was pressured to broaden the scope of Mexico's border patrols and accept a program of joint activity with U.S. officers in the border areas of Chihuahua, Sonora, and Tamaulipas. However, in addition to the serious crime problems that were used to justify these actions, these are also the crossing points for undocumented migrants — men and women who are victims of institutional crime almost as often as they are victims of offenses committed by common criminals.

The last element that contributes to insecurity and impunity throughout the country is a nonfunctional justice system. NGOs and government institutions alike report that murders of women, wherever they occur, are rarely treated with professionalism by prosecutors and judges. Not only are most cases inadequately investigated and documented, but the justice system's treatment of the families affected is truly inhuman (Lagarde y de los Ríos 2005). While punishing those who commit these murders might not stop the murders from occurring, it might serve as a deterrent.

The justice system's deficiencies in this regard have forced us to recognize that no one is even sure of the number of murders in Mexico in general. This recognition has led Congress to establish a special commission on feminicide, chaired by the feminist Representative Marcela Lagarde. This commission brought together a significant number of feminists from around the country to conduct an investigation in the eleven states with the highest incidence of murders of women. The results, along with proposals for public policies to resolve the problem, were released at the end of 2005 (see Comisión Especial sobre los Feminicidios 2005). The problem is so deep, however, that in order to make progress the women of Mexico need to participate in building a different world — one without violence, sexism, or oppression. And to do that, we must struggle against the neoliberal system that has invaded our lives.

Notes

This chapter originally appeared in *Latin American Perspectives* 33, no. 2 (2006): 104–14. Reprinted by permission of Sage Publications Inc.

1. Gender violence against women is considered here to be any act directed at members of the feminine sex that may result in injury or physical, sexual, or psychological suffering, including threats of such acts, coercion, or arbitrary deprivation of liberty either in public or in private life. These acts constitute violence even when their origin lies in custom or in the personal characteristics of those who commit them (Feministas de Chiapas 2004).

2. More than 8 million Mexican migrants work in the United States and, despite the existing salary discrimination, send remittances to Mexico that exceeded U.S. $20 billion in 2005 (Bartra 2005).

3. The report suggests that one of the reasons that neoliberalism has had less success than expected in Mexico is that the last three governments of Carlos Salinas de Gortari (1988–94), Ernesto Zedillo (1994–2000), and Vicente Fox (2000–2006) lowered trade barriers too quickly.

4. On a national level in 2000, 11.7 percent of women age fifteen and older had no education. A little more than 50 percent of women had some schooling, but only 9.4 percent had managed to get higher education. The poorest states had much lower rates. For example, in Chiapas, 28 percent of the women have had no education, and only 4.5 percent have had higher education (INEGI 2005). Such discrimination strongly affects peasant and indigenous women in particular. In Chiapas, for example, many indigenous women make craft products that they may sell directly to consumers but more typically sell through middlemen who retail them in tourist markets in Mexico or even abroad. Although there are some cooperatives that export in the solidarity market, most artisans barely recover their investment in materials, much less the value of their labor.

5. See the conclusions of the Congreso Mundial de la Familia, held in Mexico City in 2004 with government sponsorship (*La Jornada*, February 4, 2004).

6. See Delgado Wise (2006), Ruíz (2006), and Barkin (2006) for more on the causes and effects of the changes in the rural economy.

JULIA ESTELA MONÁRREZ FRAGOSO
Translated by Sara Koopman

The Victims of the
Ciudad Juárez Feminicide

SEXUALLY FETISHIZED COMMODITIES

In any analysis of feminicide in Ciudad Juárez, the first detail given — and the one that is most striking — is the way in which the bodies have been abandoned, stiff and inert, in one-dimensional, sexually transgressive settings: desert zones, empty lots, stream beds, sewers, and garbage dumps.[1] These desolate and arid spaces, full of filth, are important indicators, but at the same time the most dramatic aspect of their murders is the falsification, deception, and imitation of what these girls and women represented in their different social and cultural realities. When these nude and seminude bodies are left abandoned and neglected, their historical identities, citizenship, and territorial specificity are taken from them. They are transformed into what Laura Donaldson (1999, 3–4), referring to the collector's act of bringing objects together, calls "things" flung any which way to symbolize their value above and beyond any price due to their rarity. In the same manner, they also symbolize the women's low human value as less than women — as sexually fetishized commodities.

The testimony given by families when they identify the bodies are specific signs of the pain that is communicated from the body of the victim to the body that observes it. The testimony is a physical history of the pain. The signs that communicate pain, the visual images, should be read as a dialectical relationship between those who recognize the body and those who fail to do so. The body is mediated by pain, but it is also a body in pain that has been mediated by the assassins. The pain is part of the social construction of gender, but it is also part of the social construction of capital, and it exposes the sufferer to the vulnerability of those who observe their suffering. The physical body reveals the effects of violent power and reflects the tensions of civilization as a whole (Pincikowski 2002, 29), and of the victim's family in particular.

The anatomy of pain externalizes the anguish and grief of the relatives. As Scott Pincikowski argues in his analysis of bodies in pain and what their fragmentation means, it can be said that the bones of the condemned, dispersed and displaced, deny the possibility of an appropriate funeral. Honor and social prestige are undermined. The fragments of a body that once was an object of veneration represent signs of extreme cruelty. The blows and marks that are found on the corpses signify an entire system of pain that defines the sacrificed woman. The handcuffed hands cannot be brought together to plead for mercy; they no longer have an active role and cannot be used even to cover the eyes and face before atrocities and imminent death. The destroyed vagina evokes the action and scrutiny of male aggression and female defenselessness (Pincikowski 2002, 29–40, 95, 97). At the same time, the belongings and objects that in one way or another identify the victim attempt to retain her identity. Although the bodies have been ripped apart, they are individual bodies. They are more than "the dead women of Juárez," as they are coded. The assassinated women have become things, but they are part of the social relations that turned them into sexually fetishized commodities.

For this reason, my reflections trace a commodity analysis of the way in which these bodies were produced, distributed, consumed (Jhally 1990, 26), and thrown (out). When the violence that is exerted against women is analyzed, it is frequently said that the women are a part, and an effect, of the general cruelty of the city. As such, the problem of inequality between men and women — the ancient, violent links of gender difference — remains hidden and denied. The new links to the process of capitalism and the antagonism and exploitation of the social classes that exert violence are also left unnamed. Both relationships are overlooked in this analysis, in which two social systems have to come together for crime against women to be made concrete, and they are marked with an entire system of punishment and torture that keeps women subaltern in the face of arbitrary masculinity and in an inferior socioeconomic state that leads them to be regarded as defenseless property with little worth in the capitalist market.

The Production of a Body: Gender and Capitalism

The analysis of the production, construction, and economic exploitation of women's bodies is essential to understanding feminicide under patriarchal hegemony and capitalist hegemony. This is also a way to understand the nature of the links of an aspect that is related but is at the same time dialectic, and whereby the effects of the two processes are internalized in the bodies of the women "that is created, bounded, sustained, and ultimately *dissolved"* (Harvey 2000, 98; emphasis added). From this point of view, the body is represented and produced as a signifier of the gender system and of the economic social class system. Likewise, the body and its performativity cannot be understood if one does not take into account the body's insertion into social processes and all of the economic, political, and social forces that surround and culturally construct it. Thus, theory and experience should remain connected in this analysis to relate the micro-sphere of the physical body — of the assassinated women as much as of the assassin — to the macro-sphere of the forces that swirl around that same body and allow for systematic extermination over a decade. Leaving this knowledge out means ignoring that the culture and ideology of each society "disguises and even mystifies the dynamics of knowledge and its uses" (Keesing et al. 1987, 161) of violence in general, among which we find deadly violence against women. In this violence, the gender, social class, and race of the victim is chosen from a deadly misogynistic perspective.

If we consider women's bodies from a biological perspective and as receptacles of the various social constructs that mold them, we can, following Karl Marx, discuss the formation of the body as an *appendage of capital* through its circulation and accumulation. We can also discuss its formation as a docile body, as described through Michel Foucault's disciplinary mechanism (Harvey 2003, 123). From a feminist perspective, we have identified gender relations in the system of patriarchy. Likewise, we point to class as the positionality of the subject in relation to the circulation and accumulation of capital. At the same time, this process has to do with the ownership of the means of production and of rights to the body (Harvey 2003, 125).

Following David Harvey's analysis very closely, the body of a woman as a worker or as reserve labor is that of a person composed of a body and a will who sells her capacity to labor — that is, nothing more than a body that is transformed into a *commodity.* The extraction of that capacity to labor and the surplus value from the bodies of people and their subjectivities is part of the circulation of variable capital, which is reflected in *productive consumption, exchange,* and *individual consumption* (Harvey 2003, 125). So how, then, can we analyze all of these victimized bodies that held jobs as workers in maquiladoras, in shoe stores, in grocery stores, and of those who had not yet entered the workforce for whatever reason? Here Marx's (1979, 47) argument that these bodies represent "a mere gelatine of undifferentiated human labor" is relevant. Some were not workers as property, but they were potentially so, and as such would be subject to the conditions that reign in the labor market for a monotonous and unvarying production force.

The *productive consumption* of the commodity that is the capacity to labor in a capitalist labor market demands the mobilization of the " 'animal spirits,' sexual drives, affective feelings, and creative powers of labor to a given purpose defined by capital" (Harvey 2000, 103). In other words, the production of commodities is conditioned by the market. It is in this way that constructions of gender, race, and ethnicity are equally implicated in the variable circulation of capital and, therefore, in the division of labor and in the class system. These partial standards under which humanity is classified impose generalizations that are inadequate (Williams 2001, 279) but useful in the purchase of the capacity to labor available in each region, which has a price on the labor market according to its group value and is regulated on the basis of its alterity.

This leads to *exchange*. The body of the worker exchanges with the capitalist its commodity — the capacity to labor — which this body assumes as its capacity to dedicate itself to a set job. In this transaction between capitalism and the body of the worker, the basic condition of the contract assumes that the capitalist has the right to produce a disciplined body for production according to what the worker produces, following company guidelines to "direct the work, determine the labor process, and have free use of the capacity to labor during the hours and at the rate of remuneration stipulated in the contract" (Harvey 2000, 107). In Ciudad Juárez, everything involved in the maquiladora industry, including compulsory breaks, leave, vacation, training, supervision, and the distribution of work in response to technological changes, is determined by companies based on production needs (De la O Martínez 2001, 64).

In addition to acting as a producer or exchanger, the worker's body as an aggregate of variable capital finds itself in the position of being a consumer and reproducer in what is designated *individual consumption*. When this worker's body comes to possess money, it exercises autonomy in market practices that have to do with lifestyle, habit, and capitalist consumption (Harvey 2003, 133). The lifestyle of Ciudad Juárez clearly has been molded by processes that, over the past thirty years, have transformed the city from an agricultural economy offering tourist services into a manufacturing center of electronic and automobile parts for export. Nevertheless, Ciudad Juárez continues to carry a stigma as a perverse and lost border city. The most harmful weight of this, as Jorge Balderas Domínguez (2002, 47–65, 84–85, 95) argues, has fallen on female workers since they began to be incorporated into the workforce on a large scale in 1965. The maquiladoras were seen as saviors, for they took women out of the cabarets. Yet at the same time, the women who worked for the maquiladoras were seen as having dubious reputations because they transgressed public spaces: They became breadwinners, and when several women pooled their money, they could buy cars and go out dancing (Balderas Domínguez 2002, 100–42). That is, capitalist wages and the purchasing power they bring allowed women to transgress the patriarchal system.

Harvey says that the different bodily qualities that are codified in gender, ethnicity, social class, and other means of valuing human men and women, including the degree of respect of bodily integrity and the dignity the worker's body achieves in different places, exist in an environment that is made spatially competitive through the circulation of capital. For this reason, "uneven geographical development of the bodily practices and sensibilities of those who sell their labor power becomes one of the defining features of class struggle as waged by both capital and labor" (Harvey 2000, 109). Nevertheless, the global and the local should be viewed as analytical constructs, not as explanatory terms or empirical realities (Comaroff and Comaroff 1991, 2). To do otherwise is to commit the mistake of using industrial globalization as an explanation for everything and, at the same time, as an explanation of nothing.

Given this, we should analyze how this peculiar competitive struggle, which has repercussions on diverse bodily practices and assigns them a value on the labor market, has been maintained in Ciudad Juárez by a history and culture that has allowed for a geographically unequal valuation of workers' bodies, particularly the female worker's body. In this context we should remember how the female worker's body has been used as a monolithic explanation for a globalization process that allows for the construction of maquiladora workers as alluring victims (Fregoso 2003, 9). But beyond these arguments, it is clear that the process of industrialization and social class do not fully explain feminicide.

According to Rosa-Linda Fregoso, the feminicide in Ciudad Juárez from a feminist perspective is much more complex and goes beyond the equation of generic bodies *exploited* by capitalism, for they become generic bodies *exterminated* by a single process of industrialization from which both conditions are born (Fregoso 2003, 7). Fregoso argues that it is necessary to make clear the different structures of power in the unequal legal classifications and fragmentations of women. As such, we can visualize the power of wealth over poverty, the power of adulthood over youth, the power of a white elite over *racialized* women — in sum, "a dirty war" propped up by several factors against the disposable bodies of the women (Fregoso 2003, 2) that are exterminated by misogyny and sexual-political terrorism. It is an effective means for controlling women socially in which the power of the state over the social body is always present.

Lesley A. Sharp cites Marx in regard to commodities and fetishism.[2] Sharp argues that

> Marx recognized the social character of commodities produced within the alienating conditions of the capitalist system. Though his comments on fetishism are very brief, he emphasizes the enigmatic quality of commodities. He argues that, "At first look, a *commodity* appears to be a trivial thing, of immediate comprehension; its analysis demonstrates that it is a possessed object, rich in metaphysical subtleties and theological insinuations. Whereas with *use-value*, nothing mysterious hides within it" ([Marx] 1979, 87).[3] What is more, he argues that it is the origin of commodities, that is, the process that generates them, that remains obscure. The mystery of commodities lies in the fact that "value . . . does not include a label describing what it is," but rather "converts every product into a social hieroglyphic. Later on, we try to decipher the hieroglyphic, to get behind the secret of our own social products." (Marx 1979, 319–22; Sharp 2000, 291)

When we decipher the woman/commodity using a Marxist analysis, her consumption lies in the form of value of the *commodity*, "which is a dual thing. Its form of use-value is the form of the body of the commodity itself. . . . [I]t is the natural form of the commodity. The form of the commodity's exchange value is its social form" (Marx 1979, 1017). Commodities, on the other hand, satisfy those human needs that are independent of where they originate. In this argument I present a long quote from Marx's *Capital* and insert my comments:

> The [woman/commodity] is, in the first place, an exterior object, a thing with its own properties [her biological and gendered body] satisfying needs [patriarchal] of all kinds. The nature of these needs, which originate either from hunger or fantasy, [in the cultural construction of woman] does not modify the problem whatsoever ([Marx] 1979, 43). . . . The same body of the commodity [the body of woman] is thus of use value or a good ([Marx 1979], 44). . . . By the same token it is necessary to reduce the exchange value of the [women/commodities] to something that is common, with respect to that which they more or less represent [in terms of social class and gender, as well as of race and ethnicity]. ([Marx 1979], 46)[4]

When we read Marx in this way, we can see that, in the consumption sphere, women represent commodities that have a use value and an exchange value according to cultural constructions and the material life in which they are inserted. Thus, women are converted into items of consumption, into useful commodities whose bodies are frequently valued for their (re)productive potential (Sharp 2000, 293) and for, among other things, being zones of desire with a consumable difference (Lalvani 1995, 265). These bodies therefore need to be regulated, disciplined, and classified in their use and exchange in the different spheres of domination in which they are used and consumed. Therefore, when we ask who kills whom, we see that killing is not an act open to everyone. Rather, it is a function of patriarchy and other structures of power that are superimposed on the victim (Cameron and Frazer 1987, 63).

In this sense, those who have been assassinated have been killed because someone has (or various someones have) granted himself (or themselves) the right to consume and dispose of them. And this act is, as Marx (1979, 103) states as its referent when he says: "Commodities alone cannot take themselves to the market, or exchange amongst themselves. Therefore we have to turn to their custodians, *those who possess the commodities*. Commodities are things and, therefore, do not offer resistance to man. If they refuse to be taken, he can turn to violence or, in other words, take possession of them."

The custodians or possessors of the commodities, Marx argues, relate to each other as people whose will resides in the object. In this voluntary act, they together appropriate the commodity that is not their own by recognizing each other as private owners. This is a relationship of wills that draws on the economic and patriarchal relationship to take total possession of women. Simone de Beauvoir (1999, 156) explains: "The idea of possession is always impossible to positively realize: one never truly has anything or anyone. As such, one attempts to achieve [possession] in a negative way. The surest way of insuring that a good is mine is to impede another from using it. . . . What is more, one of the ends of any desire is to consume the desired object — which implies its destruction." This objectification of the subject is the key to an analysis of its subjection, and is vitally important for the consumption, use, and abuse of the human being. "Commodification insists upon objectification in some form, transforming persons and their bodies from a human category into objects of economic desire" (Sharp 2000, 293). As such, objectification is present in the subjection of individuals in this social system, and it allows for consumption to be instilled in them, be it economic, sexual, or murderous. This is why the images of the murdered girls and women have been twisted so that they emerge as something completely different — from the physical to the emotional; from the private to the public; as something enigmatic, unfathomable, and mysterious that must be deciphered.

In human terms, they have been converted into "the most miserable of commodities" (Marx 1977, 67).[5] The women have been turned into the product of a work of absurd fantasy of gender, class, and racial violence. Their lives are quantified in subjective fragments, or "lethal constructions" (Schmidt 2000, 308), that are part of social conventions and constructions and a way to organize people in relation to other people using nature (Taussig 1980, 4) and the social body. Nevertheless, when these fragmentations of women are seen as natural, it impedes analysis of the social construction and desensitizes the social body to the injury that has been committed against them. Isabel Velásquez puts it categorically: "Only one argument, perhaps the most important, has been absent from the discussions of the authorities, the statements in the press and the criminal experts — that the murdered women of Ciudad Juárez were Mexicans, and as such had the full right to live . . . and to move freely without being bothered or their lives put in danger . . . simply because they lived in a Republic with a constitutional government . . . and even once dead, they had the right to have the State use its force to . . . condemn the assassins . . . and for their name and their memory not to be put into doubt by public safety officers" (Benítez et al. 1999, 84–85).

Nevertheless, this gender violence is part of being "situated at the margin of the world [which is] not a favorable situation" (Beauvoir 1999, 129); of a citizenship for girls and women whose "sexual nature" has been instrumentalized as non-normative; whose racial heritage is a crack in the difference of the white social body; and whose poverty represents exclusion from material progress. All of these classifications made by the Other represent the exotic, or that which can be consumed (Lalvani 1995). The assassinated women are the ones who carry these subjectifications. They are the holders and carriers of these values, of the different structures of power over those who have the least.

The hieroglyphic analysis of the body of the assassinated woman is dual. For those who assassinate, the body is an object of the decor in which it is exhibited; it is part of a museum where the collector / collectors decorate the wide-open scene with the free exhibition of their genitals and sexuality. At the same time, the collector or collectors call for the assassinated woman to be rethought in other terms: as the one desired by the unstoppable sexual instincts of those who commit the feminicide, those who she herself convoked by doubly exposing herself, in a double life, down a trail of broken families. Her worth is also dual. Once fragmented, she becomes part of an integrated body of other divided bodies with an indissoluble value threaded with sexual and economic value: Its value is so little and so easy to replace in the processes of production that requires docile bodies, colonized bodies. At the same time, the assassinated bodies' dual value serves to ratify patriarchal restrictions on women, but those bodies also have the ability to perpetuate the social system of Ciudad Juárez, of (re)healing it and making it more pure through the example of its feminicide.

"Explaining" this feminicide as a collateral contingency of the growth of big cities, of human nature, of the psychopathology of the assassins does not take into account that human conduct is a product of man, a social product, and knowledge itself cancels out the understanding of the social order (Taussig 1980, 4) of those who construct it and benefit from it. The capitalist patriarchal system has changed her body into a subjected object with a new use and exchange value.

Her fetishization is a sign that obscures the way in which it has been produced and makes masculine domination appear given or natural. The borders of family, nation, identity, matrimony, and group belonging have been left outside those bodies. She definitely represents a new form of gender and economic oppression as part of a (re)configuration of a new capitalist, racist, and gendered modernity. Her differential consumption, according to Suren Lalvani (1995), generates a sphere of power under the control of consumerism as a sign of worth and exchange. She is represented as the exotic, and as her corpse is spread out with all of its libidinal power, she is converted into a fetishized woman / commodity. Once changed into a sexual fetish, she "absorb[s], contain[s], and exploit[s] the contradictions of modernity contributed in large extent by the phallic sphere of production" (Lalvani 1995, 265).

But through the "mark of excess" in torture and rape her corpse "could be exploited to eroticize the commodity and make consumption the equivalence of pleasure" (Lalvani 1995, 271). Following Lalvani's logic in regard to the fetishization of women, the incomplete and mutilated bodies function in their fragmentation as marks of desire for others (the assassins) who seek the exotic: immigrant, dark-skinned, rural, country girls or girls from Juárez or Juarenses; known or unknown, young maquiladora workers, students, shoe-store workers — in sum, poor women. Through these characteristics the woman has been seduced by murderous consumption, but at the same time she has been transformed in the process of seduction, like the image of an exchangeable commodity whereby human relations are transformed into things. As such, what can be exchanged among men are women.

Her assassination not only represents the construction of an other as a sensual object for death; it also symbolizes the exploitation of the female other in the sphere of exotic difference, in a discourse of racial superiority and economic development that legitimizes the consumption of things and people as a civilizing force (Lalvani 1995, 7–12). But at the same time, these women who have been converted into "things" have lost their connection with their social world and paradoxically appear as entities that are simultaneously inert and animated (Taussig 1980, 5). I can find no better way to compare the prolonged consumption with impunity of the sexually fetishized girl or woman than these two words: *inert* and *animated*. The assassinated women find themselves suspended as they wait for justice while at the same time the potential victims appear as a sort of spirit revived from death, because, as Ramona Ortiz asks, "In what society can one find . . . raped bodies without anything much happening? What makes someone think (be it an occasional or premeditated assassin, a one-timer or serial killer, alone or accompanied, Mexican or foreign) that in Ciudad Juárez you can rape and kill a woman without fear that anything will happen to you?" (Benítez et al. 1999, 101).

Is this not the transformation of women's bodies into a sexual fetish that can be tortured, mutilated, raped, and thrown away? The horror and the atrocities become part of the urban norm and part of the sexual excess of girls and women who "asked for it." As such, the collection of bodies can continue indefinitely in a logic of objectification of women who are crossed by different power structures whose acts of discrimination are not analyzed. Quite the opposite: They are considered natural. The women are not granted the right of citizenship but, rather, are marginalized and condemned to be victims of sexual assailants. The low value of the feminine body that does not adapt and that transgresses the border culture, the religious culture, the economic culture, becomes evident when that body is displayed in a brutal decor that converts it into a sign of its (in)significance. In this same sign the person who lacerated the body and exhibited it remains unidentified.

The sexual and economic benefit of these inert bodies would seem to end with death, but it continues to be present in their fetishization in prohibited spaces, in the one-dimensional scene of the women/objects that are left in the desert for long periods and evoke an entire history of suffering that remains in the collective memory of women and men — of course, with different meanings for each man and woman, since memory cannot be equally interpreted from any given social situation. Reflections on life and human dignity therefore are not at the center of the city but on its margins — in the empty lots, the sand pits, the desert where the bodies have been thrown. All of these scenes and remains of bodies reveal to us the economic functionality of violence against women as an aberrant and absurd fantasy of gender, race, and social class. All of these elements are converted into sexual coordinates intertwined in the woman as sexual fetish. It is only when the State, as the guarantor of justice, recognizes these omissions that they will become crimes against humanity and the logic of justice, though late, will be reestablished. It is at that moment that victims and their families will have justice.

Notes

1. I use *feminicide* (a concept that comes from the term *femicide* and which was translated by Marcela Lagarde as *feminicidio* 'feminicide') because it is a theoretical offering and a feminist political stand (Lagarde y de los Ríos 1999; Radford and Russell 1992; Russell and Harmes 2001). Feminicide is the assassination of a woman committed by a man, where one finds all of the elements of the relationship of inequality between the sexes: the gender superiority of man over the gender subordination of woman, misogyny, control, and sexism. Not only is a woman's biological body assassinated, but what the cultural construction of her body has signified is also assassinated, with the passivity and tolerance of a masculinized state.

2. In this section I follow the Marxist analysis traced by Sharp (2000); the only changes are the references to the Spanish editions of Marxist texts.

3. Editor's translation.

4. Editor's translation.

5. Editor's translation.

RITA LAURA SEGATO
Translated by Sara Koopman

Territory, Sovereignty, and Crimes of the Second State

THE WRITING ON THE BODY OF MURDERED WOMEN

As a place, Ciudad Juárez is emblematic of women's suffering. There more than anywhere else, the motto "Woman's Body Equals Danger of Death" becomes real.

Ciudad Juarez is also an emblematic place of economic globalization and neoliberalism, with its insatiable hunger for profit. The sinister shadow that covers the city and the constant fear I felt during each day and each night of the week I spent there continued to haunt me for months after my return to Brazil. There one can witness the direct link between capital and death, between unruly accumulation and concentration and the sacrifice of poor, dark-skinned women, mestizas, engulfed in the clefts of the joints linking monetary and symbolic economy, control of resources and death power.

I was invited to go to Ciudad Juárez in July 2004 because in the preceding year two women from the Mexican organizations Epikeia and Nuestras Hijas de Regreso a Casa (Bring Our Daughters Home) had heard me lay out what seemed to me the only plausible hypothesis for the enigmatic crimes that haunted the city: the deaths of women of a similar physical type, which were perpetrated with an excess of cruelty, exhibited evidence of gang rape and torture, and being disproportionately numerous and continuing for more than eleven years, seemed unintelligible.

My initial nine-day commitment to take part in a forum about the feminicides of Ciudad Juárez was interrupted by a series of events that resulted, on the sixth day, in the entire city's cable-television signal crashing just as I started to describe my interpretation of the crimes in an interview with Jaime Pérez Mendoza on local Channel 5. The frightening coincidence of the timing of the signal crash and the first word of my answer as to the reasons for the crimes led us to decide to get out of the city. We left Ciudad Juárez the following morning for our safety and as a protest against such censorship. We were astounded when everyone whom we talked to confirmed that our decision to leave was a wise one.

It is worth remembering that, in Ciudad Juárez, it appears that there are no coincidences. As I will try to argue, everything works as part of one complex communication machine whose messages are intelligible only to those who, for one reason or another, are able to break the code. Thus, the first problem that the hideous crimes of Ciudad Juárez pose for foreigners and distant audiences is that of intelligibility. And it is precisely in their unintelligibility that the murderers take refuge, as if using a sinister war code, an argot made up entirely of "acting out" behavior. To give only one example of this logic of signification, I turn to one of the journalist Graciela Atencio's articles on the murdered women of Ciudad Juárez. In it she questions whether it was mere coincidence that precisely on August 16, 2003, when her newspaper, the daily *La Jornada* of Mexico City, first published the news of a Federal Bureau of Investigation (FBI) report "describing a possible *modus operandi* in the kidnapping and disappearance of young women" that problems with the mail prevented its distribution in Ciudad Juárez (Atencio 2003).

Unfortunately, this was not the only apparently significant coincidence during my time in the city. On Monday, July 26, after having given my first talk and halfway through our forum — and exactly four months after the discovery of the last corpse — the dead body of the maquiladora worker Alma Brisa Molina Baca appeared. I will spare you the description of the many irregularities committed by investigators and the local press regarding Alma Brisa's remains. It is no exaggeration to say that you had to see it to believe it; you had to witness the inconceivable, the unbelievable. But I will note that the body was found in the same empty lot in the center of the city where another victim had been found the year before. That other victim was the murdered daughter, still a child, of the mother who we had in fact interviewed just the evening before, on July 25, in the bleak neighborhood of Lomas de Poleo, in the barren desert that crosses the border between Chihuahua and the U.S. State of New Mexico.[1] General comments also pointed to the fact that the year before another body had been found during the federal intervention in the Mexican State of Chihuahua ordered by then President Vicente Fox. The cards were on the table. This sinister "dialogue" seemed to confirm that we were inside the code and that the traces we were following led to a destination.

This is the interpretative path I will trace here, as well as what I was about to say when the cable-television signal crashed that early Friday morning of July 30, 2004. It is a path that describes the relationship between the deaths, the illicit results of the ferocious neoliberalism globalized across the borders of the "Great Frontier" after the North America Free Trade Agreement, and the unregulated accumulation that was concentrated in the hands of certain families of Ciudad Juárez. Indeed, what stands out the most when you take the pulse of Ciudad Juárez is the vehemence with which public opinion rejects the names that law enforcement presents as the presumed culprits. It gives the impression that people want to look in another direction and are waiting for the police to direct their suspicions to the other side — to the city's rich neighborhoods.[2] The illegal traffic to the other side is of every possible type: It includes the commodities produced from the work extorted from the maquiladora workers and the surplus that the value extracted from that work adds, as well as drugs and bodies — in short, all of the considerable capital that these businesses generate south of paradise. This illicit movement is similar to a process of constant repayment to an unfair, voracious, and insatiable tax collector who nevertheless hides his appetite and disengages himself from the seduction he exerts. The border between the misery of excess and the misery of lack is an abyss.

Two things can be said of Ciudad Juárez without risk. They are, in fact, said by everybody: the police, the attorney general, the special prosecutor, the human rights commissioner, the press, and the activists. One is that "the *narcos* (drug traffickers) are responsible for the crimes," sending us to a subject that looks like a thug and reaffirming our fear of the margins of social life. The other is that "these are sexually motivated crimes." On the day after Alma Brisa's body was discovered, the newspaper repeated that this was "yet another sexually motivated crime," and the special prosecutor emphasized, "It is very difficult to reduce the number of sexual crimes" — confusing the evidence yet again and sending the public down what I believe is the wrong path. This is how, while pretending to speak in favor of the law and rights, opinion makers and the authorities foster an indiscriminate perception of the misogynist crimes occurring in Ciudad Juárez, as well as in others part of Mexico, Central America, and the world: crimes of passion, domestic violence, sexual abuse, rape by serial aggressors, crimes related to drug debts, trafficking of women, cyber-pornography crimes, trafficking of organs, and so on. This I understand as "will of indistinctness" between these crimes and all the crimes committed against women, and the matter-of-fact look directed at them; they work as a smokescreen whose consequence is to prevent a clear view of a central nucleus that shows particular and similar characteristics. It is as if concentric circles formed by various forms of aggression are hiding in their center a particular type of crime (not necessarily the most numerous but the most enigmatic, given its precise, almost bureaucratic, characteristics): the kidnapping of young women of a distinct physical type, most of them workers or students, who are held captive for several days and tortured, gang raped (as the former Chief of Experts Oscar Máynez declared more than once at the forum), mutilated, and murdered. This is followed by the mixing or loss of clues and evidence by law enforcement, threats and attacks by lawyers and journalists, deliberate pressure by authorities to blame scapegoats who are clearly innocent — and, ultimately, the continuation of these crimes, uninterrupted, from 1993 to the present. The impunity over all these years is terrifying and can be described by three characteristics: (1) the absence of indicted perpetrators who are credible in public opinion; (2) the absence of consistent lines of inquiry; and (3) an endless repetitive cycle of this sort of crime as a consequence.

Two brave investigative journalists — Diana Washington Valdez, the author of *Cosecha de mujeres* (Harvest of women; 2005), and Sergio González Rodríguez, the author of *Huesos en el desierto* (Bones in the desert; 2002) — gathered numerous details that the police had set aside over the years and came up with a long list of places and people that, in one way or another, are linked to the disappearances and murders of women.[3]

I spoke with Diana Washington on two occasions on the other side of the border (the FBI does not let her cross the bridge without an escort), and I read Sergio González's book. What emerges is that people from "good" families — large landholders — are connected to the murders. But a crucial link is missing: What drives these respected, financially successful heads of prestigious families to become involved in gruesome and, as all signs indicate, collectively committed crimes? What could be the plausible link between these men and the kidnappings and gang rapes that would allow them to be identified and formally accused? A reason seems missing. It is precisely here, in the search for this reason, that the overused idea of "sexual motives" is insufficient. New classifications, legal categories, and clearer definitions are needed to be able to understand the specificity of a limited number of deaths in Ciudad Juárez. It is particularly necessary to state what appears obvious: that no crime committed by common outcasts would remain in complete impunity for this long, and no serious police force would speak so lightly of criminal motives, which generally are determined after lengthy investigation. Those basic truths make Ciudad Juárez shudder and become unspeakable.

Science and Life

Before I heard about the Ciudad Juárez murders, I conducted research from 1993 to 1995 on the state of mind of condemned rapists imprisoned in Brasilia (Segato 2003a).[4] What I heard these prisoners, all of them convicted for anonymous sexual assaults of unknown victims on the street, say reinforces the fundamental feminist thesis that sexual crimes are not the work of deviant individuals, or of the mentally ill. Neither are they social anomalies. They are, rather, expressions of a deep symbolic structure that organizes our acts and fantasies and makes them intelligible. In other words, the aggressors share the collective gender imaginary. They speak the same language; they can be understood.

What emerged more strongly than ever in the interviews is what Menacher Amir (1971) had already found in a quantitative analysis of empirical data: Contrary to our expectations, rapists generally do not act alone. They are not antisocial animals preying on their victims as lonely hunters; rather, they commit their crimes in the company of others. There are not words enough to emphasize the importance of this finding and its importance for understanding rape as a real act that occurs *in societate* — that is, in a communicable niche that can be penetrated and understood.

Rape as the use and abuse of the body of another without compatible intention or will is aimed at annihilating the victim's will. The achievement of this end is signified precisely by the victim's loss of control over her body's behavior and the management of it by the aggressors' will. The victim's control of her body space is expropriated. For this reason, it can be said that rape is the act par excellence of Carl Schmitt's definition of sovereignty (Agamben 1998; Schmitt 2006 [1922]): unrestricted control; arbitrary and discretionary sovereign willpower whose condition of possibility is to annihilate equivalent attributions in others and, above all, to eradicate the power of these as alterity indexes or alternative subjectivities. In this sense, this act is also tied to the consumption of the "other," a cannibalism through which the other perishes as an autonomous will and is allowed to continue to exist only as appropriated and included in the body of the one who devoured it. The remains of its existence lie only as part of the dominator's project.

Why does rape acquire this meaning? As a consequence of the function and role of sexuality in the world as we know it, rape combines physical and moral subjugation in a single action. There is no sovereign power that is only physical. Without psychological and moral subordination of the other, there is only death power, and death power by itself is not sovereignty. Complete sovereignty, in its most extreme phase, implies "to *make* live or *let* die" (Foucault 1999). With no control over life as such — that is, of the living — domination cannot complete itself. This is why a war that ends in extermination is not a victory, because only the power of colonization makes it possible to demonstrate the death power among those destined to remain alive. Sovereignty's mark par excellence is not the power of death over the subjugated but, rather, the psychological and moral defeat of the subjugated and their transformation into a receptive audience for the dominator's exhibition of its discretionary death power.

It is for its expressive rather than instrumental quality — violence whose finality is expressing absolute control of one's will over another's — that rape is the aggression nearest to torture, whether physical or moral. The expression of being in control of somebody else's will is the telos or finality of expressive violence. Dominance, sovereignty, and control are its semantic realm, not benefits of a utilitarian sort. It is worth remembering that these, nevertheless, are functions that can be exercised only before a community of the living and therefore have more in common with the idea of colonization than that of extermination. In a regime of sovereignty, some are destined for death so the sovereign power can leave its mark on their bodies. In this sense, the death of those chosen to represent the drama of domination is an expressive death, not a utilitarian death.

It is necessary yet to understand that all violence, including that in which the instrumental function prevails, somewhat exceeds instrumentality and contains an expressive dimension. In this sense, one can say what every detective knows: Every act of violence, as a discursive gesture, has a signature. It is in this signature that a subject's reiterative presence can be seen through an act. Any detective knows that if we recognize what is common to a number of crimes, we can identify the signature, the profile, the presence of an identifiable subject behind an act. An aggressor's modus operandi is nothing more and nothing less than the mark of a style across various speeches. Identifying the style of a violent act the way we identify the style of a text will take us to the perpetrator in his or her role as author. In this sense, the signature is not a result of deliberation, of will. It is instead a consequence of the enunciation's own automatism — the recognizable trace of the subject, his position and interests, in what he says, in what he expresses by word or deed (Derrida 1972).

Rape, as I have argued (Segato 2003a), is an enunciation necessarily addressed to one or many interlocutors who are present either physically in the scene or in the enunciating subject's mental landscape. It turns out that the rapist sends his messages along two axes of dialogue and not one, as is frequently argued by those who focus only on his interaction with the victim. On the vertical axis he does speak, indeed, to the victim: His discourse acquires a punitive aspect, and the aggressor takes on a moralizing profile as a safeguard of social morality, because in that shared imaginary woman's destiny is to be contained, censored, disciplined, and reduced by the violent gesture of he who reincarnates the sovereign function through this act. However, it is the discovery of a horizontal axis of dialogue that potentially represents the most interesting contribution of my research with convicted rapists in Brasilia. The aggressor addresses himself to his peers, and he does so in several ways: He petitions to be accepted into their society, and from this perspective, the raped woman becomes the immolated sacrificial victim of a ritual of initiation; he competes with his peers, showing that, because of his aggressiveness and power of death, he deserves to be part of the virile brotherhood and even to acquire a distinguished position in a fraternity that recognizes only a hierarchical language and a pyramidal organization. In the case of the ordinary rapist, he resorts to rape as a surrogate road of access to manhood that, for a variety of reasons, he cannot attain through legal — or, at least, socially authorized — violence.

This is so because in the extremely long and slow tempo of the history of gender, so long that it seems to overlap with the history of the species, producing masculinity obeys processes different from those that produce femininity. In a transcultural perspective, evidence shows that masculinity is a status that is only conditionally achieved and as such has to be reconfirmed with certain regularity throughout life. This is done through a process of tests or conquests and is above all dependent on the exaction of tribute from an other that, because of the naturalized position in this status order, is perceived as the provider of the repertoire of gestures that nourish virility. This other, by means of the very act of handing over the renewed tribute, produces its own exclusion from the caste it consecrates. In other words, the necessary condition for a given subject to obtain his masculine status as a title, as a rank, is that another subject that does not have it grants it to him through a process of persuasion or imposition, which can be effectively described as tribute. In "normal" sociopolitical conditions of the status order, we as women are the givers of the tribute, and they as men are the receivers and beneficiaries. The structure connecting these two positions recycles a symbolic order marked by inequality. The patriarchal system so reproduced underpins all scenes of social life ruled by the asymmetry of a status law. It constellates and gives meaning to its actors despite the most erratic dispositions they might display, impregnating them with the marks of the positions in the relationships contained by the structure.

In short, according to this model the crime of rape results from a commandment arising from the gender structure to guarantee the tribute that qualifies each new member for access to the virile brotherhood. It occurs to me that the tension between the two axes — the vertical one, or the consumption of the victim, and the horizontal one, conditioned on obtaining the tribute — can shed light on key aspects of the long and established cycle of feminicides in Ciudad Juárez. In fact, what took me to Ciudad Juárez was that my interpretive model of rape seemed able to shed new light on the enigma of the feminicides and allow for the organization of the puzzle's pieces so that a recognizable design emerges.

Inspired in this model, which emphasizes the importance of two interlocutional coordinates organizing fraternity membership, I tend not to understand the feminicides of Ciudad Juárez as crimes in which hatred toward the victim is the dominant factor (Radford and Russell 1992). I do not doubt that misogyny, in the strict sense of intense hatred of women, is common in the environment in which the crimes take place and constitute a precondition for their occurrence. Yet I am convinced that the victim is the waste product of the process, a discardable piece, and that extreme conditions and requirements for being accepted into a group of peers are behind the enigma of Ciudad Juárez. Those who give meaning to the scene are other men, not the victim, whose role is to be consumed to satisfy a group's demands to become and remain cohesive as a group. The privileged interlocutors in this scene are the peers: the members of this mafia fraternity, to guarantee and seal their covenant; its opponents, to exhibit power before their business competitors, local authorities, federal authorities, activists, scholars, and journalists who dare to get mixed up in their sacred domain; or the victims' fathers, brothers, or male friends. These requirements and forms of exhibitionism are characteristics of the patriarchal regime of a mafia order.

The Feminicides of Ciudad Juárez: A Criminological Proposal

I present here a list of several ideas that together paint a possible picture of the feminicides' setting, motives, ends, meanings, and occasions and the conditions that make them possible. My problem is that the analysis can be rendered only in the form of a list. Nevertheless, the issues outlined together paint a picture that makes sense. It is not a linear list of successive items but a meaningful whole: the world of Ciudad Juárez. This is why every particular element leading to the crimes need not be part of the perpetrators' discursive conscience: They are constitutive of the world where aggressors belong and make up their subjectivity. To speak of causes and effects does not seem adequate to me; to speak of a universe of intertwined meanings and intelligible motivations does.

THE PLACE: THE GREAT BORDER

As a frontier between excess and lack, North and South, Mars and the Earth, Ciudad Juárez is not a cheerful place. It embraces many tears, many fears.

It is the frontier that money has to cross, virtually and materially, to reach the firm land where capital finds itself finally safe and gives its rewards in prestige, security, comfort and health. It is the frontier beyond which capital gets moralized and reaches worthwhile, sound banks.

It is the frontier to the most patrolled country in the world, with its almost infallible tracking and close-range surveillance. Here, around this line in the desert more than anywhere else, illicit actions must be carried out in the utmost stealth and secrecy by the most cohesive clandestine organization. A rigorous pact of silence is its requisite.

This is the frontier where the great entrepreneurs "work" on one side and live on the other. It is the frontier of the great expansion and fast valorization, where terrain is literally stolen from the desert each day, each time nearer the Río Bravo.

It is the frontier of the world's most lucrative traffic—in drugs; in bodies.

It is the frontier that separates one of the most expensive labor forces from one of the cheapest.

This frontier is the background of the longest-lasting series of attacks on women's bodies with similar modus operandi known in so-called peacetime.

THE PURPOSES

The evidence that the justice system had an extremely long period of inertia around these crimes immediately points our attention to their persistent subtext: The crimes speak of impunity. Impunity is their grand issue, and as such impunity is the way into deciphering them. Although the environment I have just described, characterized by a concentration of economic and political power and, therefore, high levels of privilege and protection for some groups, is the ideal cauldron for brewing the murders, it occurs to me that we are mistaken when we see impunity exclusively as a causal factor.

I propose that the feminicides of Ciudad Juárez can be better understood if we stop thinking of them as a consequence of impunity and imagine them as producers and reproducers of impunity. This was my first hypothesis, and it is also possible that it was the first purpose of perpetrators: to seal, with collectively shared complicity in the hideous torturing and killing of captive and defenseless women, a vow of silence able to guarantee the unbreakable loyalty to mafia brotherhoods operating across the most patrolled border in the world. The feminicides also serve as proof of the capacity for cruelty and power of death required for conducting extremely dangerous business. The sacrificial ritual, violent and macabre, unites the members of the mafia and makes their bond unbreakable. The sacrificial victim, part of a dominated territory, is forced to hand over the tribute of her body for the cohesion and vitality of the group. The stain of her blood defines the assassins' esoteric belonging to the group. In other words, more than a cause, impunity can be understood as a product, as the result, of these crimes, and the crimes can be seen as a means for producing and reproducing impunity: a blood pact sealed with the victims' blood. There is also another dimension: to give proof of the capacity for the extreme cruelty and unwavering death power that highly dangerous and illicit businesses require.

In this sense, we can point to a fundamental difference between this sort of crime and the gender crimes perpetrated in the intimacy of domestic space against daughters, stepdaughters, nieces, wives, and other victims who belong to the circle of the abuser. If in the shelter of domestic space a man abuses the women who depend on him because he can — that is, because they are part of the territory that he controls — the aggressor who takes possession of the female body in an open, public space does so because he must prove that he can. The first case is a matter of affirming an existing domination; the latter is the exhibition of a capacity for domination that must be restaged with certain regularity and can be associated with the ritual gestures that renew vows of virility. Power here is conditioned on a regularly dramatized public exhibition of a predatory action against a woman's body. But the production and maintenance of impunity through the sealing of a pact of silence in reality cannot be distinguished from what could be described as the exhibition of impunity. The classic strategy that sovereign power uses to reproduce itself as such is to broadcast and even spectacularize the fact that it is above the law and can legislate. We can also understand the crimes of Ciudad Juárez in this way and suggest that they also fulfill the *exemplary function* by means of which sovereign power lets slip the crude reality of its presence in everyday life together with its underworld vitality as a ruling *second state* that is acting and shaping society from beneath the law.

This is so because, in the capacity to kidnap, torture, and kill repeatedly and with impunity, the subject/author of these crimes displays, beyond any doubt, the cohesion, vitality, and territorial control of the corporatist web that he commands and the code of norms at work in it. It is evident that the continuity of this sort of crime over eleven years requires considerable human and material resources, including the command of an extensive web of loyal associates; access to detention and torture sites; vehicles for transporting victims; and access to, influence over, or power to blackmail or intimidate representatives of public order at every level, including the federal level. What is important to note is that, as this powerful network of allies is set in motion for cover-up by those who command the corporatist crimes of Ciudad Juárez, the existence of the web is exhibited in an ostentatious display of a totalitarian domination over the area.

THE MEANINGS

It is precisely when this last function is accomplished that the crimes begin to behave as a communication system. If we listen carefully to the messages that circulate there, we can see the face of the subject speaking through them. Only when we understand what he says, to whom and with what ends, will we be able to locate the position from which he speaks. This is why we must insist that each time the sexual-motive explanation is repeated lightly, before analyzing minutely what is being "said" in these dialogic acts, we lose a chance to follow the trail of he who hides behind the bloody text.

In other words, the feminicides are messages sent by a subject/author who can be identified, located, and profiled only by rigorously "listening" to these crimes as communicative acts. It is within his discourse that we find the subject who speaks; it is within discourse that the reality of this subject is inscribed as identity and subjectivity and therefore becomes traceable and recognizable. Likewise, in its enunciation we can find the interlocutor's trail, his imprint, like a photographic negative. This is true not only for the violent "acting-out" behaviors that the police investigate, but also for the discourse of any subject, as a variety of contemporary philosophers and literary theorists have made clear.[5]

If the violent act is understood as a message, and the crimes are seen as orchestrated in a clear call-and-response style, we find ourselves in a scene where the acts of violence communicate efficiently with those who "know" the code, the well informed, those who speak the language, *even when they are not taking part directly in the enunciative action*. This is why once a communication system with a violent alphabet is installed it is very difficult to de-install and eliminate it. Violence, constituted and crystallized within a communication system, is transformed into a stable language and comes to behave in the nearly automatic fashion of any language.

To ask in these cases why there are killings in a certain place is similar to asking why a certain language is spoken there — Italian in Italy, Portuguese in Brazil. At some point, each one of these languages was established through historical processes, be they conquest, colonization, migration, or the unification of territories under one national state. In this sense, the reason we speak a certain language is arbitrary and cannot be explained by logic. The processes by which a language is wiped out, eradicated from a territory, are also historical. The problem of violence as a language is even worse if we consider that there are certain languages that, in particular historical conditions, tend to become the lingua franca and spread across the ethnic or national borders that defined their original niche.

And so we ask: Who is speaking here? To whom? What is being said? When? What is the language of feminicide? My bet is that the author of these crimes is a subject who values profit and control of territory above all else, even above his own personal happiness; a subject with an entourage of vassals who in this way makes it absolutely clear that Ciudad Juárez has landlords and that these landlords kill women precisely to show themselves as such. *Sovereign power does not affirm itself unless it is able to spread terror in a way that nobody is safe.* "Sovereign is the one for whom all men are potentially *hominis sacri*" — "nude" men who could be killed without consequences because, as a Roman juridical variety of a death penalty, they were condemned to become devoid of civil existential status (Agamben 1998) — "and *homo sacer* is the one towards whom all men act as sovereign" (Agamben 2005, 110). Is the author here aware he may be referring to women? Could the author accept as possible that all women customarily belong to this category of people that represent bare life, life that can be erased without consequences for public law and society?

He, the sovereign, addresses himself to all men in the domain: to those who should have been responsible for the victim and all of the others like her in the domestic space and to those responsible for their protection as representatives of the state. He also speaks to the men of the other, either friendly or hostile fraternities to show the array of resources he has at his disposal and the strength of his support network. To his allies and business partners he confirms that the group communion and loyalty continue unaltered. He tells them that his control over the territory is total; that his web of alliances is cohesive and trustworthy; and that his resources and contacts are unlimited.

He pronounces himself in this way during the consolidation of a brotherhood; when planning a dangerous, illicit business transaction on this patrolled border; when the doors are opened to a new member; when another mafia group challenges his control of the territory; or when there are external inspections, intrusions on his total control of the area.

The language of feminicide uses women's bodies to indicate what can be sacrificed for a higher good, a collective good, such as the constitution of a mafia brotherhood. The woman's body is the supreme index of the position of she who renders tribute, of the victim whose sacrifice and consumption will be most easily absorbed and naturalized by the community. Part of this process of digestion is the usual double victimization of she who is already victim, as well as the double and triple victimization of her family, usually represented by a mourning mother. To reduce the dissonance between the logic with which we expect life to behave and the way it really does, an almost uncontrollable mechanism of cognitive defense makes us hate those who, though unwillingly, play a part in the staging of such unbearable cruelty. Given the definitive absence of the aggressor, someone has to be held responsible for the collective distress caused in this way.

Just as it is usual for the convicted to blame their victims for their own fate and loss of freedom, in the same way the community is ever more engulfed in a misogynist cycle that, lacking appropriate support for dealing with the discomfort, leads it to blame the victim herself for the cruelty she faced. We easily choose to reduce our own suffering when confronted with testimony of intolerable injustices, alleging that "there must be a reason." In this way, the women murdered in Ciudad Juárez quickly are transformed into prostitutes, liars, partygoers, drug addicts, and all that which can inoculate us from the responsibility and bitterness of facing the injustice of their fate.

If we are to follow the track of the equivalence between women and the nude life of *sacer* humans, we may venture that the crimes of carnality and eroticism condemn them to such a verdict and to the permanent open possibility of being disposed of in a wasteland, as garbage, as residue of the real, vested life of the covenant citizens. Their sacred quality may derive from the sacrifice on which the emergence of the covenant itself depends.

Gang rape, as in pacts of blood, is the mixing of body substances of all

those who take part in it; the act of sharing intimacy in its most ferocious aspect, of exposing what is kept under the greatest of zeal — sex
itself, as the leak of the most intimate of all secretions. As the willing cut
from where blood flows, rape is the making public of the fantasy, the
transgression of a limit, a radically compromising gesture.

In the language of feminicide, the female body also signifies territory,
and its etymology is as archaic as its transformations are recent. It has
been constitutive of the language of wars, tribal and modern, that the
woman's body is annexed as part of the nation that is conquered. The
sexuality poured over it expresses the taming act, the taking possession
of, when inseminating the woman's body territory. This is how the mark
of territorial control by the lords of Ciudad Juárez can be inscribed on
the body of the city's women as part of or as an extension of the domain
they declare as their own. Rape as sexual domination implies, in conjunction, not only physical control over the victim, but also moral reduction of the victim and its associates. Moral reduction is a requisite
for domination to be consummated, and sexuality in the world we
know plays a fundamental part in the moral chart.

What, then, does *feminicide* mean in the sense that Ciudad Juárez
gives to the term? It is the murder of a generic woman, of a type of
woman, simply for being a woman and being of this type, in the same
way genocide is a generic and lethal attack on all who belong to the same
ethnic, racial, linguistic, religious, or ideological group. Both crimes are
directed at a category, not a specific subject. Indeed, this subject is
depersonalized as a subject, for the category it belongs to is more relevant than its individual biographical or personality traits.

But it seems to me that there is a difference between these two kinds
of crimes that should be further examined and discussed. If in genocide
the rhetorical construction of hate toward the other leads to the act of
his or her elimination, in feminicide the misogyny that lies behind the
act is a feeling more like that of hunters for their trophy: a contempt for
that life or the conviction that the only value of that life lies in its
availability for appropriation.

As such, the crimes seem to speak of a truly beastly *primae noctis* (the
right of the landlord to rape a woman on her wedding night) by a feudal
and postmodern baron with his group of acolytes; as an expression par
excellence of his absolute domain over a territory, where the right to a
woman's body is an extension of the lord's right to his fiefdom. Nevertheless, in the more than terrible contemporary postmodern, neoliberal,
post-state, post-democratic order, the baron has become capable of controlling his territory in an almost unrestricted way as a consequence of
the unruly accumulation characteristic of the frontier's expansion re-

gion, exacerbated by globalization of the economy and the loose neo-liberal market rules in effect. Its only regulating force is the greed and predatory potency of his competitors, the other barons.

Regional micro-fascisms and their totalitarian control over the province accompany the decadence of the national order on this side of the Great Frontier and require, more than ever, the urgent application of internationalist-oriented forms of legality and control. The mysterious torturing and murdering of the women of Ciudad Juárez indicate that decentralization, in a context of de-statization and neoliberalism, cannot but install a provincial totalitarianism, in a regressive conjunction of postmodernity and feudalism, where the female body is once again icon and annex of territorial domain.

The Conditions of Possibility: Asymmetry and Siege

The extreme asymmetry that results from local elites' unregulated extraction of wealth is essential to establishing a context of impunity. When the inequality is as extreme as it is in an unrestricted neoliberal regime, there is no real chance to separate legal from illicit business. Inequality becomes so extreme that it allows for absolute territorial control at a sub-state level by certain groups and their webs of support and alliance. These webs establish a true provincial totalitarianism and come to mark and express, without a doubt, the regime of control in force in the region. The torturing and murdering of women in Ciudad Juárez seem to me to be a way to signify this territorial control.

One thing that strongly characterizes totalitarian regimes is enclosure — that is, the representation of totalitarian space as a universe with no outside, encapsulated and self-sufficient, where the siege strategy of the elites hinders inhabitants' access to a different, external, alternative perception of reality. A nationalistic rhetoric that asserts itself in a primordialist construction of national unity (as in the case of "Mexican-ness" in Mexico, "tropical civilization" in Brazil, or the national ontology of a so-called national self in Argentina) benefits those who hold territorial control and monopolize the collective voice.

These metaphysics of the nation are based on an anti-historical essentialism and, no matter how popular and revendicative they may seem to be, work with the same logic that sheltered Nazism. This same kind of national ideology can also be found in places where a regional elite consolidates its domain over the space and legitimizes its privileges in a primordial regionalist rhetoric — that is, using its identification with an ethnic group or with a supposedly rock-solid cultural heritage. Powerful nativist appeals put pressure to create a feeling of loyalty toward the symbols of territorial unity with which the elite also designs its own heraldry. Popular culture, in a totalitarian context, is a confiscated culture: The people are the property of the manor, and the authorities are the owners of discourse, of traditional culture, of the wealth produced by the people, and of the totalized territory.

Like national totalitarianism, one of the principal strategies of regional totalitarianism is to turn the collective away from any discourse that might be called non-native, not issued and sealed by the commitment to an internal loyalty. "Foreigner" and "outsider in town" are transformed into accusations, and the possibility of speaking "from the outside" is barred. Therefore, the rhetoric is one of a cultural heritage that must be defended above all else and of a loyalty to territory that predominates and excludes other loyalties — for example, those of abiding by the law, of struggling to expand rights, and of activism and international mediation to protect human rights. This is why, if placing a premium on inwardness and using well-disguised techniques of media siege are the totalitarian leaders' sure strategy, the outer side is always the basis for action in the field of human rights. In a totalitarian environment, the value most hammered away at is the "we." The idea of "us" becomes defensive, entrenched, patriotic, and anyone who infringes it is accused of treason.[6] In this kind of patriotism the first victims are the others inside the nation, the region, the locale — always the women, the black people, the First Nations/indigenous people, and the dissidents. These inside others are coerced to sacrifice, and postpone their complaints and the argument of their differences in name of the sacralized and essentialized unity of the collective.

It is by articulating in public discourse these "patriotic" values (of a provincial totalitarianism) that the media of Ciudad Juárez disqualify, one by one, foreign views of the local cruel practices on women. When we "listen" to the subtext of the discourse of the news media, when we read between the lines, we hear: "Better a local murderer, no matter how cruel, than a foreign avenger, even if he is in the right." This well-known basic propaganda strategy builds up, every day, the totalitarian wall around Ciudad Juárez and has contributed over all these years to holding back the truth from the people and the neutralization of the law, from the municipal to the federal level, that resist a prosthetic articulation with the local powers that be.

It is impossible not to think of Ciudad Juárez when reading Hannah Arendt:

Totalitarian movements have been called "secret societies set up in broad daylight" (Koyré 1945). . . . The structure of the [totalitarian] movements . . . reminds one of nothing so much as of certain outstanding traits of secret societies. Secret societies form hierarchies according to degrees of initiation, regulate the life of their members according to a secret and fictitious assumption which makes everything look as though it were something else, adopt a strategy of consistent lying to deceive the non-initiated external masses, demand unquestioning obedience from their members who are held together by allegiance to a frequently unknown and always mysterious leader, who himself is surrounded . . . by a small group of initiated who are in turn surrounded by the half-initiated who form a "buffer area" against the profane world. Totalitarian movements and secret societies have also in common the dichotomist scission of the world between "blood-bondage brothers" and an indefinite and inarticulate mass of sworn enemies . . . distinction based on the absolute hostility towards the surrounding world. . . . Maybe the most clear resemblance between secret societies and totalitarian movements lies in the importance of ritual. . . . [Nevertheless], this idolatry does not prove the existence of pseudo-religious or heretic tendencies . . . [but] are simple organizational tricks, very much practiced in secret societies, who also force their members to keep secrecy for fear and respect towards truculent symbols. People unite themselves more firmly through the shared experience of a secret ritual than by simple admission to a secret's knowledge. (Arendt 1998 [1949], 425–27)

But, what state is this? What leadership is this that produces the effect of a regional totalitarianism? It is a *second state* that desperately needs a name in the codes of law—a name that could serve as a basis for the juridical category finally able to frame by the law its owners and the support web they control.[7]

The feminicides of Ciudad Juárez's are not ordinary gender crimes. They are corporative crimes and, more specifically, crimes of the second state, of a parallel state. As a phenomenon, they are more like the rituals cementing the unity of secret societies and totalitarian regimes. They share an idiosyncratic characteristic of the abuses of political power: They appear to be crimes without a personalized subject carried out against victims who are also not personalized: A secret force abducts a certain type of woman, victimizing her, to reaffirm and renew its capacity for control. Therefore, they are more like state crimes, crimes against humanity, where the parallel state that produces them cannot be classified for lack of efficient legal categories and procedures.

This is why it would take the creation of new juridical categories to make these crimes legally intelligible, classifiable. They are not ordinary crimes — that is, gender crimes with a sexual motivation or resulting from power relationships in the domestic sphere — as law enforcement, authorities, and many activists frivolously argue. They are crimes that we could say are of the second state, or corporative crimes, where the expressive dimension of violence prevails.[8] Here I understand the "corporation" to be the group or web managing resources, rights, and duties of a parallel state, firmly established in the region and with tentacles that reach to the country's top administration.

Let us, for a moment, invert the terms and say that the telos, or ends, of capital and the "commandment of capitalization" is not the process of accumulation, as this would mean falling into a tautology (accumulation's final goal is accumulation; concentration's final goal is concentration). We would be trapped in a circular argument. If we were, instead, to say that the ends of capital were the production and reproduction of difference by means of a progressive expansion of hierarchical distances to the point of exterminating some as an uncontested expression of success, then we would conclude that only the death of some can appropriately and self-evidently serve as an allegory for the place and position of all who are dominated, the dominated people, the dominated class.

It is in exclusion and in its signifier par excellence — the capacity to suppress the other — that capital, as an expression of the one and most contemporary form of power, is consecrated. What could be more emblematic of the role of submission than the body of the mestizo woman, the poor woman, the daughter and sister of others who are poor and mestizo? Where could otherness, produced precisely to be defeated, be better signified? What trophy would serve as a better emblem of the returns of optimal businesses, beyond the reach of any rule or restriction? This doubly other woman thus emerges in the scene as the place of production and a signification of the last form of totalitarian territorial control (of bodies and property, of bodies as part of properties) through the very act of her humiliation and suppression.

We find ourselves, then, facing the unboundedness of both economies, symbolic and material. The depredation and pillaging of the environment and the labor force works hand in hand with systematic and corporative rape. Let us not forget that *rapiña*, the Spanish word for pillage, and *rapinagem*, the Portuguese word for voracious looting, share a root with *rape*.

If this is so, we can not only assert that a large-scale understanding of the economical context helps us to throw light on the events of Ciudad Juárez, but also that Juárez's humble dead, from the small scale of their situation and localization, wake us up and guide us into a more lucid rereading of the transformations the world undergoes nowadays, while it becomes, at every moment, more inhospitable and terrifying.

Epilogue

A cautious examination of my personal reasons for getting involved in the case of Ciudad Juárez is, in the end, necessary.[9] As part of my results I have understood that even if the greatest suffering is that of the victims themselves, their mothers and next of kin, the atrocious crimes against Ciudad Juárez's women are the obligatory jurisdiction of all legal codes and an unavoidable concern for all who value justice and collective well-being. This is so in two ways. On the one hand, the theoretical, ethical, and legal issue of the feminicides is similar to the great issue of the Holocaust and its dilemmas. Both crimes are a heritage and a lesson that belong to all of humanity. Its perpetrators are not beyond the limits of our common humanity; nor are its victims gifted with an idiosyncratic and essential quality that distinguishes them from all other peoples massacred across history. Historical conditions that can transform us into monsters or the accomplices of monsters threaten us all, and the menace of becoming monsters hangs over us all, without exception, as does the threat of becoming victims. All it takes is the creation of a strict and exact frontier between an "us" and a "them" for the process to begin. As in the case of racism, it is the humanity of the supposedly "not affected" that deteriorates without notion or remedy and plunges, unaware, into an inexorable decadence.

But this is not the only reason I say we are facing a problem that concerns us all. As I have argued, in the particular case of the feminicides of Ciudad Juárez, I understand these to be crimes perpetrated against us, addressed to us and for us, the law-abiding citizens. What puts us into dialogue with the perpetrators is deliberate and intentional. I am saying this not in general but in the strict sense that I am convinced that these crimes are directed at us, thrown our way as a declaration of that sovereign power acting in partnership with the state persists and continues in force underneath the statutory surface. They tell us about the permanent reissuing of a second law whose judges and prosecutors act as shadow authorities of the state. In other words, I am not saying that we are involved simply because the crimes affect us, make us suffer, offend us. Rather, I mean that the exhibition of a discretionary power over the life and death of those who live in that limit territory is represented and inscribed on the bodies of women as a document, as an edict, the unappealable sanction of a decree, as the staging of a dialogue with all who seek shelter under the law. These murders are aimed at exhibiting *for us* an intense capacity to produce death, an expertise in cruelty, and a sovereign domain over a territory to tell us that this is a matter of an occupied jurisdiction in which we cannot interfere. It is precisely because we disagree with this, because we think that Ciudad Juárez is neither outside Mexico nor outside the world—that we have to resist the submissive position where the murders prevent us from engaging in an active opposition to the regime they impose on us.

WHAT TO DO?

Just when I thought that I had done my job correctly as an interpreter of social text and had offered my contribution to an understanding of what could well be called "the enigma of Ciudad Juárez," I remembered, once more, the phrase that has haunted me since the day Lourdes Portillo's documentary *Señorita Extraviada* (Missing Young Woman; 2001) introduced the subject into my life: Decipher me or I will devour you. Unconsciously, I associated the Sphinx's interpellation that assailed the kingdom of Thebes with the defiant encounter between rational faculties and Ciudad Juárez's infamies.

When it came time to take final stock, the Sphinx's mocking challenge came back with all its menacing power: "Decipher me or be devoured." Full of doubt, I remember Oedipus, the hero who, we are misled to think, defeated the Sphinx by deciphering the enigma she put to travelers, today transformed into an innocent riddle of children's folklore. It was actually Oedipus who was skillful, wise, and intelligent enough to find the correct answer. He understood. He managed to make sense of it. But curiously, this saved neither him nor Thebes from their tragic fate.[10] It was actually after this act of apparent understanding, of making intelligible, deciphering, unveiling that the tragic pattern followed. This is, I believe, our situation now in Ciudad Juárez. It is possible that we have taken a step toward understanding the facts. We can see an image, pale but recognizable, in the scattered pieces that make up this sinister charade. Nevertheless, the discovery, yet again, of a body in a "cotton field" four days before the public reading of this epilogue on November 25, 2004, the international day against Violence against Women, seems to reinforce our uncertainty. This new find also coincides, dreadfully, with the exact anniversary of a similar discovery in another empty lot of Ciudad Juárez in 2003. An interlocutor who is recalcitrant and hostile to interventions does not desist from pronouncing himself.

Let us suppose that the enigma has been deciphered, and we know what it means. Even so, like the tragic hero we plunge deeper and deeper into a destiny we are unable to stop. I was pondering this when I received a book by Federico Campbell, *La memoria de Sciascia* (Sciascia's memory). The following extract is from the chapter "Nunca se Sabrá (We will Never Know)," in which he comments on the book *Negro sobre negro* (Black on black), a collection of Leonardo Sciascia's articles in Italian newspapers between 1969 and 1979: "We will never know any truth about the criminal acts that have even the slightest bit to do with the management of power." He then illustrates this maxim with numerous examples taken from recent Mexican and Italian history:

> We will never know who murdered Pasolini, we will never know who poisoned Pisciotta, we will never know who riddled Manuel Buendía [the Mexican journalist murdered May 30, 1984] with bullets, we will never know who ordered the massacre of Tlatelolco, we will never know if Enrico Mattei's death was an accident or a crime, we will never know who set the bomb in the Banca dell'Agricoltura in Piazza Fontana, we will never know who should be charged with the killing of the 10th of June 1971 in San Cosme, we will never know how and by whose hands the editor Feltrinelli died, we will never know why the residents of El Mareño, Michoacán were killed off, we will never know who signed Huitzilac's death sentence in 1927, we will never know who shot Salvatore Giuliano and Francisco Villa, we will never know if the deaths of Benjamin Hill and Máximo Ávila Camacho were intentional poisonings or not, we will never know if Carlos Madrazo's and Alfredo Bonfil's airplane crashes were truly accidents, we will never know who organized the holocaust of Topilejo, we will never know who murdered Ruben Jaramillo in 1962, we will never know who, under whose orders, and why, the members of the *ejido* San Ignacio de Río Muerto, Sonora, were murdered in 1975, we will never know who ordered the murder of journalist Héctor Féliz Miranda's (alias El Gato) in Tijuana in 1988, we will never know by whose orders Francisco Xavier Ovando, one of the leaders of the Cuauhtémoc Cárdenas' candidacy for the Presidency of the Republic, and young militant Román Gil Heráldez were gunned down on July 2nd, 1988. (Campbell 2004 [1989], 23–25)

Nevertheless, and here Campbell is quoting Sciascia directly, "we did find out very quickly, in a matter of a few hours, where the bomb that killed the agent Marino came from: a clear sign that those responsible had no connections with the hyperpower."

In my heart of hearts I wonder whether, and am afraid that, the tragic nature of human destiny may be the pattern structuring personal lives and histories. If tragedy has one characteristic, among many, it is that it does not shelter the possibility of justice without distorting its nature.

What if justice is not possible, but some occasional degree of peace is? Would any peace be enough? Could we resign ourselves to the women's murders of Ciudad Juárez simply stopping one day and slowly transforming into a thing of the past, without justice ever being done?

I ask these questions seriously, honestly. I ask them first of all of myself, in deepest privacy. If we were told that the only way out is an armistice, would I, would you, be able to accept it? And would we be able not to accept it? I am still perplexed by this question, because, yes, Sciascia was right: A decade of impunity indicates that the crimes of Ciudad Juárez are crimes of power, and therefore it may be that we can only negotiate their decrease and cessation.

Notes

1. Alma Brisa's remains were found amid sunflowers on the same plot of land in the center of the city where the body of Brenda Berenice, daughter of Juanita, one of the main collaborators of the Epikeia project, was found.

2. For example, in November 2004 in the main plaza of the neighborhood of Coyoacan, in Mexico City, I witnessed a protest of mothers and relatives of the victims who demanded both an end to impunity for the real murderers of women and the liberation of "*el cerillo*," a youngster jailed and, according to them, falsely accused of the crimes. The attorney Irene Blanco, whose child suffered an attack, is also well known for her work defending Latif Sharif, who was falsely accused of the crimes, as is the work of the mothers against the jailing of the Los Rebeldes (Rebels) gang, for the same reason.

3. Also published in Spanish in Mexico and Spain, *Harvest of Women* compiles Washington's column for the *El Paso Times* newspaper. González Rodríguez was beaten and left for dead on a street in Mexico City in 2000 while he researched his book. He was hospitalized for a month and lost all his teeth.

4. See the chapter "La Célula Violenta que Lacan no Vio: Un Diálogo (Tenso) entre la Antropologia y el Psicoanálisis (The Violent Cell That Lacan Did Not See: A [Tense] Dialogue between Anthropology and Psychoanalysis)" in Segato 2003b.

5. See various forms of contemporary "listening" to a text in authors such as Mikhail Bakhtin, Jacques Lacan, Emmanuel Levinas, and others in Patterson 1988.

6. I like the treatment of this difference in Jean Améry's essay "How Much Home Does a Person Need?" (Améry 1980 [1977]).

7. Giorgio Agamben (2005) adheres to the notion of a "dual state" as adequate to speak of totalitarian systems such as fascism and Nazism: They had a constitutional frame, but secondary rules — those of a second state — hold the system together, issue the orders, and command the affairs.

8. I further developed this idea about the need for a new juridical category

able to grasp the specificity of these crimes among all feminicides, framing the corporate elements involved in them in Segato (2007).

9. Text I read on the presentation of the book *Ciudad Juárez: De este lado del Puente* (Mexico City: Epikeia, Nuestras Hijas de Regreso a Casa e Instituto Nacional de las Mujeres, 2004) and Rogelio Sosa's play *Lacrimosa*, featured by Lorena Glinz, together with the Spanish anti-corruption attorney Carlos Castresana and Isabel Vericat, at Museo del Chopo, Mexico City, November 29, 2004.

10. "*Oedipus*, feet walking towards wisdom, the famous Oedipus who knows of the famous enigma, but does not know that *tyché* (divine cause, evasive to human logic, and the one that refers to the arbitrariness of human fate and of history) is what rules everything, as Iocasta uselessly anticipated him" (Vincentini 1999, 61). Therefore, even in deciphering it, he gets trapped in the terms of the riddle. Indeed, Oedipus and all his family belong to the enunciation, "Which is the being that is *dipous, tripous, tetrapous at the same time?*" put by the Sphinx, and deciphering its apparent meaning does not dispel the hidden plot of the properties of the structure of history.

ANGÉLICA CHÁZARO, JENNIFER CASEY,
AND KATHERINE RUHL

Getting Away with Murder

GUATEMALA'S FAILURE TO PROTECT WOMEN

AND RODI ALVARADO'S QUEST FOR SAFETY

After suffering ten years of brutal domestic violence, with the police and the courts ignoring her pleas for protection, Rodi Alvarado fled her native Guatemala and sought refuge in the United States. Alvarado is not alone in her suffering. Since 2001, more than 2,200 women have been murdered in Guatemala (Amnesty International 2006). These gender-based murders, frequently executed with extreme brutality and sexual violence, have been labeled "feminicides."[1] Perpetrators of the feminicides enjoy widespread impunity for their crimes.

In the United States, grants of asylum to women who suffer human rights violations related to their gender ("gender-based asylum") remain controversial. Opponents cite the "floodgates" argument, contending that if the door to refugee protection is opened to women fleeing gender-based harm such as domestic violence, the United States will be flooded with such individuals. Although historical experience and statistics demonstrate that the floodgates argument is without substance,[2] it persists. Rather than focus on turning away individual refugees based on fear of opening the floodgates, a more sensible and humane response would be to address the conditions that force women like Rodi Alvarado to flee their homelands in the first place. Until then, the few women like Alvarado who are able to flee will continue to seek the lifesaving protection asylum provides, while countless women will remain in their home countries, with their physical integrity and very lives at risk.

This chapter examines the underlying conditions that cause women like Alvarado to flee their home countries. It seeks to provide a framework for the Guatemalan state's dismal record for protecting women's lives, examining the conditions that give rise to the feminicides, including a legacy of military violence, a history of impunity, and systemic discrimination against women.

Rodi Alvarado's Plight and Her Quest for Safety

Rodi Alvarado was born and raised in Guatemala. The circumstances underlying her flight demonstrate the failure of her home country to provide any meaningful protection for women who are victims of violence. In 1984, at sixteen, Alvarado married Francisco Osorio, a former soldier who was five years her senior. Almost immediately after they were married, her husband began to threaten her and to carry out violent assaults. Those assaults continued without respite over a ten-year marriage. Osorio raped and sodomized Alvarado, infecting her with sexually transmitted diseases; broke windows and mirrors over her head; dislocated her jaw; and tried to abort her child by kicking her violently in the spine. In addition to using his hands and his feet against her, he resorted to weapons, pistol-whipping her and terrorizing her with his machete. Alvarado tried to flee the family home on several occasions, but her husband always tracked her down—one time beating her into unconsciousness in front of their two children to punish her for trying to escape. He threatened to "cut off her arms and legs, and . . . leave her in a wheelchair, if she ever tried to leave" (U.S. Department of Justice 1999).

Alvarado's attempts to secure the protection of the authorities were just as futile as her attempts to hide from her husband. Neither the police nor the courts of Guatemala intervened even once over the entire course of this decade-long brutal marital relationship. The police did not come when telephoned by a desperate Alvarado, and they never took any steps to arrest Osorio or require him to appear in response to written complaints that she filed. Osorio enjoyed the same impunity within the court system; when Alvarado went before a judge, he told her that he would not "interfere in domestic disputes" (U.S. Department of Justice 1999). The police had communicated essentially the same thing, telling Alvarado that they would not provide any assistance because she should "take care of it at home."

Desperate to save her life, Alvarado finally fled to the United States—a difficult decision because she was forced to leave her two children behind with relatives. In September 1996, an immigration judge in San Francisco granted her asylum.

Unfortunately, the granting of asylum was not the end of Alvarado's ordeal. The Immigration and Naturalization Service (INS) appealed the grant to a higher immigration court, the Board of Immigration Appeals (BIA). In June 1999, the BIA reversed the decision of the immigration judge, by a divided 10–5 vote, and ordered that Alvarado be returned to Guatemala. The denial of protection to Rodi Alvarado set off a firestorm of protest by refugee rights and women's rights activists across the country, who saw it as a dangerous precedent cutting back on protections for female asylum seekers. This vocal activism and outrage led Attorney-General Janet Reno to become personally involved. In December 2000, the U.S. Justice Department issued proposed regulations to address gender claims, and Reno "vacated" the BIA's decision in Alvarado's case, directing the BIA to re-decide the case once the regulations were issued in final form.

At the time of this writing, the regulations have still not been issued. The failure of the BIA and of subsequent attorneys general to grant asylum is all the more notable in light of the fact that the U.S. Department of Homeland Security (DHS), the successor agency to the INS, reversed its position in 2004 (after opposing asylum for Alvarado for eight years). The DHS not only filed a brief urging the attorney-general to recognize Alvarado as a refugee but endorsed the issuance of regulations that would mandate such a result. It remains to be seen whether the Justice Department, under the direction of Attorney-General Alberto Gonzales,[3] will take a similar position and work with the DHS to finalize regulations, pending since 2000, so that they do in fact support a grant of asylum to Alvarado.[4] [Editors' note: In October 2009 the DHS endorsed Alvarado's request for asylum.]

In 1996, Rodi Alvarado was forced to flee Guatemala due to the impunity her batterer enjoyed. That same year marked the signing of the peace accords that ended Guatemala's thirty-six-year civil war. Ten years later, Alvarado was still in the United States awaiting word on her immigration case, while back in Guatemala violence against women had reached epidemic levels, with the crisis of impunity, a legacy of the civil war, continuing unabated. The Guatemalan feminicides constitute the clearest manifestation of the lack of protection from life-threatening violence Guatemalan women suffer. Alvarado barely escaped becoming another feminicide statistic. However, her story contains many of the root causes of the feminicides discussed later, including socially and legally accepted domestic violence, unresponsive police and courts, and a partner whose cruelty was partly rooted in his wartime experiences. Rather than focus its energy on denying protection to refugees like Alvarado, the United States should turn its attention to the root causes of violence and impunity that result in the flow of women fleeing for their lives.

The Case of Claudina Velásquez

The persistent threat to Guatemalan women's lives is amply reflected in the rising number of their deaths.[5] The case of Claudina Velásquez illustrates the individual injustice engendered by each feminicide. On Friday, August 12, 2005, the nineteen-year-old law student Claudina Isabel Velásquez Paiz left for class at the University of San Carlos. She arrived at school and attended her two Friday morning courses, human rights and constitutional rights. When she did not come home that evening, her parents began searching hospitals and police stations for her. They contacted the Policía Nacional Civil (National Civil Police; PNC) to assist in the search. However, they were informed that the police would not begin searching for their daughter until she had been missing for twenty-four hours. Midday on Saturday, August 13, Claudina's parents were called to identify their daughter's body at the morgue. She had been murdered, raped, and brutally beaten. She died as a result of two bullet wounds to the head.

Information obtained from Claudina's friends and family revealed terrible inadequacies in the investigative and prosecutorial processes. According to witnesses who heard the gunfire, Claudina was shot sometime in the early-morning hours of August 13, 2005. However, the authorities never established the time of her death. It was not until 11:30 p.m. the same day, after her body had been in the morgue for many hours, that an agent from the Public Ministry (the Guatemalan equivalent of the district attorney's office) arrived to take Claudina's fingerprints. Although skin and fluid samples were taken from Claudina's body, no analysis was conducted. The clothing that she was wearing at the time of her death was turned over to her family. No forensic analysis of the clothing was conducted.

Statements obtained from witnesses indicated that Claudina spent the afternoon of August 12 in a condominium building in Ciudad San Cristobal in the municipality of Mixco. Although the building had private security, the Public Ministry never searched or took as evidence the registry of entrances and exits for August 12–13. There was further information that Claudina had been seen accompanied by other people in a supermarket on the night of August 12. However, the Public Ministry did not view or take control of the supermarket's surveillance videos; nor did it request a statement from the store manager on duty the day of the murder. Five days after Claudina's murder, the primary suspect, without having been summoned, made a voluntary statement at the Public Ministry. Human rights advocates close to the case remarked on the failure of the authorities to take the suspect's fingerprints and to take him into custody — even though the advocates believed there was a sufficient basis for issuing an arrest warrant.[6]

The way in which Claudina's case was handled demonstrates a number of failings in the investigative and prosecutorial processes that are characteristic of the authorities' handling of feminicides, including delay in initial investigation, a complete lack of forensic analysis, and a failure to pursue relevant evidence or suspects. Rather, investigators labeled Claudina a "nobody," based on the fact that she was wearing a bellybutton ring and sandals, to legitimate lack of due diligence in the investigation.[7] The lack of response by authorities, a pattern that has repeated itself in nearly all of the other feminicides, allows those responsible to enjoy impunity for their crimes.

Sadly, the savage beating and sexual violence inflicted on Claudina before she was shot is also common to many of the Guatemalan feminicides. While the actual number of murders involving sexual violence is unknown, as the Guatemalan authorities do not currently classify murders in a way that takes into account this type of gender-based violence (Amnesty International 2005, 10–11), several nongovernmental organizations (NGOs) and other groups have presented their own investigations and analyses of the killings (Amnesty International 2006, 3–4). For example, the Human Rights Ombudsman reported that while most murdered men were killed "with no intimate physical contact between the victim and the perpetrator," the majority of murders of women were marked by rape, torture, and mutilation (Amnesty International 2006).[8] According to Angélica Gonzalez of Guatemala's Red de la No Violencia Contra las Mujeres (Network of Non-violence against Women), a broad coalition of women's organizations, "Sexual aggression, the mutilation of body parts like breasts, torture, and the dumping of victims in empty lots are trademarks of the killings" (Paterson 2006a). In some cases, the bodies are placed and mutilated in a way thought to be sending a message of terror and intimidation, leading the Special Rapporteur on Violence against Women to label these "exemplary" killings (Amnesty International 2005, 11).

Theories behind the Killings

The lack of proper investigation and prosecution of the recent murders increases the difficulty of pinpointing who is behind the feminicides. Several different theories have emerged, ascribing blame to different societal factors or agents, including domestic violence and backlash against women in the public sphere, an overall increase in the general crime rate, gangs and organized crime, the security forces, and even the victims themselves.

According to the Network of Non-violence against Women, one-third of all murders are the consequence of domestic violence (Amnesty International 2005, 12). The United Nations Rapporteur on Violence against Women points to the unstable and vulnerable post-civil-war circumstances as predisposing heads of household "to experience sexual and domestic violence as well as stigmatization" (Ertürk and Commission on Human Rights 2005, para. 26). The surge in violence is also viewed as a backlash against women's increasing presence in the public sphere (Ertürk and Commission on Human Rights 2005, para. 22).

Ironically, the former Special Prosecutor for Crimes against Women did not view the rise in murders of women as being motivated by their gender. She attributed the skyrocketing number of killings of women to the general increase in crime, stating that the "violence is not gender violence" (Federación Internacional de Derechos Humanos 2006, 28). Government officials most frequently cite the young members of Guatemalan gangs (known as *maras*) as being responsible for the murders. The head of the Unit on Aggression against Women of the Servicio de Investigación Criminal (Criminal Investigative Service) has said, "The majority of the deaths can be attributed to gang members who, as a result of jealousy or other personal problems, have killed their live-in partners, wives, or girlfriends."[9]

While gang violence may be a factor, the authorities tend to categorize all of the feminicides as gang-related without having carried out proper investigations. According to the Centro de Reportes Informativos sobre Guatemala (Center for Informative Reports on Guatemala; CERIGUA), inadequate investigations leave the government with no real knowledge of who is committing the crimes and why ("Femicides on the Rise" 2006). Moreover, the disproportionate focus placed on the gangs may "result from an intention to cover up the responsibility of those in power in these acts" (Federación Internacional de Derechos Humanos 2006, 28). An insidious alliance between criminal elements and the still present counterinsurgency structures from the war years continues to thrive,[10] and there is evidence that private security forces and the police themselves are committing some share of the murders. The Human Rights Ombudsman reported twenty-three police officers to the authorities for their involvement in crimes against women (Federación Internacional de Derechos Humanos 2006, 32), and police officers are thought to be involved in at least ten of the murders (Ertürk and Commission on Human Rights 2005, para. 58).

Investigations by the police and the prosecutors have focused on the "character" of the victims rather than on the motives for their murderers (Amnesty International 2005, 21–22). Blaming the victim for her own death is a persistent practice in the investigation of feminicides.[11] By linking the victims to gang violence, officials place responsibility for the murders on the victims themselves, in effect blaming the women's presumed choice of acquaintances for their deaths.

Contextualizing the Violence: "Feminicide's Waiting Room"

Feminicide is only the most extreme expression of violence against Guatemalan women and must be viewed in the context of their systematic oppression.[12] Conditions in Guatemala, which include a high incidence of violence in the home, a thirty-six-year legacy of war violence targeting women, and deeply rooted patriarchal traditions enshrined in the legal code, have set the stage for this epidemic of violence against women.

VIOLENCE IN THE HOME

Rodi Alvarado's attempts to obtain state protection from horrific abuse by her husband were futile. Her experience is not unique. A U.S. State Department report found that in 2004 in Guatemala City alone, 10,000 reports of family violence were received by the prosecutor's office, with only 370 reaching trial (U.S. Department of State 2005). In the first nine months of 2005, 13,700 reports of family violence were made (U.S. Department of State 2006). Because the Human Rights Ombudsman and prominent women's rights NGOs estimate that 90 percent of incidents go unreported, it is fair to assume that the actual incidence of family violence is exponentially higher.[13] With one-third of the feminicides thought to result from domestic violence (Amnesty International 2005, 12), and the police often failing to respond to battered women's requests for assistance, battered women have an acute susceptibility to being murdered.[14]

A LEGACY OF GOVERNMENT-SANCTIONED VIOLENCE AGAINST WOMEN

The current wave of violence against women cannot be viewed in isolation from the internal civil conflict characterizing Guatemala's recent history. Beginning in 1960, Guatemala suffered a thirty-six-year armed internal conflict, during which at least two hundred thousand people were killed. The state and its representatives were later found to be responsible for 93 percent of the acts of violence (CEH 1998, 37). The conflict was marked by pervasive state-sponsored violence, including physical, psychological, and sexual torture; disappearances; and massacres of indigenous communities in Guatemala's highlands.[15] Women constituted a quarter of the victims of the conflict and suffered forms of violence unique to them as women. While the Peace Accords of 1996 provided for the prosecution of wartime atrocities, the majority of offenders have escaped justice (United Nations Committee against Torture 2006, para. 16; translation by the authors). This pattern of impunity continues unabated, complicating efforts to seek justice for today's crimes against women.[16]

During the conflict, agents of the state, including members of the Guatemalan military and the Patrullas de Autodefensa Civil (Civil Defense Patrols; PACs), used sexual violence as a weapon of war systematically and with complete immunity (CEH 1998, paras. 2350, 2478),[17] with women suffering 99 percent of the sexual violations (CEH 1998, para. 2376). A generation of young men forcibly recruited into the army was indoctrinated in the use of sexual violence as a weapon (Recovery of Historical Memory Project 1999).[18] Rapes were carried out during military operations in rural areas as well as during detentions of suspected guerrilla supporters in the cities (Recovery of Historical Memory Project 1999, 170).[19] Sexual assaults were so widespread in the highland combat zones that one local official commented it would be difficult to find a Maya girl of eleven to fifteen who had not been raped (Reproductive Health Response in Conflict Consortium 2002, 112).[20] It is estimated that rape was an aspect of one in every six killings during the conflict (Feminicidio en América Latina 2006, 11). A truth commission charged with reexamining the human rights violations during the war concluded that rape was carried out as a show of power, a show of victory over adversaries, a bartering tool (with women's rape accompanied by the often broken promise that a family member, often a child, would not be killed), and as war plunder (Recovery of Historical Memory Project 1999, 77–78).

Sexual violence was used in conjunction with other practices that reinforced the notion of women as men's servants, sexually and otherwise. In many cases, women were forced to cook and dance for their assailants before being assaulted and murdered (Recovery of Historical Memory Project 1999, 73).[21] While the Peace Accords of 1996 have long since been signed, the war against women seemingly continues, with the attitudes and practices of violence against women developed during the conflict persisting nearly ten years later and embodied in today's feminicides.[22] One prominent Guatemalan NGO hypothesizes:

> In this case we could be looking at a repetition of the phenomenon of murders of women that took place during the war, as a product of a post-conflict era that could not guarantee non-repetition [of the violence]. The lack of punishment for the perpetrators of sexual violence and torture against women . . . has permitted the conditions in which persons who learned from the lived experience of the war—be it because they were victimizers or because as children or adolescents they witnessed these events as normal—reproduce the violence of the past, focusing once again on women (Federación Internacional de Derechos Humanos 2006, 27n6).

Moreover, as discussed later, recent police reforms and joint police–military initiatives mea.1 that, in Guatemala, the current police force is composed of the same men who patrolled the country during the war years. This affects both the ability of communities to work with police forces to end violence against women and the attitudes of the police in addressing such violence.

VIOLENCE SANCTIONED BY LAW

Underlying the violence facing Guatemalan women is a legal system that sanctions gender-based discrimination. Through the ratification and passage of international, regional, and domestic instruments and commissions, Guatemala has committed itself to the protection of women's rights.[23] Article 4 of the Guatemalan Constitution guarantees equal rights for men and women. However, significant portions of Guatemalan law rendering women vulnerable to violence fail to reflect this foundational commitment.

Civil Laws Until recently, Guatemala's patriarchal culture was explicitly codified within certain articles of its Civil Code, which dates to 1963. Women's rights groups were successful in pushing for the reform on these provisions in 1998 (Morales Trujillo 2002),[24] but the assumptions underlying the now defunct provisions still hold true for many Guatemalans, contributing to women's vulnerability to violence. Until the 1998 reforms, the Civil Code provided that a husband had the duty to protect and support his wife, while she had the right and duty to care for and raise minor children and oversee domestic tasks (Morales Trujillo 2002). In addition, husbands could legally object to their wives' working outside the home (Morales Trujillo 2002). Only husbands could legally represent the married couple, and they were the sole administrators of the household's financial resources, as well as of any of the family's assets. Even when parents had joint custody, fathers were still the sole legal representatives of their children and the administrators of their assets. While women are now free to engage in formal employment without the permission of their husbands, the current Labor Code continues to place the work of women and minors in the same category, separate from the norm — the labor of men.[25]

Criminal Laws A recent report describing the Guatemalan criminal code as "a series of anachronistic provisions that reflect the persistence of discrimination against women" (Federación Internacional de Derechos Humanos, 28) accurately reflects the current state of affairs. Among the gaps in the Guatemalan Criminal Code are provisions to effectively prevent and punish domestic violence. While Guatemala's minister of national security recently affirmed the connection between the feminicides and domestic violence, the Guatemalan Penal Code still treats domestic violence as a minor offense.[26] Although the law prohibits intrafamily violence, it does not provide for criminal penalties for abusers.[27]

When violence against women occurs in a family setting, perpetrators can be charged with assault only if signs of physical injury from the abuse persist for ten days (U.S. Department of State 2006). One prosecutor explained: "Family violence does not constitute a crime; as a consequence, a case cannot be initiated unless there are injuries. In that case, it should be determined how much time will be required for the injuries to heal in order to establish whether or not a case should be opened. However, when the woman appears and there are no injuries present, there is nothing that can be done" (Inter-American Commission on Human Rights 2003a, para. 299).[28] This approach requires the violence to be particularly grisly, ignoring other forms of violence, including psychological violence. Moreover, it decreases the possibility for criminal or judicial intervention at a time when it could actually prevent a woman from being murdered by her partner. This approach also helps explain why half of the victims who filed complaints in 2005 with the Public Ministry failed to follow up and why 90 percent of incidents are estimated to have gone unreported (U.S. Department of State 2006).

The Law to Prevent, Sanction, and Eradicate Intrafamily Violence of 1996 does allow for the exclusion of the batterer from the family home, social services for victims, and the issuance of orders of protection (Congreso de la Republica de Guatemala 1996). In the face of impunity, however, such restraining orders are often entirely ineffective (Federación Internacional de Derechos Humanos 2006, 28). Advocates point to cases in which women with protective orders literally in hand were killed by their husbands (Federación Internacional de Derechos Humanos 2006).[29]

The Guatemalan Criminal Code also offers insufficient protection to victims of sexual crimes. Guatemalan laws currently do not recognize rape occurring within marriage as a crime. Therefore, spouses and live-in partners cannot be prosecuted for such an act. This serves to reinforce the idea that women have the obligation to sexually satisfy their husbands or partners.[30] Despite significant momentum to eliminate them, laws allowing sexual predators to evade justice remain in force. In December 2005, Article 200, which allows a rapist to escape prosecution if he marries his victim,[31] was temporarily suspended by Guatemala's Constitutional Court, following a challenge by the Human Rights Ombudsman's office (CERIGUA 2005b). However, the court's decision was not retroactive, and those who committed the crime before the law was overturned can still use the marriage exception to escape responsibility (U.S. Department of State 2006). Article 176, which criminalizes sexual intercourse with a minor only if the girl is "honest," also remains good law (CERIGUA 2006a). This focus on the victim's perceived character and conduct rather than on the perpetrator's act has also emerged as an undercurrent in the government's investigation and reporting of the feminicides.

Women face procedural obstacles, as well. According to the Guatemalan Code of Criminal Procedure (Congreso de la Republica de Guatemala 1992), the initiation of prosecution for rape and other sexual crimes depends on the victim.[32] Furthermore, if an offender obtains a pardon from his victim, he is released from criminal responsibility if his crime falls under a certain category, consisting primarily of sexual crimes against women, including rape, sexual abuse, and abduction. Amnesty International notes that these provisions can lead victims, "exposed to pressure or coercion, who are unaware of their rights, or who lack funds for legal assistance or faith in the justice system, into not filing complaints and may also encourage prosecutors to dissuade victims from filing complaints" (Amnesty International 2005, 24).

Government Responses to Violence against Women

While certainly a contributing factor, the legal framework itself does not fully explain the levels of violence that Guatemalan women experience. Even if the Guatemalan government were to enact legislation placing the country in compliance with its international obligations and its commitment to gender equality in its own Constitution, the enforcement of such laws would be complicated by factors such as the failings of the police and the unwillingness and inability of the Public Ministry to prosecute crimes of violence against women.

In theory, the Guatemalan police force offers the first line of defense against the murders of women. While the laws surrounding sexual violence and violence against women in the home provide insufficient protection, the laws on murder are unambiguous, presumably guaranteeing police attention. In practice, however, the Guatemalan police force's response to the feminicides has been widely criticized, and recommendations for decreasing the violence consistently call for police reform. While such reform is badly needed, it should be informed by an understanding of the police force's historically determined limitations. The PNC was created in 1997 as part of the negotiation of the peace accords (Neild 2002). Its predecessor, the Policía Nacional (National Police; PN), was infamous for its corruption, abuse, and incompetence (Washington Office on Latin America 2002). After the recent discovery of nearly a century of secret PN files, researchers have begun to document the force's complicity in the terror inflicted on the civilian population (Watts 2005).[33] Prioritizing the rapid deployment of the new police force, the Guatemalan government incorporated most of the old PN into the new PNC (Washington Office on Latin America 2002, 62). More than 90 percent of officers initially underwent the "recycling" process, and as of 2002, the majority of the beat cops and the entire police leadership were still drawn from former police personnel (Neild 2002, 3).[34] It is the legacy agency of this infamous police force that is now charged with protecting a civilian population and investigating the violent deaths of women.[35]

Not surprisingly then, the PNC has been widely criticized for its investigation of the feminicides. Amnesty International's report on the feminicides from 2005 chronicles the PNC's shortcomings. They include delays and insufficient efforts by police to locate women who have been reported missing; lack of coordination between the Missing Persons Unit and the Homicide Unit; frequent failure to protect, examine, or preserve the crime scene once a body has been discovered; and failure to gather necessary forensic and other evidence. As recently as March 2006, Renato Durán of the Office of the Special Homicide Prosecutor said that prosecutors have no material evidence in 95 percent of cases, due to poor police work and a lack of forensic evidence (Lakshmanan 2006). Specifically, the police have demonstrated extremely poor data collection, including the omission of location and time of the discovery of the bodies and of evidence regarding gender-related forms of violence found on the bodies. As one report notes, "[An] almost total absence of sex-disaggregated data means that gender-related violence is generally under-recorded and often rendered almost invisible" (Amnesty International 2005, 5). Finally, the police have demonstrated a failure to follow up on crucial evidence and a failure to act on arrest warrants.

Even in cases in which abductions are witnessed and immediately reported, family members have been unable to convince investigators to take immediate action. Consequently, women who are reported as having been abducted are often found dead before the police take any action whatsoever. Despite the repeated recommendation by organizations such as Amnesty International to implement an urgent search mechanism for missing girls and women, none has been created (Amnesty International 2006).

More than a lack of resources, a lack of will on the part of investigators underlies the poor investigations of Guatemala's feminicides, as shown by the persistent practice of blaming the victim and the reported hostility toward family members.[36] The United Nations Committee against Torture recently expressed concern about the lack of investigations of Guatemala's feminicides, stating that "the fact that these acts aren't investigated exacerbates the suffering of the families that call for justice; furthermore, the families complain that the authorities commit gender discrimination during the investigation and judicial process" (United Nations Committee against Torture 2006, para. 16). Families are discouraged from pressing charges with comments such as, "If she is already dead, what are you looking for?" (United Nations General Assembly 2006). Those who demand justice suffer threats and harassment, and many fear for their lives.[37] As recently acknowledged by a Guatemalan delegate to Convention on the Elimination of All Forms of Discrimination against Women (CEDAW), the protection for witnesses and families of victims is a "significant weakness" in the Guatemalan legal system (United Nations General Assembly 2006).

While the investigation of murders of women remains highly inadequate, the PNC is hardly inactive. Much of its energy is siphoned into policing the young members of gangs that have become a feature of Guatemalan life since the signing of the peace accords.[38] As discussed earlier, members of the maras are frequently cited as being responsible for the murders of women. However, the wholesale nature of the PNC's current war against the maras makes it very unlikely that the gang members who do in fact kill women will be investigated for their crimes.[39] Instead, the indiscriminate arrest and detention of the young gang members redirects attention from the social ills underlying the existence of the maras and has done nothing to stop the murders of women or to bring down the crime rate in general.

The difficulties women at risk of being murdered face in gaining access to justice are likely to increase with the current trend toward merging police and military functions.[40] Joint military–police patrols have been approved by the Guatemalan Congress since 2001 to battle gangs and drug trafficking, "despite the lack of any indication that they are effective" (Neild 2002, 28),[41] and continue to be deployed in areas of the capital with the highest crime rates (U.S. Department of State 2006, 4).[42] One report found that in practice, there is no clear distinction between the tasks of the police and those of the army when it comes to security.[43] Yet neither the police nor the military have ever proved effective at targeting violence against women, particularly that rooted in intrafamily violence. Rather, government actors were themselves responsible for a majority of the violence against women during the war and have been implicated as perpetrators of some of the feminicides. Addressing violence against women is likely to demand even less of the PNC's energy as gangs and drug traffickers are transformed into quasi-military threats, to be dealt with in a military fashion, an approach that in Guatemala historically has perpetuated forms of violence unique to women.

Inadequate policing is just one aspect of the deficient state response to the rise in feminicides. Even when police investigations have occurred, the rate of prosecution of crimes against women remains dismally low. The Public Ministry is charged with investigating crimes and prosecuting offenders. According to the U.S. Department of State (2005), its efforts have been hampered by "inadequate training and equipment, excessive caseloads, and insufficient numbers of qualified investigators." The alarming lack of prosecution of the feminicides in Guatemala fits squarely within an ongoing pattern of impunity. Of the approximately 250,000 complaints filed with the Public Ministry during 2005, fewer than 3 percent were prosecuted, and significantly fewer received convictions (U.S. Department of State 2006). Further, files of the public prosecutor reveal only fourteen successful prosecutions for the over 1,500 women killed between 2003 and early 2006 (Lakshmanan 2006). Guatemala's Network of Non-violence against Women has documented only fifteen sentences handed down for the more than 2,000 feminicides in Guatemala between 2000 and 2006 (Paterson 2006a). In terms of the 665 deaths documented in 2005, Amnesty International reported that only two resulted in convictions, with no arrests made in 97 percent of the cases.[44]

These figures replicate the impunity of the war years, when the Guatemalan Historical Clarification Commission (CEH 1998, 36) found that both military tribunals and the ordinary justice system "were incapable of investigating, trying, judging and punishing even a small number of those responsible for the most serious human rights crimes, or of providing protection to the victims."[45] With 93 percent of the war violence attributed to the state, the wartime massacres remain the greatest symbol of government impunity. Three democratically elected presidential administrations later, the war crimes continue unpunished, and those responsible for the killing remain active in the state's affairs.[46] Recently, the Guatemalan government announced the creation of the Comisión Nacional para el Abordaje del Femicidio (National Commission to Address Femicide).[47] The stated mission of the commission is to develop strategies for the government to address the feminicide crisis. The government has pledged its commitment to the issue, yet it has devoted scant resources to existing law enforcement and investigative institutions and has failed to effectively address their respective systemic failures. While the creation of the commission needs to be viewed positively, it is unclear how another institutional structure will improve the government's response and overcome issues of duplication and official incompetence (Amnesty International 2006, 12).

Conclusions

The impunity granted the perpetrators of violence against women renders them particularly powerful because they know that women cannot pursue help through the expected channels. The Guatemalan government has an obligation to reform and rebuild the state to end this general climate of impunity.

To start to overcome the disadvantages that women seeking justice for gender-based violence face, members of the Guatemalan Congress should invalidate the law that criminalizes sexual relations with a minor only in cases in which the victim is considered "honest" and follow the Constitutional Court's lead and abolish Article 200, which allows a rapist to escape prosecution if he marries his victim.

Even with adequate laws, the challenges to slowing the increase in violent murders of women are substantial. The Guatemalan government must take a variety of concrete steps aimed at stemming the epidemic levels of violence against women (Amnesty International 2005, 29–30). To start, the government must take immediate steps to establish a central, unified database of missing persons accessible to every official body responsible for law enforcement, investigation, and prosecution of these crimes. An urgent search mechanism for missing women and girls must also be created. Investigators must be trained in acceptable methods of collecting, protecting, and processing forensic evidence, and a system of oversight should be implemented for all investigations. Gender-related violence should be fully reflected in official reports and statistics. Furthermore, given the link between some of the feminicides and organized crime and security forces, including the PNC, the government should expedite the creation of a mechanism to address the illegal activities of clandestine security groups and those undertaken by structures within the state (Ertürk and Commission on Human Rights 2005, para. 68, recommendation 1).[48] Finally, current efforts to train judges and prosecutors in gender discrimination and violence against women should be supported and expanded by the Guatemalan state.

Recent statements by then President Óscar Berger and Supreme Court President Beatriz de León regarding the need to eradicate feminicides and the establishment of the National Commission to Address Femicide are encouraging because they recognize that women's murders *are* a separate phenomenon. However, they must also be accompanied by significant resources and real action. Otherwise, public statements and commissions provide scant relief to the women like Rodi Alvarado and Claudina Velásquez who continue to be abused and murdered on the basis of their gender.

Notes

This chapter is based on Center for Gender and Refugee Studies 2005, 2006b. For more information on the Center's campaign to stop the violence against women in Guatemala, see http://cgrs.uchastings.edu/campaigns/femicide .php.

1. For a more in-depth discussion of the use of this term, see Amnesty International 2006; U.S. Department of State 2006.

2. Canada, which has accepted gender-based asylum cases since 1993, has kept statistics on the number of gender claims. It has reported that since such claims have been recognized in Canada, they have made up only a very small percentage of the overall asylum claims filed: see Musalo and Knight 2002. In addition, after asylum was granted to Fauziya Kassindja, a young woman fleeing female genital cutting, the INS kept statistics on the number of female-genital-cutting claims; it also reported that there was no significant explosion of claims (U.S. Department of Justice 2000).

3. *Editor's note:* Gonzalez was succeeded by Michael B. Mukasey, who in 2009 was in turn succeeded by Eric Holder.

4. In July 2009, the Obama administration reversed a Bush administration position and opened the legal path for granting asylum to women victims of human rights abuse due to their gender (Preston 2009).

5. One significant and fundamental problem in addressing the feminicides is the lack of any standard system for collecting data on violence against women in Guatemala. Furthermore, many crimes go unreported either because the victims feel that nothing will come of it or because they fear reprisal. One report estimates that 75 percent of crimes committed in the country are never reported, with 51 percent of victims not reporting because they do not believe that anything will be done and 12.8 percent not reporting because they fear reprisals from the victimizers (Federación Internacional de Derechos Humanos 2006; excerpts translated by the authors). Despite any discrepancies in statistics, it is clear that the rate at which women are killed continues to rise.

6. Affidavit of Ana María Méndez, human rights activist and friend of Claudina Velásquez, October 2005, on file at the Center for Gender and Refugee Studies, Hastings College of Law, University of California, San Francisco.

7. The term used in Spanish is *una cualquiera*, which translates literally as "a nobody." However, *una cualquiera* also has a sexual connotation when used in reference to women who are deemed to have loose morals; this term would have the English equivalent of "slut" or "tramp." In the case of Claudia Velásquez, authorities told the family that they had been reluctant to investigate because her bellybutton ring and sandals indicated that she was *una cualquiera*. In another case, authorities immediately categorized an unknown woman found naked in a riverbed as *una cualquiera* or even a prostitute because she was wearing red nail polish (Portenier 2006).

8. See also U.S. Department of State 2006.

9. "En lo que va del año se reportan 405 asesinadas" (So far this year, 405 women reported murdered), *Diario Siglo Veintiuno* (Guatemala City), November 3, 2004.

10. International efforts to bring the *clandestinos* (clandestine security groups) to justice have been thus far unsuccessful. The Comisión de Investigación de Cuerpos Ilegales y Aparatos Clandestinos de Seguridad en Guatemala (Commission for the Investigation of Illegal Bodies and Clandestine Security Apparatus; CICIACS), appointed by the United Nations in 2004, aimed to prosecute the *clandestinos* but was found to be unconstitutional by Guatemala's highest court. Efforts to revive CICIACS have since stalled. The illegal armed groups created during the internal armed conflict have been able to maintain their structural relations with the state and have developed and strengthened their links to organized criminal networks (Hernández 2005).

11. As illustrated by the case of Claudina Velásquez, investigators are quick to look for signs that the victim is a "nobody" to legitimate a lack of due diligence in such investigations. The practice of placing responsibility on the victims themselves is not limited to individual investigators. As recently as

2004, Guatemalan President Oscar Berger said, "We know that in the majority of the cases, the women had links with juvenile gangs and gangs involved in organized crime" (Amnesty International 2005, 21n7). While in public statements Berger has indicated that the feminicides are the product of societal inequalities and discrimination, it is unclear whether he has truly receded from his original position (CERIGUA 2006d; see also Morales Trujillo 2002; idem, interview by Katherine Ruhl, Red de la No Violencia contra Las Mujeres, San Francisco and Guatemala City, tape recording, July 2006).

12. The quote in the subhead is from a Guatemalan news article titled "Violencia intrafamiliar: Antesala del femicidio (Intrafamily violence: Femicide's waiting room)" (CERIGUA 2006c).

13. U.S. Department of State 2006. A study of the Guatemalan urban poor found that violence between spouses was so widespread that it was an assumed occurrence within Guatemalan households. In the vast majority of cases studied, men were the perpetrators, and women were the victims (Moser 2001).

14. The U.S. Department of State (2006) has found that in practice, the police often fail to respond to requests for assistance related to domestic violence. Women also face high levels of violence outside the family setting. In fact, women in state custody may even fare worse, with 80 percent of women in detention reporting abuses of some kind (U.S. Department of State 2006). Reports of rape increased 40 percent between 2001–5 (this may reflect improved recordkeeping of crime statistics but is nevertheless alarming). In 2005, twenty-nine cases of police rape were filed with the Internal Affairs Department of the Guatemalan police (U.S. Department of State 2006). Women are also at risk in the workplace, with one-third of the domestic workers Human Rights Watch interviewed for a study in 2002 reporting having suffered some kind of unwanted sexual approach or demand by men living in or associated with the household. None of them had reported the incident to the police (see Human Rights Watch 2002, 79).

15. The extent of state-sponsored violence has been well documented (see, generally, Schirmer 1998; see also Schlesinger and Kizer 1999, x).

16. The United Nations High Commissioner for Human Rights recently stated that the lack of prosecution of high-level officials has "encouraged the current crime wave sweeping Guatemala" (Guatemalan Human Rights Commission 2006).

17. Up to 1 million civilian men were recruited into PACs between 1981 and 1995, when the president called for the dismantling of this armed civilian force. As of 2002, the PACs had not yet been fully dismantled, with Amnesty International reporting that they remained "a virtual alternative power structure in rural Guatemala" (Amnesty International 2002).

18. "During the entire period of the internal armed confrontation, the Guatemalan Army illegally forced thousands of young men into the army to participate directly in hostilities . . . and included minors under the age of fifteen" (CEH 1998, 37n46). Testimony asserting that soldiers were promoted

based not on how well they carried out orders but, instead, on the brutality they demonstrated highlights the danger women faced during the war years. "The ability to kill, to take initiative during massacres, and to demonstrate cruelty in the course of operations were implicitly valued by the army and other security forces. Internal competition to ascend the ranks was an added incentive for agents and officers to become increasingly involved in repression. A perverse system was created in which disregard for human life was a prerequisite for promotion" (CEH 1998, 37n46).

19. The report goes on to state, "Many perpetrators viewed rape as something natural, and of little significance, in the course of violence against women and communities."

20. In discussing rape and sexual violence as a deliberate strategy of war, Monica McWilliams (1999, 115) argues, "In such situations, the range of permission from the dominant group — military or paramilitary — to subordinate the 'other' is so extensive that, for women caught up in the conflict, religion or ethnicity offers a second incitement."

21. This brings to mind Catherine MacKinnon's (1998, 53) assertion that "men do in war what they do in peace, only more so, so when it comes to women, the complacency that surrounds peacetime extends to wartime, no matter what the law says."

22. Yakin Ertürk, the United Nations Special Rapporteur on Violence against Women reported that "the *modus operandi* [in the abduction and killing of women] is reminiscent of torture methods used in the counterinsurgency" (Ertürk and Commission on Human Rights 2005, para. 30).

23. In 1996, the Guatemalan government and the Guatemalan National Revolutionary Unit, the umbrella guerrilla group, signed the Agreement on Social and Economic Aspects and Agrarian Reform as part of the Peace Accords. Recognizing that the elimination of discrimination against women is essential for Guatemala's economic and social development, the agreement obliged the government to revise national laws and regulations to eliminate discrimination against women in all spheres. In a section on the rights of indigenous women in the Agreement on the Identity and Rights of Indigenous Peoples, the parties committed themselves to promoting "the dissemination and faithful implementation of the Convention on the Elimination of All Forms of Discrimination against Women [CEDAW]," which Guatemala ratified in 1982. Despite these agreements, and Guatemala's further obligations as a signatory of the Inter-American Convention on the Prevention, Punishment, and Eradication of Violence against Women, laws that limit women's access to justice remain in place.

24. The discriminatory Civil Code norms were repealed only after the Inter-American Commission on Human Rights determined that they, as well as other provisions, violated articles of the American Convention on Human Rights.

25. Until a reform was passed in 1999, a woman could work outside the home only "when this [did] not prejudice the interests and care of the chil-

dren or other attentions in the home." (Human Rights Watch 2002, 48). A Constitutional Court case in 1993 upholding the discriminatory articles repealed in 1998 and 1999 argued that the articles were not discriminatory against women: "In marriage there is a role for each of the spouses, those that are determined by the State within the traditional Guatemalan values and the diversity of conceptions, customs, and national beliefs in relation to marriage. The state has regulated the institution [of marriage] with precise norms to give certainty and legal security to each of the spouses" (Human Rights Watch 2002). While this provision has been repealed, provisions of the current Labor Code place women in the same category as children. For example, Title IV of Chapter 2 of the code is titled, "Work of Women and Minors," and Article 147 of Chapter 2 states, "The work of women and minors should be appropriate to their age, physical conditions or physical state, and their intellectual and moral development."

26. Trujillo, interview by Katherine Ruhl.

27. According to Trujillo (ibid.), the existence of a family or spousal relationship is not an aggravating factor in sentencing and is not an element of the crime. She also explained that, if abusers are charged, they are often charged only with a minor offense, which is punishable by a prison sentence of about ten days or a fine.

28. "La violencia intrafamiliar no constituye delito; en consecuencia, no puede iniciarse un proceso a menos que existan lesiones. En ese caso, debe determinarse el tiempo que requerirá la curación para establecer si corresponde iniciar o no un proceso. Sin embargo, cuando la mujer comparece en general ya no hay lesions presentes, por lo que nada puede hacerse."

29. While Guatemalan law provides for police protection and intervention in cases of violence in the home, "in practice . . . the PNC often failed to respond to requests for assistance related to domestic violence," and while there were social services for domestic violence victims, "there were insufficient funds for this purpose" (U.S. Department of State 2006.

30. This legally enshrined expectation of sex from domestic partners is reflected in the violence women suffered during the internal conflict, where they were often forced to cook and clean for the soldiers who raped them (Recovery of Historical Memory Project 1999, 73).

31. On the other side of the spectrum, until 1996 women could be imprisoned for sexually satisfying someone other than their husband. This criminalization of adultery flowed in only one direction; a man could only be imprisoned if he knew that his female lover was married, but not solely for the act of having sex outside of marriage (Villaseñor Velardi 1996, 68).

32. In the United States, the prosecutor generally has the ultimate discretion in pursuing charges of sex crimes. While the victim's willingness to cooperate may be a factor (the prosecution may drop the charges in some jurisdictions if a victim does not wish to cooperate), the onus is on the state to prosecute the crime. In Guatemala, sexual violence cannot be investigated by public action; it requires the victim to file a complaint. Thus, a public pros-

ecutor cannot pursue a case without the active participation of the victim (Amnesty International 2006, 9; Federación Internacional de Derechos Humanos 2006, 28).

33. A truth commission sponsored by the Catholic church found that the P N's Criminal Investigation Department, despite several name changes over a period of twenty years, maintained as its basic function "political persecution rather than public safety" (Recovery of Historical Memory Project 1999, 23).

34. When the P N C was created, 70 percent of the P N officers had not received any type of police training. New P N C officers were offered six months of training, while officers who were being recycled received only three months (Vela et al. 2001, 153). The three-month training has been criticized as "patently insufficient to inculcate new values and adequate skills in police officers accustomed to operating within past corrupt and repressive forces" (Washington Office on Latin America 2002). In February 2005, the ranks of professors at the police academy was thinned, with old professors substituted by former military men who completely lacked the human rights/due process training the previous professors had attempted to pass on to recruits (Investigation on Feminicides (Maldonado 2005, 48).

35. Further blurring the lens between the present and the past, President Óscar Berger announced his plan to boost the police force with the addition of three thousand former soldiers (B B C News 2006).

36. Trujillo, interview by Katherine Ruhl.

37. For instance, the family of Jairo González, featured in the B B C broadcast "Killer's Paradise" (Portenier 2006) was forced to go into hiding after demanding justice for their murdered loved one. Giselle Portenier, the producer and director of "Killer's Paradise," reports that they continue to live in fear for their lives. According to Angélica González of Guatemala's Network to Oppose Violence against Women, investigators "frequently focus their probes on family members of victims rather than examining the bigger picture" (Amnesty International 2006, 10–11; Paterson 2006a).

38. There are differing opinions on the nature, makeup, and actions of the maras. By P N C standards, the maras are composed of approximately two hundred thousand persons, while local organizations believe that there are no more than thirty-five thousand gang members in the country (Federación Internacional de Derechos Humanos 2006, 35).

39. All suspected gang members have become presumed felons, with critics accusing the police of indiscriminate and illegal detentions when conducting anti-gang operations in high-crime neighborhoods. In stark contrast to the lack of arrests in cases of feminicide, gang members have been arrested on the basis of false charges and in some instances without a warrant and not during the commission of a crime (U.S. Department of State 2006).

40. As observed in an article on violence against women in societies under stress, "In countries in which the 'security' services have a heightened perception of their 'military' role and the police culture predominantly subscribes to traditional views about the subordinate role of women, the more laissez-faire

attitudes toward domestic violence add yet another set of barriers to the help-seeking process" (McWilliams 1999, 138).

41. In these joint missions, "members of the military are in the majority, giving rise to a continuation of the practices employed during the war years, and to a conception of security linked exclusively to a systematic militarization of Guatemalan society" (Federación Internacional de Derechos Humanos 2006, 34).

42. It is interesting to note that, according to one report, "Even though sixty-seven percent of Guatemalans associate the military with criminal acts, fifty-two percent support their involvement in fighting crime" (Neild 2002, 28).

43. The blurring of civilian and military lines would not at first glance seem to affect the government's response to violence against women. However, the sense of themselves as a "military" branch among police officers (stemming from the fact that they are led and staffed by the same pre-Peace Accords force and often conduct joint patrols with the military) affects their willingness to work with the prosecutor's office (Public Ministry), which is considered a "civilian" entity. One report quotes a police official explaining his unwilling-ness to work with prosecutors "*porque son civiles* (because they are civilians)" (Maldonado 2005, 50). Clashes between the PNC and the Public Ministry render the scene of the crime an object of permanent dispute, and when evidence is gathered, it is often lost between the two entities' competing forensics labs (Investigation on Feminicides (Maldonado 2005, 50).

44. Some reports claim that none of the 665 killings that occurred in 2005 have been solved (Frenkiel 2006). However, Amnesty International (2006, 4n18) reported that the murders of María A. López Camas, Suly Niseyda Leonardo and Maria C. Menchu Taca in 2005 had resulted in two convictions.

45. Ten years later, violence around the war deaths continues, with "sub-stantial threats made in 2005 against the lives and safety of persons involved in exhumation of secret mass graves containing victims of the internal armed conflict" (U.S. Department of State 2006).

46. General Efraín Ríos Montt, the leader of the "scorched earth" campaign that devastated mostly indigenous communities and under whose short re-gime in the early 1980s the highest number of victims were recorded, ran for president in 2003 and served as president of the Guatemalan Congress (analo-gous to the U.S. Speaker of the House) until 2002. His ability to rally support in the face of the overwhelming evidence against him speaks to Guatemala's entrenched culture of impunity (Recovery of Historical Memory Project 1999, 291). During Ríos Montt's sixteen months of leadership in 1982–83, "the Guatemalan army destroyed some 400 towns and villages, drove 20,000 rural people out of their homes and into camps, killed between 50,000 and 75,000 mostly unarmed indigenous farmers and their families, and violently displaced over a million people from their homes" (Schlesinger and Kizer 1999, 10).

47. In November 2005, the government announced its intention to create a

national commission on feminicides. The National Commission to Address Femicide was introduced in March 2006 (CERIGUA 2005a, 2006e).

48. It also is critical that the Guatemalan Congress reject draft legislation to transfer jurisdiction to military courts for crimes by current and former military personnel and, instead, establish a mechanism by which to investigate and address the problems posed by clandestine and private security forces.

MARTA FONTENLA
Translated by Sara Koopman

Femicides in Mar del Plata

Masculinist violence is maintained and reproduced by the state, not only when it fails to take measures to prevent and protect women from violence, but also when it allows for impunity and contributes to the propagation of violence through the direct involvement of state institutions and state actors. Crimes and disappearances of women in prostitution in Mar del Plata and other places fall under the definition of femicide and the continuum of violence, as do other crimes whereby deaths follow a similar pattern, accompanied by impunity, throughout Argentina.

In Mar del Plata, femicide began in 1996 with the murder of Adriana Jacqueline Fernández, the first in a series of crimes against and disappearances of women that have yet to be solved. As I write this article, only two low-ranking police officers of the Province of Buenos Aires have been sentenced, not for the disappearances and deaths, for which their participation could not be proved, but for their conspiracy in crimes related to the promotion and facilitation of prostitution. Neither did it prove possible to establish the links among organized prostitution networks that operate similarly throughout Argentina. Women might be prostituted on the streets, in brothels, in bars, and in hotels, but regardless of whether they can have freedom or are enslaved and deprived of their freedom, they are always under the control of these networks. On the streets they have to pay the police officers who collect the money for the trafficking network either directly from the women or from their pimps. Although this does not prevent violence, those women who refuse to pay suffer even greater violence and threats of detention by the police.

To remain open, brothel managers pay bribes to the police and other state agents. On the street, the connections with police officers and those in power are plainly visible. Often there are emotional relationships between police officers and prostitutes, as in the cases of the women who were killed and disappeared in Mar del Plata (Silvana Caraballo and María Esther Amaro) and in Rosario (Sandra Cabrera).

The drug-trafficking circuit is also linked to prostitution. A large number of women use drugs or are drugged to keep them(selves) in that situation or are used for drug trafficking. One modus operandi that continues to increase is the kidnapping and "forced disappearance" of women and girls for prostitution networks. They end up in brothels, as did Marita Verón, kidnapped in Tucumán in daylight and "disappeared," and Fernanda Aguirre, kidnapped in Entre Ríos, among others. The way the networks operate resembles the last military dictatorship. Women are kidnapped, "disappeared," and murdered with the complicity of their clients, police, and judicial authorities. To date, there is no national or local registry of the women murdered and disappeared under these circumstances.

Mar del Plata Cases: Judge Hooft's Decision

The only investigation that has yielded any results was conducted by the Criminal and Correctional Transitional Court Number 1 of Mar del Plata under Dr. Pedro Federico Hooft, who investigated the cases of forced disappearance of Silvana Caraballo, Verónica Chávez, and Ana María Nores.[1] This decision illustrates the network of complicity and links among pimps and different state agents. The case was originally addressed by Department Court Number 7 and was transferred to Hooft at the end of September 1998, when the province's criminal justice system was reorganized.

During the first phase of the investigation, the police were in charge. Since there had been no progress, Hooft requested that the attorney-general of the Supreme Court of the Province of Buenos Aires name judicial examiners. The examiners started the investigation in March 2001 virtually from scratch, although they had evidence of phone calls that demonstrated the existence of multiple and regular communications of this kind among segments of organized prostitution in Mar del Plata and police, judicial, and municipal agencies. An article by the Argentine news agency Telam on November 23, 2003, reported that, according to a report resulting from the investigation of kidnappings, homicides, and other serious crimes by the attorney-general of the Supreme Court of the Province of Buenos Aires, Eduardo Matias de la Cruz, regarding the incoming and outgoing calls from the offices of the

Army's commander-in-chief, thousands of telephone connections were verified. Eighteen of them were linked to the case of the women in prostitution in Mar del Plata.[2]

As a result of information obtained from the searches conducted at the brothels, it was possible to link the disappearance of Ana María Nores, Silvana Caraballo, and Verónica Chávez. According to the report drafted by the Centro de Apoyo a la Mujer Maltratada (Battered Women's Support Center; CAMM), by August 9, 2002, there were records of at least twenty-eight female victims who were presumed to be involved in prostitution and who had either been "disappeared" or murdered. The file shows that from 1997 to the beginning of 1998, at least eight male police officers coordinated crimes related to organized prostitution, such as facilitating its promotion and protection on the streets and in brothels, as well as providing surveillance and security. These police officers fulfilled certain functions within the criminal organization. They were in charge of forcibly collecting a weekly amount from each woman, watching over the women, and checking car registrations of the clients, among other things. The police also collected a weekly sum from the brothels.

A witness testified that Silvana Caraballo and the police officer Lines Ayala were lovers and that rumors were going around about the involvement of police officers, judges, and other influential people in these cases. The mother of Verónica Chávez testified that Caraballo had been "beaten up for doing a lousy job . . . and that she liked prosecutor [Marcelo] García Berro."[3] According to her mother, the day before her disappearance "Verónica . . . said that she was working at the coat check of a bar where the prosecutor had been on the day of its opening." Another witness stated: "Marcelo [García Berro] used to call Verónica Chávez and drive her around in a Corsa [and] after the disappearance he never called again." According to another testimony, "The girl that disappeared [Chávez] has a baby girl. . . . [T]he prosecutor was her client. . . . [T]hey saw his car's plates" and "Ayala [one of the police officers found guilty] had black parties [gatherings that feature excessive sex, drugs, and alcohol and that occasionally end with some kind of violence or a woman's murder] with [Chávez], and the prosecutor participated in them. . . . There were drugs and alcohol at those parties in Sierra de los Padres. . . . Police officers participated, too, as deliverymen. . . . Other girls who subsequently disappeared had also participated in those parties. . . . To get them to participate in these parties they sweet-talked them, tempting them with a lot of money. . . . Some parties were held at private homes. . . . Ayala was also involved with María Esther Amaro [who was murdered] . . . who was pregnant, and Ayala was the father. . . . Ayala had been charged several times for collecting from the girls and for beating them up. . . . The witness Liliana Lesdesma, who testified against Ayala, said she heard him say: "You accused me, and they took me off the streets, but I'm coming back, and I'm going to get back at you for what you did to me." He apparently said this to a girl who filed charges against him. Her name is unknown. Another witness testified that she "met Chávez and Caraballo . . . and [knew] because she saw . . . that they got into fancy cars and got back out after a few minutes, which made you suspect that Verónica and Silvana were informants or were performing some other type of tasks." Another woman testified that Silvana Caraballo "used to date a young police officer" and that a "police officer in narcotics offered her a job as an informant." The witness said she thought that an "organization in which the police are involved [was] responsible for the deaths and disappearances of the girls of Mar del Plata."

In his statement, Police Inspector Juan José Arteaga stated that he could not understand how the facts could not be brought to light. To "take the girl the way [Caraballo] left the apartment," he clarified, "it would have had to be a very well-known person; to disappear a body, you have to have access to important means." Arteaga said that he "never believed the story that a psychopath from the street was committing the crimes. You have to have time and resources, and you have to work with the girls on the street." Police Inspector Carmelo Impario added, "The way I interpret it is that some of these [disappeared] girls may have switched sides; they were victims of mafia activity and of their possible protectors. . . . As to the dead and mutilated women, my interpretation is that they were a message to the other women that worked the same way . . . as a warning to them."

Just reading these statements, which are only excerpts from the court decision, the responsibility of the police and of judicial authorities in the exploitation of prostitution is clearly evident, as is the well-founded suspicion of their involvement in the crimes being investigated. Nevertheless, because of the requirements for establishing legal truth, it was necessary for the two police officers to accept the evidence resulting from a (plea-bargained) summary judgment in which the district attorney and the attorneys for the accused agreed on sentences of four years and four years and two months, respectively. In this case, there are still four more accused, including police officers and the managers of a brothel. All are currently fugitives.

Different Cases, Same Actors

The cases of murders and disappearances of women in prostitution and of those trafficked into forced prostitution have similar characteristics. The analysis of some judicial and journalistic investigations suggest the connection between state agencies and human- and drug-trafficking gangs that operate throughout Argentina. If we examine a few case examples — the disappearances of Nores, Caraballo, and Chávez in Mar del Plata; the murder of Sandra Cabrera in Rosario; the murder of Natalia Melmann in Miramar; the murder of Leyla Nazar in Santiago del Estero (Dársena crimes); the disappearances of Marita Verón and Fernanda Aguirre in Tucumán and Entre Ríos, respectively; and the triple crime in Cipolletti — we find a number of similarities.[4]

In the case of Natalia Melmann (Miramar), two low-ranking Buenos Aires police officers were sentenced to life in prison based on the evidence collected. Melmann was kidnapped and taken to a private party before she was raped and killed. Her murder on February 4, 2001, occurred on Police Inspector Carlos Grillo's birthday: "Some suspect that when Grillo was chief of the Miramar division, police officers tended to gather and celebrate in intimate parties at the Copacabana house, where they took the women. The presumption is that Natalia was taken by force after refusing to participate" (Peker 2003).

In most of the cases, police officers and other public officials from state agencies are involved in prostitution networks, in private parties in which women are forced to participate (Chávez, Nazar, Melmann), and in brothels like the ones at Sierra de los Padres and La Perla (Mar del Plata), in Rioja, and in the Province of Buenos Aires.

In the cases investigated by Hooft, and in the Rosario case, the victims had links to police and judicial authorities. In the case of Sandra Cabrera, Diego Parvluczkl, a member of the police force's Dangerous Drugs Division, was charged with the crime. He declared, "She used to give me certain information about the streets relevant to my work." He denied having any emotional relationship with the victim, but Cabrera's father stated that Cabrera and Parvluczkl "had been lovers since 1997." (La Voz del Interior 2004).[5] As stated earlier, in the criminal case overseen by Hooft, Police Inspector Carmelo Impario testified that he believed some of the girls might have pocketed money or switched gangs and were victims of mafia actions and of their possible protectors. He also regarded the murder and torture of women as a form of warning or message for other women who work the same way.

The journalist Gustavo Ragendorfer stated that "the triple crime of the Cipolletti girls was in reality a settling of scores between two gangs of pimps. One of the gangs, connected to the police, was going to kill three prostitutes connected to the other gang, but the hit men made a mistake, and the police covered up the previous murders. It was a scandal" (Peker 2002, 12).

María de los Ángeles (Marita) Verón was kidnapped and disappeared in Tucumán in daylight in 2002. Since then, her mother, Susana Trimarco, has searched for her in prostitution rings throughout Argentina. Trimarco received information that her daughter had been moved to Rioja to be prostituted; then she heard that her daughter had been sent to Spain. Susana Trimarco says, "I think we have to stop being hypocrites. This is not about judicial or police negligence but about a machinery of complicities and cover-ups that involves the criminal justice system, the police, and the political elite of Rioja . . . that for years has been functioning here with fluid contacts in neighboring provinces." As to the stories she has been told, it turns out that women, girls, and adolescents are prostituted; that the disappearance of the Swiss tourist Annagreth Würgler in the District of Coronel Felipe Varela, in La Rioja Province, had to do with VIP prostitution; and that three young women between twenty and twenty-three escaped from the José C. Paz brothel, where they had been locked up. (They avoided the nearest police station because its officers were clients of the brothel, and they escaped from a second police station because those police were protecting the owner of the bar.) Among other things, Trimarco asks, "How did they end up in that place? Who handed them over? Who are their kidnappers? Where were they being prostituted? Who were the clients? To answer those questions you have to unmask people in power, and nobody wants to open that door" (Sandá 2005, 12).

The investigation headed by Attorney-General Eduardo de la Cruz looked into the possibility that some of the women disappeared in Mar del Plata in the past few years are alive and have been moved to Spain by organizations involved in human or drug trafficking to work as prostitutes or to be used as "mules."

Actions Taken to Clear Up the Crimes

CAMM has initiated the most important actions aimed at solving the murders and disappearances in Mar del Plata.[6] On September 17, 1997, CAMM launched a campaign with the slogan, "No One Life Is Worth More than Another." It also drafted a petition and collected signatures, organized marches, delivered public talks on prostitution, handed out flyers, held roundtables, and carried out interviews of the authorities, judges, and prosecutors involved in the proceedings. On July 18, 1998 — the one-year anniversary of Ana María Nores's disappearance — the group organized a march along with the Grandmothers of the Plaza de Mayo, the Permanent Assembly for Human Rights, the National Women's Gathering of Mar del Plata, and labor unions. CAMM has received the support of numerous organizations and national as well as international women's rights groups.

On February 9, 2001, CAMM organized a large demonstration, which received widespread support from the community of Mar del Plata. It also drafted the report that Judge Hooft cited in his decision. In the city of Buenos Aires, the Raquel Liberman Assembly distributed flyers denouncing the murders and disappearances and demanding that they be investigated.[7] At the Sixteenth National Women's Gathering in La Plata in 2001, several feminist groups from the federal capital, from La Plata, and from Mar del Plata organized a roundtable entitled "Prostitution and the Crimes in Mar del Plata."

Every March 8 and November 25, we (members of CAMM) distribute flyers in Buenos Aires and hold *escraches* in front of the Mar del Plata House.[8] Besides the investigation carried out by Judge Hooft and the judicial examiners of the Attorney-General's Office for the court of the Province of Buenos Aires, Senator Elisa Carca has tried to make the provincial Senate aware of the situation but has encountered resistance on the part of other legislators.[9] Carca believes that this resistance stems from discrimination against women in prostitution but also from police involvement and the efforts to protect public figures who were clients of the victims.

Senator Carca has questioned the investigation undertaken by Prosecutor Carlos Alberto Pelliza, charging that he is not the appropriate person to conduct the investigation. The presence of Pelliza, as well as that of the accused police agency is, for Carca, evidence of a lack of willingness to conduct an in-depth investigation into the crimes. If involvement by police officers is suspected, either through their actions or through cover-ups, how can they be expected to uncover evidence of their own complicity?

In a meeting on December 5, Attorney-General De la Cruz informed Senator Carca that he had relieved Pelliza, along with some police officers, from their investigative duties. De la Cruz also informed Carca of the appointment of a group of prosecutors to work exclusively under his orders, noting that he believed the number of murdered and disappeared women to surpass twenty-five and that he suspected the involvement of local police and staff from the federal justice system, as well as influential political figures. Besides noting that Hooft had been the only judge to show any genuine interest in the case, de la Cruz indicated that he did not have any direct evidence of involvement of the Juárez Cartel in the cases and that the investigation had progressed significantly.

Hooft detained eight police officers and charged Federal Prosecutor García Berro with concealing evidence. To date, two men have been sentenced. The federal justice system has jurisdiction over García Berro's case. (He was appointed prosecutor for the Federal Oral Criminal Tribunals of San Martín.) Because no official data are available, the exact number of women who have been "disappeared" and murdered in Mar del Plata is still unknown. De la Cruz reported to Carca that by 2001 twenty-five more victims of femicide had been reported; other sources estimated somewhere between twenty-seven and forty-two victims.

The Law

It is difficult to calculate the number of kidnappings, assassinations, and forced disappearances of women throughout Argentina from or for organized prostitution rings on the streets or in brothels. Some people estimate that the situation is comparable to the time of the latest military dictatorship. It is one of the biggest human rights problems the country faces.

Since the unconstitutional Reform of 1999 (Act 25.087), legislation in Argentina has regressed in the area of human rights protection for people involved in prostitution and for those trafficked for sexual exploitation. The law has also retreated from prosecuting pimps and human traffickers. Proposals for reforming the Penal Code — both the one introduced by the nation's attorney-general (the Freixas bill) and taken up by Senator Jorge Alfredo Agundez and the one proposed by Deputy Hernan Damiani — followed the current trend of designating prostitution as work and point to the consolidation of a system of impunity around forced prostitution.

The Reform of 1999 departed from Argentina's abolitionist tradition, which was ratified in the Convention for the Suppression of the Traffic in Persons and of the Exploitation of the Prostitution of Others of 1949. The convention establishes that the procurement of prostitution should be criminalized in all its forms (individual and organized), regardless of the age of the victim. It also maintains that the person in prostitution should never be criminalized and that even in the case of adults, consent should be irrelevant to the definition of the crime committed by the traffickers, pimps, and others.

Along with the Reform of 1999, the proposed reform bills are not useful for prosecuting the crimes or for protecting the victims; nor do they address demand, which is the root cause of these femicides. By insisting on an element of coercion, violence, abuse, or vulnerability affecting the ability of victims older than eighteen to consent, the burden of proof is placed on the victims, who have to demonstrate that they "do not/did not accept" the situation they found themselves in and that they did not consent to their own exploitation.

This trend has been strengthened by the approval by the United Nations of the Convention against Transnational Organized Crime and the Palermo Protocols of 2000,which establish that, for the crime of trafficking to occur, the element of "coercion" or "force" of victims older than eighteen must be present, along with criminal association and the transport of victims across national borders. This makes it virtually impossible to prosecute the crime of trafficking.

Argentina has adopted the new regulatory system promoted by European countries (with the exception of Sweden) whereby pimps become "lawful entrepreneurs." Some countries in Latin America consider the Palermo Protocols' definition of trafficking to be ineffective for combating the crime and protecting the victims. Both Colombia (in 2005) and Peru (in 2004) have amended their penal codes to reflect a redefinition of trafficking that considers the victim's consent irrelevant. The regulation of prostitution and its consideration as work (another form of regulation) consolidate the exploitation of women in prostitution, smuggling, and trafficking for prostitution.

Femicide and Prostitution

The murders of women in Mar del Plata and other parts of Argentina fit the definition of femicide. It is also clear from the murders and forced disappearances that prostitution is paradigmatic of social, sexual, and political violence against women. Women in prostitution are victims of social stigmatization, discrimination, abuse, and physical and psychological violence by pimps and clients who profit from the prostitution of others, or the exchange of money for access to women's bodies.

Femicide represents the extreme form of patriarchal domination. The failure on the part of civil society (except for a few human rights groups and individuals) to react to crimes such as the murder and disappearance of women, the impunity that surrounds these crimes, society's negation of femicide, the justification on the part of clients of prostitution, and lax legislation all contribute to furthering and consolidating the climate of impunity. The combination of the absence of a strong social movement to counter gender-based violence and the state's complicity, negligence, and failure to investigate the crimes make it unlikely that women's murders and disappearance will end any time soon. These are not isolated cases; nor can they be attributed to a serial killer. Femicide exists because of a network of complicity among clients, pimps, and institutions within the state.

Violence against women is rooted in male domination as much as it is perpetuated by a perspective that considers prostitution a legitimate form of work rather than a practice that abuses, exploits, and objectifies women.[10] It is a perspective that is congruent with the current stage of neoliberal patriarchy in which commodification not only reaches all aspects of life (including people's intimacy), but also has high levels of legitimation.

Notes

This chapter originally appeared in *Feminicidios e impunidad*, ed. Silvia Chejter. Buenos Aires: Centro de Encuentros Cultura y Mujer, 2005.

1. Decision issued by Judge Hooft in December 2004 in the case of three disappearances in Mar del Plata, in which two police officers — Lines Ayala and Oscar Orlando Iturbure — were sentenced.

2. "Rastreo de llamadas telefónicas implican a militares," *La Capital*.

3. All of the quotes are from Judge Hooft's sentence, December 2004 The legal case file is in the Criminal and Correctional Court (in transition no. 1) of the Judicial Department of Mar del Plata in the Buenos Aires Province. The case remains in the court in the event that the fugitives are found. If the case is closed, the file will be sent to the archives.

4. On February 6, 2003, in the area of La Darsena, near the provincial capital of Santiago de Estero, the bodies of nineteen-year-old Leyla Nazar (who had disappeared twenty days before) and Patricia Villalba were found mutilated and devoured by wild animals. Leyla was involved in prostitution in bars and near candy stores. The crimes surprised local managers, merchants, and members of the Catholic Church, who blamed rural police, senators, and high-ranking officials, as well as Mercedes Araqonés de Juárez, wife of the governor. On November 9, 1997, in Cipolletti, a province of Rio Negro, Maria Emilia Gonzalez went for a walk with her sister Paula and a friend Veronica Villar. They disappeared. Two days later, their bodies were discovered lying by the side of a road. Veronica's hands were tied with her shoelaces and had a handkerchief stuffed in her mouth. She also had a deep

cut in her neck. A short distance away and partially buried in the ground were Maria Emilia and Paula, with hands tied and mouths gagged. Both had been severely beaten and then shot, the former in the head near her ear and the latter in the back and head.

5. "Detienen a un policía acusado de matar a una prostituta," *La Voz del Interior*.

6. Roundtable at the 16th National Women's Meeting, La Plata, about prostitution and the crimes of Mar del Plata, August 18, 2001, published in *Brujas* magazine, año, no. 29 (November 2002). Information on the actions taken by CAMM and Elisa Carca were summarized in the presentations given by Ana de Mare of CAAM and Diana Staubli, Carca's adviser.

7. The Raquel Liberman Assembly was active between 1996 and December 2000.

8. *Translator's note*: An *escrache* is a type of public demonstration in which activists go to the residence or place of work of someone they want to denounce to make the person visible to the public. The term comes from the chalk messages often left in front of the house or office. *Escraches* have been commonly held in Argentina since 1995. For more information, see http://es.wikipedia.org/wiki/escrache (accessed January 15, 2008).

9. Request for reports from Senator Elisa Carca, Martín Vega, and Eduardo Sigal to the Senate of the Province of Buenos Aires, 2000. The parliamentary report is located in file no. F-1121/00–01, p. 213–14, Parliamentary Information Section of 12–21–2000, Senate Library, Buenos Aires,

10. "No hay lucha sin cuerpo y sin palabra," *Brujas Magazine* (Buenos Aires), año, no. 31 (October 2005).

HILDA MORALES TRUJILLO
Translated by Sara Koopman

Femicide and Sexual Violence in Guatemala

Since the year 2000, voices have been raised in alarm in Guatemala over the appearance of women's corpses without explanations for the causes of death. The women's bodies show signs of having been treated with hatred and cruelty. The corpses show multiple wounds caused by bladed weapons and firearms, and some of the women were strangled, dismembered, and raped, raising specters of the forms of gender-based violence committed during the armed conflict that ended with the Peace Accords signed in December 1996. Violence against women has existed across time and has been considered a normal phenomenon, inherent in the context of a patriarchal and authoritarian system that discriminates, oppresses, and enslaves women. If the problem had not reached the size it has recently, and if the women's movement did not have the level of organization that it has achieved since the signing of the Peace Accords, the authorities probably would not pay attention to these violent deaths of women.

In the course of seven years, about three thousand women have been murdered in Guatemala, and no one has been identified as responsible in the majority of the cases (see table 7.1).[1] Thus, these crimes against women remain in total impunity. The problem is similar to that in Ciudad Juárez, Mexico, which is better known internationally, and increases in violent deaths of women are also coming to light in other Latin American countries, including Costa Rica, Colombia, El Salvador, Honduras, and Peru. It is for this reason that the women's movement demands that the authorities fulfill their responsibility of offering better security for women and of prosecuting the guilty. The women's movement has again taken up the arguments made by Jill Radford and Diana Russell, who first named this problem "femicide."

TABLE 7.1. Violent deaths of women in Guatemala

Year	Assassinations of Women
2000	213
2001	302
2002	317
2003	409
2004	497
2005	624
2006[a]	590+
Total	2,950

Source: National Civil Police, Guatemala City, 2006.
Notes:
[a]As of November 2006. This statistic is not a total, since women's corpses appear daily, and the compilation of statistics is delayed.

The Concept of Femicide

According to the feminist movement, *femicide* is a relatively new term for the most extreme manifestation of violence against women. Its use addresses a concern for identifying the increase in violent deaths of women that has been seen in recent years, on a large scale, in some Latin American countries. However, the act of killing a woman for being a woman — whether a woman is considered one's "own" through marriage or family ties or even one of several women who have transgressed the established patriarchal order — has existed since time immemorial. These acts are based on the belief that women have no autonomy; that they do not own their own bodies or their own lives but are, instead, things or goods that belong to men, who can dispose of them as they please.

Killing a woman, or several women, for being of the feminine gender is a problem that must be analyzed not only from a legal perspective, but also from a sociological and political perspective. The position and condition that men and women hold and maintain in society affects how men assume the right to mistreat and kill women.

From the perspective of legal history, the killing of women has sometimes been taken into account and sometimes not in the keeping of crime statistics. In ancient Roman law, when a man killed his wife, the act was called *uxoricide*, which comes from the Latin *uxor* (woman, wife, consort) and *coedere* (to kill). The act has also been called *conyugicidio* (conjugicide), although this term can also be used to mean a woman killing her husband. This terminology has fallen into disuse. The term used today is *homicide*, which from a linguistic perspective, leaves women invisible as victims, because *homicide* comes from the Latin *homicidium* (*homo* 'man') and *coedere* (to kill). Spanish-speaking feminists argue that the language has been built on the basis of the masculine, as such, the feminine has been considered alternative. The law uses androcentric language, with man as its paradigm for humans, excluding and making invisible the existence of women. Legal norms use feminine language only when referring to acts related to the biology, anatomy, or physiology of women — for example, legal acts related to maternity or the reproductive organs or to sex itself, such as in cases of rape when men and boys are excluded as victims (as is the case of the Penal Code of Guatemala, which has been in effect since 1972). The consideration of the murder of another person — that is to say, *homicide* — makes clear the lack of a focus on gender in legal terminology.

Currently, the majority of penal codes use the legal form *parricide* to describe the form of homicide in which a murderer is related to the victim in one of the ways covered under the law. Originally, *parricide* referred exclusively to the murder of one's father. Its use was later expanded to cover cases in which the victim was someone who served as a father substitute (a stepfather or a mother's companion) or when a mother, wife, husband, or descendant was killed. Sanctions are greater in these cases than when the victim is a stranger or there is no family tie.

For centuries, violence against women went unnoticed. It was considered a natural act in all societies, by women as well as by men. However, because internationally organized women have argued before universal and inter-American human rights bodies for the need to expressly recognize that violence against women exists and is a violation of human rights, international and national legal instruments and mechanisms have been elaborated that make violence against women visible as a problem that affects women's dignity, worth, and human condition. These instruments and mechanisms define the phenomenon as *gender violence*, or as a phenomenon in which women are attacked physically, psychologically, and sexually for being women. This definition recognizes that gender is a social construction used to differentiate the roles socially assigned to men and women that translate into discrimination, oppression, subordination, and the exclusion of people of the feminine gender. However, given the way the term *gender* is twisted and misunderstood, it is preferable to keep using the term *violence against women*.

Among these new legal instruments it is worth highlighting the

Vienna Declaration and Program of Action, which came out of the World Conference on Human Rights, held in Vienna in 1993, where it was emphasized that women's human rights are part of universal human rights. Based on that declaration and program, the United Nations issued the Declaration on the Elimination of Violence against Women in December 1993. The Comisión Interamericana de Mujeres (Inter-American Commission of Women; CIM) issued its own Declaration on the Elimination of Violence against Women during its twenty-fifth Assembly of Delegates. In June 1994 at Belém do Pará, Brazil, the Assembly of the Organization of American States (OAS) adopted the Inter-American Convention on the Prevention, Punishment, and Eradication of Violence against Women, also known as the Convention of Belém do Pará. This convention defines violence against women as "any act or conduct, based on gender, which causes death or physical, sexual or psychological harm or suffering to women, whether in the public or the private sphere" (Asamblea de la Organización de Estados Americanos 1994, Article 1).

Nevertheless, the considerations, effects, and concepts of statutory law have demonstrated a blind spot when it comes to the massive number of deaths of women in various countries at the hands of men whom they knew and did not know; who were family members and who were not. The phenomenon exceeds the meaning of terms such as *aggravated homicide*, *assassination*, and *parricide*, for they do not point to the reality of these cases or the possibility of judging such acts across eras of universal history, during which femicide has been state policy. It has been so openly and directly, such as in the Middle Ages, when women were killed during the Inquisition under the accusation of being witches, and it has been covered up or, at least, tolerated by the state in other eras and other parts of the world.

The term *femicide* can be understood as the corollary to *homicide*. The first term refers to killing a woman, and the second, as is known, refers to killing a man, though *homicide* legally is understood as the act of taking a person's life without regard to his or her sex. In contrast, *femicide* has been normalized to mean the act of killing a woman for being a woman. It implies different characteristics and constitutes a demonstrative crime as a maximum sanction and expression of extreme violence inflicted on women who subvert the patriarchal order by attempting to break out of the traditional canon of submission, subordination, and inhibition of their own autonomy. It is understood, as international and regional instruments regarding violence against women affirm, that the causes of such violence lie in the historically unequal relations of power between men and women.

Jill Radford and Diana Russell (1992) were the first to advance the term *femicide* theoretically based on concrete acts, especially the massacre of fourteen female students by an individual in Canada. They systematically laid out the acts that constitute femicide, defining it as an act of killing a woman because she is a woman. Based on their arguments, Ana Carcedo and Montserrat Sagot (2002) developed specific concepts: intimate femicide for assassinations committed by men with whom the victims had an intimate, familiar, household, or similar relationship; non-intimate femicide for assassinations committed by men with whom the victims had not had a relationship, although the act was preceded by a sexual attack; and femicide by association for assassinations of women who were in the "line of fire" of a man trying to kill a women and who put themselves in the way to try to stop the act.

In studying cases in Ciudad Juárez, Mexico, Marcela Lagarde y de los Ríos (2004) named these acts *feminicide*, which for her means a repeated violation of women's human rights that culminates in assassination and constitutes genocide against women that is characterized most of all by impunity. According to Lagarde, who bases her theoretical construction on the studies by Radford and Russell, feminicide "occurs when the historical conditions generate social practices which allow for attacks on the integrity, development, health, liberty and life of women. . . . It is shaped by an ideological and social environment of machismo and misogyny, of normalized violence against women, of an absence of laws and government policies, which creates an insecure coexistence for women, puts their life at risk, and favors a set of crimes" against women (Lagarde y de los Ríos 2006, 26). All manifestations of violence against women can be placed within Lagarde's arguments. Indeed, at a forum on the violent deaths of women held in Guatemala, the Mexican attorney Alicia Elena Pérez Duarte y Noroña indicated that Lagarde's definition has to be interpreted in two ways: In a broad sense, it implies all of the manifestations of violence against women, and in a strict sense, it implies the violent deaths of women that remain in impunity.

According to research done in Guatemala, *femicide* "is a political term that not only includes individual aggressors but the state and legal structure, given that since femicide does not exist in the statutes as a crime, it does not receive the legal and sociological treatment appropriate for cases that characterize it: when a person is assassinated and is a woman. On the other hand, the state, through its inability to fulfill its duties, contributes to impunity, silence and social indifference" (Congreso de la Republica de Guatemala 2005, 16).

Unpublished research conducted by the Grupo Guatemalteco de Mujeres (Guatemalan Women's Group) analyzed several cases of murdered women and, following Russell and Radford's definition closely, determined that not all of the violent deaths of women in Guatemala are cases of femicide. Nevertheless, the research also stressed the lack of data for the cases analyzed that would allow for definitive conclusions.

The arguments advanced by these different authors make clear the need to consider and address the problem. Although Lagarde has argued for the need to elaborate a national and international criminal classification in the law along the lines of genocide, it seems to me that we first need to deepen our understanding of the characteristics and circumstances of the violent deaths of women to be able to insist on its recognition under statutory law. Meanwhile, prevention and sanction actions are urgently needed to keep this problem from continuing.

When discussing the problem of violent deaths of women committed in the context and with the characteristics described here, the most widely used term within the Latin American and Caribbean Feminist Network against Domestic Violence and Sexual Violence, and the one officially used by the CIM and the Committee of Experts on Violence of the Monitoring Mechanism of the Convention of Belém do Pará, is *femicide.*

Femicide, an Ever Present Problem

Over the course of ten years, Ciudad Juárez, Chihuahua, Mexico, has seen violent deaths of hundreds of women who were first disappeared and whose killers have remained in impunity. The cases of femicide in Ciudad Juárez have attracted attention and concern from the international community, which often has cast the phenomenon in the context of a border region whose population has a great deal of migratory mobility and where manufacturing companies show a preference for employing women with scarce resources.[2] Ciudad Juárez's murdered women make manifest the state's inability to protect the lives of women and to carry out criminal investigations and prosecute the criminals.

From 2000 to 2006, approximately three thousand violent deaths of women were reported in Guatemala.[3] In the majority of cases, investigations were inadequate or nonexistent, and the perpetrators have remained in impunity. This, in turn, has kept Guatemalan women in a state of alert and terror. The argument has been made that the violent deaths of these women correspond to the more generalized violence that exists in Guatemala, but this does not address the special characteristics of these killings — notably, the evidence of cruelty found on the corpses of the majority of the assassinated women.

In the Central American region, women's organizations in Honduras, Costa Rica, and El Salvador have also reported increases in violent deaths of women in recent years. In the face of these atrocious and inhumane acts, the women's movements in Guatemala and elsewhere in Central America are advocating for greater attention from society and the state. They are also demanding from the state more responsible intervention in identifying and adjudicating those who are guilty for these crimes, as well as greater guarantees of women's safety.

Femicide and Armed Conflicts

Femicide is a phenomenon that is present during periods of armed conflict, as well as in times of "peace," as has occurred in Guatemala, El Salvador, and Peru and as is occurring in Colombia. In times of war, women are considered trophies on whom the vengeance and unbridled hatred of enemies can be enacted. Today, wars are carried out everywhere; there are no well-defined battlegrounds. This has placed women in greater danger, as the parties involved in conflicts unleash their instincts and as assault, rape, and death are privileged as strategies of war. In Guatemala, the internal armed conflict between the army and the Unidad Revolucionaria Nacional Guatemalteca (Guatemalan National Revolutionary Unity; URNG) lasted approximately thirty-six years. According to the "truth reports," when soldiers arrived in rural communities, they killed the men and forced the women to cook for them, serve them, and dance for and with them; they also assaulted, raped, and, finally, killed women and sometimes burned them. All of this was done with the consent and approval of the commanding officers. (CEH 1999; Recovery of Historical Memory Project 1999). Nevertheless, and despite the recommendations of the Comisión para el Esclarecimiento Histórico (Historical Clarification Commission), the state has not disseminated the truth reports as widely as necessary, preventing the wounds of the past from being healed through compensation to surviving victims, judgment of the guilty, and the initiation of a culture of dialogue in schools and universities.

Femicide can be an isolated act in which a violent death is due to the circumstance of being a woman or it can be a matter of massive, violent indiscriminate deaths of women. Both cases follow from contempt for the feminine, misogyny, or hatred of women. Women's contributions to economic, social, and cultural development are more visible in this century than in other eras, which makes us think that contemporary assassination of women is an attempt to restrict the autonomy that we have been able to achieve and build with great effort, obstacles, and sacrifices.

Statistics reflect an increase in femicides, even when not all of the violent deaths of women are clearly documented. Even if there were in fact fewer such deaths, it would not diminish the horror and the environment of fear that is lived in Guatemala and that is made manifest in the bodies of women. In effect, most of the corpses show signs of torture; wounds made with bladed weapons and firearms; and mutilation. There have been cases in which a woman's extremities, head, and trunk have been left in different areas.

The authorities and public opinion have both associated the victimizers with members of youth gangs (*maras*), organized crime, drug trafficking, and domestic violence. For its part, organized civil society also associates the murders of women and the generalized violence that exists in Guatemala with the training in a culture of violence that has its roots in forms of repression that were used during the war. It is for this reason that the Historical Clarification Commission, installed as a result of the Peace Accords, recommended that the contents of its report *Memória del silencio* (*Memory of Silence*) be widely disseminated, including to schools and educational centers at all levels, with the aim of keeping the horrors of war from being repeated. This is a task that the state has yet to take on. As a result, we still frequently see, as we did during that era, that pregnant women are killed and that victims are subjected to torture, rape, and other sexual abuse in a continuum that once signified, and still signifies, violence against women. The difference in the current violence lies in the great number of women who have been assassinated without knowledge of who killed them and without any meaningful response from the state.

The costs of the femicides are reflected in the suffering and the emotional instability lived by the daughters, sons, mothers, fathers, and other family members of the women, together with the re-victimization these family members face when they approach the justice system and confront its negligence, indifference, and irresponsibility. For these reasons, under the Inter-American Convention on the Prevention, Punishment, and Eradication of Violence against Women and the Convention of Belém do Pará, the Guatemalan state is responsible for the tolerance and lack of appropriate intervention in the crimes that are committed daily against women.

After several years of presenting the claim of the femicide of María Isabel Véliz Franco before the Inter-American Commission on Human Rights, the case was accepted in October 2006. The Guatemalan state will now have to establish the circumstances surrounding María Isabel's death, deepen the investigation, and file charges so that her assassination does not remain in impunity. The admissibility of the claim is exemplary and serves as a support for family members of other victims to keep exerting pressure for their cases.

It is worth noting that the majority of the victims of femicide are women of reproductive age — that is, from sixteen to thirty-two. It is in this age range that women often obtain middle and high levels of education, although young girls, adult women, and seniors are also on the lists of femicide victims. The PNC itself admits that the majority of the victims are students and housewives, and it can also be said that the women affected belong to the middle and working classes.

The wave of misogynist violence has yet to provoke outright indignation among civil society. Beyond the organized women's movement and a few other exceptions, civil society remains unperturbed by these acts. If a story ran on the news today saying that the corpse of a street vendor, a newspaper seller, a university student, or even a doctor or lawyer had been discovered, no voices of outrage would be heard.

Countering Gender-based Violence

The Red de la No Violencia Contra las Mujeres (Network of Non-violence against Women), which brings together ten women's organizations, was established in 1992 after the assassination of the union leader Dinora Pérez, which has remained in impunity. The network and other women's and human rights organizations, including the Fundación Sobrevivientes (Survivors Foundation) and the Centro de Acción Legal en Derechos Humanos (Center for Legal Action on Human Rights), have turned to the international community, obtaining recommendations from Yakin Ertürk, the United Nations Special Rapporteur on Violence against Women, as well as from Susana Villarán, the former Women's Rapporteur of the Inter-American Commission on Human Rights; the European Parliament; and 110 members of the U.S. Congress. Yet the Guatemalan state has taken no action that responds to the magnitude of the problem.

The Network of Non-violence against Women played an important role in lobbying for approval of the Law to Prevent, Sanction, and Eradicate Intrafamily Violence and has sought mechanisms for the law to be effectively applied by the administrators of justice.[4] In the years that the law has been in effect, administrators generally have shown a reluctance to comply with its mandates. They have made the crucial process for filing complaints more difficult and sent women in a sort of pendulum swing from one institution to another before their complaints are accepted. As a result, measures of protection are not always granted with the speed required. The network also took the initiative, beginning in 1998, to develop the regulations of the law and advocate for their approval. The regulations were approved in November 2000. Through these regulations, the Coordinadora Nacional para la Prevención de la Violencia Intrafamiliar y contra las Mujeres (National Coordinator for the Prevention of Domestic Violence and Violence against Women; CONAPREVI) was created, bringing state representatives together with representatives of the network. Although the budget provided by the state is insufficient, CONAPREVI has developed the Plan Nacional para la Prevención y Erradicación de la Violencia Intrafamiliar y Contra las Mujeres 2004–2014 (National Plan for the Prevention and Eradication of Interfamilial and Violence against Women), which aims to promote research, establish a system for tracking statistics, strengthen institutions so that complaints receive better attention, and create shelters with comprehensive services for abused women and their children. This institution has become the reference point for women's organizations in civil society that want to institutionalize public policies to stop violence against women.

In 2003, the Network of Non-violence against Women presented a complaint against the Guatemalan state before the Inter-American Commission on Human Rights for its lack of appropriate intervention to stop violence against women in general, and the lack of investigation and punishment of the femicides specifically. Rapporteur Susana Villarán visited Guatemala in 2004 in response to this complaint; United Nations Rapporteur Yakin Ertürk was likewise asked to come to Guatemala by members of the network who are also part of CONAPREVI.

The Sector de Mujeres (Women's Sector), formed during the negotiations that led to the Peace Accords, has also spoken out against violence against women and the femicides. In the struggle against impunity, members of Non-violence against Women, the Women's Sector, and other women's organizations have worked together to speak out publicly in organized marches protesting violence against women. We have also carried out actions before the authorities to demand that they carry out their role by administering justice and providing security for women and that Congress approve the reforms that we have proposed and modify the Penal Code regarding crimes committed against women.

Another significant action that was first put forward by the Network of Non-violence against Women and that has also been advanced by CONAPREVI is the need to have a single statistical registry to be able to reliably track statistics of domestic violence and violence against women. The use of such a registry is being considered by the authorities of the Instituto Nacional de Estadística (National Statistics Institute), but there is still resistance from the institutions that would be responsible for recording the data. Some administrators of justice have argued that filing such statistics will not aid in resolving cases. This shows us that a culture of statistical record keeping does not exist in state institutions and that this issue is also affected by a desire to hide the reality of violence against women. Having reliable data would make it possible to clarify how many women have died violently and the circumstances in which those crimes have occurred — and, therefore, to place greater emphasis on public policies to stem the tide of femicides.

Conceiving of the violent and massive number of deaths of women as *femicide or feminicide* is a theoretical tool. It can assist in helping us to name the problem; it can also be used to classify such acts as a prosecutable crime at a national and an international level — for example, at the International Criminal Court, where gender was taken into account in the drafting of the Rome Statute. But what is most urgent now is to stop the indiscriminate killing with impunity of women and to get society to reject it, as well as to raise the awareness of those who are responsible for the security policies and the administration of justice of the state.

Notes

1. According to information supplied by the PNC. These statistics are not reliable, however, because the figures reported by different institutions that receive and process complaints do not match up.

2. The most recent data from the Colegio de La Frontera Norte regarding the violent deaths of women in Ciudad Juárez states that 22 percent were workers in the *maquilas*.

3. According to statistics from the PNC.

4. The law was approved in Congressional Decree 97/96, October 1996.

MONTSERRAT SAGOT AND
ANA CARCEDO CABAÑAS

When Violence
against Women Kills

FEMICIDE IN COSTA RICA,

1990–99

Over the past decade, violence against women has been acknowledged as an important social problem. However, despite increases in visibility, services for affected women, and international treaties and national laws, such violence has continued to cause more deaths and injuries among women age fifteen to forty-four than malaria, AIDS, or war (Carcedo and Zamora 1999).

Regardless, in Western societies, ideas of peace and safety have been closely associated with the institution of the family, to the point that many have still found it difficult to accept the fact that many women, girls, and boys have been abused within their homes. But the truth is that for many, especially women and girls, the family has been the most violent social group, and the home, the most dangerous place.

While under-reporting has made an exact estimate of the size and impact of violence based on gender inequity difficult to ascertain,[1] research has begun to unveil the terrible and oppressive situation that some survivors, especially from incest, call the "best-kept secret." For example, studies conducted in the United States show that during the Vietnam War, more women died at the hands of intimate male partners than U.S. soldiers died in the war, with an average of 3,500 women a year, compared with 57,685 soldiers in twenty years of U.S. intervention (Morgan 1989).[2]

This is merely a small example of the magnitude of the war against women. Other studies conducted in the same country have clearly shown how the so-called domestic-violence syndrome is systematic and disproportionately directed against women. For instance, it has been shown that since the 1970s, 63 percent of all murdered women have been killed by husbands, fiancées, or partners, and most of these murders have occurred in the victims' own homes (see Dobash and Dobash 1979; Strauss, Gelles and Steinmetz 1980). Similar data have been reported for Canada and Brazil, where 60–78 percent of all murders of women were the acts of male partners (United Nations 2000; Statistics Canada 1993).

Other sources, such as the Hopkins Report, "Ending Violence against Women," have estimated that around the world, at least one in three women has been beaten, forced to have sex, or in some way abused at some point in her life (CHANGE 1999). We refer to these studies, since there are fewer studies conducted in Latin America on gender violence, mainly due to a lack of resources and reporting protocols for victims of violence, as well as few databases or resources to collect these data.

One study conducted in Colombia by the Instituto Forense de Bogotá (Forensic Institute of Bogotá) found that a fifth of the cases of physical injuries presented for evaluation by forensic medicine were due to conjugal violence against women (United Nations 1991). An evaluation of hospital emergency services in Santiago, Chile, from September to November 1986, found that 73 percent of the 2,618 women seen for injuries had been hurt by family members (Heise et al 1994).

Even if in Costa Rica there are few systematic studies on the theme of gender-based violence, statistics that have been available reinforce the data previously presented. In 2000, the Rompamos el Silencio (Let's Break the Silence) phone line of the Instituto Nacional de las Mujeres (Women's National Institute) received 12,183 calls, 94 percent of which were from women affected by violence and asking for support. According to data from the Departamento de Planificacion del Poder Judicial (Planning Department of the Judicial Power), 26,437 requests for protection from domestic violence were received in 1999, a 26 percent increase over 1998. During the same year, the Delegacion de la Mujer (Women's Precinct) attended to 5,188 cases, most related to violence against women within the family (Proyecto Estado de la Nación 2000). According to the Encuesta Nacional de Violencia contra las Mujeres (National Survey on Violence against Women), 58 percent of the women in the country have experienced at least one act of physical or sexual violence since age sixteen, and most of these acts were perpetrated by close males (see Sagot 2004).

In a study conducted by the program "Mujer No Estás Sola (Woman You Are Not Alone)" of the Centro Feminista de Información y Acción (Feminist Center for Information and Action), five thousand women from its support groups found that the severe aggression they experienced put them in danger of death. Fifteen percent of these women were attacked or threatened with firearms; 31 percent, with knives; and 24 percent, with glass, other instruments, or fire. Obviously, danger of death is an integral part of these women's daily lives. In fact, 58 percent of them revealed to have felt at some time being in danger of dying at the hands of the aggressor, and 47 percent have desired or attempted to commit suicide as a result of violence. Finally, 48 percent of these women have had to leave home at some time out of fear of death (Carcedo 1994).

Situations experienced by victims of gender-based violence and the kinds of responses they encountered when searching for help indicate what, in a previous work, we called the "total social conspiracy," in which each actor has a role he interprets, with no need of a director (Carcedo 1994). If in Costa Rica people from any other social group had been so systematically raped, threatened, and even murdered merely because they belonged to that social group, it would have been publicly denounced as a brutal violation of human rights and personal integrity. However, in the case of women, until very recently such "total social conspiracy" has allowed these deaths to be presented only as isolated cases in newspaper pages. Social awareness of the seriousness of the problem has increased, and some preventive actions have been initiated, but in 2000, at least twenty-three women died due to domestic and sexual violence.

From this perspective we developed the idea of conducting systematic research on murders in Costa Rica of women for reasons related to gender inequity. This is the first research of its kind conducted in the country.

Our aim was to analyze the characteristics and factors associated with women's murders in Costa Rica due to gender inequity from 1990 to 1999. Our specific objectives were (1) to collect the available statistical data on murdered women due to gender inequity from 1990 to 1999; (2) to analyze the relationships between the women and their murderers; analyze the place, form, and conditions of the murders; and document previous help sought by the women and responses received; and (3) to develop proposals for prevention and protection of women at risk of death from violence based on gender inequity.

Theoretical Framework: Gender Socialization, Violence, and Femicide

In all known cultures, gender is a major determinant of the organization of social relations. To a great extent, observed differences between women and men in most societies can be attributed to cultural patterns derived from gender relations. For instance, masculinity and femininity are expectations that are socially constructed and not categories determined by biological condition. Similar to social behaviors associated with social class or ethnicity, gender exerts a powerful influence on the social relations of human beings, their life prospects, their opportunities, and their access to social resources.

All societies establish precise mechanisms for human beings to learn the behaviors, attitudes, and expectations considered appropriate to each sex. This learning process is called gender socialization. Gender socialization fulfills a series of important functions of social control. First, it imposes on each person a self-definition as male or female. Second, it imposes a definition of the world and one's position in it. Third, it defines others and the kind of intersubjective relations established. Finally, the gender socialization process fosters acquisition of proper gender characteristics and discourages acquisition of characteristics associated with the opposite sex (Andersen 1988).

This process, however, is not neutral. Gender socialization does not occur in a void. Socialization's central objective is to lead people to adapt to the norms of a society structured on a basis of gender inequity and oppression. While the degree of oppression and inequity varies widely across cultures, in no contemporary society is the general condition of women equal or superior to that of men (Chafetz 1988; Chow and Berheide 1994).

Gender socialization fulfills the function of reproducing and justifying social hierarchies for each individual, especially the sex hierarchy and existing institutionalized patterns of domination and oppression, for "the transmission of oppression ideology is socialization's central element" (Sagot 1994, 129–40). As part of the entire social and cultural machinery that tries to teach women to live in oppression, gender socialization is a violent process. The violence expresses itself in many ways, from the subtlest forms of manipulation of and psychological pressures for women to repress traits considered improper to their gender to more blatant aggression, such as physical and sexual violence.

In addition to being one of the fundamental elements of the socialization process, violence against women is also a structural part of the gender-oppression system. The use of violence against women is both a means to control them and one of the most brutal and explicit forms of their subordination. As mentioned previously, the positions of women and men are structured as a hierarchy in which men control both the main resources of society and women. There are many ideological, moral, political, economic, and legal grounds for the exercise of men's authority over women. Although it has varied historically and culturally, the use of violence is one of the main and generalized practices that support such exercises of authority.

As Rebecca and Russell Dobash (1979) say, while men's legal right to exert violence against women is no longer explicitly sanctioned in most Western societies, the heritage of ancient laws and openly accepted social practices continue to generate conditions that allow for the general maintenance of that kind of violence. Although laws do not explicitly support violence against women, inaction, policies of indifference, and contradictory institutional procedures continue to reflect the ideal of women's subordination and men's right to dominate and control them, even resorting to violence.

This complex social web of permissiveness and domination leads to daily practices of systematic violence against women that affect survivors' integrity and quality of life, and can end in death. Deaths of women at the hands of husbands, lovers, fathers, fiancées, acquaintances, and others are not unexplained cases of deviant or pathological behavior. On the contrary: They are the result of a structural system of oppression. These deaths are femicides, the most extreme form of sexual terrorism, caused primarily by a sense of ownership and control of women.

DEFINITION OF THE CONCEPT

Drawing from Jill Radford's and Diana Russell's (1992) definition of *femicide*, we have used the following conceptual categories for the operational ends of our research: *Femicide* refers to the murder of women because they are female. Femicide is the most extreme form of violence based on gender inequity, understood as violence, forcibly exerted by men against women, to obtain power, domination, or control. It includes murders resulting from intrafamily violence and sexual violence. Femicide can take two forms: intimate femicide and non-intimate femicide.

Intimate femicide is the murder of a woman at the hands of a man with whom she has or has had intimate relations—that is, family, friends, or similar relations. Non-intimate femicide is the murder of a woman at the hands of a man with whom she did not have and has never had intimate relations. Non-intimate femicide often involves a sexual attack against the victim. In addition, femicide by connection refers to a woman murdered "in the line of fire" by a man trying to kill another woman: a relative or other woman trying to interfere or in some other way involved in the femicide.

Methodological Strategy

This is a retrospective exploratory study based on the collection of existing data relative to the murders of women in Costa Rica due to gender inequity from 1990 to 1999. As there is no central database for the information, we had to resort to using various sources.

The first task involved is elaborating a list of women murdered by gender violence, following the criteria established by the definition of *femicide*. No institution uses the category "femicide" in its records. Therefore, for our list we had to know, for each intentional death of a woman, her relationship to the killer and her form of death. The elaboration of the list was not a simple task and required the use of many sources and methodological procedures, as described in the following.

We began by using the *Libro de diagnósticos de causas* (Book of diagnostics of causes) of the Sección de Patología Forense del Organismo de Investigación Judicial (Forensic Pathology Sector of the Judicial Research Organ; OIJ) to collect information relative to women murdered and their causes of death. With this information, we arrived at our initial list of murdered women.

As secondary sources, we referred to the Costa Rican newspapers *Extra*, *La Nación*, *La Republica*, and *La Prensa Libre*. There we looked for information about each woman's death, and this in many cases provided data on who the killer or suspect was and his relation to the woman. In newspapers we also found data for many murders regarding previous aggression suffered by the woman, pleas for help, the form of death, how the body was found, eventual witnesses, other people injured, and what the murderer did after the murder.

As a third source, we used the *Anuarios estadísticos del* OIJ (Statistical yearbooks of the Judicial Research Organ), which present data on murders and relations between victim and aggressor. Our review of the yearbooks added to the data obtained from the Forensic Pathology Sector and national newspapers.

With the data collected from these three sources, we constructed a *tentative* portrait of femicides from 1990 to 1999 and elaborated a matrix of relevant information on the women. However, to establish whether a murder was a femicide or not, we needed more information, which was obtained from other sources.

In a second phase of the research, we collected data from judicial investigations. The source was the *Libro de casos entrados del* OIJ (Book of entered cases of the Judicial Investigation Organ). With the case number obtained from the book, we went to the Expedientes de Homicidios (Murder Files). With this fifth source, we completed the information on the defendant for each case, if available.

The Expedientes de Homicidios are located in the offices of the Judicial Investigation Organ in each province. For practical reasons, we limited this part of the study to deaths in San José, where the largest number of women's murders occurs (29 percent) and where the Expedientes de Homicidios were easier to access. We arrived at sixty-two homicide cases, and this was useful for us to confirm the data collected from other sources.

Information on the women's murderers was completed with data from the Instituto de Criminologia del Ministerio de Justicia (Criminology Institute of the Ministry of Justice). Finally, to allow comparisons between the data relative to femicide and those corresponding to other kinds of murders, with both female and male victims, as well as violent deaths, we referred to the *Estadisticas vitales de la* OIJ (Vital statistics of the OIJ) and the OIJ yearbooks.

DATA ANALYSIS

With the information collected and confirmed according to established criteria, we conducted a statistical analysis searching for significant relationships and changes over the time period. Some of the analyzed results were relationship of the murders of women to murders in general; relationship of the murders of women to murders of men; relationship of murders of women in general to femicide; characteristics of the murdered women and aggressors; relations and situations of higher risk; nationality; other people injured in the attack; weapons used; sexual attack associated with femicide; murderers' antecedents; suicides; frequency of femicides according to province; victims' ages, relations to the murderers, and place of death; and criminal sentence.

Given the previously mentioned limitations to precise information, this research could not arrive at the identification of all women's murders, which would allow establishing with absolute certainty which ones were femicides and which were not. In this sense, we adopted a conservative stance and excluded murders that did not appear in the OIJ yearbooks and did not have at least two corroborating sources. All women's murders classified as "femicides" were corroborated by at least two sources, were the result of violence based on gender inequity, and fell under the conceptual definition of femicide. There were also eight other women's murders that we suspected were products of femicide, but the available information did not allow for certainty. In those cases, we employed the analytic category "suspect of femicide."

To the extent that we were able to broaden our research, there were still fifty-three women's murders (17 percent of the total) without enough data on the circumstances. In some occasions, only a qualitative analysis or a successful police investigation would have been able to establish what had happened and whether they were cases of femicide. In these situations, we adopted the category "indeterminate."

Research Findings

According to the statistics of the OIJ, from 1990 to 1999 homicides were the cause of 1,885 deaths in the country, representing a yearly average of 188. The rate relative to the total population, which was 4.7 per 100,000 inhabitants in 1990, increased in 1999 to 6.7 per 100,000 inhabitants. The most frequent victims of homicide were men (86 percent). This asymmetry was found in all countries throughout the world. In fact, men were more involved in violent acts, particularly in homicides, both as victims and as perpetrators.

The second great asymmetry is related to the murderers. In this case, women's participation was lower and, in relative terms, had slightly decreased throughout the decade. From 1990 to 1994, women were murderers in 7.5 percent of cases, and in the five following years, in only 5.5 percent. The asymmetry was also seen in the fact that, in the past ten years, women represented 14 percent of the homicide victims and 6 percent of the murderers. These figures clearly pointed out the gendered manifestations of violence in which men not only "kill each other" more often; they also are more often the murderers than the victims, a pattern contrary to that of women.

The unequal participation of women and men in homicides is to be expected. As gendered beings, society assigns women and men different roles and consistently prepares them to develop and relate to other human beings and the environment differently. That way, violence is easily accepted and even encouraged behavior in men. In the construction of traditional masculinity, violence is the preferred strategy for approaching conflict. In contrast, for women aggressive behavior is considered improper; it is not encouraged and is even repressed. The gendered aspect on homicides — that is, the fact that the percentage of female murderers is smaller than that of female victims — is not coincidental. What helps explain this is precisely the sexual hierarchy that allows these crimes, femicides, to occur simply because the victims are women.

MEN'S MURDERS, WOMEN'S MURDERS: TWO DIFFERENT PORTRAITS

Circumstances associated with men's murders (1990–99) have to do in most cases with quarrels, personal disputes, thefts, or drugs and only in small part with intrafamilial and sexual violence (7 percent) or so-called crimes of passion, which have been increasing throughout the decade. As table 8.1 shows, in 1999 the causes first mentioned accounted for 67 percent of homicides of men, while intrafamilial and sexual violence accounted for 8 percent and "crimes of passion" for 1 percent. On the other hand, the most frequent causes of women's homicides were domestic violence, sexual violence, and "crimes of passion" (45 percent). Only a small number of cases of murders of women were due to quarrels, thefts, personal disputes, or drugs. In 1999, as table 8.2 shows, most victimizations resulted from "crimes of passion" and family problems.

Given the circumstances of men's murders, it comes as no surprise that a third died at the hånds of people with whom they had no relation; by contrast, only a very small minority of women (9 percent) were killed by people unknown to them.[3] There were also few murderers of women who were not identified (19 percent).[4] As we will see, the most frequent killers of women were people close to them, and these women were also frequently killed at home.

HIDDEN FIGURES

This research found forty-four homicides of women (14 percent of the total) that did not appear in the OIJ yearbooks. Of these homicides, the Forensic Pathology Sector subjected twenty-six to autopsies and considered them homicides. Three cases were declared homicides by the courts. However, the under-recording of intentional women's deaths was still larger in cases of femicide. This added up to the general under-recording in cases of violence against women.

Relative to femicide — murders of women by men in intrafamily and sexual violence — the categories employed by the OIJ, as already mentioned, do not allow for its identification according to the terms defined in our study. Of the fifty homicides of women reported during the decade as perpetrated by people whose relation to the victims were unknown, this research was able to determine that at least thirteen (26 percent) were perpetrated by partners, former partners, fiancées, or clients. These errors in the identification of the relations of murderers to the female victims distorted information and effaced the precise elements that may determine whether a murder can be considered femicide.

This study found an under-recording in the official sources of sixty-

TABLE 8.1. Homicides of men by cause, Costa Rica, 1999 (absolute figures and percentages)

Cause	Total	%
Intrafamilial violence	15	6.94
Crimes of passion	3	1.39
Theft	49	22.68
Personal disputes	47	21.76
Quarrels	36	16.67
Sexual violence	3	1.39
Drug problems	13	6.02
Other	50	23.15
Total	216	100.00

Source: Based on data from *OIJ Statistical Yearbook*.

TABLE 8.2. Homicides of women by cause, Costa Rica, 1999 (absolute figures and percentages)

Cause	Total	%
Intrafamilial violence	13	38.24
Crimes of passion	6	17.65
Theft	4	11.76
Personal disputes	4	11.76
Quarrels	2	5.88
Other	5	14.71
Total	34	100.00

Source: Based on data from *OIJ Statistical Yearbook*.

one femicides (33 percent of the total) over the decade. This means that, for every two femicides identified in the OIJ yearbooks, one was not recorded, either because it was impossible to identify as such or it was not recorded as homicide.

As table 8.3 shows, femicides accounted for most homicides of women in the decade (58 percent). These data were consistent with research conducted in countries such as the United States, Canada, Brazil, and Mexico. In fact, violence based on gender inequity caused more than half of women's homicides. In addition, we must consider a significant number of homicides (17 percent) lacking enough information to determine

TABLE 8.3. Homicides of women and femicides, Costa Rica, 1990–99

	1990	1991	1992	1993	1994	1995	1996	1997	1998	1999	Total	%
Homicides of women	32	39	27	29	30	32	27	26	34	39	315	100
Femicides	21	16	13	20	18	20	17	12	21	26	184	58
Possible femicide	0	0	0	1	1	2	1	1	1	1	8	2
Not femicide	6	15	6	5	4	8	4	7	7	8	70	22
Indeterminate	5	8	8	3	7	2	5	6	5	4	53	16

Source: Based on data from many sources, including *Libro diagnósticos de causas del OIJ*; *Extra*; *La Nación*; *República*; *La Prensa Libre*; and *Expedientes de Homicidios*.

whether they are femicides. These opened the possibility that the real percentage of femicides may be larger than what we found in this study. Even with the number of indeterminate cases, one can be sure that, for each woman's homicide that was not femicide, there were almost three that were.

GENDER VIOLENCE WITHOUT EQUIVALENCE IN THE MALE POPULATION

Taking into account only women's homicides in which we know all circumstances (perpetrator, relationship, and form of death) — that is, excluding "indeterminate" cases — the percentage of femicides increases to 70 percent of the total. That means that most of the homicides of women in Costa Rica from 1990 to 1999 were an extreme manifestation of violence based on gender inequity and, therefore, femicides. They were neither casual homicides nor homicides in which the victim could be female or male. They were homicides in which the victim's identity as female was a necessary condition for their occurrence.

Femicide is a serious social problem that is unparalleled in the case of men. In few cases have men died at the hands of female partners, daughters, or other relatives. From 1994 to 1999, only thirty men died in these conditions, which amounts to 2.7 percent of the total homicides of men during the same period. It is worth noting that the murders of men included cases of a woman's self-defense against an aggressor or protection of her children from abuse, whereas in the former cases, the murder of a female partner or relation by a man was a culmination of intra-familial or sexual violence.

Data demonstrate that a considerable number of men were dying in the domestic space, for, as in other places, men are more prone than women to involve themselves in quarrels and violence in general —

violence being a common approach to men's conflict resolution. Even if we view all men's homicides in the decade as resulting from intrafamily violence (eighty), "crimes of passion" (fifty-nine), and sexual attacks (twelve),[5] perpetrated by either other men or women, they all represent only a very low percentage of men's homicides.

In 1990–99, 315 homicides of women and 1,614 homicides of men involved intrafamily and sexual violence, and 131 homicides of women and 1,463 homicides of men did not (*estadísticos vitales de la* OIJ). If we were able to eliminate homicides due to intrafamily and sexual violence both in the cases of women and in those of men, intentional violent deaths of women would decrease by 58 percent, whereas those of men would decrease by only 9 percent.

Any expression of violence in a society is undesirable, and violent deaths of men and women, regardless of their number, are manifestations of serious social problems we need to confront. However, the results from this research show that homicide, as a problem of the safety of citizens, does not have the same characteristics for men as for women because its causes, scenarios, and dynamics are different. This is a reality that has been taken into consideration in international forums on crime and citizens' safety (Johnson 2000).

INCIDENCE OF FEMICIDE

The number of murders of women was similar in the first and second halves of the 1990s (157 in 1990–94; 158 in 1995–99). However, there was a 12 percent increase in the rate of femicides in the same time period (88 in 1990–94; 96 in 1995–99). This finding means that, while the total number of intentional women's deaths remained constant, that of femicides increased. In that sense, femicides represented a growing proportion of the total number of women's homicides (56 percent in the first half and 61 percent in the second half) (*Libro diagnósticos de causas*; *Libro de casos entradas del* OIJ; *Expedientes de Homicidios*; *estadísticos vitales de la* OIJ).

FEMICIDE'S IMPACT

From 1990 to 1999, violence based on gender inequity caused more deaths among women than AIDS, and the same is true for mothers' mortality, as table 8.4 shows. That is why the Organización Panamericana de la Salud (Panamerican Health Organization) has declared violence against women a public health problem.

Women's life expectancy has increased from forty-three years in 1930

TABLE 8.4. Deaths of women by femicide, AIDS, and mother's mortality, Costa Rica, 1990–99

	1990	1991	1992	1993	1994	1995	1996	1997	1998	1999	Total
Femicide	21	16	13	20	18	20	17	12	21	26	184
AIDS	8	6	3	5	5	14	10	15	4	4	74
Mother's mortality	12	28	18	15	31	16	23	29	12	15	184

Source: Based on data from many sources, including *Libro diagnósticos de causas del OIJ*; *Extra*; *La Nación*; *La República*; and *La Prensa Libre*.

to eighty in 2000 (Centro Centroamericano de Población 2001), even though premature death of girls represents a total loss of 7.345 years. Femicide's profound impact, however, goes beyond its effects on public health and the country's economy. Above all, women's murders represent a violation of the most fundamental human right: the right to bodily integrity. The quality of life of abused women, considered apart from their health, does not reach the minimum standard to which all people are entitled. On the other hand, when a woman dies because of gender violence, it greatly affects the family's quality of life and emotional well-being.

FEMICIDE'S VICTIMS

The average age of women murdered by violence based on gender inequity during this time period was thirty. In fact, most were twenty to thirty-nine. This means that women were most at risk during their reproductive years. The fact that the major targets of the murderers were young adult women explains the kind of relationship that exists between killer and victim, as will be analyzed next.

Dangerous Relations: Femicide's Victims and Murderers Data show that, in femicide cases, couples were at higher risk (even when the relationship had ended). As table 8.5 shows, women's partners or former partners accounted for 61 percent of femicides, followed by other relatives, who were responsible for 17 percent of these crimes.

Data show that people who said that they loved and protected the victim — that is, their partners, spouses, and other relatives — were exactly the individuals who represented the highest risk to women. Partners, former partners, or relatives perpetrated 78 percent of the femicides. This is not a parallel phenomenon in the case of men, as stated previously.

On the other hand, it was not easy to know the characteristics of

TABLE 8.5. Femicides according to relation between murderer and victim, Costa Rica, 1990–99

	Total	%
Partner or former partner	113	61.41
Other relatives	31	16.85
Lovers	13	7.07
Acquaintances	8	4.35
Clients	3	1.63
No relationship	6	3.26
Unknown	10	5.43
Total	184	100.00

Source: Based on data from many sources, including *Extra*; *La Nación*; *La República*; *La Prensa Libre*; and *Anuarios estadística del OIJ*.

murderers apart from their relationship to victims. As the murders often happened in situations of violence against women, we know more about the women than about their aggressors. This is partly due to the fact that criminal processes have focused on the consequences of violence, not on the aggression itself. Judicial investigations do not begin by analyzing acts of aggressors; rather, they begin by focusing on the victim's body in search of evidence. For instance, 185 men perpetrated 184 femicides; in one of them, there were three female victims. Another case involved two male perpetrators, and yet another involved three male perpetrators. In seventy-nine of these cases, the average age of the murderer was thirty-five.

The Closer, the More Dangerous   Intimate femicides in the past decade were, in each case, the culminating point of a history of domestic aggression. It is not surprising, then, that most murders occurred in women's homes (Figure 8.5). As indicated, eighty-nine of the femicides occurred in the victims' houses or near them; twenty-two occurred on streets; and twenty-seven occurred in desolate places, such as empty beaches. Another seventeen cases occurred in hotels, bars, and unexpected situations, such as a jail, a marital visit, a clergyman's house, and a rural police precinct.

From 1990 to 1999, eighty-nine women were killed in their homes; twenty-seven were killed in "desolate places"; twenty-two were killed in the street, and seventeen were killed in other places. The myth that the highest risk to women are attacks by strangers in desolate places there

TABLE 8.6. Femicides according to weapon or method used, Costa Rica, 1990–99

	Total	%
Knives and other blades	65	35.33
Firearms	60	32.61
Asphyxia or strangling	26	14.13
Blows	14	7.61
Other	5	2.72
Unknown	14	7.61
Total	184	100.00

Source: Based on data from many sources, including *Libro diagnósticos de causas del OIJ*; and *Libro de casos entrados del OIJ*.

fore has been proved false, since these places accounted for only 15 percent of the femicides during the decade. This research confirms that what women learned as a personal safety strategy — that is, to avoid dark and remote places — did not necessarily protect them from danger, since they were less likely to lose their lives in these places than in their kitchens, bedrooms, and beds. In addition, although some women's bodies were found in public and desolate places, the women had been killed at home and taken to those places in an effort to simulate attacks by strangers (see *Libro diagnósticos de causas del* OIJ; *Extra*; *La Nación*; *La República*; *La Prensa Libre*; *Anuarios estadísticos del* OIJ; *Libro de casos entradas del* OIJ).

Consistent with this, the weapons most used in femicide were easy to find in any house: kitchen knives, scissors, and other kinds of blades. Table 8.6 shows that these were the weapons employed in 35 percent of the femicides in the decade.

It is worth noting that use of a knife, strangling, and blows, which were the most employed methods, imply physical contact, repeated or prolonged attacks, or the use of force; taken together, these exclude the possibility of accidental death. This was in contrast to what happened with firearms. A single shot could cause a woman's death without touching her. However, the contact methods used by murderers in femicide cases only cause death if there is decision, persistence, and, occasionally, brutality.

Brutality The categories employed by the OIJ to classify weapons and methods used in general homicides fall short of what happens in cases of femicides. Frequently, murderers in femicide use more than one weapon and more than one method and, above all, there is a level of brutality seldom found in other homicides, both of women and of men. Brutal force is precisely one of the characteristics of femicide, be it intimate or non-intimate.

In some cases, women were killed with sixty-seven, forty-eight, or thirty-seven knife stabs, with many bullet impacts, with brutal blows that broke the neck, during sleep (three), while pregnant (six), or when on the floor; who were beaten, stabbed, burned, and buried; and who were beheaded (two), raped and murdered, or murdered and then raped (twenty-two). There were men who carefully planned the murders (three), associated with other men to perpetrate or hide murders (three), killed from behind (seven), and resorted to using various weapons to kill their victims (eleven). At least sixty-one murderers in femicides (33 percent of those identified as such) acted with brutality, employed a combination of methods, and planned femicides or perpetrated them in moments when the women were defenseless.

The brutality and premeditation excluded self-defense and accidents. Means used often exceeded those required to cause death. Even so, some murderers argued that they had not intended to kill their victims; they "just wanted to teach them a lesson." Such is the case of a man who, in 1998, killed his wife with a knife out of jealousy in a San José hotel, then argued that "it was an accident" and his intention had been "to teach her a lesson."[6] Brutality speaks of a desire to hurt that is out of measure and of hatred in such cases.

It is worth noting that the most brutal femicides in the decade were perpetrated by partners or former partners — in other words, they belonged in the category of intimate femicides: thirteen of the sixteen who repeatedly stabbed their victims, nine of the eleven who employed multiple methods, and five of the six who killed pregnant women. This indicates how dangerous violent relations on the part of the partner can be, which leads one to analyze the dynamics of control within the couple as very different from aggressive situations that occasionally can happen between people in other relationships.

Control   Many murderers in intimate femicides were men who resented being left by their partners, even when, occasionally, they themselves had left their partners and married or lived with other women. Others killed women within the context of arguing, jealousy, or desire in some way to control them or their daughters. Still others killed their former partners when they refused to return. Others were acquaintances who killed women for not accepting sexual advances. Finally, some were acquain-

TABLE 8.7. Femicides because of immediate control by type
of control, Costa Rica, 1990–99

Type of Control	Total	%
Separation	34	33.66
Sexual attack	24	23.76
Jealousy	21	20.79
Other	15	14.86
Refused sex	7	6.93
Total	101	100.00

Source: Based on data from many sources, including *Instituto de Criminología del Ministerio de Justicia*; *Libro de casos entrados del OIJ*; and *Libro diagnósticos de causas del OIJ*.

tances or strangers who felt they had a right to control and use a woman's body simply because she was a woman and attacked her sexually.

This sense of property was not incidental, and it is not simply a characteristic of these murderers. It was the same kind of control identified throughout the world in studies on abusive gender relations (CHANGE 1999).

Of the total femicides in the decade, in 101 cases (55 percent) the murders occurred as a result of some of the attempts at control mentioned here. In other words, most femicides were an ultimate consequence of an explicit intent on the part of the aggressor to control the women and their lives, bodies, or acts. Of the 101 femicides in which such desire for control was present, 33 percent occurred when the women left or attempted to leave the men; 24 percent occurred during a sexual attack; 21 percent occurred because of jealousy on the part of the aggressor; and 7 percent occurred when the women refused sexual propositions or advances from partners or acquaintances (table 8.7).

More women were killed when leaving or attempting to leave their partners. This circumstance presented a challenge, since neither separation from the aggressor nor returning to him reduced the danger for a woman. People who have suggested that women should return to their partners to avoid greater harm do not understand the potential for ensuing danger. Such acts of submission on the part of women did not tip the scales in favor of the life of those who were killed. Such results were consistent with those found in other countries, such as Canada, showing that the moments of highest danger for abused women were those of separation and reconciliation (Statistics Canada 1993).

On the other hand, strangers were not the only individuals who tried to exert control over women through sexual attack. Of the thirty-three femicides in which there was some form of sexual aggression (18 percent of the total), only thirteen cases (39 percent) were by strangers or unknown men. In all other cases, the aggressors were partners, former partners, acquaintances, or other male relatives.

Final Reflections: Causes of Femicide

Despite some common-sense ideas in the country, neither a general increase in violence nor migration seem to have been direct causes of femicides from 1990 to 1999. Our study challenges the theory suggesting that violence against women is merely another expression of social violence. In other words, violence against women based on gender inequity cannot be explained solely by the category of violence in general. Even if women were indeed affected by all forms of violence — and a relationship has been established between political violence and some manifestations of violence against women, such as rape — social violence is neither a direct cause nor a prerequisite for violence against women based on gender inequity.

As an expression of gender violence, femicide is rooted in the unequal power structure of society that gives women a subordinate position to men, and the practice expresses itself in all domains: material, institutional, and symbolic. The social structure of gender inequity allows men to exercise power over women. In turn, gender socialization enhances men's internalization of power relations over women and the construction of abusive and violent masculine identities. This is the foundation that buttresses and engenders femicide.

There are, however, other specific factors that also have fostered femicide, including, first and foremost, the social tolerance of daily violence against women based on gender inequity. A significant part of femicides, particularly intimate femicides, is bred by relationships marked by aggression and control of women, and many social actors (authorities, community, family) consider these forms of violence acceptable and even natural.

Another factor that has fostered femicide is the impunity of both the aggressors and the authorities who do not fulfill their duty to curb daily violence against women. Despite progress during the past decade, these forms of impunity are an expression of the state's inefficiency and, in some cases, of officials' lack of will in watching over the integrity of abused women. Both forms of impunity have created a vicious cycle in terms of women's demands for protection and justice, in many situations leaving them without fundamental instruments for their defense.

The third, related factor is the lack of political will to confront gender-based violence adequately and specifically. In institutions, the risk that abused women are exposed to has often been minimized, as reconciliation with aggressors is often promoted, thereby denying women's right to live free from violence. This family-centered approach, which places the family's integrity above the rights or interests of its individual members, historically has been an obstacle to the full exercise of human rights by violated women. The same holds true when the interests of the child are privileged over or seen as contrary to the rights of the mother, which results in the view that women should sacrifice their rights to defend those of their sons and daughters.

Undoubtedly, femicide is the most extreme act within the continuum of gender violence and, at the same time, a consequence of such violence. It is a form of violence directed at women *because* they are female. If femicide is not yet statistically a daily occurrence, its risk is, for it is inscribed in the everyday frequency of aggression women experience in Costa Rica.

Such risk is fed both by the violence of aggressors and by the lack of responses society offers to abused and violated women, especially in moments when their lives are in danger. However, these responses cannot be constructed without an explicit, active, and effective will to deter the everyday impunity of the aggressors and to grant women justice, protection, and solidarity.

Notes

1. According to studies conducted in the United States, only 2 percent of cases of child sexual abuse in the family, 6 percent of cases of child sexual abuse outside the family, and 5–8 percent of sexual abuse or rape of adult women are reported to police. Compare this with the reporting of 61 percent of cases of robbery and 82 percent of cases of theft. In Latin America, according to studies conducted for the case of intrafamily violence, we estimate that 15–25 percent of cases are reported.

2. See also *Enciclopedia multimedia Encarta 97*, DVD, Microsoft Corporation, 1997.

3. Data corresponding to the 1991–99 period. The data include only homicides with identified murderers.

4. Ibid.

5. According to the OIJ's classification.

6. *La República*, January 17, 1998.

ADRIANA CARMONA LÓPEZ, ALMA GÓMEZ CABALLERO,
AND LUCHA CASTRO RODRÍGUEZ
Translated by Sara Koopman

Feminicide in Latin America in the Movement for Women's Human Rights

Gender violence appears as a set of threats, assaults, mistreatment, injuries, and harm associated with the exclusion, subordination, discrimination, and exploitation of women. It is exacerbated when it and all other forms of social, economic, legal, cultural, and political violence against women are tolerated and promoted; it is exacerbated even more when it is not considered a social problem but is naturalized and normalized or, alternatively, is regarded as a series of unrelated shocking and extraordinary acts. Gender-based violence is exacerbated when no legal and policy mechanisms are created and no processes are advanced for its eradication.

Violence against women is inherent to gender oppression in all forms: discrimination, inferiorization, devaluation, exclusion, segregation, exploitation, and marginalization, among others. It is a political mechanism for domination — one that is understood as the control and natural supremacy of men and institutions over women and that implies subjection, subordination, punishment, harm, and, in the most extreme form, elimination of women. Recent phenomena have made visible an extreme form of violence against women, inspiring diverse academic investigations into the assassinations and disappearances of women and girls in specific places such as Ciudad Juárez, Mexico. These investigations, in turn, have allowed researchers to identify a modality of gender-based violence as feminicidal violence.

Defining Feminicide

Femicide has been defined as "the murder of women and girls because they are female" (Russell 2001b, 15). Feminicidal violence has proliferated given the situation of gender inequality and men's power and control structure over women and girls that allows them to decide the moment of their death, motives used to justify assassination, violent acts exerted on the victim's body, familial relationship between victim and victimizer, lack of investigation or justice by institutions that impart justice, and responsibility or complicity of the state.

The Ley General de Acceso de las Mujeres a una Vida Libre de Violencia (General Law of Women's Access to a Life Free from Violence), approved by the Mexican Senate on December 15, 2006, defines feminicide as the most extreme form of violence against women, which has been expressed as violence of class, ethnicity, ideology, and politics. Culminating in death, this violence has been accompanied by impunity and the absence of justice.

The following forms of feminicide have been distinguished (Monárrez Fragoso, Diaz de la Vega Garcia and Morales Castro 2006):

Intimate feminicide. The assassinations of women "committed by men with whom the victim had or in the past had an intimate, familial, household, or other similar sort of relationship" (Carcedo and Sagot 2002). Intimate feminicides are subdivided into child feminicide and familial feminicide.

Child feminicide. The assassinations of girls by men or women in the context of a relationship of responsibility, trust, or power because of their role as adults in relation to a minor child.

Familial feminicide. The assassination of one or more members of a family, committed by a man, based on familial relationships between the victim or victims and the victimizer (Russell 2001a).

Feminicide of stigmatized occupations. The assassination of women for being women within their particular occupation or because of the unauthorized work that they do. Victims of this form of feminicide include women who work in bars and nightclubs as dancers, servers, and prostitutes.

Systematic sexual feminicide. The assassination of women who are kidnapped, tortured, and raped. Their nude or seminude corpses are left in the desert, in empty lots, in sewer pipes, in garbage dumps, and on train tracks. Through these cruel acts, the assassins strengthen the unequal gender relations that distinguish the sexes by emphasizing otherness, difference, and inequality.[1] Systematic sexual feminicides are subdivided into organized systematic sexual feminicide and unorganized systematic sexual feminicide.

Organized systematic sexual feminicide. The assassination of women in which the assassins may act as an organized network of people involved in sexual feminicides. The assassins consciously and systematically practice a method of killing directed at women's and girls' sexual and gender identity over a long and undetermined period of time.

Unorganized systematic sexual feminicide. The assassination of women accompanied, though not always, by kidnapping, torture, rape, and the disposal of the corpse. The assassins presumably kill only once over a certain period of time. They may be men who are unknown to the victims or close friends or family members of the victims. The victims are left in lonely places, at hotels, or inside their homes.

The factors surrounding systematic sexual feminicide have also been analyzed by various academics, who have identified shared factors that may help to explain these murders: (1) maquiladora employment; (2) migration; (3) significant gang presence; (4) drug trafficking and established cartels; and (5) the Mexican political context.[2] The Mexican sociologist Julia Monárrez Fragoso (2002) has argued that structural causes and criminal factors coalesce to create violence against women. Mercedes Olivera (2006) has attributed the cause of the feminicides in Ciudad Juárez to a context of structural violence produced by the neoliberal system and the institutionalization of patriarchal power throughout the Mexican nation.

Structural factors mediating violence against women include unemployment, extreme poverty, disintegration of the rural economy, and social polarization imposed by the neoliberal economic model. This system has created a social context in which hypermasculinity — especially the exaggerated, aggressive, and violent aspects of masculine identity — is fomented. Alcoholism, narco-corruption, ungovernability, impunity, and the insecurity that make the daily lives of men and women in Mexico stressful are also components of sexist violence.

Feminicide in Ciudad Juárez and throughout Latin America

In Mexico, the Comisión Especial para el Seguimento del Feminicidio del Congreso de la Unión (Special Congressional Feminicide Monitoring Commission) presented research on feminicidal violence in ten states of the Republic of Mexico, including detailed information on each state. Despite the occurrence of feminicides in other Mexican states, we have been concerned that state authorities were using these figures to minimize what is happening in Chihuahua. Recently, Marijke Velzobor Salcedo, director of the Regional Office of the United Nations Development Fund for Women, declared that crimes against women happened not only in Ciudad Juárez but also in various countries of Latin America, and with similar patterns. She emphasized that homicides of women with characteristics similar to those of Ciudad Juárez have been found in Guatemala, El Salvador, Honduras, Costa Rica, Bolivia, Argentina, and Colombia, and that the most serious case of feminicide in Latin America is that of Guatemala. Guatemala is a multicultural and multilingual country of 12 million inhabitants. It is culturally rich and diverse, with values that derive from the Mayan, mestizo, Garifuna, and Xinca cultures (Alvarez Asencio 2004).[3] However, it is also a society that has been besieged by violence for long periods of its history.

In 2007, United Nations Rapporteur on Violence against Women Yakin Ertürk issued the preliminary conclusion that a grave problem existed in Guatemala's capacity to investigate the more than three hundred fifty known violent deaths of women. She questioned the capacity of the attorney-general and the Policía Nacional Civil (National Civil Police), the government institutions charged with carrying out criminal investigations, to determine the causes of the women's deaths and criminally prosecute those responsible. "The impunity of those who cause the violence has generated more violence," she said. "There are multiple structures of power and a lack of confidence in the apparatus of the state" (Ertürk 2004, 22). Meanwhile, women continue to suffer the consequences of this failure through violent deaths. The Guatemalan feminicide victims' ages are closely linked to their reproductive age (biological vitality and physical condition) — that is, the age of the victims has been between thirteen and sixteen. They did not have their own transportation; instead, they had to use bus transportation, thus losing control over their surroundings. With little power over their lives at such a young age, women fall victim to feminicides more easily. As shown in figure 9.1, feminicides in Guatemala were mainly recorded as deaths by firearm, steel weapon, and physical assault and strangulation. This chart also shows the significant number of cases where the cause of death was unknown, therefore providing little faith in a government charged with protecting human rights.

In the context of impunity in Guatemala, the way in which the multiple violent deaths of women have been occurring takes on new importance. These acts have been increasing and contain characteristics of misogynist behaviour manifested in torture, mutilation, rape, and assassination, which are the same type of systematic violence seen in Mex-

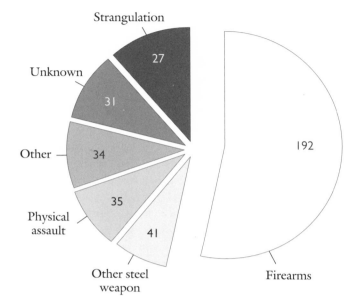

1. Methods of Feminicides *(Source: Procuraduría deDerechos Humanos de Guatemala. Based on reports from departmental morgues).*

ico. Despite the passing of the Ley contra el Femicidio y otras Formas de Violencia contra la Mujer, Ertürk has argued that the assassinations of women over the past few years in Mexico and in Central American countries, especially in Guatemala, show similar patterns and cannot be considered isolated acts or internal matters. She also has argued that women have been victims not only of criminal violence but also of bands of human traffickers and of serious abuses in the domestic sphere. In her annual report before the United Nations Commission on Human Rights, Ertürk formulated concrete critiques of the impunity, socioeconomic inequities, and machista values that perpetuate gender violence, all of which can be found in Chihuahua, Mexico, where the cases of feminicide first raised international concern and involvement.

CHIHUAHUA, THE BIG STATE

Chihuahua, particularly Ciudad Juárez, has gained international attention for the disappearances and assassinations of women and girls. These acts of gender violence have included discrimination, deficiencies in the prosecution and administration of justice, accusations of violation of due diligence, torture of detainees, fabrications of guilt, lack of certainty in closed cases, doubtful identifications, cases deemed cold, and the harassment, dismissal, and defamation of family members of victims and of human-rights defenders and nongovernmental organizations (NGOs).

Although the State of Chihuahua holds a high rank in terms of employment, a study of poverty indicators by the Instituto Nacional de Estadistica Geografia e Informática (National Institute of Statistics and Geographical Information; INEGI) pointed to a marked difference between the minimum wage and the poverty line. Nearly a million and a half residents of Chihuahua — that is, 49.18 percent of the population — live in extreme poverty below the level of basic subsistence. In Chihuahua, the largest territory in Mexico, more than a third of the population in the major cities do not hold steady jobs or have medical insurance. Chihuahua ranked first in Mexico for rates of adolescent pregnancy, youth addiction, and anorexia, and 67.7 percent (nearly seven in ten) of women older than fifteen living in Chihuahua at some point have been victims of community, family, paternal, educational, work, or intimate violence. This statistic exceeds the national rate of 67 percent. Moreover, assassinations and disappearances of women and girls have continued in the State of Chihuahua. According to the Casa Amiga Centro de Crísis (Friendly House Crisis Center), which monitors feminicides, in Ciudad Juárez alone there were thirty-five feminicides in 2005; twenty feminicides in 2006; and eight feminicides in 2007, with twenty more women violently assassinated. In 2008 sixteen hundred people were violently assassinated in Ciudad Juárez, and young women have continued to disappear. In 2009 nearly three thousand people were killed.[4]

In this decade, disappearances and feminicides in Chihuahua City have added to the numbers of those in Ciudad Juárez, leading diverse civil-society organizations, including Justicia para Nuestras Hijas (Justice for Our Daughters) and the Centro de Derechos Humanos de la Mujer (Center for Women's Human Rights), repeatedly to issue denouncements of the criminal justice system to fully investigate these crimes. In her United Nations report, Martha Altolaguirre (2003) noted that she was directing her attention to a worrisome series of disappearances in the City of Chihuahua that perhaps shared characteristics with the crimes in Ciudad Juárez. During a hearing in October 2002, representatives of the organization Alto a la Impunidad: Ni una Muerta Mas (End the Impunity: Not One More Death) reported the disappearance of fifteen women and girls in the City of Chihuahua and pointed specifically to the discovery of one victim's corpse, although the case had not yet been effectively investigated. They also argued that other disappearances had been improperly investigated to such a degree that the file for one victim, who had disappeared in 1998, was only six pages long (Altolaguirre 2003).

The pattern of the assassinations committed in the City of Chihuahua is very similar to that in Ciudad Juárez, coinciding even in the irregularities of their investigations and the authorities' impunity and complicity. In addition to these obstacles, families and organizations in Chihuahua have had to confront a constant policy of minimizing the situation. For instance, various officials have continued to make declarations that delegitimize the victims, citing their lifestyles as justification for their disappearance or assassination. They have also attempted to minimize the problem by arguing that this type of violence is present in other states in Mexico.

This official discourse increased after María López Urbina, special prosecutor for crimes related to the murders of women in Ciudad Juárez, Chihuahua (Fiscal Especial para la Atención de Delitos Relacionadas con los Homicidios de Mujeres en el Municipio de Juárez, Chihuahua, issued her "Final Report on Women's Homicides in Ciudad Juárez" (López Urbina 2006). The report was presented on February 16, 2006, by Mario Álvarez Ledesma, subsecretary of human rights, victim services, and community services with the Procuraduría (Attorney-General's Office). The report can be summarized as follows: Feminicide does not exist in Ciudad Juárez; there are no serial murders; the number of disappearances is insignificant; instead, there is a serious problem of domestic violence; and, finally, this is all a myth created by women's NGOs and academics (Monárrez Fragoso 2006a).

The document "Feminicidal Violence in Ten Entities of the Republic of Mexico" (Comisión Especial para Conocer 2005b) called for the review and monitoring of investigations and administration of justice in Mexico's feminicide cases. It determined that 1,205 women were murdered in Mexico in 2004 and that, among Mexican states, Chihuahua ranked sixth in the number of murdered women in that Mexican state. This minimizes the serial and systematic nature of the feminicides in Chihuahua and blurs the distinct types of feminicides that exist across Mexico and Latin America.

THE PROBLEM OF STATISTICS IN CIUDAD JUÁREZ

The assassinations of women in Ciudad Juárez have taken the forms of intimate feminicide and systematic sexual feminicide. Of the ninety-five victims of intimate feminicide, nineteen fell into the subcategory of child feminicide and twelve fell into the subcategory of familial femini-

TABLE 9.1. Categories of feminicides and assassinations of girls and women in Ciudad Juárez, Mexico, 1993–2005

Category	1993	1994	1995	1996	1997
Feminicides					
Intimate feminicide[a]	8	5	7	7	10
Systemic sexual feminicide[b]	9	7	20	22	17
Feminicide based on sexuality stigmatized occupations[c]	3	2	3	3	0
Assassinations					
Organized crime and narco-trafficking	1	1	5	4	4
Community violence[d]	0	4	8	3	3
Negligence[e]	0	0	2	0	1
Not specified	3	2	4	5	5
Total for the year	24	21	49	44	40

Source: Elaboration by Julia Monárrez Fragoso from Femicide Database, 1993–2005, El Colegio de la Frontera Norte.
Notes:
[a]This category includes infant and familial feminicide.
[b]This includes organized and unorganized feminicides.
[c]Included are women working in nightclubs as waitresses, dancers, and sex workers.
[d]This category includes assassinations due to robbery or child or juvenile violence.
[e]From information available, there is no evidence of premeditation, although it is possible that this presumption will be dismissed during the judicial process.

cide. There were 112 cases of systematic sexual feminicide (also called serial feminicide). Twenty-eight other assassinations with sexual components did not present a systematic and concerted pattern of serial assassination. Nevertheless, the violence exercised on victims' bodies, whether by known or unknown assassins, spoke of extreme sexual abuse. Sexual violence and the death of girls and women represented 150 cases in these two types of feminicide combined.

According to the Feminicide Database, 1993–2005, compiled by El Colegio de la Frontera Norte, women and girls age 10–29 accounted for 239, or 54.1 percent, of the total 442 cases. Added to these were 84 cases of women age 30–39, whose numbers made up 19 percent of the cases. This puts the median age of the victims at 26 (Comisión para Prevenir 2005). Regarding women's economic activities or occupations outside the home at the time of death, there was information compiled for some

1998	1999	2000	2001	2002	2003	2004	2005	Total Cases	%
8	7	13	10	16	16	5	14	126	28.5
17	7	9	15	6	7	6	8	150	33.9
2	4	0	3	1	0	2	2	25	5.7
2	1	8	4	5	0	3	3	41	9.3
8	3	2	5	9	4	2	4	55	12.4
0	0	1	2	1	1	0	1	9	2.0
2	3	4	1	3	0	2	2	36	8.1
39	25	37	40	41	28	20	34	442	100

cases. Among those employed, 2 were security guards; 22 were unemployed; 51 were employed in nonspecified work; 35 were students; 2 were indigent; 25 were minors; seven were drug traffickers; 46 were maquiladora workers; 38 were dancers, sex workers, or bar waitresses; 8 were professional women (3 teachers, a model, a reporter, a nutritionist, and a doctor); 17 were business owners; and 45 were homemakers. For 144, their occupation was unknown (Monárrez, 2005c, 193). The marital status of the victims was known for only 270 cases. Assassinations of minors accounted for 117 of the cases; single, divorced, separated, and widowed women accounted for 54 of the cases; and married women and those in common-law relationships accounted for 99 of the cases. Table 9.1 shows data from 1993 to 2005 of the total number of feminicides listed by the Colegio de la Frontera Norte.

MAJOR PROBLEMS GUARANTEEING THE RIGHT TO JUSTICE, DUE PROCESS, AND NONDISCRIMINATION FOR ASSASSINATED AND DISAPPEARED WOMEN IN CHIHUAHUA

As mentioned repeatedly, there were serious problems regarding thorough and serious investigative casework in these feminicides. The lack of efficient criminal investigations showed that the authorities did not consider these pandemic feminicides sufficiently serious and patterned crimes; for this reason, the crimes remained in impunity and continued to be committed. Unfortunately, the lack of attention to the recommendations of the Inter-American Commission has had consequences and translated into the expansion of feminicide to Chihuahua and to other cities across the state.

At the same time, however, facets of Mexican society such as women's and feminist organizations began to question, document, and galvanize support to stop feminicides by fortifying networks of people to address this misogynistic violence. As a result, organizations in Chihuahua and families of murdered and disappeared girls and women have made positive contributions toward denouncing feminicide in the State of Chihuahua by advancing proposed solutions. In the City of Chihuahua, legal assistance has been initiated by attorneys of the Center for Women's Human Rights, making it possible for people not directly related to the murdered women to examine case files of criminal investigations. Before this legal aid began, women and social organizations — who had struggled with this issue and for years and denounced the authorities' irregularities and complicity in the cases of Ciudad Juárez — had been unable to document and make visible the human rights violations. The group Justice for Our Daughters proposed the intervention of independent experts to identify unidentified bodies, conduct criminal investigations, and prepare legislative proposals for systematic and concrete change.

JUSTICE FOR OUR DAUGHTERS

Justice for Our Daughters, an NGO, has brought together family members of women disappeared and killed in the State of Chihuahua, as well as *coadyuvantes* (legal assistants) and advisers. It was formed in March 2002 in Chihuahua, and the process of *coadyuvancia* began.[5] Criminal investigations were followed by the obtaining, reading, and systematizing of the case files.

The primary activities of Justice for Our Daughters have been defending the human rights of feminicide victims and their families; accompanying victims' families to legal- and social-protest activities; carrying out archival and field research; acting and coordinating with state, national, and international NGOs; issuing national and international denunciations to human rights organizations and the media; establishing dialogue with the local, state, and federal levels of the Mexican government; and publicizing and publishing these activities and research results.[6] As an outcome of work on the disappearances and feminicides in Ciudad Juárez and Chihuahua, we, the authors, established the Center for Women's Human Rights in recognition of the broader gender and sexual violence women confront in their lives throughout Chihuahua.

CENTER FOR WOMEN'S HUMAN RIGHTS

The Center for Women's Human Rights, an NGO legally registered in 2006, was founded by human rights activists. It has participated since 1997 in denouncing the feminicides in Ciudad Juárez and is part of Mujeres de Negro (Women Wearing Black) network and its "Ni una Más (Not One More)" campaign. The center also has been the legal representative, or *coadyuvante*, for more than twenty cases of assassinated and disappeared women from Ciudad Juárez, the City of Chihuahua, and other municipalities in the state.

Its primary objectives have been to incorporate human rights and gender perspectives into legislation and public policy in Chihuahua; to promote a comprehensive response to violence against women and girls from human rights and gender perspectives; to denounce the feminicides and disappearances of girls and women in Chihuahua nationally and internationally; to litigate cases at the appropriate local, federal, and international levels; to share knowledge of human rights and gender theory with state authorities to incorporate these perspectives into law and social policies; to promote women's access to justice with a gender focus; to promote the creation and strengthening of organizations and networks for the defense and promotion of human rights, particularly those of women; and, finally, to promote women's empowerment as subjects who can define their own identity.

WOMEN DRESSED IN BLACK AND THE "NI UNA MÁS" CAMPAIGN

In the City of Chihuahua, a network of fifteen organizations with their own objectives and autonomy have struggled together since 1997 for women's human rights, in particular the right to live without violence. Since 2001, this network has been called Women Dressed in Black. It has been involved in holding a permanent denunciation campaign against the government for not thoroughly investigating feminicides; in contributing to making feminicide internationally and nationally visible; and in placing permanent "Cross Monuments" to symbolize the untimely murders of women and girls in the plaza in front of the State Capitol in Chihuahua and at the Santa Fe International Bridge in Ciudad Juárez, which links the city to El Paso, Texas. Women Dressed in Black did this during the first Exodus for Life protest, a 360-kilometer

(217 mile walk from Chihuahua to Ciudad Juárez, in which participants marched across the Chihuahuan desert behind a six-foot-tall cross made of railroad ties, and at times even carried the cross.

In the legislative arena, Women Dressed in Black has prevented the repealing of the Penal Code of Chihuahua in matters of sexual crimes, domestic violence, and other violence against women and girls.[7] It designed a proposal for a Women's Institute of Chihuahua, which was successfully implemented. Women Dressed in Black has campaigned on behalf of the security of life and integrity of women and created public awareness about the disappearances. It has also created public policies for the prevention and eradication of women's murders and advocated for adequate economic and personal resources to investigate these crimes and end the classifications that often negatively stigmatize the victim. The network has continued to demand transparency in investigations, including denouncing torture for extracting confessions, punishing actual perpetrators of crimes, and recognizing inefficient officials guilty of impunity. Ultimately, it has worked to demand better services for victims, create legal reforms, and guarantee women's rights. Despite all the network's efforts, however, girls and women have continued to disappear and have still been murdered, and this pattern has extended into other parts of Mexico and into other Latin American countries.

DISAPPEARED WOMEN

We recognize that the Unidad Especial de Investigaciones de Personas Ausentes o Extraviadas (Special Unit for the Investigation of Missing or Lost Persons), the agency responsible for investigations that recently opened in Ciudad Juárez and Chihuahua, has improved its performance. Nevertheless, its name reflects the way in which disappearances have been conceptualized. "Lost persons" is a discriminatory and moralistic concept that defines victims as people with unruly habits. Moreover, in the Mexican cultural context, getting "lost" carries a connotation of disability or distraction by the victim; in other words, it indicates carelessness on the part of the victim, placing responsibility on the victim or her family. This does not apply in the case of disappearances of girls and women that end in feminicide. Consequently, gender discrimination is reflected in the way disappearances of women are investigated, as well as in the classification of their files according to different types of "risk." Such classifications came to light in a hearing by the Inter-American Commission on Human Rights in October 2004 and, unfortunately, are still used as criteria.[8]

Since 2000, disappearances of young women in the City of Chihuahua have occurred repeatedly. In 2002, mothers of murdered and disappeared girls and women, alerted by events in Ciudad Juárez, decided to organize and insisted on attention from the authorities. With assistance from Lucha Castro Rodríguez, they learned about their right to legal assistance. They learned to follow investigations into their daughters' disappearances or murders by closely monitoring case files and investigating police assigned to their cases. Consequently, the authorities picked files up off the floor, so to speak, where they had been forgotten for years. When the work on these cases was finally organized, the mothers discovered that

The authorities did not look for the disappeared women. The case file for Miriam Gallegos, for example, was twenty-one pages long two years after her disappearance. In the case of Erika Carrillo, the file was six pages long after a year and three months. The police lost critical time. During the first few days after a girl or woman disappeared, police did not investigate, and this is the most essential period for investigations.

Contradictory statements were made without the district attorney asking the individuals making the statements to clarify their comments.

Witnesses changed their statements. This happened without the district attorney advising them of the consequences of making false statements.

False statements were made primarily to discredit the victims and their families and were done with impunity. There were no legal consequences for those who made such statements.

Spontaneous statements were made without an investigative strategy to lead to a clarification of the acts.

Statements were made by minors without parents or guardians in attendance, including occasions when they were intimidated by the investigating authorities.

Harassment of witnesses took place without consequences.

Unjustified delays in proceedings occurred with various justifications, such as lacking travel expenses or vehicles.

Unjustified depositions were taken for four missing girls — Julieta, Minerva, Yesenia, and Rosalba — between February 22 and March 13, 2001. The mothers of these young women were taken to brothels in Ojinaga, Reynosa, Monterrey, Durango, and Nuevo Casas Grandes, with no reason other than to justify looking for them and to keep them from attending the protest marches they had planned for those days.

Investigations were restarted under the pretext of changes in personnel, leading to a double victimization of the families who had to tell their stories all over again.

Investigations were conducted without cross-checking information about disappearances, femicides, and other crimes of gender violence.

Investigations lacked scientific foundation. Only close family members of the victims were deposed, which was often a widespread practice.

Numerous inaccuracies, inefficiency, and sheer apathy or ignorance have plagued investigations into disappeared and murdered girls and women in Ciudad Juárez and Chihuahua, making the possible rescue of those who have gone missing unfeasible. In the feminicide cases, lack of expeditious investigations and transparency has made finding the perpetrators of the crimes nearly impossible. The authorities' other errors have included leaking information to the media prematurely or unethically. In a rush to justify their actions before the public, the authorities have violated fundamental human rights by publishing, in great detail, the addresses of young women who left their homes. They have also given the press details of judicial proceedings related to minors and, by arriving late to crime scenes, authorities repeatedly enabled the press to photograph corpses at crime scenes and trample on crime scene evidence. Such leaking of information and carelessness has created an unethical and lackadaisical protocol for investigating these crimes, fostered potentially dangerous situations for victims and their families, and compromised investigations into disappearances.

KIDNAPPINGS

Repeatedly, the authorities at all levels have told us, as the attorneys and *coadyuvantes* in these cases, that searching for the young women was done as a social service for humanity because disappearance is not a crime. Before January 2003, cases of kidnapping were filed with the Procuraduría General de Justicia del Estado (State Attorney General; PGJE), but these claims were rejected by Manuel Ortega, the Assistant Attorney General at the time, who stated in a report to us (the authors) that by investigating these disappearances, the investigations would "dividir la continencia de la causa [divide the continence of the case]." This phrase is not judicially or legally logical, nor is it linguistically logical; it is a nonsensical argument that Ortega made to avoid any responsibility in investigating these kidnapping-disappearances.[9] In a clearly discriminatory fashion, victims' family members were informed that the crimes could not be classified as kidnappings because the families had not requested the rescue of their disappeared daughters and that kidnapping was unlikely when the families were so poor.[10] However, in legal terms, kidnapping is defined as the intent to harm a victim and does not necessarily imply seeking economic gain.

DISCRETIONAL CLASSIFICATION OF DISAPPEARANCES

Classifying disappearances as "high risk" or not has played a role in deciding whether to begin a search or inquiry immediately. This has discriminated against those whose behavior did not conform to culturally acceptable moral codes but who had an equal right to life. In February 2007, the spokeswoman of the Subprocuraduría (Regional Attorney-General's Office) for the North Zone declared, "There are currently fifty-five women who have been reported lost. Fifty of these cases have now been resolved, leaving five in the same state [status]. We do not currently consider any of these reports to be high risk" (Aguilar 2007, 1).

TRIALS OF THOSE PRESUMED TO BE RESPONSIBLE

Far from searching for those responsible for feminicide through scientific and transparent investigations, the authorities' tendency has been to rush to get results by any means necessary. The cases that have been resolved in Ciudad Juárez and Chihuahua have not satisfied citizens. They have lacked credibility, especially when it has been possible to establish that torture has been used. In some cases, individuals implicated in the crimes have been able to build networks to denounce their incarceration and have been acquitted. In other cases, they have continued to serve questionable sentences.

In September 2003, the federal government invited a special delegation from the United Nations Office on Drugs and Crime (UNODC) to visit Ciudad Juárez to analyze investigations and judicial proceedings regarding women kidnapped and assassinated in a sexually violent way. The resulting report emphasized fundamental deficiencies in judicial proceedings that have undermined efficient investigations by destroying the credibility of the judicial system. This system has regularly produced violations of fundamental rights of victims' families and the accused, as well as a nearly total lack of serious investigations into accusations of torture used to obtain confessions and use of such confessions as evidence against the accused.

The United Nations report requested judicial review of cases with accusations of violations of victims' fundamental rights, application of the United Nations Convention against Torture, and adoption of the Istanbul Protocol (Manual on Effective Investigation and Documentation of Torture and Other Cruel, Inhuman, or Degrading Treatment or Punishment). The report also urged radical reform in practically all areas of investigation and prosecutorial procedures, emphasizing the need for external bodies to strengthen supervision of the state judicial system. According to Amnesty International, the authorities in the State of Chihuahua have not implemented the recommendations of the UN report that was given to them. The two cases of documented torture and forced confession below point to these failures.

Case 1: Cynthia Kiecker and Ulises Perzábal Fabricated guilt occurred in the case of Viviana Rayas, last seen on March 16, 2003, in the City of Chihuahua. She had been working on a school project with a study group. At 5:30 in the afternoon, she headed home by bus but never made it to her house. Although the case was filed as a kidnapping, authorities considered that there were insufficient motives to consider it as such. A body was found on May 28, 2003. At first, Rayas's parents accepted that the body was their daughter's because they were shown a blouse and jacket they recognized. But they never saw the body and therefore were not entirely sure.

Cynthia Kiecker and Ulises Perzábal were later detained. In this case, the prosecutor of the City of Chihuahua argued that they had signed a statement confessing to assassinating Rayas, although both stated they had been tortured before they signed the confession. Evidence points to huge irregularities in the investigations and confession. The document they signed stated that they had killed Rayas using blows to the neck, but the autopsy revealed she died by strangulation. Friends of Kiecker and Perzábal, present when they were apprehended, were also kidnapped, tortured, and threatened by police.

The arrests of Kiecker and Perzábal led to a campaign of attacks, threats, and illegal arrests of various people. Only after organizing several mobilizations did the oppression against their friends end, although Kiecker and Perzábal were incarcerated. In December 2005, Kiecker and Perzábal were acquitted of all charges and finally freed from prison.

Case 2: Jesús Argueta and David Meza Neyra Azucena Cervantes is another case of a young girl that was "resolved" through the fabrication of guilt. Neyra Azucena disappeared on May 13, 2003, in the City of Chihuahua after leaving class at a computer school. In July 2003, a body was found that was presumed to be Neyra's. This presumption was based on ministerial actions taken on July 14 by Rocío Sáenz, Coordinator of the Sexual Crimes and Crimes against the Family Unit. Sáenz showed Neyra's mother and stepfather, Patricia Cervantes and Jesús

Argueta, clothes that had been found at the crime scene; when they recognized the clothes, Sáenz, without a court order, detained Jesús Argueta and his nephew, David Meza, and subjected them to a polygraph test because, she claimed, the men had become nervous during questioning. Meanwhile, Patricia Cervantes was asked to go to an office downtown. When she returned for her husband and nephew, she was told that they had been taken to C-4 (the PGJE center where expert tests are done and unidentified corpses are kept) to conduct expert tests. When she reached C-4, she was told that no one knew where Argueta and Meza were.

Both men were held incommunicado and tortured for several hours. Finally, Argueta was set free, but Meza was forced to sign a confession in which he stated that he had killed his cousin Neyra. Because Meza was not in Chihuahua when Neyra disappeared, the police version stated that he had paid two men to kidnap her and that he then came to the city to rape and kill her and take her body into the mountains. After a long campaign for his freedom, Meza was declared innocent in May 2006 and released from prison.

Such cases of disappearance, feminicide, scapegoating, and torture indicate a criminal justice system that is plagued with inconsistencies, impunity, apathy, and corruption. As we have outlined throughout this chapter, this sexual violence is rooted in structural systems and laws that must be changed. We fear that the pattern of violence, oppression, and complicity in Mexico will continue across Latin America. It must be stopped because it affects us all.

Classification of the Crime of Feminicide as a Crime against Humanity

Feminicide in the region leads organizations and international human rights groups to ask seriously which mechanisms should be generated to guarantee women's human rights to live free from violence. One of the primary recommendations made in the case of Ciudad Juárez and Chihuahua City is to consider feminicide a problem of gender violence. Indeed, the aim is to foster comprehensive measures that allow for the prevention and eradication of gender violence, emphasizing implications of the sexual violence characteristics of these cases.

As mentioned, we should keep in mind the various criteria that consider rape a form of torture. According to Joan Fitzpatrick, "Humanitarian law obliges occupying forces to protect the civilian population, and [that] soldiers that commit rape can be punished as war criminals.

This situation is an interesting contrast with the rape of women in times of peace, as it is only beginning to be considered that the fact that governments do not take preventative and punitive measures to combat this practice implies state complicity in the violation of human rights" (Fitzpatrick 1994, 544, 548).

In the past few years, the fact that states have not taken effective measures against violent crimes — whether committed by officials and state employees or by private citizens — generates contradictions and inconsistencies. Acts condemned in one context receive very little or no attention in other contexts. For some time, violence against women by agents of the state has been recognized as a form of torture (European Human Rights Tribunal 1998). In special International Criminal Courts, some acts of rape and aggravated sexual assault are charged as rape and as torture. International courts consider acts such as torture, genocide, crimes against humanity, and war crimes consistent with "inhumane treatment" that "deliberately cause[s] great suffering to health and body" (Gardam 2001, 25). In some communities, an act of rape committed by a private citizen (for example, domestic violence committed by a husband) is considered comparable to the murder of a young woman committed with sexual motives. Human-rights organizations consider states responsible for bringing to justice perpetrators of crimes based on gender, independent of the context (IAHRC 2001).

The close connection between certain types of violence against women and torture and the fact that the right not to suffer torture is intangible make clear the emphasis that states should place on the need to prevent violence against women and to pay attention when it is committed. Likewise, it is worth noting recent advances in international law in this area, such as the Rome Statute of the International Criminal Court and Resolution 1325 of the United Nations Security Council regarding women, peace, and security, which address the same acts of violence against women in different juridical and factual contexts. Ultimately, we believe that the discussion of the classification of feminicide as a crime against humanity can move forward from a recognition of states' obligations to respond with due diligence to acts of gender violence and to appropriately recognize both private and state aggressors for these violent crimes against humanity.

Notes

1. At the same time, the state, backed by hegemonic groups, has reinforced patriarchal domination and subjected victims' families and all women to permanent and intense insecurity. This has occurred because of a continuous and unlimited period of impunity and complicity in which the state neither recognizes the guilty as such nor grants the victims justice.

2. According to Alejandro Gutierrez, the maquiladora industry "accelerated changes in family roles in Juárez with the intensive use of female labor, which notably changed traditional social roles." He also notes that fifty thousand persons arrive each year in Ciudad Juárez and require housing and public services, yet investment goes to infrastructure for industrial development and not for poor areas of the city; that the estimated six hundred to eight hundred gangs operating in the city generate a significant number of homicides; that two thousand people make up the drug-trafficking network in Ciudad Juárez that reaches into the neighboring city of El Paso, Texas, which has fourteen large banks and numerous currency-exchange centers where "illicit operations could be carried out" and that may have direct ties to the feminicides; and that two different governors in power — Francisco Barrio Terrazas of the Partido Acción Nacional (National Action Party) and Patricio Martínez Garcia of the Partido Revolucionario Institucional (Institutional Revolutionary Party; PRI) — were not "capable of stopping the wave of homicides . . . [and] show[ed] similar characteristics when they . . . tried to minimize or hide the brutal reality of these crimes" (Gutierrez 2004, 67).

3. *Editor's note*: This source was initially consulted on May 4, 2004. The more recent population estimate is from http://en.wikipedia.org/wiki/ Guatemala (accessed May 13, 2008).

4. *Editor's note*: The updated figures for murders of women and victims of feminicide are from Esther Chavez Cano, director of Casa Amiga, who has compiled a list of feminicide victims since 1993.

5. *Coadyuvancia* in this context means the victim's right to participate directly in investigations under way by the Public Ministry. The shared information can be presented in any relevant judicial proceeding. Translation by the editors.

6. The families of the murdered and disappeared women and girls who make up this organization form an autonomous group of leaders who direct its work.

7. The majority of the members of the PRI in the Chihuahua legislature approved a penal code that reduced penalties for violators and characterized familial violence as cyclical. Because the new penal code in effect reversed the progress we (Carmona, Gómez, and Castro) had made in these types of cases, we successfully fought to change the penal code and abolish the changes. Translation by the editors.

8. The document "La situación de los derechos humanos de las mujeres en

Ciudad Juárez y en la Ciudad de Chihuahua" was presented by Lucha Castro Rodriguez at the 121st session of the Inter-American Commission on Human Rights, October 2004.

9. The accusations were dismissed in an accord signed by the Office of the Attorney General in Chihuahua. Translation by the editors.

10. *Editor's note*: Kidnappings for ransom of members of wealthy families are common throughout Mexico. This is the phenomenon that the authorities cited to claim that the disappearance of a poor girl would not be considered a kidnapping as it is popularly understood in Mexico.

PART II

Transnationalizing Justice

Translated by Sara Koopman

Testimonio

JULIA HUAMAÑAHUI, SISTER OF LUZMILA,

DISAPPEARED IN 2005

Julia is approximately thirty-eight years old. She comes from a very large and poor family in the mountains. From an early age her parents handed her over to work as a domestic servant. During her adolescence she suffered sexual violence from her brother-in-law. Later, she took on the raising of her four-year-old sister, Luzmila, who, at eight, was also a victim of sexual violence from her brother-in-law. In 2005, Luzmila, who was twenty-four years old and five months pregnant, was found in the Villa swamps, brutally murdered. Luzmila's murder is under investigation. The only suspect is Ulises, Luzmila's partner and the father of the child that she was expecting.

My brother-in-law opened the door and said that my [older] sister had given birth. Then he came over to my bed. . . . I had never had sex before. He said, "Even if you scream, no one will hear you. It's a big house. . . . I like [women] who are virgins." I was so scared. He cornered me and then grabbed me and started pulling off my pajamas, and then he slapped me. "If you resist, it'll be worse for you," he said. So that was the first time he sexually abused me.

I didn't want to tell anybody, because he said, "They won't pay attention to you because you're of legal age now, and they don't pay attention to those who are of legal age [adults]." I wanted to leave, but I was afraid. So I stayed, and he started abusing me again. . . . He said, "I don't want you to say anything to anyone, because if you do, I'll kill your entire family." Then he hit me with a belt. He said, "I can abuse you whenever I want. Whenever I want, I can be with any of you." I ended up pregnant that last time he raped me.

How did you feel when you found out that your brother-in-law had also abused Luzmila?

More than anything, I felt afraid, and since then I have felt terror. He has always terrified me, and even now I am extremely afraid of him. I sometimes imagine that he could still be in that room. After the rape I went to the district attorney's office and reported the crime, that he had raped both me and my little sister, who was only eight years old. I asked them how it was possible that the rapes had happened so long ago and there had been no movement on the investigations. The district attorney's office called the police officer who had received the report, and the police officer claimed there was no report, which was why they hadn't worked on the case. After that they came to the house and gave him [the brother-in-law] a summons, and that's when it started . . . I mean the threats — they wanted to disappear Luzmila and my baby. . . .

After a few years Luzmila met Luis and married him. Julia told us some details about this relationship.

Luzmila tells me, "One time he hit me, Julia, when I was naked, and he threw me out onto the street, naked. He told me, 'Oh, Luzmila, how have you been able to withstand so much?'" And instead of supporting her, he hit her more and also hurt her psychologically.

Guilt, Distrust, and Sadness: The Feelings of Family Members

I wanted to be alone to harm myself. . . . I was so traumatized.

Luzmila and I got along well, and I really miss her. It wouldn't have mattered if she had gone, I don't know, on a trip — I mean, if I knew that she was fine, but it's not like that.

Of all of my siblings, they killed the one I loved the most. I'm really distrustful. I just don't trust anyone right now. I don't even trust my daughters or my sons with my husband or with anyone. I'm like that. Wherever I go, I take my kids or I leave them with my girlfriend but never with my husband or near other people, no.

Really, I was very depressed. I mean if you could see my heart, you would see it is bleeding and bleeding from all the sorrow I feel.

Opinion about the Actions of Legal Authorities in Feminicide Cases

Well, I feel like I'm not listened to. But I say, if I had money they would listen to me. I've always felt like the legal system doesn't listen to me. I went and told them that I was the one that raised my sister. I was the one there with her, in the good times and the bad.

And the legal system just pushes me aside. They look for excuses, for the "but's" and the "nos": "You, no; him, yes." When the rape happened, it was the same thing: We were the ones who were lying; he was the innocent one, the good man. And now with all this, it makes me feel the same way — that the people who have treated my sister badly are the ones who should be in jail, but the authorities don't care at all.

I think that for a person who is poor, there is no justice.

The police said, "This bitch, your sister is a prostitute," and that she had been with several men. That made me feel bad, of course, the police claiming that she deserved to die because she was with several men. I said to them that my sister did not deserve to die like that, because I will always remember her as I raised her. And that's when the police started asking questions like, "Who were they?" "What did I have to confess?" And [they said] that it seemed like my sister was going down the wrong path.

When I went before the female judge and wanted to tell her that I had investigated such and such a person, I wasn't allowed to say the person's name as a civil party/person. The only right, I mean, of being able to say, "Your honor, you know what: Why don't you investigate her [Luzmila's] husband?" Naturally he doesn't want anyone to know that he was an abuser or they would suspect him in her murder. If he had never mistreated her, these things never would have happened. She was a girl who was coming out of one problem and went right into another, plus the problem that she was being beaten.

But I want justice to be done so it doesn't happen to others, to other young women, but not just young women. It could be a girl or my daughter or an adult. Here, though, there is only a case if a child has been raped, not if the person is an adult.

So then I ask, how is it that they listen to him [Luzmila's husband]? I want them to listen to me. I am the one who raised her. I know everything about her, I say; that's what I want them to hear. "You don't hear me," I say. "You just say come here, go there." It's as if they're playing with me.

In this case, it's as if she is the guilty one, and it shouldn't be like that, because then no one is going to want to file a report because it seems like just a waste of time and money. So why am I going to file a report if they don't even pay attention to me?

HÉCTOR DOMÍNGUEZ-RUVALCABA AND
PATRICIA RAVELO BLANCAS
Translated by Sara Koopman

Obedience without Compliance

THE ROLE OF THE GOVERNMENT, ORGANIZED CRIME,

AND NGOS IN THE SYSTEM OF IMPUNITY THAT MURDERS

THE WOMEN OF CIUDAD JUÁREZ

One of the most frequently asked questions regarding the feminicides in Ciudad Juárez, and one of the most difficult to answer, is, "Why haven't these murders stopped happening?" For those of us who have followed accounts of the violent acts in this city and the response carried out (or not carried out) by the government and various sectors of society, it is significant that no promise, program, reform, pronouncement, or recommendation has been enough to put a stop to this infamy. The terms commonly used to explain this lack of response are: *impunity, negligence, ungovernability, corruption, misogyny, classism, racism*, and *xenophobia*. Some of these terms apply to judicial institutions and some to social vices. We will discuss here three principal hypotheses regarding the deficiencies that maintain the current state of impunity: the Mexican government's relationship with organized crime; a politics more concerned with the city's image than with combating the impunity that the society of Ciudad Juárez and the local government have put into place; and the extrapolation of human rights entities and organizations from the creation of policies that protect women in civil society.

The Mexican Government and Organized Crime

Governmental institutions find it impossible to solve and prevent the feminicides in Ciudad Juárez because they have submitted to the will of more powerful groups that control them through corruption, threats, or blackmail. Various publications that try to explain this phenomenon of feminicides attribute the impunity in these cases to the Mexican government's inability to fight organized crime.[1] This implies that the perpetrators of the feminicides act with the protection of the authorities, as do drug traffickers, human traffickers, kidnappers, and other areas of organized crime. The question that arises when we establish this relationship is: In what way is the raping and killing of women incorporated into the activities of criminal business? Diana Washington Valdez (2005) and Sergio González Rodríguez (2002) both point to the large orgies held by recognized magnates in the border communities, some tied to the politically powerful. In the review we conducted of 444 forensic files from 1993 to 2006, published on the website of the Mexican Senate, we found thirty-six cases of murdered women who had been subjected to torture, mutilation, and wounds that are recognizably practices of sadistic pornography (González and Ravelo 2006).

Rita Laura Segato (2004), for her part, suggests that these murders are hate crimes carried out as part of initiation rites among what are called *fratrias*, or brotherhoods of criminals that require proof of loyalty through the commission of these kinds of misogynistic acts. Alfredo Corchado and Ricardo Sandoval (2004a) attribute these murders to current and former police officers' belonging to a drug-trafficking mafia known as *La línea* (the line), who carry out these macabre orgies as part of their celebrations when they successfully pass a shipment of drugs into the United States.

Police participation in organized crime has been amply documented. Washington Valdez (2005), González Rodríguez (2002), and Héctor Domínguez-Ruvalcaba and Patricia Ravelo (2006), as well as the documentaries *Señorita Extraviada* (Missing Young Woman; Portillo 2001) and *La batalla de las cruces* (The battle of the crosses; Bonilla and Blancas 2005) present numerous facts implicating officers of various police entities in the disappearances of women—or, at least, their complicity and negligence.

This direct participation of the police agents in the perpetration of crimes is only one part of the complex system of impunity that involves the entire justice system. Edgardo Buscaglia, who was a member of the Commission of Experts from the United Nations Office on Drugs and Crime, argues in the judicial audit of September 2003 that the impunity of the judicial system in the State of Chihuahua is one of the strongest determining factors in the violence against women because of "the systematic abuse of procedural and substantive discretion." In other words, the criminal acts do not fit into the penal code of either Mexico or Chihuahua, which "means that contradictory legal criteria are used in the same type of cases," and it is for this reason that "human rights are abused, [and] procedural deadlines are ignored" (Buscaglia 2005, 108). This commission of experts has recommended "demanding administrative liability, and criminal liability as appropriate, from the officials responsible for the misconduct or negligence of undue delays" (Buscaglia 2005, 113).

It is worth recalling that in 2004 María López Urbina (who held the now defunct title of special prosecutor for women's homicides, named by the attorney general) reviewed more than one hundred fifty deficient investigations of women's murders carried out by the Chihuahua State authorities. At least seven of the cases were directly addressed by López Urbina. The conduct of more than one hundred state officials who were involved in the initial investigations of these crimes was found possibly to imply administrative or criminal liability due to negligence. However, because the investigation of these crimes was to be done by the state authorities themselves, there was grave concern that those responsible would not be held accountable for their actions (Amnesty International 2003). López Urbina drew up a list of eighty-one officials accused of negligence, not only for having committed administrative errors, but also for violating the Law of Public Employee Responsibility, along with other codes within each entity and institution. After questioning, no official was found guilty, and at any rate the sanctions that were applied to some were light (such as temporary suspensions) and almost all were exonerated. Of these, the most serious case was that of Suly Ponce, who was in charge of the Office of the Special Prosecutor for Women's Homicides until 2002. Ponce participated in eighty-four cases. She was administratively liable in fifty-nine of the cases and criminally liable in forty-four. There is a detailed tracking of the ineffectiveness with which she acted while serving as an agent of the Public Ministry (District Attorney's Office) and, later, as a prosecutor (Minjares and Rodríguez 2006). Mothers and family members of murdered and disappeared women have consistently pointed to Ponce's negligence.

These efforts to combat impunity appear to respond to the principal claims made in the report "Intolerable Killings" (Amnesty International 2003) — namely, the irresponsibility of the institutions of justice in handling these cases, including a lack of coordination of records and files; negligence in investigation; fabrication of guilt through torture; and reprisals against human rights organizations. In light of the complete lack of results from the efforts of López Urbina, one can say that the recommendations of the Amnesty International report were not followed and that this Prosecutor's Office barely tried to demonstrate that the Mexican government responds to its internationally contracted commitments on human rights issues, operating under the motto,

"Obey, but Do Not Comply," which has characterized the Mexican judicial authorities since colonial times (Paz 1982, 40).

What interests inspire the Mexican government to neglect this fundamental aspect of the application of justice and ignore the international laws to which it has committed, even to the point of facing global shame for being one of the countries with the highest levels of human rights violations? The answer must lie in the submissive relationship that the Mexican government maintains with criminal organizations. Recent reports from the U.S. government, published in the magazine *Proceso*, claim that the Sinaloa Cartel and the Juárez Cartel enjoyed the protection of former President Vicente Fox's administration. In addition, the Gulf Cartel, the mortal enemy of the Sinaloa Cartel, has become so strong that it operates as a state within a state (Esquivel and Appel 2006; Ravelo 2006). These reports are based on Federal Bureau of Investigation and U.S. Drug Enforcement Administration investigations and allow us to conclude that more than negligence on the part of the Mexican government, there exists an impotence before the forces that have corrupted almost all official sectors. In other words, the Mexican government cannot be considered an autonomous entity. Rather, it is dependent on the criminal forces that control the border.

Cleaning Up the Image of Ciudad Juárez

In the most hegemonic sectors of society (the political class, some entrepreneurial groups, the media, intellectuals, and academe), the prevailing opinion is that the victims of the violence are less of a priority than the city's image and economic development. For this reason, mentioning or denouncing these crimes is considered antisocial and unethical behavior. A generalized process of censoring any reference to violence in Ciudad Juárez has developed. This means, primarily, that the victims are devalued. In this regard, Buscaglia (2005, 112) notes, "In those countries where violence against women is high and [the perpetrators] enjoy impunity, the value of my life and the value of the lives of my family members is diminished, the value of my citizenship is diminished, and the value and legitimacy of the State itself is diminished." He recommends that "victims' family members should gain full access to the process, legal recognition as legitimate civil parties able to take legal action and file appeals" (Buscaglia 2005, 112–13). And, he goes on to say, "A strong, forceful response from the State to minor crimes against women is extremely important in order to prevent major crimes." In addition to the affected parties' having access to the criminal procedures, the right of a civilian to information is fundamental, though this is what the policies focused on Ciudad Juárez's image work to eliminate. Broad and transparent access to information about judicial procedures and actions of the state, from our point of view, would clean up the city's image better than what the Chihuahua government is currently doing. While supported by hegemonic sectors, the government points to the research on violence in Ciudad Juárez, as well as to some journalists and local, national, and international civil-society organizations, as being responsible for "tainting" the city's image.

This process of "invisibilization" is one of the major mechanisms through which the government and those it protects maintain a state of impunity. The process of invisibility works to create the myth of Ciudad Juárez as the victim, substituting the actual victims of violence for an abstract victim and thus hiding the various interests of organized crime and the government. The media that support this line of thought insist that the main objective of forensic agents and those who do research on feminicide (including some journalists and human rights organizations) is to defame Ciudad Juárez society as a criminal society. The media do so to enflame public opinion, thereby substituting indignation about the crimes for indignation at the supposedly unjust accusation that is said to have offended the middle class of Ciudad Juárez.

This complaint regarding the city's image has been made at public events, on television programs, in statements by politicians and officials, and even by the local academic community, who claim that talking about the violence has antisocial ends that range from profiting from the pain of the family members to sensationalism and strengthening the agendas of political groups with interests that are not those of the community. We consider this claim itself primarily to be a political posture sustained by paying close attention to appearances; it manifests itself through censure and witch hunts as a way to solve the problem of a bad reputation.

This willingness to censure has been evident in the scandal surrounding the song "Pacto de sangre (Blood pact)" by the group Los Tigres del Norte (Tigers of the North). The video for the song shows bodies of the murdered women, which, according to the video's critics, offends the sensibilities of those in mourning. So these sectors come to consider any attempt at analysis of or complaint against the precarious administration of justice and consequent permissiveness toward crime to be obscene and improper. In the face of such obscenity (i.e., what is not appropriate to show on screen), it is prescribed that media images should submit to the norms of decency or the control of the visible. If we look at the history of censorship, we find that displeasure at the display of public infamy is characteristic of most totalitarian power.

Figures we now praise for their efforts to denounce injustices were once similarly reproached — for example, Bartolomé de las Casas, who in his time stirred up anger similar to that which is now coming from those who proclaim themselves to be defenders of the city's image.

Whom does it bother, for whom is it inconvenient that Ciudad Juárez is presented as a violent city? Undoubtedly those who are affected economically by the city's "negative" image are sectors such as the tourist industry. In a wider sense, the growing knowledge of the violence inconveniences those who consider themselves owners of the city, those who assume for themselves the privilege of dominating the public sphere and from there raise their own interests to the level of priority for the collective. This sector believes it is neither victim nor perpetrator of the violence and would be capable of negating its existence if the bloody facts were not so evident.

In effect, some social sectors in Ciudad Juárez interpret as "myth" (i.e., a lie) the finding of remains, of marked bodies, of women who have been mutilated, raped, burned, tortured, disfigured, murdered in their homes, buried, or thrown into the desert, trash dumpsters, empty lots, and cotton fields. The evidence has been brought to light, shown, documented by the mothers and family members of the murdered women; by civil-society organizations; by the academic community; by national and international human rights organizations; by legislators, journalists, artists, and intellectuals. In spite of all of this, a policy of disinformation and confusion is reinforced, presenting as myth what is a solid truth — which adds to the uncertainty and desperation. Despite these efforts at denial, the attorney-general of the State of Chihuahua reported 364 homicides of women committed between 1993 and 2006.

The Mexican Government and Human Rights Organizations

The dialogue between human rights organizations and the government has virtually ended. While human rights organizations focus on justice systems (in the classic style of Amnesty International, against prison systems, disappearances, and torture), the government turns a deaf ear to those recommendations, refusing to uphold agreements it has signed in various international forums.

Mexico is a signatory of the following declarations and international conventions relating to kidnapping and homicide: the Regulations of the Organization of American States; the American Convention on Human Rights; the Universal Declaration of Human Rights; the International Covenant on Civil and Political Rights; the International Covenant on Economic, Social, and Cultural Rights; the Convention on the Elimination of All Forms of Discrimination against Women; the Convention on the Rights of the Child; the Inter-American Convention to Prevent, Punish, and Eradicate Violence against Women (Convention of Belém do Pará); the Inter-American Convention to Prevent and Punish Torture; the International Convention on Forced Displacement; and the United Nations Declaration on the Protection of All Persons from Forced Disappearance (WOLA 2007).

National and international bodies began to intervene in Ciudad Juárez at the end of 1997, when the Comisión Nacional de Derechos Humanos (Mexican National Human Rights Commission; CNDH) received a complaint presented by Congresswoman Alma Angélica Vucovich Seele, which described thirty-six crimes against women committed in 1996–97. The document was presented by Vucovich Seele in her capacity as president of the Commission on Gender Equality of the House of Representatives of the 57th Congress and was based on a complaint filed by the Coalition of Non-Governmental Women's Organizations of Ciudad Juárez. After analyzing twenty-four records of murders of women in the city, the commission published Recommendation 44/98 on May 15, 1998, which urges the government of the State of Chihuahua to undertake a timely investigation of the facts. Moreover, the Instituto Nacional de Estadística Geografía e Informática (National Institute of Statistics and Geographical Information; INEGI) was asked to conduct a study to better understand the public-safety issue. With regard to judicial procedures, the commission recommended that the three governmental levels (municipal, state, and federal) work together and create coordination agreements to fully investigate the rapes and homicides. The objective was to hold the public servants who were involved in the coordination of previous investigations responsible for the omissions that occurred. In terms of prevention, the Human Rights Commission recommended, among other things, the establishment in short order of a state public-security program for those municipalities with high crime rates, such as Ciudad Juárez (Comisión Especial para Conocer 2006d, 156–57).

Asma Jahangir, the United Nations Rapporteur on Arbitrary, Summary, and Extrajudicial Executions, reported on her visit to Mexico in 1998 that "the lack of action taken by the government to protect the human rights of its citizens, because of their sex, has generated a state of insecurity for the majority of women living in Ciudad Juárez." This has meant, indirectly, that the perpetrators of the crimes are protected and enjoy impunity. Jahangir was the first representative of an international body to make any statement about the situation (Comisión Especial para Conocer 2006d, 157).

Another international representative who visited our country was Dato Param Cumaraswamy, the United Nations Rapporteur on the Independence of Judges and Lawyers. In May 2001, he expressed his concern over the murders in Ciudad Juárez and the inefficiency, bias, and negligence with which the authorities were acting in regard to the cases. On July 27, 2002, Juan Méndez, president of the Inter-American Commission on Human Rights, came to Ciudad Juárez to assume the Rapporteurship on Migration. At that time, he was informed by the nongovernmental organizations (NGOs) that the majority of the disappeared and murdered women were migrants. This information was corroborated by Martha Altolaguirre, who visited Ciudad Juárez in February 2002 as the Special Rapporteur on Women's Rights. The reports of the two rapporteurs were included in the National Human Rights Commission Report presented in March 2003 and titled, "The Situation of the State of Women's Rights in Ciudad Juárez, Mexico: The Right to Be Free from Violence and Discrimination" (Altolaguirre 2003). Its main recommendations include coordination among the three governmental levels to stop the murders and other forms of gender-based violence; incorporation of a gender perspective into the design and implementation of public policies; development and implementation of an action plan to respond to pending cases of disappeared women to ensure that all reasonable possibilities are investigated; and cross-referencing of data related to the disappearances with data in murder cases to identify possible connections or modus operandi, among other things (Comisión Especial para Conocer 2006d, 158).

Two international reports have been issued: the report by the Expert Commission from the United Nations Office on Drugs and Crime, presented in September 2003, which is the only report that reveals information about networks of organized crime (drug trafficking in particular); and the Amnesty International report "Intolerable Killings," issued August 11, 2003, which analyzes the lack of diligence on the part of the state to prevent, investigate, and punish crimes against women and mentions the commitments that the Mexican state contracted when subscribing to the institutional norms of human rights. Amnesty International argues that the pattern of murders and disappearances of women in Ciudad Juárez and Chihuahua are not only a violation of the victims' right to life and physical safety, but are also an attack on the rights of all women in the community, especially the youngest and poorest. The report concludes that the authorities have failed in their duty to act with due diligence in the four areas imposed by international

law: investigation of crimes, punishment of those responsible, reparation of damages to the victims, and crime prevention. This is the only
report that includes the cases of the City of Chihuahua (Comisión
Especial para Conocer 2006d, 158–59).

The phenomenon of feminicide in Ciudad Juárez has mobilized some
civil society groups in the United States. Most groups have formed
explicitly in solidarity with the murdered and disappeared women, including the Coalition against Violence toward Women and Families in
El Paso, Texas; the group Amigos de las Mujeres de Juárez (Friends of
the Women of Juárez) in Las Cruces, New Mexico; and the Mexico
Solidarity Network in Chicago. The situation has also generated expressions of solidarity from legislative groups in the United States. A group
of members of the U.S. Senate and House of Representatives presented
a Joint Bill on the Murders of Women in Ciudad Juárez and Chihuahua,
in which they expressed their condolences to the families of the murdered young women in the State of Chihuahua and declared their desire
to promote "greater U.S. participation in the efforts to stop these
crimes."[2] They also appealed to President George Bush and to Secretary
of State Colin Powell to include the investigation and prevention of
these crimes as a topic in the bilateral agenda between the U.S. and
Mexican governments and to continue expressing concern over the kidnappings and murders to the Mexican government. They also expressed
concern about the harassment suffered by the families as well as by the
human rights advocates who work with them and about the impediments that have prevented the families from receiving prompt and adequate information about their cases. The proposal also supported efforts to identify the victims through forensic analysis, including DNA
tests. It condemned the use of torture as an investigative method in
these crimes and recommended that the U.S. ambassador to Mexico
visit Ciudad Juárez and the City of Chihuahua to meet with the victims'
families, women's rights organizations, and the Mexican state and federal officials responsible for the investigation and prevention of these
crimes (WOLA 2007).

In a special report issued in November 2003, the Mexican National
Human Rights Commission ratified the voices of organizations as to
the "intolerable weight of negligence, neglect, omissions, and even discrimination and deception, that has characterized the conduct of agents
of the authorities responsible for investigating and clarifying the cases of
murders and disappearances of women in Ciudad Juárez" (Comisión
Especial para Conocer 2006d, 159).

NGOs observe governmental actions and publish declarations and
recommendations following international human rights organizations'

models of observance. This practice has established a symmetrical relationship in which the actions and declarations of each organization are systematically and mutually disqualified or minimized by the Mexican government. Instead of becoming agents of change in their own country, they become yet another party in the political conflict around the ensuing violence. Spokespeople for the state government constantly express disagreement with the reports of Amnesty International and other human rights organizations, making them intolerable to governmental institutions. This confrontational relationship paralyzes any political means of access or advancement toward enforcement of justice. This situation arises from the lack of existing international mechanisms to monitor the enforcement of social justice and human rights.

While human rights organizations insist on holding the state responsible for the violence against women, the government views these organizations as a threat to its interests (which often get confused with the interests of criminal organizations). The actions of Amnesty International, since its inception, have been oriented toward enforcing international pacts signed by the governments that do not enforce them, given that there are very limited instruments of coercion against those governments. However, when sanctions against countries that violate human rights are enforced, they are frequently enforced very selectively against governments that are declared enemies of the dominant economic policies in the world, as is the case with Cuba. Perhaps this explains the very small number of cases in the international courts against the Mexican government for allowing feminicides to happen.[3]

The anti-governmental politics of Amnesty International responds to state-perpetrated forms of human rights violations during the Cold War — that is, the violation of civil (political) rights of political prisoners. Since the inception of Amnesty International, human rights violations have diversified and now include kidnappings, disappearances, and murders, among other abuses, and are committed not only by those who accuse others of dissidence but by those who dictate the interests of organized crime, the ultimate forces behind the illegal economy. In the globalized world, it is not the state that holds power; rather, it is the interests of the market that work according to corporate statutes that operate above formal law and even control states. The lack of consideration of these new power relationships established by neoliberalism suggests to us that some reflection is needed on the frameworks of responsibility and the means to guarantee the enforcement of human rights in an environment where it is not the state but market forces and organized crime that order and regulate society. This is not to say that in this context Amnesty International uses obsolete methods and anachronistic assumptions to solve problems that belong to another era while refusing to restructure its conceptual framework. Rather, Amnesty International seems to play the political role of highlighting the inefficiency of some state models by its promotion of a liberal, democratic, and capitalist way of organizing the state. The ideology of human rights must then be a political agenda in a globalized world (Hardt and Negri 2000).

The number of violent deaths committed by organized crime is high. Many executions of men and some homicides of women are related to drug trafficking or some other type of organized crime. According to the information provided by the state attorney general's Homicide Department, of the 1,419 murders committed against men from 1995 to 2002, 15 percent were directly related to drug trafficking. Of the 321 women murdered from January 1993 to July 2003, twenty-four were connected to drug trafficking — that is, 7.5 percent of the cases (Instituto Chihuahuense de la Mujer 2003). These data have significant implications as to the nature of a *culture of terror* (Ravelo 2005a).

In 2004, Chihuahua was the state with the sixth-highest number of homicides of women, the seventh-highest number of homicides of women up to age 14, and the sixth-highest number of homicides of women age 15–59 (Comisión Especial para Conocer 2006d).[4] But when measured using other indicators (type of victim and serial murder pattern with rape), the feminicides of Ciudad Juárez occupy the highest rank.

In regard to the maquiladora industry, Amnesty International recommends that labor-protection laws be enforced and that companies participate in ensuring the safety of their workers. Ever since the maquiladoras were built in Ciudad Juárez in the mid-1970s, the workers have enjoyed few benefits and have had scarce means of labor protection and safety. But a serious issue that the Amnesty International report does not address, and that is one of the foundations of human rights, is the need to establish dignified standards of living for all. The standard of living imposed on the workers by low salaries is a risk factor. This has many implications, for, according to our interviews and observations, the workers have to supplement the $50 that they earn per week (in salary plus overtime hours). Some do this by selling candy, clothing, or trinkets; others do it by working as table dancers, as domestic workers in El Paso on their days off from the maquiladora, or by offering massage services, and sometimes sexual services, in Ciudad Juárez and El Paso (Ravelo and Sánchez 2005).

There have also been cases in maquiladoras of employees involved in organized-crime networks, facilitating retail drug traffic within the factories or selling the drugs directly (usually cocaine), as is done by some supervisors. According to the local press and the interviews we have conducted, and as confirmed by our observations, this activity has led to violent homicides of men and women — voluntary (intentional) as well as manslaughter (circumstantial).

Let us bear in mind that, as of April 2002, at least thirty of the murdered women had worked in a maquiladora or had gone to seek work in one. The business policies regarding work schedules facilitate the kidnapping and murder of women. Claudia Ivette González disappeared when she was sent home for having arrived two minutes late to the factory for which she worked; Sagrario González Flores disappeared on the way from the factory to her house; Lilia Alejandra García Andrade's body was found abandoned in front of the factory where she worked. Claudia Ivette González's funeral was paid for by her employer; Sagrario González Flores's mother, Paula Flores, followed the procedures set out by the Mexican Social Security Institute to have her daughter recognized as officially deceased en route to her job and obtained a pension. And the owner of the Plástico Promex maquiladora for which Lilia Alejandra García Andrade worked coordinated a group of businessmen to collect $25,000 to be offered as a reward for information leading to her killer.

But there is no legislation, and there are no controls that regulate a company's responsibility to prevent kidnappings and murders and to protect the life of its workers and employees, who have no other type of protection, such as unions. The rate of unionization is very low; lawsuits are usually individually based; and few lawsuits are processed through any kind of local union. The workers and their families feel more comfortable going to religious and other types of community groups than to unions and labor institutions to get information about their rights. Ciudad Juárez has independent groups, such as the Committee of Workers in the Struggle, CETLAC (Comité de Obreros en Lucha), CISO, the Workers' Ministry (Pastoral Obrera), Center for Working Women (Centro de la Mujer Obrera), and others that provide labor-related legal aid in working-class neighborhoods to factory workers, mobile vendors, shoe shines, and small-businesses and service workers. They also participate in local, national, and international actions. In October 2006, some of these groups organized the Border Social Forum, which brought together hundreds of participants from around the world, mainly from civil society organizations. Although the forum's main themes were migration and the environment, the issue of the feminicides was addressed by various panels.

This landscape allows us to draw attention to three important omissions made when indicating the agents of human rights violations: organized crime and the restrictions it places on the government; the maquiladora industrial system; and some NGOs. Thomas W. Pogge (2005, 11) observes that in the case of "an ordinary criminal assault . . . though the victim may be badly hurt, we would not call this a human rights violation. A police beating of a suspect in jail, does seem to qualify." However, the human rights violations involved in feminicide go far beyond the actions of the government, which has classically been the interlocutor and object of scrutiny of Amnesty International. Since its inception in the 1970s, Amnesty International has played an important role in liberating political prisoners, abolishing the death penalty, combating torture, and advancing petitions for asylum. Its principal objects of critique are governments. Governments are fundamentally facilitators and violators through negligence and tolerance of crime. This emphasis needs to be revisited because the government is now a subordinate agent, dominated by leaders of organized crime.

Conclusion: The Need to Accept and Move beyond Obsolescence

Organized crime must be recognized as an economic force that transforms culture and politics. The dialogue about the violence in Ciudad Juárez needs to convene with and engage the criminal agents (the mafia bosses and the police officers who protect and work for them), the economic sectors that finance them, the politicians and officials who are mixed up in the networks of organized crime, and other sectors that are involved. The globalized world has moved beyond the agendas of NGOs such as Amnesty International. First, by their own definition, they are developed in reference and in contrast to the state. They are formed as entities that monitor and enforce international laws and are interlocutors with governments, focusing their efforts on the errors that governments commit. When we analyze the development of organized crime we have to conceive of a more complex political framework. The state is no longer the sole sovereign power responsible for abuses against its inhabitants, for it is also beholden to the transnational forces that rule the global economy, including the globalized network of organized crime. This new development requires a restructuring of human rights discourse to accommodate the economic and political influence of organized crime. When seen from this wider perspective, the NGOs' recommendations only distract attention from efforts to combat violence because they are aimed at redressing violations through formal channels without taking into consideration that human rights violations are now occurring in an extra-governmental space. An example of this inadequacy is the limited definition of *disappearance* used by Amnesty International:

1. There are reasonable grounds to believe that a person (the victim) has been taken into custody by the authorities or their agent.
2. The authorities deny that the victim is in their custody or the custody of their agent.
3. There are reasonable grounds to disbelieve that denial. (Clark 2001, 85)

If we define *disappearance* as kidnapping, being cut off from communication, torture, sexual abuse, and murder committed by unidentified agents who enjoy the protection and tolerance of the state, we must conclude that (1) there exists an agent that acts beyond the will of the state, which is the will of organized crime, for whose logic of power this type of death serves a purpose; (2) there is a stubborn concealment of the identity of the aggressor, which goes beyond merely denying that the disappearances have happened; (3) if one cannot believe in the capacity (or the innocence) of the state institutions, then all recommendations with respect to the disappearances and deaths of women have to take the uselessness of the state as a starting point. The impossibility of locating the aggressor, and the strong suspicion that an organized criminal group is involved, challenges us to consider a nongovernmental human rights approach that also pursues nongovernmental actions. However, it also suggests the need to abandon legal frameworks that themselves no longer have mechanisms for effectively rendering justice. International courts cannot intervene in state sovereignty, and the laws of asylum protect only the politically persecuted, not the victims of disappearances carried out by nongovernmental agents.

Notes

1. The most widely published works on this subject are González Rodríguez 2002; Washington Valdez 2005. See also Bonilla and Blancas 2005; Portillo 2001.

2. House Concurrent Resolution 90, "Murders of Young Women in Ciudad Juarez and Chihuahua, Mexico — Condolences," May 3, 2006, p. 3720–23, http://frwebgate.access.gpo.gov (accessed August 20, 2009).

3. Complaints have been presented against the Mexican government regarding the feminicides and disappearances of women: by Silvia Arce, Laura Bernice Ramos Monárrez, Claudia Ivette Gonzalez, and Esmeralda Herrera Monreal in Ciudad Juárez and by Paloma Angélica Escobar Ledezma in Chihuahua City.

4. It should be noted that 2004 was the only year in which a comparison of feminicides could be conducted at the national level, because this was the only year in which comparable data could be found for the whole country. "In general terms, in spite of the fact that there has been a reduction in the number of homicides of women in some areas during 2004, in other areas the number has stayed the same, and in some areas it has increased. However, 2003 saw an alarming increase in the number of murders of women." In that year, Chihuahua reported one of the lowest levels of homicides of women (nineteen cases, compared with thirty-seven in 2001, for example). For this reason we consider the comparison to be slanted (Comisión Especial para Conocer 2006d, 49, 107).

WILLIAM PAUL SIMMONS AND REBECCA COPLAN

Innovative Transnational Remedies for the Women of Ciudad Juárez

More than four hundred women have been brutally murdered in Ciudad Juárez, Mexico, since 1993, and more than 140 of these murders have been classified as "sexual homicides." The Mexican authorities and others have offered a plethora of theories to explain the crimes and have arrested several alleged suspects, but the crimes have continued with impunity. The victims' families have grown increasingly frustrated with the local, state, and federal authorities. In the summer of 2006, when the Mexican federal government announced that it had closed, without any progress, the fourteen cases that it had been examining, several family members expressed the belief that international remedies were their last hope. Some international organizations such as the Inter-American Commission on Human Rights (IACHR) and the Convention on the Elimination of all Forms of Discrimination against Women (CEDAW) have increasingly given attention to the murders. The IACHR issued a much publicized report on the femicides in 2003, and CEDAW issued a thorough and detailed report in 2005. Such reports can play an important role in documenting human rights violations and often shine a much needed international spotlight on a given human rights situation, but by themselves these reports are unlikely to lead to substantial improvements in human rights on the ground. Additional alternative transnational remedies must be pursued.

The past two decades have witnessed a "human rights cascade" with the simultaneous strengthening of a number of international human rights regimes. This chapter will analyze four different alternative international remedies that could be pursued for the women of Ciudad Juárez, including (1) contentious cases in the Inter-American Court of

Human Rights; (2) individual petitions to the Human Rights Committee overseeing the International Covenant on Civil and Political Rights; (3) filing civil suits in U.S. federal courts under the Alien Tort Statute (ATS); and (4) withholding or issuing loans by the Inter-American Development Bank (IADB).[1] For each of these, we will examine previous precedents within the institutions, as well as the fine points of regulations and laws and their potential effectiveness for the Juárez situation. Rarely has such a wide range of potential remedies been examined side by side, especially in relation to a specific human-rights situation. This chapter, we hope, will be of assistance to activists, attorneys, and scholars in deciding which remedies should be pursued in other concrete situations. Legal precedents in this case could also potentially lead to significant advances regarding human rights worldwide.

The appropriate remedy will vary depending on the given situation, but it must be successful in putting pressure on those, usually the state, that have the most power to make changes. The ideal remedy would be swift and would not interfere with other actions being taken simultaneously in other jurisdictions. It would ideally address both the immediate crimes and the structural factors that have fueled the crimes, such as gender discrimination, poverty, and corruption. In considering any remedy for such abuses, it is vital that the remedy allow a voice for the victims and provide agency for their families so that they are not revictimized by the legal process. In most cases, these remedies will be effective only if the "envelope is pushed" — that is, if the institutions are used in innovative ways. It will be important to consider whether such expansions in institutional power might lead countries to withdraw or ignore a regime's jurisdiction. Such a backlash would significantly damage the regime's institutional prestige.

The Mexican Government's Failure to Adequately Investigate and Prevent the Femicides

In the Ciudad Juárez situation, remedies should concentrate on putting pressure on the Mexican government. Some commentators have argued that the transnational corporations that operate the maquiladoras in Juárez could be found culpable for the murders, but the link between the maquiladoras and the murders appears to have been exaggerated. Several scholars and activists have also suggested that the local police may have been directly complicit in these murders (Ensalaco 2006; Washington Valdez 2005), but we argue that even if it cannot be shown that they are directly complicit, the Mexican government and some of its agents should be held accountable because of the systematic failure to investigate and prevent these murders.

The failures to investigate and prevent these crimes have been well documented by family members of the victims, journalists, nongovernmental organizations (NGOs), the Mexican government, and international organizations. The IACHR documented missing evidence from case files, failure to seal off crime scenes, case files that contained only a few sheets of paper, as well as very little follow-up on older cases. In one case, the "ground was dug up [by the authorities] in the vicinity of the discovery [of the body], apparently to conceal any evidence" (CEDAW 2005, para. 90). Family members have reported returning to crime scenes several months after the initial police investigation and finding clothing and other evidence that the police had not gathered (2003b, para. 48). This has led to a local practice called "*rastreo*," in which the families and friends of missing and murdered women join together to comb through the surrounding desert looking for remains and other clues (Schmidt Camacho 2004, 43–48). Moreover, there have been systemic delays in processing missing persons cases, as well as a failure to submit missing persons cases to the homicide prosecutor in a timely manner. Information has been withheld from the victims' families; family members have been denied the means to identify their loved ones; and, in some cases, the remains have not been returned to the families. In addition, family members, attorneys, and reporters have been harassed and threatened when they have criticized the investigations.

The failure to adequately conduct investigations is often linked to the failure to prevent crimes as a culture of impunity is established that perpetuates crimes. Also, the systemic delays in investigating missing persons cases signal a failure to adequately prevent these crimes, especially in several well-known cases in which women were observed being forcibly abducted but the authorities were slow to initiate an investigation. The commission has also noted that the Mexican government has failed to take recommended and obvious operational measures to prevent further violence, such as initiating special training programs for law-enforcement officers, and has failed "to install more lights, pave more roads, increase security in high-risk areas and improve the screening and oversight over the bus drivers who transport workers at all hours of the day and night" (IACHR 2003b, para. 157). The Mexican government, when it has acted, has failed to provide enough attention to the more general problem of violence against women and its roots in gender discrimination and instead has focused on the so-called serial killings. Finally, the state failed to increase its outreach efforts to civil society groups and to conduct general educational campaigns to prevent violence against women.

This list of negligent behavior on the part of law-enforcement officials is only a sample of the complaints that the victims' families have voiced. The commission's special report concluded "the response of the Mexican State to the killings and other forms of violence against women has been and remains seriously deficient. As such, it is a central aspect of the problem. Overall, the impunity in which most violence based on gender remains serves to fuel its perpetuation" (IACHR 2003b, para. 69). Amnesty International (2003, 71–72) concluded that the investigations show "a pattern of intolerable negligence" and that "the pattern of non-compliance with the minimum requirement of the 'due diligence' standard has been so marked that it calls into question whether the authorities have the will and commitment to put an end to the murders and abduction in Chihuahua and the violence against women they exemplify." The CEDAW report found "systematic violations of women's rights, founded in a culture of violence and discrimination that is based on women's alleged inferiority, a situation that has resulted in impunity" (CEDAW 2005, 261). The Mexican government's commissions have reached similar conclusions. A 1998 report by Mexico's Comisión Nacional de los Derechos Humanos (National Commission on Human Rights; CNDH) documented a series of inadequacies in the investigation and concluded that the impunity resulting from the local government officials has perpetuated the crimes. A spokesman for the CNDH says that its 2003 report "provides evidence of everything said so far by international and local groups regarding negligence and carelessness in the conduct of the investigations" (Latin American Weekly Report 2003). One activist was led to declare that "the governor and his attorney general had 'declared war' on civil organizations [attempting to publicize and stop the femicides] instead of declaring war against the criminals" (Wright 2005, 286). Clearly, a case can be made that the Mexican government has violated the due diligence to investigate and prevent violence against women as laid out in previous international legal cases. The question remains as to which transnational remedy or remedies would be most effective in holding the government accountable.

Inter-American Court of Human Rights

One of the most effective potential international remedies for the women of Ciudad Juárez would be to bring action against Mexico in the

Inter-American Court of Human Rights. The court came into existence in 1978 and is the final arbiter in violations of the American Convention on Human Rights. Mexico ratified the convention in 1981 and agreed to the court's jurisdiction on December 16, 1998. The convention is binding on ratifying states and ensures, inter alia, the right to life (Article 4); the right to humane treatment (Article 5), which includes the protection against torture and "cruel, inhuman, or degrading punishment or treatment"; the right to equal protection (Article 24); and the right to judicial protection, which includes "simple and prompt recourse, to a competent court or tribunal" for violations of the rights guaranteed by the convention (Article 25). The Inter-American Court of Human Rights might also hear cases stemming from Article 7 of the Inter-American Convention on the Prevention, Punishment, and Eradication of Violence against Women (the Convention of Belém do Pará), which Mexico ratified in 1998. This treaty prohibits any form of violence against women, "physical, sexual, and psychological," that occurs in the public or private sphere (Article 1), and Article 7 requires states "to apply due diligence to prevent, investigate and impose penalties for violence against women."

Increasingly, international legal institutions, including the court, have held that states can be held responsible for the actions of non-state actors in specific cases. In the Inter-American system, this responsibility stems from Article 1 of the convention, which creates positive obligations on states: "The states [that are] parties to this Convention undertake to respect the rights and freedoms recognized herein and *to ensure* to all persons subject to their jurisdiction the free and full exercise of those rights and freedoms" (emphasis added). From this duty to ensure rights comes the corollary duty to put in place a legal system that will provide effective recourse for human rights abuses. As the court ruled in an advisory opinion: "Any state which tolerates circumstances or conditions that prevent individuals from having recourse to the legal remedies designed to protect their rights is consequently in violation of Article 1(1) of the Convention."[2] In the context of the Ciudad Juárez case, the Mexican government could be in violation of the convention for failing to provide security for the women of the city once the government knew that human rights violations were likely and for failing to provide due diligence in investigating, prosecuting, and punishing the perpetrators. The court ruled in its very first contentious case, "An illegal act which violates human rights and which is initially not directly imputable to a State (for example, because it is the act of a private person or because the person responsible has not been identified) can lead to international responsibility of the state, not because of the act itself, but because of the lack of due diligence to prevent the violation or to respond to it as required by the Convention" (*Velasquez-Rodriguez v. Honduras* 1988). Of particular note is the requirement to provide an adequate investigation. The court held, "Where the acts of private parties that violate the Convention are not seriously investigated, those parties are aided in a sense by the government, thereby making the State responsible on the international plane" (*Velásquez Rodríguez v. Honduras* 1988, para. 177). The court offers three possible avenues for seeking remedy for human rights abuses: contentious cases, advisory opinions, and provisional measures (see Simmons 2006). The best-known procedure is a contentious case, which is similar to a trial in the usual sense whereby a state is "accused" of violating parts of the treaty and can present a defense of its actions.

CONTENTIOUS CASES

The convention permits only states or the commission to bring contentious cases to the court, and to date no state has brought a case to the court. Thus, it would be up to the commission to bring such a case. Under the commission's modified Rules of Procedure of 2001, a case will automatically be sent to the court if the state has not complied with the previous recommendations of a commission's ruling, "unless there is a reasoned decision by an absolute majority of the members of the Commission to the contrary."[3] Since several cases related to the Ciudad Juárez murders have already been filed with the commission and the commission's rulings are rarely complied with, it is most likely that the commission will ultimately send a contentious case to the court in the Juárez situation.

Once a contentious case is brought to the court, it normally proceeds through three distinct phases. First, the state almost invariably files preliminary objections as to why the case should not be heard by the court. The most commonly used objection is that the victims have not exhausted all local remedies before submitting a case to the commission, as required by Article 46 of the convention. In this case, Mexico might claim that it was providing remedies for the women and that its investigation is ongoing. However, the court has ruled in several cases that, to clear the hurdle of admissibility, the domestic remedy must be both adequate and effective. In this situation, Mexico's failure to effectively act for more than a decade, as well as the ongoing harassment of lawyers, victims' families, and activists, should lead the court to decline to wait for domestic remedies to become more than a "senseless formality" (*Velásquez Rodríguez v. Honduras* 1988, para. 68).

Once the case clears preliminary objections, it proceeds to the merit phase, where the claim and relevant laws are considered. It is in this phase that the court would have to consider the state's responsibility for the actions of non-state actors, as discussed earlier, and violations of specific articles of the convention and of Article 7 of the Convention of Belém do Pará.

If the country is found to be in violation of either convention, then the case proceeds to the reparations phase. In its first two decades, the court was criticized for the modest monetary sums it awarded to victims, especially in cases of disappearances and loss of life (Saul 2004). Recently, the court has increased the amounts of monetary damages that it has awarded and has increasingly awarded creative non-monetary remedies. Often, these remedies have had the purpose of giving agency to the victimized — or, at least, recognizing the humanity and dignity of the victim. The court has ordered the state to restore the integrity or identity of the victim by exhuming remains, investigating disappearances, or even locating children separated from their parents. Victims' families are often given agency through the ability to oversee the investigations of the states, as well as the capacity to work with the court to ensure compliance with reparations orders. For example, in *Myrna Mack v. Guatemala* (2003), the court found that Guatemala had violated the right to life, right to fair trial, and right to humane treatment in the assassination of Myrna Mack Chang, an anthropologist and human rights activist. Guatemala accepted unconditional responsibility for the killing. As for reparations, the state was ordered to investigate the case, prosecute and punish the perpetrators, and publish the results of any investigation. What is striking is the extent to which the state was also ordered to honor and memorialize the victim, including the establishment of an educational grant in the victim's name. The court ordered that "the state must also name a well-known street or square in Guatemala City in honor of Myrna Mack Chang, and place a prominent plaque in her memory at the place where she died or nearby, with a reference to the activities she carried out." (*Myrna Mack v. Guatemala* 2003, para. 286). Finally, the state was ordered to pay more than $750,000 in damages and expenses to her family. A similar ruling could go a long way toward restoring the subjectivity of the women of Ciudad Juárez and assist with what one prominent scholar describes as "a vital struggle to retrieve the subjectivity of the victimized women from the brutality of their deaths, to establish their value and social meaning in *life*" (Schmidt Camacho 2004, 47).

The court's increased attention to memorializing the victim could be attributed to the changes in its procedures in 1997 that allow the victim the right to directly address the court (*locus standi in judicio*) during the reparations stage. The court's awarding of reparations seems to have changed dramatically, with monetary damages increasing substantially and almost all of the cases involving creative uses of non-monetary damages occurring after 1998. Changes to the court's rules of procedure that took effect on June 1, 2001, included allowing the victims or their relatives to address the court at all stages of contentious cases. The President of the Court noted that this change "marks a major milestone in the evolution of the inter-American system for the protection of human rights" (Cançado Trindade 2002, 12), and this granting of increased agency to the victims surely will lead to dramatic changes in the court's jurisprudence in contentious cases.

A final striking feature of the court's jurisprudence is the compliance rate by states. States have almost universally complied with the orders of the court. Christina Cerna (2004, 203) writes: "They [states party to the Convention] have accepted the judgments of the Inter-American Court of Human Rights and, this is surprising, because the decisions of the Commission still generally remain unobserved in comparison. . . . The most remarkable development in the evolution of the Inter-American human rights system, and I cannot emphasize this enough, is that it has become accepted." Finally, recent rulings by the court led Trinidad and Tobago to withdraw from the court's jurisdiction, and Peru unsuccessfully attempted to withdraw when faced with potentially adverse decisions by the court (Helfer 2002). After years of work by NGOs and others, Mexico finally acceded to the court's jurisdiction in 1998. For it to withdraw now would be a major blow to the court's legitimacy. Equally damaging would be the government's overt refusal to comply with an order from the court. However, such backlash in this case would be highly unlikely, as the Mexican government has recently made several highly publicized statements on human rights and has taken several concrete steps forward in respecting human rights, such as establishing the CNDH and making some substantive improvements to the investigation in Ciudad Juárez. Further, Mexico sought the assistance of the court through two different advisory opinions in the past decade. Therefore, it is highly unlikely that Mexico would withdraw from the jurisdiction of the court or refuse to comply with a ruling by the court.

Human Rights Committee

If a regional human rights court promises such effective remedies, one might expect an international human rights body with the backing of the United Nations to be just as effective, if not more so. Of the quasi-

United Nations treaty-based human rights committees, the Human Rights Committee (HRC), the Committee to Eliminate Racial Discrimination, and the Committee against Torture allow individual petitions against a state party. Here we will discuss the HRC, which oversees the International Convention on Civil and Political Rights (ICCPR). Optional Protocol 1 to the ICCPR allows individuals to submit written communications to the HRC alleging violations against their government. It could be argued that the women in Ciudad Juárez have suffered violations, at minimum, of Article 6 (the right to life), Article 7 (cruel, inhuman, or degrading treatment), and Article 9 ("right to liberty and security of person") of the ICCPR.

Individual communications proceed through three stages. The first stage is the receipt of a written communication from the complainant and transmission of the complaint for response by the state party; the second stage is the determination by the HRC of the admissibility of the communication, which usually hinges on the exhaustion of domestic remedies; and the final stage is the determination by the HRC of the merits of the communication. The HRC can also issue orders for interim protection for the authors of the communication while the committee considers the complaint. These protections are often individually tailored to the needs of the authors and have included "urgent medical procedures, stays on executions and stays on extradition."[4] Such interim measures, which are also available from the Inter-American Court of Human Rights, should be an important factor in deciding which forum would be best for the women of Ciudad Juárez.

At first glance, the HRC appears to be a promising alternative for effective remedies for the women of Juárez. It is well established. As of 2003, 149 states were party to the ICCPR, and 104 were party to the Optional Protocol 1. The HRC has a rich body of jurisprudence with approximately 1,200 final views issued as of 2006 on a wide range of human rights issues. It can also issue orders for interim measures to protect those who bring a communication before it. Mexico ratified the ICCPR in 1981 and ratified Optional Protocol 1 in 2001. However, the HRC has heard precious few cases on affirmative duties of a state or on violence against women, and it suffers from severe structural shortcomings.

STATE DUTIES UNDER THE ICCPR

Article 2 of the ICCPR lays out the affirmative obligations of state parties. Paragraph 1 states that each state must take measures to "respect and to ensure to all individuals . . . the rights recognized in the present Covenant," and Paragraph 2 requires each state "to adopt such laws or other measures as may be necessary to give effect to the rights recognized in the present Covenant." Paragraph 3 obliges each state to ensure an "effective remedy" for any rights violated. The HRC in its general comments (authoritative interpretations) has interpreted Article 2 to extend state responsibility to the actions of private actors. For example, in its interpretation of Article 7 of the ICCPR, the HRC wrote that it prohibited torture or cruel, inhuman, or degrading treatment "whether inflicted by people acting in their official capacity, outside their official capacity, *or in a private capacity*" (emphasis added). In General Comment 6, the HRC concluded, "State parties should also take specific and effective measures to prevent the disappearance of individuals . . . [and] should establish effective facilities and procedures to investigate thoroughly cases of missing and disappeared persons in circumstances which may involve a violation of the right to life." This interpretation led the committee to find Colombia in violation of Article 6 (right to life) and Article 9 (right to security of person) for failing to investigate the alleged abduction of two university students by a section of the state police force (*Elcida Arévalo Perez et al. v. Colombia* 1989).

Nevertheless, the HRC has issued very few rulings holding states accountable for the actions of private actors. The case that is clearest on state duties to prevent crimes is *Delgado Páez v. Colombia*, which involved a Colombian teacher of religion and ethics who made complaints against the Apostolic Prefect and the education authorities concerning discrimination against him based on his teaching of liberation theology. As a result of these complaints, Delgado received death threats, which he reported to a wide range of authorities. Subsequently, he was physically attacked. The HRC noted the difficult situation in Colombia but concluded that the state was responsible for the personal security of citizens of the state under Article 9 and had not taken "appropriate measures to ensure Mr. Delgado's right to security of his person." Based on *Delgado Páez*, it can be argued that the Mexican government must take the appropriate measures to protect the women of Ciudad Juárez — that is, they are responsible for the safety of the women currently living in Juárez and the surrounding areas.

The HRC has made several pronouncements on the rights of women in its General Comments (4 and 28) and in a number of its responses to periodic reports by state parties,[5] but it has issued precious few rulings on individual complaints dealing with women's rights. In General Comment 28, the HRC concluded, "The State party must not only adopt measures of protection but also positive measures in all areas so as to achieve the effective and equal empowerment of women" and "State parties are responsible for ensuring the equal enjoyment of rights without any discrimination . . . [and must] put an end to discriminatory actions both in the public and the private sector which impair the equal enjoyment of rights." The General Comment also mentions "domestic and other types of violence against women, including rape" in its discussion of Article 7, which prohibits torture and "cruel, inhuman or degrading treatment or punishment" (para. 11). Many of its responses to periodic reports by states single out domestic and sexual violence against women and call on the state to take specific measures to prevent these crimes. For example, in its response to Kenya's periodic report in 2005, it called on the government to "sensitize society as a whole to this matter, ensure that the perpetrators of such violence are prosecuted and provide assistance and protection to victims" (para. 11). Nevertheless, the HRC's final views on women's rights have been confined to such questions as tribal rights for women (*Lovelace v. Canada*), entitlement to public services (*Vos v. the Netherlands*), and the status of immigrant women (*Aumeeruddy-Cziffra v. Mauritius*). Several scholars have suggested that the HRC could issue views on sexual violence or domestic violence (see, e.g., Vesa 2004), but to date there have been no final views from the HRC interpreting the relevant ICCPR articles in connection with specific situations of domestic or sexual violence.

STRUCTURAL WEAKNESSES OF THE HRC

Scholars and legal practitioners have pointed out a litany of problems that reduce the HRC's power to serve as an effective remedy for human rights violations. The committee's proceedings are time-consuming, taking on average twelve to eighteen months for a communication to be declared admissible, and cases average three to four years from initial receipt of a communication to final view. The HRC also has adopted an unnecessarily restricted interpretation of its requirement that communications must be filed by a victim or on behalf of a victim, thus preventing NGOs from serving as authors of communications on behalf of victims.

More important, the HRC's rules of procedures do little to restore voice or agency to the victims, and their final views rarely lead to effective change in the human rights situations. The HRC conducts its proceedings completely through written submissions. The complainants submit written documentation of the alleged abuse or abuses, and the state is invited to provide a written response within six months. The committee can, and often does, request further written information from the parties, but no witnesses are questioned; nor are representatives called to give an oral account of the state's actions. Furthermore, the HRC lacks fact-finding ability, which severely limits the amount of information available to it, as well as its ability to ascertain the truth in any given situation. The committee then holds closed meetings and submits its final views, often with little legal analysis, to the state and to the individual. Often these findings are not publicized, and they rarely provide guidance on which specific measures the state should take to remedy the situation. Until recently, the HRC exercised very little over-sight of its final views after they were issued. The process itself is so abstract that it most clearly resembles advisory opinions or authoritative interpretations that seem to take little account of the specific case at hand. This view is further reinforced by the almost rote nature of most opinions in which the wording of comparable opinions mirror each other in great detail.

The biggest drawback of the HRC is the lack of binding status for its final views. It could be argued that its views should be binding because the HRC "monitors implementation of the ICCPR," a binding treaty. Recently, the HRC has been more forceful in asserting that its views have some legal force, but state practice belies these claims. The HRC's website claims that "several countries have changed their laws as a result of decisions by the Committee on individual complaints under the Op-tional Protocol. In a number of cases, prisoners have been released and compensation paid to victims of human rights violations."[6] The best estimate, though, is that approximately 85 percent of final views lead to no substantive change in the human rights situation. Most commenta-tors would agree: "It must be frankly admitted that compliance with the HRC's views by state parties has been disappointing" (McGoldrick 2001, 202). For example, in a recent case in which the HRC issued interim measures to prevent deportation of a suspected terrorist from Canada, the Canadian courts ruled that "neither the Committee's views nor its interim measures requests are binding on Canada as a matter of international law, much less as a matter of domestic law" (Harrington 2003, 61). Overall, one commentator concluded that "the Committee's views are inept instruments to achieve greater protection of rights by all states" (Hakki 2002, 96).

The HRC has taken several steps to increase publicity for, and com-pliance rates of, its final views. In 1990, it appointed a Special Rappor-teur for the Follow-Up of Views, and it now requests that countries found in violation of the ICCPR submit a report on the steps taken to address the violations. Such follow-up measures are also supposed to be addressed in the countries' periodic reports to the HRC. The HRC also appends a summary of state actions in responses to final views in their annual reports to the General Assembly of the United Nations and the

United Nations Economic and Social Council. However, "the [United Nations] bodies have not taken up any significant supervisory role" (Nowak 2005, 899) and thus have not applied any pressure on the governments to comply with the final views. Without added pressure from the United Nations, the committee's efforts so far have not resulted in increased compliance rates.

Even though they are not legally binding, the HRC's final views can increase publicity for a human rights situation and put a modicum of pressure on a national government to institute reform. However, considering the current local, national, and international pressure on the Mexican governance, coupled with the structural weaknesses of the HRC, a final view on the feminicides would probably accomplish little. In other cases, in other countries, the HRC can and does play an important role, especially in areas that lack effective regional human rights bodies. From the foregoing structural weaknesses and the HRC's seeming inattentiveness to women's issues, it appears the committee would not be an appealing alternative for the women of Ciudad Juárez.

Alien Tort Statute

The Inter-American Court of Human Rights and the Human Rights Committee have both been faulted for their lengthy procedures, and both are limited to making rulings against national governments and therefore cannot hold specific individuals in the Mexican government directly accountable for the femicides. Another promising potential remedy would be to file a civil suit against specific local Mexican officials as third parties to the femicides in U.S. federal courts for their failure to adequately investigate and prevent these crimes. We argue that this could be done based on a once obscure American law, the Alien Tort Statute (ATS). We argue that a suit under the ATS could succeed and would potentially be a very innovative remedy for the women of Ciudad Juárez, but such a suit, as we argue below, would most likely require a very innovative but plausible interpretation of what constitutes "acquiescence to torture" in international law.

The ATS is a deceptively simple one-sentence statute that reads: "District courts shall have original jurisdiction of any civil action by an alien for a tort only, committed in violation of the law of nations or a treaty of the United States" (28 U.S. Code, Section 1350). Parsing the wording shows that the act covers an action initiated by a non-U.S. citizen, only for a civil tort, and it must involve a violation of the law of nations or U.S. treaty. The ATS was passed by the first U.S. Congress as part of the

Federal Judiciary Act of 1789 but lay virtually dormant before being given new life in 1980 in the groundbreaking case, *Filártiga v. Peña-Irala*.

In *Filártiga*, it was alleged that Américo Norberto Peña-Irala, while serving as inspector-general of police in Paraguay, had kidnapped and tortured to death the seventeen-year-old son of Dr. Joel Filártiga because of Filártiga's opposition to Alfredo Stroessner's government. On learning that Peña-Irala was living in the United States, Filártiga and his daughter brought suit in U.S. Federal District Court claiming civil damages under the ATS and several other statutes and treaties. The Second Circuit Court of Appeals ultimately held that "having examined the sources from which customary international law is derived, the usage of nations, judicial opinions and the works of scholars we conclude that official torture is now prohibited by the law of nations" (*Filártiga v. Peña-Irala* 1980, 884) and thereby actionable under the ATS. The District Court then granted a default judgment in favor of the Filártigas, and each of the plaintiffs was awarded $5 million in punitive damages.

Since then, dozens of ATS cases have been heard in federal courts. Originally cases were mainly brought against foreign government officials, but increasingly cases are being brought against individuals and multinational corporations. In 2004, the Supreme Court, in its first ATS case, *Sosa v. Alvarez-Machain*, limited its scope to a narrow range of human rights norms, basically those that are "specific, universal, and obligatory." While there is still some controversy over which abuses would be actionable, it is safe to say that "torture, genocide, crimes against humanity, and war crimes" (*Sosa v. Alvarez-Machain* 2004, 762) would meet this *Sosa* test. In the past two years, several large settlements have been granted under the ATS, including two cases involving abuses during the Salvadoran civil war of the 1980s. In a much publicized case, three Salvadoran refugees brought claims against the former minister of defense of El Salvador and the director-general of the El Salvador National Guard for torture under the ATS (for two plaintiffs, as the third was not an alien) and the Torture Victim Protection Act. After several appeals — most notably, on a statute of limitations claim — the plaintiffs were awarded $54.6 million in a jury trial. In another recent case, a jury found the former deputy minister of defense of El Salvador liable for the torture of four Salvadorans and awarded them $5 million in compensatory damages and $4 million in punitive damages.

The next major controversy in ATS jurisprudence appears to be whether the statute allows for third-party liability — that is, whether an individual can be held accountable for the actions of another individual. The most common theory advanced in these cases is that a corporation or an individual aided and abetted a human rights abuse. The federal courts have been split on such liability, with some ruling that there is no aiding and abetting liability under the ATS, while most courts have ruled that aiding and abetting liability and other third-person liability can be found using a range of legal theories. In a separate article, William Paul Simmons (2007) shows that even if aiding and abetting liability was sustainable under the ATS, it would not apply to Juárez. Instead, we offer a government official's acquiescence to private acts of torture as an innovative application of third-party liability for that situation. Recall, that torture is one of the universal, specific, and obligatory norms that meets the *Sosa* test.

STATE DUTIES TO PREVENT TORTURE

While torture has been defined in a plethora of international documents and cases, the authoritative international definition can be found in Article 1 of the Convention against Torture (CAT).[7] The CAT had been approved by 136 countries as of 2004; it has been referred to in dozens of national and international cases; and its definition of torture has been labeled "customary international law." The CAT defines torture as "any act by which severe pain or suffering, whether physical or mental, is intentionally inflicted on a person for such purposes as obtaining from him or a third person information or a confession, punishing him for an act he or a third person has committed or is suspected of having committed, or intimidating or coercing him or a third person, or for any reason based on discrimination of any kind, when such pain or suffering is inflicted by *or at the instigation of or with the consent or acquiescence of a public official or other person acting in an official capacity*" (Article 1; emphasis added). Under the CAT, state parties have the affirmative duties, inter alia, to "prevent acts of torture" (Article 2) and "ensure that its competent authorities proceed to a prompt and impartial investigation" (Article 12). Nor can states "expel, return (*refouler*) or extradite a person to another State where there are substantial grounds for believing that he would be in danger of being subjected to torture" (Article 3).

It is increasingly clear that these affirmative duties of a state apply to acts of torture committed by public officials *and* private individuals. After all, from this definition, torture need not be directly perpetrated by the public official but could be at the "instigation of" an official or with the "the consent or acquiescence" of an official. The Special Rapporteur on Torture of the United Nations Commission on Human Rights has written that the consent or acquiescence language "makes the State responsible for acts committed by private individuals which it did not prevent from occurring or, if need be, for which it did not provide appropriate remedies" (Rodley 2001, para. 73). However, very few international institutions have found states accountable for acquiescing to torture by private individuals. The best-developed jurisprudence on acquiescence to torture can be found in recent U.S. nonrefoulement cases.

ACQUIESCENCE, OR A GOVERNMENT'S "WILLFUL BLINDNESS" TO PRIVATE ACTS OF TORTURE

The Foreign Affairs Reform and Restructuring Act of 1998 (FARRA) was drafted in part to comply with Article 3 of the CAT, which prohibits the refoulement of immigrants who fear torture when they return to their own country. Acquiescence was clarified in the Code of Federal Regulations (CFR): "Acquiescence of a public official requires that the public official, prior to the activity constituting torture, have *awareness* of such activity and thereafter breach his or her legal responsibility to intervene to prevent such activity," (8 CFR 208 1208.18[a][7]). This case law on acquiescence to torture is still in an early stage, as FARRA was enacted only in 1998. The authoritative interpretation of acquiescence is in cases in the federal circuit courts on appeal from immigration courts. The standard to determine acquiescence is made more difficult to decipher in circuit court cases because of the strict standards required for a circuit court to overturn a ruling by the immigration courts. "The administrative findings of fact are conclusive unless any reasonable adjudicator would be compelled to conclude to the contrary" (8 U.S. Code, Section 1252[b][4][B]). Rarely are these cases overturned, and when they are, they are usually returned to the immigration courts for a final determination based on the evidence.

Nonetheless, several circuit courts have recently agreed on a willful blindness standard to help determine when a state has acquiesced to torture, and some general principles are beginning to emerge as to what constitutes a state's "willful blindness" to torture by private individuals (cf. Freshwater 2005, 601–606).

First, it is clear from non-refoulement cases that the government must take appropriate steps to prevent acts of torture committed by private individuals as well as public officials. The Ninth Circuit has been perhaps the clearest on this issue. In *Azanor v. Ashcroft* (2004, 1019), a case considering whether the practice of female genital mutilation might constitute torture, the court wrote, "INS regulations and the Senate's official understandings to the Torture Convention clearly establish that a petitioner may qualify for withholding of removal by showing that he or she would likely suffer torture while under *private parties'* exclusive custody or physical control." Similarly, in *Reyes v. Ashcroft* (2004, 787), the court opposed an immigration judge's ruling that the "Torture Convention requires that someone in the government or acting on behalf of the government torture the respondent." To interpret the CAT in this way "contravenes the plain language of the governing regulation" and "effectively excised the phrase 'or with the consent or acquiescence of' from the regulation" (*Reyes v. Ashcroft* 2004, 787).

Second, acquiescence to torture is not a form of strict liability whereby the state is responsible for all torture in its jurisdiction even if it was not aware of it. A state must either have actual knowledge of, or be willfully blind to, torture. In *Adeniyi v. Bureau of Immigration* (2004), the Circuit Court threw out a CAT challenge because there was no evidence that the state of Nigeria was aware that a family member would punish a man for his religious beliefs. The court wrote, "There is no indication in the record that any authorities were aware of what was happening in Famola's village. Once again, his failure to report any of his uncle's actions to the authorities undermines his claim that they would not take any action to protect him" (*Adeniyi v. Bureau of Immigration* 2005, 465).

Third, if the state is actively involved in fighting the perpetrators of the abuses, it will be less likely to be acquiescing in torture. For example, the Third Circuit held that governmental acquiescence could not be found when the government of Uganda was "in continuous opposition" with the Lord's Resistance Army, which was alleged to be perpetrating acts of torture" (*Lukwago v. Ashcroft* 2003, 183). Other cases show that if the government reacts in a timely manner and takes steps to conduct an investigation, even if it has not solved a crime, it will be less likely to be acquiescing.

Fourth, several non-refoulement cases suggest that a state's failure to adequately investigate or prevent domestic violence or sexual violence qualifies as acquiescence to torture. In *Ali v. Reno* (2001), the Sixth Circuit upheld the decision of the Bureau of Immigration Appeals decision in a domestic-violence case that the Danish police had not acquiesced in violence because they had investigated and arrested family members but were then asked by the applicant not to punish her brothers. Nevertheless, the court wrote, "This is not to say that domestic violence of the sort alleged in this case could never be the basis for relief under the Convention against Torture. In different circumstances, such as a situation in which the authorities ignore or consent to severe domestic violence, the Convention appears to compel protection for a victim" (*Ali v. Reno* 2001, 598).

Although the courts did not side with the appellants in these cases, based on the factual patterns, it is becoming clear what kinds of questions the courts will ask to determine whether a government "would turn a blind eye to torture" (*Ontunez-Tursios v. Ashcroft* 2002, 355). General government corruption and under-funding of law enforcement will most likely not count as acquiescence to torture. The failure to solve crimes is also not sufficient to show government acquiescence, but failure to respond in a timely fashion, failure to follow up on leads, and failure to take operational steps to prevent torture all will contribute to a finding of acquiescence. Thus, a plausible argument can be made that a state's failure to conduct an adequate investigation or to take preventative measures can constitute acquiescence to torture, which is equivalent to torture as defined by the CAT and is thereby actionable under the ATS.

LEGAL HURDLES WITH THE ATS

Several practical hurdles that have been fatal to ATS cases on other issues would need to be addressed in bringing such a suit for the femicides. We believe that these hurdles could be met adequately for a suit to proceed. First, federal courts need to exercise personal jurisdiction over a defendant in order to hear a civil suit. This typically means that the individual must be within the court's jurisdiction to receive a summons to appear in court — that is, he or she must receive "sufficient notice of the complaint and action" against him or her (*Doe v. Qi* 2004, 1276). In most instances, then, the individual must be in the United States to be sued under the ATS. But considering that Ciudad Juárez is a border town whose officials frequently visit the United States for business and personal reasons, this should be less of a problem than it has been with defendants from far-flung areas of the world.[8]

Another potential hurdle is the Foreign Sovereign Immunities Act (FSIA), which lays out the circumstances in which government officials from foreign countries can be sued in U.S. courts. On this issue, the circuit courts have been split. Some have ruled that the FSIA applies only to national governments, so that all government officials, besides heads of states, can be sued under most circumstances. But the more plausible interpretation of the FSIA is that it applies only to government officials acting in their official capacity. Under this interpretation, the FSIA "will not shield an official who acts beyond the scope of his authority" (*Chuidian v. Philippine National Bank* 1990). Recently, it has been argued that any act that violates the law of nations cannot legally be within the scope of any government official's authority (cf. *Doe v. Qi* 2004). So if a government official's failure to investigate and prevent crimes constitutes torture under the definition found in international law, such actions or inactions could not constitute valid government authority, and no defendant could be granted foreign sovereign immunity for such action or inaction.

Other hurdles common in ATS cases would most likely not be applicable in a case related to the femicides. The statute of limitations for ATS cases is generally considered to be ten years, and there are provisions for extending the statute of limitations "where extraordinary circumstances outside plaintiff's control make it impossible for plaintiff to timely assert his claim" (*Forti v. Suarez-Mason* 1987, 11549). U.S. federal courts also invoke the principles of *forum non conveniens*, which basically means that a court will not hear a case if there is a more convenient legal forum to hear the case. It is not clear how the pending cases in the IACHR would be viewed by a U.S. federal court, but since those cases are against the Mexican government as a whole and are not civil suits, they should not be seen as a competing forum. As with cases in the HRC and the Inter-American Court of Human Rights, it will have to be shown that the plaintiffs have exhausted all domestic remedies, but again, the failure of the state to stop the impunity would weigh heavily against it on such a challenge. Finally, some ATS suits have also been dismissed because they deal with a political question, immunity for heads of state, immunity for acts of states, and interference with the Torture Victims Protection Act. We hold that none of these would be substantial obstacles in this case.

The ATS offers several advantages for the women of Ciudad Juárez. Most important, U.S. federal courts would provide a neutral forum that would allow the victims' families to voice their complaints against local Mexican government officials and call them to account for their actions during the femicides. A federal district court would allow the introduction of a wide range of evidence documenting the failures of the local government officials and the workings of the local law-enforcement agencies, as well as personal testimony from the victims' families. If the defendants chose to testify, they would be open to cross-examination by the families' attorneys. Concerted attempts have been made to further silence those family members who have demanded justice through harassment, threat, and disregard. The ATS could allow a forum for the victims' families to voice their suffering. Such "litigation provides victims with access to a narrative forum that enables the victim to name her experience and to situate it within a larger policy or practice of repression" (Van Schaack 2004, 2318–19).

A case involving the ATS would not address the larger structural factors, but it could provide some needed satisfaction for the families. Very few ATS cases have resulted in large settlements for the families, but even the potential of such a settlement could provide additional pressure on the government to take more steps to investigate and prevent the femicides. Unlike the Inter-American Court of Human Rights, an ATS claim could serve to localize accountability. A ruling by the Inter-American Court of Human Rights against Mexico as a whole could lead the national and local governments to continue to blame each other, with neither side accepting responsibility. Finally, proceedings in federal district courts, though often criticized for their glacial pace, would most likely be quicker than international remedies, especially in the early stages of a case. The defendants would be required to provide a much quicker response to the plaintiffs' claims.

The World Bank and the Inter-American Development Bank

Another possible remedy would be to attempt to leverage the enormous power of international financial institutions (IFIs) to improve the human rights situation in Juárez. The past decade has seen a wide-ranging debate as to the extent that IFIs can be used for human rights purposes — after all, IFIs are established for economic motives and not for advancing human rights. However, many scholars and activists have argued that IFIs should be employed for improving human rights or, at minimum, should not finance projects that worsen human rights situations.

When considering IFIs the ones that most readily come to mind are the Bretton Woods institutions, especially the World Bank. Many have suggested that the World Bank could withhold loans to states with poor human rights records or provide monies to target specific human rights abuses. But the World Bank is constrained by its original Cold War-era Articles of Agreement, which restrict lending "to considerations of economy and efficiency and *without regard to political or other non-economic influences or consideration*" (emphasis added).[9] Strict adherence to this provision limits the bank's concern with human rights unless "such violations are so pervasive as to have negative economic effects" (Morais 2000, 88). Not surprisingly, there have only been a few instances in which the World Bank has withheld loans even partially for human rights reasons, such as the suspension of a loan in 1972 to Chile. Conversely, the World Bank has backed several infamous projects that have had deleterious effects on human rights, such as the Chad–Cameroon Pipeline. In response to pressure from activists and others, the World Bank has made several procedural changes to increase its transparency and sensitivity to the concerns of affected peoples. For instance, it created an Inspection

Panel "for the purpose of providing people directly and adversely affected by a Bank financed project with an independent forum through which they can request the Bank to act in accordance with its own policies and procedures" (Hunter 2003, 3; cf. Wahi 2006). The bank has also issued several important Operational Directives and Policies on the environment, displaced persons, and gender. However, these directives and policies have been strictly interpreted within the bounds of the original Articles of Agreement so that it is quite clear that human rights issues in general and gender issues in particular remain peripheral issues for the bank.

INTER-AMERICAN DEVELOPMENT BANK

For the victims of Ciudad Juárez, and others who live within the Americas, the IADB could also be used to promote human rights. The IADB, established in 1959, was the first regional development bank. It was specifically created to "contribute to the acceleration of the process of economic and social development of the regional developing member countries, individually and collectively" (Inter-American Development Bank 1959, Article 1.1). Throughout its history, the IADB has an admirable record of developing its own capacity so that it has positioned itself to play a major role in the economic development of Latin America (Scheman 1997, 88–89). Its mandates and policies have overtly attempted to improve on weaknesses within the Bretton Woods institutions, especially "their lack of specialization and knowledge of local conditions" (Barria and Roper 2004, 622). The IADB is also much less controlled by donor nations. For example, recipient nations have a majority of the votes in the bank's deliberations, and the bank's independence is further guaranteed by its solvency. The bank is capitalized at more than $100 billion, and its excellent repayment rate and high credit rating ensures a steady source of income without further replenishment for years to come. The IADB annually lends approximately $6 billion–$7 billion to Latin American countries, an amount that surpasses that given by the World Bank to the region (Barria and Roper 2004, 631, 634). The IADB lends mostly to governments but has shown an increased willingness to provide loans to private entities, especially large banks. Although civil society organizations can receive loans when guaranteed by their government, this type of lending is sporadic and has not been substantial.

The Eighth (and last) Replenishment of 1994 was key in changing the IADB's focus to the social sector. It requires that "50 percent of the projects be in social sectors, including those of civil society and the environment" (Scheman 1997, 90). In its annual report for 2005, the IADB divided its lending into three areas: social development, competitiveness, and reform and modernization of the state. Almost half of all monies went to social development. Many of these loans went to projects to benefit the environment, urban development, education, and health. Throughout its work, the IADB has been very sensitive to the needs of the poor and marginalized and has undertaken several projects intended to reduce income inequality. In June 2006, the president of the IADB announced the Building Opportunity for the Majority initiative, which is specifically aimed at helping the region's poor through infrastructure projects, as well as affordable housing, micro-credit projects, digital connectivity, and other projects, each with well-specified benchmarks. The IADB has also been much more attentive to human rights concerns than the World Bank. It has withdrawn funding from or suspended funding to several high-profile projects because of human rights concerns, such as the Camisea Gas Pipeline in Peru and the Maya Lands Case in Belize. It is not surprising that a recent empirical study has shown that, of the regional development banks, the IADB is most sensitive to civil and political rights when determining aid (Neumayer 2003, 111).

The IADB categorizes Mexico as a Group A country—that is, as one of the most developed countries in the region. Group A countries receive the largest share of loans but the least per capita. Countries in Group A can receive 50 percent of a project's cost, or 60 percent if the project specifically targets low-income populations (Barria and Roper 2004, 630). The IADB is currently funding a range of projects in Mexico —most notably, a program to assess and maximize the benefits of remittances from migrants to the United States. It also funds projects to strengthen local governance, improve rural water supplies, and finance small exporters. A major initiative has been Mexico's Oportunidades program, which received $1.2 billion and which the IADB calls "one of the pioneering conditional cash transfer programs in the world" (Inter-American Development Bank 2006). The Oportunidades program is a conditional cash-transfer program to the poorest people in Mexico to ensure that their children stay in school and receive better health care. "It has had a substantial positive long-term impact on the education, nutrition and health of its beneficiaries, especially children, and has alleviated extreme poverty."[10]

SPECIFIC IADB INITIATIVES AFFECTING HUMAN RIGHTS

Several recent initiatives of the IADB have direct relevance to the human rights situation in Juárez and elsewhere. First, the Modernization of the

State Strategy Document of 2003 is essential for understanding the current views of the IADB on human rights concerns. This report directly links economic development to democratic governance and democratic governance to human rights. So, while the raison d'être of the IADB remains development, development cannot be separated from a focus on human rights, which is enmeshed in the need for government reform. While this strategy explicitly broadens the IADB's mandate to the human rights field, it narrows the type of human rights concerns that will be privileged and the methods that will be employed. In general, the IADB has privileged institutional reforms, especially those that tie in with its four "areas of action": (1) democratic system; (2) rule of law and justice reform; (3) state, market, and society; and (4) public management. Human rights have perhaps been most apparent in the area of rule of law and justice reform. However, since this area has been identified as part of governance reform, it mostly concentrates on an institutional perspective, with such initiatives as strengthening the independence and capacity of the judiciary, modernizing administrative and judicial institutions and procedures, widening access to justice, and protecting citizens' security. The IADB has provided funding for specific programs, such as training judges, providing more law-enforcement officers, providing technical assistance, creating community-based violence-prevention programs, and offering workshops. Most, if not all, of these have had a citizen-participation component and have grown to involve civil society organizations (Biebesheimer 2005, 276).

Second, violence prevention has been a growing issue for the IADB. The Organization of American States Summit statement from Quebec in 2001 identified that violence "impedes development, [and] reduces foreign and domestic investment." (Inter-American Development Bank 1999). The IADB has supported innovative violence-prevention programs, such as Call and Live, in which the IADB teamed up with the Ricky Martin Foundation and the International Organization for Migration to combat human trafficking in Peru through media campaigns and hotlines. The IADB has also partially funded a community policing initiative in Bogotá and citizen-security initiatives elsewhere in Colombia, in Chile, and in Guyana.

Third, the IADB's Women in Development unit united with the bank's Social Development Division to create a Violence Reduction Group that has given special emphasis to violence against women, including domestic violence. This group, among other things, conducts research, identifies best practices, and "support[s] governments in the design of national and municipal prevention strategies" (Inter-American Development Bank 2007). Its projects have included conducting surveys, training social workers, and conducting public-information campaigns. In the past few years, the IADB has undertaken a series of domestic-violence programs in Ecuador, Honduras, Colombia, Suriname, and Guyana. These programs generally have been small in scale, usually costing less than $200,000.

RIGHTS-BASED DEVELOPMENT

The IADB has shown a willingness to push the envelope and take on projects and initiatives that the World Bank and others would claim are outside the scope of an international financial institution. Many of these initiatives are aimed at addressing just the type of issues that are at stake in Ciudad Juárez, but an even more broadly based and multifaceted program would be needed there. Such a program is unprecedented in the IADB's history and would require further advances beyond the bank's current thinking. However, we believe that if NGOs and governments pushed it, the IADB would be willing to entertain such a program that would combine several of its previous initiatives.

Such a program would have to include traditional legal capacity-building projects such as access to justice and increased judicial independence; radical improvements in the police forces; and public-information campaigns. It would also have to include innovative violence prevention programs such as community policing and community involvement in the planning of violence prevention strategies. A major component would have to be the empowerment (economic and otherwise) of local women and supporting local and national NGOs fighting the femicides. These groups would need considerable autonomy over their resources and important oversight over any government reform efforts. Indeed, the local women's groups and families of the victims should play the predominant role in designing such a project. Currently, the IADB is not considering such a program, but the family members of the victims could work with local, national, and international NGOs to pressure the Mexican government to request a loan to fund one. Such a project could provide more of a holistic approach to remedying the femicides and might be able to address the various types of structural violence (corruption, gender inequality, lack of political efficacy) that sustain both the femicides and the impunity for the perpetrators.

For such a project to be initiated and to be successful, the IADB would have to modify some of its current guiding principles. First, the IADB is reluctant to lend money to governments that have not demonstrated "a high level of political will and support for reform and show a genuine commitment to key rule of law principles, including democracy, respect for human rights, anti-corruption, and judicial independence" (Biebesheimer 2005, 287–88). Such a principle increases the likelihood of success of the IADB's projects and reduces the risk that its projects will add to human rights abuses, but it also basically prevents the bank from addressing the worst human rights abuses in the region. The IADB has the capacity, legitimacy, and moral authority to involve itself in such projects. It understandably avoids becoming involved in local political controversies and believes that involving itself with a country that is hesitant to initiate reforms would embroil it in such issues. However, several commentators have noted that the IADB's reluctance is eased when there is a regional consensus that an issue is a human rights abuse. In this case, the jurisprudence of the Inter-American Court of Human Rights on states' duties to investigate and prevent crimes as, well as the adoption of the Convention of Belém do Pará on violence against women, should ease the IADB's worries that the Juárez situation involves a local political issue.

Finally, the IADB, like all international financial institutions, has adopted what Stephen Golub (2003, 3) has called the rule-of-law orthodoxy — that is, a " 'top-down,' state-centered approach [that] concentrates on law reform and government institutions, particularly judiciaries, to build business-friendly legal systems that presumably spur poverty alleviation." These reforms are mostly controlled by the top levels of the judiciary and the bar and are concentrated in the capital cities. They often offer workshops for top officials, build courthouses and other legal buildings, install technology, and reorganize the judiciary. Although these programs can be effective in reforming the highest levels of the judiciary, there is serious concern about whether these programs reach the majority of a country's population (cf. Hammergren 2006). The model needed in Ciudad Juárez is more in line with the "legal empowerment" approach recommended by Golub. This would include building the capacity of civil society organizations; empowering the marginalized in society; addressing structural barriers to legal reform, such as poverty and discrimination; implementing alternative dispute-resolution programs; and increasing legal-aid programs. The women in Juárez need to be legally empowered in a substantive way so that they can effectively guide the reforms needed to stop the impunity, and the IADB has the capacity to fund just such a project.

Conclusion

Since 1993, hundreds of women in Ciudad Juárez have been brutally murdered, and many of these have been raped or subjected to other types of torture. Many more women have been subjected to torture in the form of extreme domestic violence. Although it is still not clear who is perpetrating many of these crimes, it is clear that the Mexican authorities have not taken sufficient steps to investigate and prevent them.

The human rights situation in Juárez is complex and multifaceted. It is grounded in myriad social, cultural, demographic, economic, and political conditions, some of which are idiosyncratic to the Mexican border town while others are endemic to Mexico and beyond. Therefore, a comprehensive set of remedies should be pursued. The exact remedies to be pursued should, of course, be determined by the families of the victims.

Nevertheless, this review leads to some general conclusions. Institutions based on United Nations treaties such as the Human Rights Committee would add little pressure to that already being placed on the Mexican government and would not provide "victims with access to a narrative forum that enables the victim to name her experience and to situate it within a larger policy or practice of repression" (Van Schaack 2004, 2318–19). We believe that contentious cases in the Inter-American Court of Human Rights offer the best hope for remedying past human rights abuses, especially in relation to the "serial" killings that have garnered much of the international attention. Such a case could lead to reforms in law enforcement and provide reparations to individual families. The court could order creative reparations that would serve to memorialize the victims and encourage agency for the victims' families. A civil suit under the U.S. Alien Tort Statute could provide a forum for the victims' families and could put direct pressure on local government officials. However, such a civil suit would most likely not address the structural factors behind the femicides. A broad-based project partially funded by the Inter-American Development Bank, as outlined earlier, could lead to reforms that would address such structural violence. Transnational remedies should not be seen in isolation; they require concomitant actions by those closest to the situation. The murders in Ciudad Juárez would not have drawn such national and international attention if it were not for the heroic efforts of the victims' families and of other women, including social workers such as Ester Chávez Cano, journalists such as Diana Washington Valdez, and international activists such as Lourdes Portillo. Any transnational remedy should not be seen as supplanting the efforts of grassroots groups who will be the ones who effect real change through continued and constant pressure on the local and national government.

The victims of the femicides have been silenced by these crimes and erased further by the actions and inactions of the government officials.

This silencing is not limited to Juárez but is indicative of gender violence in many jurisdictions. "Perpetrators of gender violence know that they 'act with virtual total assurance that, as statistics confirm, their acts will be officially tolerated, they themselves will be officially invisible, and their victims will be officially silenced'" (Nessel 2004, 141). Concerted attempts have been made through harassment, threat, and disregard to further silence those family members who have demanded justice. In rushing to create precedents in international law and debating abstract areas of law, it is imperative that the victims and the families are involved and at the forefront of all aspects of any legal proceeding. The mothers of the victims have played crucial roles in this fight and should continue to do so. Anything less than keeping the victims and their families in the forefront risks re-victimizing the victims. Therefore, it seems fitting to end with the voice of the mothers who have banded together to form Justicia para Nuestras Hijas (Justice for Our Daughters). In an open letter, they wrote:

> We are humble women who live in the *colonias* of Chihuahua. We use public transportation, we work for less than the minimum wage, and most of us have only received a primary education. We are mothers of young women who have disappeared. Some of us have finally found our daughters: raped, murdered, and disposed of anywhere. Others of us are still looking for our daughters. We are united today in our suffering, suffering loss of a daughter or the terrible anxiety of not knowing where our daughters are. Our daughters, the disappeared, are captive somewhere, and are in grave danger. Our murdered wanted to be happy: they had dreams, plans, all cut short by their killers. Along with our desperation, our pain, and our anxiety at having lost a daughter, or of not knowing what has happened to her, we have to add the mistreatment we have incurred at the hands of investigating officials. (Quoted in Schmidt Camacho 2004, 56–57)

Notes

1. William Paul Simmons has previously published articles on remedies for the femicides through the Inter-American Court of Human Rights (Simmons 2006) and the Alien Tort Statute (Simmons 2007). Recently, three other legal scholars have considered transnational human rights remedies for the femicides in Ciudad Juárez. Grace Spencer (2004–2005) explored the possibility of bringing a case in American federal courts under the Alien Tort Statute (ATS) for the abysmal working conditions in the maquiladoras. However, she does not consider whether a case could be brought under the ATS for Mexico's failure to investigate and prevent the murders, as outlined here. Joan

Robinson (2005) and Mark Ensalaco (2006) discuss whether Mexico can be held accountable for the actions of non-state actors in the Juárez case through an analysis of *Velásquez Rodriguez v. Honduras*, Judgment of July 29, 1988, Inter-American Court of Human Rights, OEA/Ser. C. 172 (1988).

2. Exceptions to the Exhaustion of Domestic Remedies (Articles 46.1, 46.2a, 46.2b, of the American Convention on Human Rights), Advisory Opinion OC-11/90, Inter-American Court of Human Rights, OEA/Ser. A. (1990).

3. Rules of Procedure of the Inter-American Commission on Human Rights, Article 44, available online at http://www.cidh.oas.org/Basicos/basic16.htm (accessed August 21, 2009).

4. Australian Human Rights Center, "Communicating with the Human Rights Committee: A Guide to the Optional Protocol to the International Covenant on Civil and Political Rights," available online at http://www.austlii.edu.au (accessed July 13, 2009).

5. These reports are submitted every five years to the committee, which also receives information from NGOs and other sources before issuing concluding comments that summarize the human rights situation in the country in relation to the ICCPR and frequently offers suggestions for improving the human rights situation in the country.

6. Available online at http://www.2ohchr.org/English/bodies/HRC/procedure.htm (accessed August 21, 2009); cf. Ghandhi 1998, 401.

7. Available online at http://www.unhchr.ch (accessed July 13, 2009).

8. A recent district court case granted personal jurisdiction over Osama bin Laden, ruling that he could be served "in a place not within any juridical district of the United States" as long as the "means" are "not prohibited by international agreement" (*Mwani et al. v. Bin Laden* 2005).

9. World Bank's Articles of Agreement, Article 3, sec. 5, http://siteresources.worldbank.org/EXTABOUTUS/Resources/IBRD/Articlesofagreement.pdf (accessed August 21, 2009).

10. IADB, "Social Sectors," available online at http://www.iadb.org/news/articledetail.cfm?font=2&artid=2880 (accessed July 13, 2009).

DEBORAH M. WEISSMAN

Global Economics
and Their Progenies

THEORIZING FEMICIDE

IN CONTEXT

The murders of women in Ciudad Juárez require an analysis that considers a range of theories related to political economy and the socioeconomic injustices that global economic liberalization produces. Theories about the murders must be examined through the perspective of daily life in Ciudad Juárez, a city transformed by global economic policies that favor the flow of capital and unfettered markets over the interests of workers drawn to Ciudad Juárez in search of a better life. The city has plunged headlong into an export economy, and its salient characteristic has been the degree to which this change has implicated the demise of social controls. These circumstances invite scrutiny of the murders in Ciudad Juárez (as well as in other localities whose rates of gender violence have soared) with attention to this context.

Such an approach seeks to bring into perspective a more nuanced understanding of the relationship between socioeconomic systems that contribute to and depend on the subordination of poor communities and gender oppression in the form of gender-based murders. Without undertaking this task, femicide is more likely to recede into distant and garish spectacles while the root causes remain unrevealed and unaddressed. Furthermore, any attempt to understand femicides without appreciating the political-economic context may result in the distorted portrayal of Mexicans, or of Juárez residents, as murderous people without morals, governed by corrupt forces, and better kept on the other side of the border.

Economic Liberalization and
the Production of Victims

The living conditions in Ciudad Juárez have disrupted socioeconomic norms, producing a state of crisis and anxiety that impedes social cohesion. Vast numbers of people live in essentially permanent conditions of indigence, without the possibility of relief or prospect of remedy. Indeed, intolerable living conditions have created insecurity and fear. The reach of market influences has extended beyond the economic and entered the realms of daily life. These circumstances have given rise to the conditions described as "a set of social processes by which large bodies of populations are irreversibly kept outside or thrown out of any kind of social contract" (de Sousa Santos 2002, 1050).[1]

This is particularly true for female maquila workers. In the maquila sector, the image of women possessing inherent tendencies within (or outside of) the labor force has been constructed as a means to justify low wages and has taken on new purpose. Although women were previously recruited by maquila managers as ideal workers who worked hard and produced at low cost, new stereotypes have developed related to the characteristics of women on the assembly line. Maquila managers were once concerned with formulating descriptions of women as model labor recruits; now, women are represented as unsuitable for training and unworthy of any investment by virtue of their gender. They are denounced as flighty, irresponsible "girls [without] any responsibilities" who "just come [to Ciudad Juárez] to meet friends, boys, [and] have fun" and are demonized as rash and untrustworthy (Wright 2001a, 103).[2]

Violence is perpetrated against women whose place in the hierarchy of market values renders them readily interchangeable cogs in the wheel of production. They are vulnerable precisely because they are easily expendable; they are deprived of human rights because they are denied their humanity. Women are more easily excluded from the social contract by the employment strategies that cast them as culpable for the general state of labor's exploitation. Low-wage jobs in the labor-intensive export zones have been perceived as the result of the employment of women. Maquila women generally are disparaged as the cause of workplace instability, high turnover, and the justification for labor flexibilization.

In these circumstances, where segments of the population are understood as excluded from the social contract, it is reasonable to perceive the murderers as individuals who believe themselves to be acting out the mandates directed by society and to interpret their actions by the conditions that produced them. This is the social enactment of the disdain for poor working women, their status assigned according to their economic function. This phenomenon occurs in circumstances where market values both predominate and determine human value to the exclusion of other measures of social worth. Such circumstances may be evident in the depiction of female maquila workers whose condition of disposability in the workplace has extended to the shallow graves where their bodies lie.

Economic Liberalization and the Production of Perpetrators

Social disorganization theories propose that structural factors, including economic insecurity, stressful working conditions, the lack of community kinship and absence of social support networks, and uprootedness are the sources of the multiple ways in which communities experience social disruption and fall victim to high crime rates (Shaw and McKay 1969, 315).[3] Conditions of poverty and inequality have been demonstrated to produce "alienated individuals [who] have little to gain by conforming" (Lynch et al 2000, 128). These theories have applicability to Ciudad Juárez, which suffers from structural violence, both physical and psychological, experienced as a deprivation of physical, mental, and emotional needs and which acts to erode the values of poor communities from within.

The factors that underlie social disorganization theories are at work in Ciudad Juárez. Crime has soared as never before in Mexico's history (Dillon 1998b, A1). Migrants who come from the south looking for work, unfamiliar with the north and without the resources of kinship networks, often live in squalor, on the streets, and at the margins of society, where they are vulnerable to crime and drugs. The uninhabitable housing that proliferates in Ciudad Juárez has been associated with a high incidence of violent crime and social disorganization. The transient nature of shantytowns creates residential rootlessness and instability, further contributing to crime and ineffective law enforcement. Communities that suffer from such circumstances are less likely to possess the means to deter crime.

Residents of Ciudad Juárez experience the effects of privatization daily in realms of hopelessness. The structural adjustment policies imposed during the 1980s required privatization of state-sector systems, including transportation, health care, pensions, and much of the education system; the elimination of government subsidies; and the reduction of government spending on those social programs that remained.

The cost of food and medicine has increased; staple items in the Mexican diet have quadrupled in price. Adequate health-care systems are lacking, and the transportation system is overburdened and inadequate. The closing of schools and the lack of health care serve to deny the possibility of a better future for children. Populations suffering such conditions become fearful and experience a loss of control. Powerlessness and resentment loom large.

Workers produce what they cannot buy and live within sight of a well-being they cannot reach. Maquila work is alienating, fragmented, and dangerous, and it has taken its toll on the physical and mental well-being of workers. The pressures of just-in-time production schemes, inequitable wages, lack of opportunity for advancement, and chronic insecurity have contributed to the creation of a frustrated, humiliated, and increasingly hostile workforce. Unemployment in Ciudad Juárez has increased even as maquilas have created jobs in the export zone.

The sociopsychological consequences of structural violence serve to authorize lawlessness as the moral order shifts and societal norms lose their legitimacy. Such circumstances are everywhere in Ciudad Juárez, where crime and violence, particularly street crime, kidnappings, and public killings, have become almost daily occurrences, prompting social commentators to note that "there has been a total crack in society" (Ochoa and Wilson 2001, 3, 6).[4] The increases in suicide, accidents, mental illness, and delinquency have all been attributed to economic policies and market reform.

Parallels in Guatemala

The focus on social disorganization as an explanation for the murders of women is a denigration of neither the people nor the place. Indeed, the pattern of increased violence and rising crime rates in Ciudad Juárez is consistent with recurrent violence in other countries similarly caught up in economic liberalization projects. The murders in Ciudad Juárez are replicated elsewhere, sometimes in similar form, such as the case of the epidemic gender murders of Guatemala. Since 1999, there has been an epidemic of gruesome killings of women in urban areas of Guatemala. Aside from the striking similarities related to the fact of femicide, it is not difficult to discern parallels between these murders and the murders of women in Ciudad Juárez.

The economic transformation is similar: As in Juárez, Guatemala has adopted policies encouraging direct foreign investment and is home to many foreign-owned corporations. As in Ciudad Juárez, women were recruited as the ideal maquila workers. Once employed, they have been subjected to oppressive conditions in the maquilas. They have been discriminated against in terms of wages and training and are considered a fungible workforce that is easily replaced. They are forced to work overtime and subjected to verbal and physical abuse in the maquilas. In addition to the specific abuse and harassment suffered in the workplace, many Guatemalans also suffer the consequences of government decentralization, privatization of industry and services, and the inexorable slide toward an export economy.

Labor protections are not enforced by the state, and there is little evidence that a state apparatus exists for this purpose. Collective action on the part of workers has been met with violent resistance. Young women in their teens and early twenties have been targeted, beaten, and terrorized as a result of anti-union efforts (Rodríguez-Garavito 2005). Many women and girls in Guatemala live with gender-based violence: Violence against women in the family, rape, and sexual harassment in the workplace are commonplace. Women have been victims of horrific crimes followed by wholly inadequate police response and the phenomenon of victim blaming. As in Ciudad Juárez, public-security issues and breakdown in the rule of law are frequently cited as among the main concerns of the population at large.

Of course, there are differences, but these differences still have many of their sources in political-economic considerations. Guatemala experienced a civil war that began in 1962, a conflict not unrelated to the coup sponsored by the U.S. Central Intelligence Agency in 1954, designed to thwart the process of socioeconomic reform that was then under way in Guatemala. The military focused on subduing popular movements, especially labor unions and workers' groups, and committed daily human rights violations to ensure control of economic resources on behalf of corporations such as the United Fruit Company (Holland 2005). The intermittent violence that has plagued Guatemala since 1954 continues to be a function of the response of the army in defense of landowners and corporate interests to the demands of farmers and workers who have struggled for land rights and living wages.

Of the hundreds of thousands of Guatemalans who either were killed or disappeared during the period of civil war and its aftermath, a quarter of the victims were women. Rape and sexual violence were an integral part of the strategy to destroy civil resistance. The current rash of femicides in Guatemala over the past five years bears the same signs of sexual violence that were the hallmarks of the crimes that went unpunished during the civil war. The combination of civil war atrocities that often targeted women and the expendable nature of the female maquila worker contributes to the current epidemic of femicide. As in Ciudad Juárez, formal governance structures are lacking in human and financial resources to protect and promote women at all levels of society (CEDAW 2006, "Concluding Comments," para. 17). Like their counterparts in Ciudad Juárez, women in Guatemala have been rendered subjects ineligible for the protection of law.

The violence against women in Ciudad Juárez and in Guatemala is conceived as a type of deviance; the people of the place are represented as naturally violent. But the idea of deviance to describe the murders may also be used to describe political-economic relationships in effect in export zones throughout Latin America. To put it another way, current global economic policies that depend on the demise of the domestic economy, the consolidation of cheap labor, and the production of poverty are neither natural nor inevitable. Instead, they reflect an outcome with a long history of exploitation of the many for the benefit of the few and should be seen as outside acceptable moral standards. Indeed, the murders of women illustrate that the synthesis of abstract virtues such as free markets and efficiency with privatization and the abandonment of social-welfare programs results in despair and death.

Gender Conflict in Context: Economic Liberalization, Gender Relations, and Backlash

It is crucial to examine the function of gender conflict as a motivation for homicide to obtain a comprehensive account of femicide. Such an analysis must consider the relationship of market institutions and global capital to gender conflicts, thereby avoiding the imaginary divide between the global economy and violence against women. The development of the export economy has restructured relations between men and women in families and communities in ways that affect survival strategies, social expectations, and the very idea of the future. An examination of these changes helps to untangle myths from reality with regard to the concept of gender backlash, and further clarifies how such a phenomenon is produced.

ECONOMIC LIBERALIZATION AND THE PRODUCTION OF BACKLASH

The murders in Ciudad Juárez are often attributed to acts of reprisal against women perceived to be responsible for the loss of men's jobs. Similarly, increased employment of women outside the home is said to contribute to heightened domestic violence within the home. These theories may rest on a distortion of cultural characteristics even as they describe the consequences of the loss of identity and economic devastation as a result of chronic unemployment. To be useful, such theories must begin with an analysis of gender violence that considers the use of gender renderings both historically and in context. In historical terms, Mexican women have often been portrayed as "long-suffering objects of gratuitous violence" (Stern 1995, 7),[5] while the image of Mexican men has been deeply etched in the discourse of machismo, hot-bloodedness, and violence. Similarly, violence in Guatemala has been represented as a natural phenomenon (Grandin 2004). As historical depictions, such constructions are misleading and contribute to the blurring of the relationship of violence to economic conditions (Stern 1995, 155–56; Stevens 1971).[6] These characterizations suggest that crime is cultural and serves to separate gender injustices from questions related to political economy.

Gender relations in Mexico have not been static. Rigid characterizations of the responses to women's employment deny the possibility of a variety of reactions to women's increased role in the labor market, including those that have led to waning machismo. Backlash theories tend to eclipse other studies of gender relations that suggest that men accept women as co-workers and recognize the importance of the contributions of women's wages. If, in fact, gender backlash contributes to the murders of women, there has been little effort to consider how the dynamic is produced or to examine the way in which both men's and women's identities are constructed in current economic conditions. Without such consideration, the possibilities for community agency and solidarity against destructive economic forces are limited.

Escalating conflict in gender relations cannot be attributed simply to the increasing presence of women in the workforce. Women have long worked outside the home, and the jobs they are taking are not all jobs previously held by men (Eckstein 1998; Gonzalez de la Rocha 2001; Stern 1998).[7] Certainly, men whose identities are linked to their ability to provide financially for family needs have been affected by the failure to fulfill such roles. The impact of the loss of the central feature of one's productive life cannot be measured. But as studies demonstrate, it is the cumulative affect of rising unemployment among men coupled with the demise of income-producing alternatives for working-class families in general that have contributed to catastrophic conditions affecting gender relations (Gonzalez de la Rocha 2001).[8]

Without attention to context and absent sufficient interrogation of underlying social structures, backlash theories reflect the type of totalizing thinking about gender violence that stereotype men as universal perpetrators of violence and women as universal victims without agency. Because such theories discourage investigation into the production of gender animosity, they contribute little to an understanding of the sources of gender violence. Rather than sorting through the complicated experiences of violence for women and men, backlash theories, which often offer little more than incomplete descriptions, serve to discourage affinities between poor working men and women.

ECONOMIC LIBERALIZATION AND THE
TRANSFORMATION OF HOUSEHOLD RELATIONS

Notwithstanding the siting of transnational factories in the export zone, economic conditions have deteriorated and unemployment has increased for residents of Ciudad Juárez. The loss of resources and diminution of opportunities to provide for basic family needs have affected households in drastic ways. It has weakened the family as a site for managing economic exchanges outside the workplace. Poor households are no longer able to rely on social-exchange networks and norms of reciprocity that often develop through relationships formed in the workplace but function in the realm of non-work-related activities and personal spaces. These networks extend from household to household and often have served as a means of survival outside of the formal economy through bartering, exchanges, and the sharing of resources. Their loss has created further impoverishment.

Unemployment has disrupted day-to-day patterns and disturbed social dynamics vital to stable familial relationships. The well-being of individuals is deeply affected by the loss of jobs, because a crucial element in their lives is now absent. Those outside the workplace are divested of a range of social interactions in which the ability to communicate and mediate disagreements is exercised. The stigmatization of unemployment and loss of place in the working world engenders a disorientation that affects relations within the family.

The new household regimens that have developed have empowered neither men nor women. The exploitation and discrimination against female workers taint any rewards associated with employment and increase the difficulty of meaningful acquisition of power within families and society. When family income is inadequate for subsistence, women can hardly appreciate the benefits of diminished hierarchies within the family that often occur as a result of their increased employment outside of the home.

Mercedes Gonzalez de la Rocha (2001, 86–87) has examined the impact on families and household dynamics in urban Mexico in which members are dependent on wage labor and who found themselves lacking an adequate subsistence base. She notes that the collapse of routines that affect physical and emotional well-being, coupled with a process of social isolation and stigmatization, has adversely affected households (Gonzalez de la Rocha 2001, 90). Entire families have experienced instability and uncertainty as new economic arrangements have transformed the roles of both men and women. The division of tasks and the fruits of their accomplishments under the previous social structure may not always have been allocated in a manner that served men and women equally, but it did assume purpose and achieve household order, self-respect, and a semblance of economic stability (Stern 1998, 60).[9] Long-established household arrangements based on the performance of certain tasks, whether collectively undertaken or performed according to gender-ordered dictates, have plunged into disarray. The household and familial obligations that bound men and women together in a common endeavor have been rendered either unnecessary or impossible to fulfill. Male members of the family who grew corn and other food staples are no longer able to carry out such tasks. Their migration north in search of work as wage laborers has not been successful, either. Female members on whom the family relied to provide food from family crops have also been drawn into a wage-labor economy inadequate to meet family needs. As the market economy has eviscerated previous household arrangements, there have been few opportunities to develop constructive alternative conventions by which men and women can discharge mutual responsibilities toward each other and their families.

Daily routines have been so disrupted and unemployment is so rampant in Ciudad Juárez that the immigration of household members may appear as the only solution. Households thus suffer further destabilization. The transition from the "resources of poverty" to the "poverty of resources" has hindered family members from fulfilling obligations within the home to each other (Gonzalez de la Rocha 2001, 89). These community characteristics correlate with gender violence. The stress and disorder of the market has been replicated in households and has manifested itself in increased rates of divorce, separation, household volatility, and gender violence.

State Impunity in Context: Economic Liberalization, Governance, and the Rule of Law

Demands on the state from victims' families and various human rights groups expose the acute failures of state systems, including legal systems, that have contributed to gender violence and the lack of accountability for criminal acts. Human rights groups have directed their denunciation against the highest levels of the federal government, as well as against local officials, for failure to investigate the murders in a timely fashion, for negligence and incompetence, and for apparent indifference to women's rights. Such condemnation accurately describes the state's dereliction, lack of political will to correct its deficiencies, and role in contributing to an environment that provides tacit acceptance of the murders. But without considering the determinants of the failures of the state, the implications of the state's inadequacies and the solutions that might address them cannot be fully developed.

Calls for reform urge the state to respond to the crimes, prevent further murders, and provide justice to victims' families primarily through rule-of-law strategies and the restructuring of Mexico's justice system. These demands, however, avoid key questions of political power and obscure from view the *Realpolitik* of market-based governance that has supplanted the functions of state government and redirected legal systems. Economic globalization strategies have impaired the ability of the state to perform traditional functions and contributed to delegitimizing the rule of law as a means of addressing gender violence. Not only has the control of economic systems moved beyond the boundaries of the state, but state systems affecting security and crime have been subordinated to the governance mechanisms of the market.

ECONOMIC LIBERALIZATION AND THE FUNCTIONS OF THE STATE

The demand for state accountability, as formulated in the context of the murders of Ciudad Juárez, evokes a conceptual notion of the state as a concentrated political and juridical entity with the resources and authority to intervene for the benefit of the polity. This account overlooks the ways in which conditions imposed by international financial institutions weaken the state's ability to discharge such functions.[10] Although the sovereign state is understood to be the entity responsible for public safety, the stranglehold of economic liberalization policies and conditions attached to the use of International Monetary Fund and World Bank funds, as well as agreements with the United States requiring cuts in public spending and the privatization of public functions, raises questions related to the capacity of government to carry out its responsibilities. The willingness of Mexico's administration to implement structural-adjustment programs that began almost two decades ago has weakened the power of the government to protect its citizens.

The loss of resources to support public functions, including policing, has an evident role in the inability of the state to respond to the increasing levels of violence. Rising crime has, in part, been attributed to the inability of the attorney general to handle a sufficient number of criminal cases (Davis 2004; López-Montiel 2000).[11] In some Mexican cities, the salaries of the police are among the lowest; officers must often use their own pay to purchase their uniforms, and guns and police equipment are lacking (López-Montiel 2000, 86). State tax policies, which could potentially mitigate the problems of police and judicial corruption associated with poor pay and lack of investigative resources, are manipulated by international financial institutions and transnational corporations. Economic globalization that transfers profit on exports out of Mexico has made it all but impossible to acquire and redirect wealth to the state institutions on which victims rely for effective law enforcement. Gustavo Elizondo, the mayor of Ciudad Juárez from 1998–2001, described the paradox of the export zone: "Every year we get poorer and poorer, even though we create more and more wealth" (quoted in Thompson 2001, A1).

These conditions have produced a mass exodus of law enforcement from city and state police agencies, and the situation is expected to worsen (Corchado and Sandoval 2004b).[12] As the crime rate increases, the criminal justice system remains incapable of providing protection to residents. Resources with which to train staff in the use of forensic laboratory equipment and to pay for crime-prevention technology are insufficient. Crime investigators have been laid off, and the police academy for training new recruits for Ciudad Juárez has been periodically closed (Corchado and Sandoval 2004b; Nathan 2004). The low pay for law-enforcement officials creates ideal conditions for widespread corruption among police officers.

Moreover, police privatization schemes are proliferating throughout Mexico (Santillán 2002, 23–25).[13] This has led to gaps in policing authority, as well as to violence and corruption in the absence of public accountability. However, police security among the maquila-owned factories is state of the art: The areas are fenced in and guarded around the clock by police and private security guards.

Certainly, difficulties with police practices are not new. There is a history in Mexico of police complicity with criminals in a range of illegal activities. Yet it would be unduly facile to describe the current situation in Mexico as one that wholly emerges from this experience. Current economic policies that reduce public funds for training and for police salaries and that have replaced corporatist policies with authoritarianism, as well as the increased militarization of society, have contributed to the present crisis of corruption in law enforcement agencies. As the authority of the state has weakened, corruption has increased, and organized crime has developed an "alternate state" (Periera and Davis 2000, 3, 6).[14] Militarization, repressive police tactics, and state impunity in response to the increased violence are not only a consequence of the growing insecurity brought about by current economic policies but are also a result of the reduction in the police force.

Demanding that the state act while ignoring challenges to economic policies masks how poverty and crime are generated and fails to recognize that the state's efforts to respond to the problems have been severely undermined. Strategies for crime prevention and human rights protections can thus no longer be linked to the political project of a state whose authority often falls short in its ability to solve problems created by actors and circumstances outside its boundaries. Transnational corporations that contribute to the conditions in which human rights abuses are committed may act in ways that avoid the reach of traditional state governance. Such institutions often exact conditions from host countries that facilitate the maximization of profit with little regard to costs to human rights. The dependence of the state on transnational economic actors weakens government incentives to prevent and seek redress for human rights violations. Under these circumstances, demands to enhance law enforcement without combating the economic conditions that contribute to corruption and malfeasance may only serve to encourage the development of a police state with excessive and unregulated powers and use of torture. In the end, it may be that the term *impunity* ought to describe not simply the state but also the multinational corporate actors who act contrary to the interests of the majority of Mexicans.

ECONOMIC LIBERALIZATION AND THE RULE OF LAW

The murders in Ciudad Juárez have been largely attributed to the shortcomings of Mexico's legal system. Mexican courts have been described as weak, and corruption and malfeasance have plagued judicial processes (Periera and Davis 2000). As a result of the pressures of local and international human rights groups, a federally appointed special prosecutor was assigned in January 2004 to examine the legal system's handling of the criminal cases, and federal police were authorized to share responsibility for security in Ciudad Juárez (Bourdreaux 2003, A3).[15] Within six months, the special prosecutor issued a report with findings of at least eighty-one instances of official misconduct within the justice system.[16] But progress has been insufficient, and recommendations call for increased authority for the special prosecutor, the incorporation of gender perspectives into policing and judicial practices, and judicial review of those cases that have already been prosecuted.

The legal system continues to be criticized for the failure to treat the murders as a pattern of violence against women rather than as individual criminal acts. The legal system's failure to provide redress has been described along gender fault lines, with little reference to the relation between the rule of law and economic globalization. While these proposals advance important and necessary themes in ending violence against women, they do not address the relationship between the legal system and new economic policies that are at the root of the social costs of economic inequalities and other conditions that give rise to the murders.

Transformation of Mexico's National Laws   Mexico's legal system has undergone significant transformation since the 1980s. During the mid-1990s, legal reforms were implemented pursuant to World Bank directives to ensure the responsiveness of Mexico's judicial system to economic-liberalization strategies (Dakolis 1996; Gilman 2003; Slover 1999; J. Vargas 2004; Zamora 1995). The reforms urged a strengthened Constitutional Court system, more independent judges, efficient administration of justice, and improved access to the justice system. Implementation of legal reform, however, has been driven by market needs, primarily concerned with defining and enforcing private rights, resolving investment and expropriation disputes, and creating legal mechanisms to facilitate market reforms. In this regard, lawmaking and legal reforms have been undertaken as a crucial project to accomplish the tasks of economic globalization.

To attract foreign investors, Mexico has had to alter its national legal processes. It has committed to binding privatized investor-state arbitration. New laws opened Mexico's natural resources and banking system to foreign investment and control. Similarly, Mexico's once strong consumer-protection laws have been weakened.

Labor laws with the greatest potential to provide safeguards for maquila workers have been undermined. Labor laws in Mexico are of historic significance and are known as some of the most expansive and progressive in the world. Federal labor laws derive from Mexico's Constitution, which provides comprehensive protection for workers, a focus on class interests instead of individual rights, and protection of workers from management. Mexican labor laws target women for specific protection, providing benefits throughout pregnancy and during the breast-feeding period and providing the right to day care. Mexico has also ratified several international treaties protecting workers' rights.

Nevertheless, these formal rights have not been enforced in Mexico. Since the economic liberalization trend began, new arguments have been made for reforming labor law in terms that suggest that strong labor protections undermine the ability of transnational firms to lower costs and compete effectively. Proponents of economic liberalization and institutions financing such projects have pushed for reform of labor laws and reduction of workers' benefits to conform to the new employment strategies of the export zone. Mexican labor-law specialists have reported that U.S. labor practices, which serve to discourage union-organizing drives, have been adopted with increasing frequency.

Such reform has not been easy to accomplish, given the constitutional nature of labor-law protections, but changes have been implemented that encroach on workers' rights. As advocated by the World Bank, pension systems have been fully privatized. Monitoring of occupational health standards has moved to voluntary compliance mechanisms, and while domestic industries have attempted to cooperate with such programs, maquilas have responded poorly, if at all. Laws governing workers' housing have also been weakened. In 2004, former Mexican President Vicente Fox proposed a labor-reform package that would have curtailed workers' rights to strike, to bargain collectively, and to call for a vote to gain representational rights or supplant a pre-existing union (Human Rights Watch 2004).[17] Although the proposal did not gain momentum, it would have been a major setback for Mexican workers.

Even without formal legal changes, the practice of disregarding existing laws has been invigorated with new strategies formulated by transnational corporate management. Rights to maternity leave and child care have been undermined by corporate policies that seek to reduce labor costs. Mostly U.S. maquilas have defended their discriminatory hiring practices against pregnant job applicants by claiming that Mexican laws only apply to current employees. This distinction is disavowed by Mexican labor lawyers and is an analysis at odds with U.S. labor laws. Other protections, such as overtime and the legal work week, are rendered inapplicable because workers are forced to work excess hours to earn sufficient wages on which to survive, and thus have no incentive to seek redress.

NAFTA and the Rule of Law   In addition to domestic labor reforms, supranational legal developments have altered legal rights for Mexican workers. Although the North American Free Trade Agreement (NAFTA) does not incorporate new substantive labor-law standards, its corresponding labor-side accord, the North American Agreement on Labor Cooperation (NAALC), does address such issues.[18] The NAALC, which is said to encourage parties to enforce their own domestic labor laws, has been criticized as an administrative labyrinth that fails to bind private employers and provides workers with no tangible solutions for labor-law violations.

The NAALC's jurisdiction covers eleven enumerated areas of labor law. Nevertheless, it is nearly impossible to ascend the NAALC's administrative levels, where enforcement powers may materialize. At the higher levels of the dispute mechanism, protections for workers narrow, and certain categories of protection are eliminated from review. Moreover, the most progressive Mexican labor laws, which are not recognized in the United States, lose their utility, as only "mutually recognized labor laws" may be reviewed. There is no jurisdiction to adjudicate violations related to the rights to form a union and to strike and those against unlawful termination or employment discrimination.

No cases affecting core rights of workers, from a denial of the right to unionize to wage claims, hazardous working conditions, and discrimination against pregnant women, have made their way through all of the enforcement levels of the NAALC process (Holt and Waller 2004).[19] Female workers have not benefited from the NAALC because it limits claims regarding employment discrimination and equal pay to the second tier of labor rights and, therefore, renders them ineligible for the imposition of sanctions. Labor issues affecting women, such as family leave, child care, discriminatory treatment by unions, and sexual harassment, are excluded from the agreement altogether. The NAALC's disappointing results have been attributed to the reluctance of the United States to pressure the Mexican government because of concerns that labor protections interfere with economic liberalization strategies and the needs of transnational corporations.

Law reform has been accomplished not only by the refashioning of state courts and processes that have constitutionalized market-driven ideologies, but also by the relocation of adjudication processes to sites outside the nation-states into realms controlled by private transnational institutions and actors "organized around one great lex mercatoria" (Sassen 2000, 38). These reforms have taken precedence during the emergence of the export zone and have contributed to the conditions in which the murders of women occur, indicating the need for context and specificity in making demands for improvements to the law.

Conclusion

It is difficult to set forth blueprints for ending the egregious conditions plaguing Ciudad Juárez and Guatemala where the circumstances of economic globalization are manifested in their most extreme manner. The structural formation of the export economy seems to defy consideration of even modest alternatives. As Chandra Talpade Mohanty (1997, 3–4) has noted, "Almost total saturation of the processes of capitalist domination makes it hard to envision forms of feminist resistance which would make a real difference in the daily lives of poor women." Furthermore, the difficulty in framing an analysis that implicates political economy in the murders of women in Mexico and Guatemala is made more challenging by the need to propose legal solutions that might address these concerns.

This is undoubtedly an ambitious project. It requires incorporating current scholarship on the effect of economic liberalization on legal systems and the rule of law to gender violence and the murders at issue. It demands attention to existing global governance structures in which transnational corporations have supplanted national governments as the determinants of economic and institutional models, as well as their corresponding legal frameworks. Failure to attempt to do so would be tantamount to capitulation to such problems and to abandoning the law as a realm within which to contest these circumstances.

Human rights organizations that demand stronger legal systems in response to femicides must first acknowledge the ways in which law has acquiesced to market forces and thus contributed to the socioeconomic conditions that produce violence. The task must be to invigorate the debate about the relationship of human rights and legal systems to economic globalization and develop approaches that will raise the prominence of gender, poverty, and inequality in the search for legal solutions. Advocates must use the framework of human rights law not only to criticize the role of the state, but also to hold accountable transnational corporations and international financial institutions as violators of such rights. In doing so, it is not sufficient to graft gender perspectives onto the current laws that govern market relations without questioning the premises that underlie economic liberalization.

Notes

Substantial portions of this chapter were originally published in "The Political Economy of Violence: Rethinking the Gender-Based Murders of Ciudad Juárez," *North Carolina Journal of International Law and Commercial Regulation* 30 (2005).

1. These conditions are described as "societal fascism."
2. Quoting a maquila supervisor who denounced female workers for their lack of family orientation.

3. Clifford Shaw's and Henry McKay's theories have been ratified by current research, which focuses on the role of community characteristics as opposed to those of individuals in understanding crime (see Meares 2002).

4. Quoting Mexican writer and journalist Carlos Monsiváis with regard to the impact of neoliberal reforms on the unprecedented crime wave affecting Mexicans.

5. Stern characterizing this notion as a stereotype with a grain of truth.

6. Stern suggests that such stereotypes avoid the critical issues involving the social analysis of masculinity, economic, social and power relations. Stevens criticizes the social science literature of machismo for its inevitable description of the Mexican male as aggressive and antisocial.

7. Eckstein notes that women in Latin America in the nineteenth century, like women in the twentieth century, have always worked but also always earned less than men. This is not meant to dispute that, historically, there was a rigid system of gender subordination in Mexico, as Stern notes.

8. Describing household instability and diminished survival capacity due to a lack of resources in poor urban households in Mexico.

9. Describing gender patterns of hierarchical complementarity by which men and women performed separate but essential and interdependent household functions.

10. For an examination of the ways in which global economics interferes with the role of the state generally, see Ewelukwa 2002, 603, 617. Saskia Sassen (2000) notes that structural adjustment programs entail the "4 'Ds' — deregulation, deflation, devaluation, and denationalization" (Ewelukwa 2002, 612) and affect the role of the states with regard to public welfare functions.

11. Davis notes budgetary constraints as a factor inhibiting law enforcement and the judiciary's ability to properly respond to crime.

12. Corchado and Sandoval note that in May 2004, more than five hundred state and local police serving Ciudad Juárez left the force.

13. Santillán notes that the emphasis on free trade and open markets has led to the rise of private security forces employed by foreign companies, which have found easy profitability.

14. Pereira and Davis describe the shrinking and decentralization of the state, along with increased repression.

15. Bourdreaux notes the use of federal agents to assist local police.

16. In July 2003, President Vicente Fox announced a plan to enhance law-enforcement efforts in Ciudad Juárez that included the appointment of a special prosecutor and special commissioner, both of whom have released reports after initial investigations (Comisión para Prevenir y Erradicar la Violencia contra las Mujeres en Ciudad Juárez, *Primer informe, Fiscalía Especial para la Atencíon de Delitos Relacionados con los homicidios de mujeres en el Municipio de Juárez, Chihuahua*, June 2004, available online at http://www.almargen.com.mx/archivo/fefuno.pdf, accessed May 11, 2005).

17. Human Rights Watch describes the terms of the proposals that would

make certifying union registration much more difficult and would require strikers to publicly disclose their names, inviting retaliation.

18. North American Agreement on Labor Cooperation, September 14, 1993, Article 27-41, 32 ILM 1499, 1502, entered into force January 1, 1994. For an analysis of the NAALC, see Otero 1995.

19. Holt and Waller note that of the twenty-six cases sent to the National Administrative Office (NAO) of the U.S. Department of Labor, none has moved past the first stage of investigation, report, and non-binding recommendations. The NAO was created to handle cases filed under the NAFTA labor agreement. For a listing of NAFTA claims filed as of 2001 and their outcome, see Human Rights Watch 2001.

Searching for Accountability on the Border

JUSTICE FOR THE WOMEN OF

CIUDAD JUÁREZ

The driving force of Ciudad Juárez is the community of corporations running a number of factories that employ a large number of the residents of this fluid city. Young women migrate to Juárez at a rate of forty thousand to sixty thousand a year to seek jobs in the maquiladoras, which pay higher wages than elsewhere in Mexico (Livingston 2004). The reputation of Juárez and other industry-led border cities would lead one to believe that law is only to be found within the walls of the *maquila*. However, this "law" is the one set by the corporation, not necessarily in compliance with international or national labor standards. Outside the factories, drugs, crime, prostitution, and rape are an everyday reality. To better understand Juárez, one must understand what life is like for a majority of its residents: "Many of the residents of Juárez live on the outskirts of the city in colonias, or shantytowns, in makeshift houses constructed from discarded wooden pallets, cardboard boxes, or cement, without running water or telephones" (Livingston 2004, 63). With crime and poverty a daily part of life in Juárez, one could ask: Are these contributing causes of feminicide in the city?

   This chapter focuses on a dimension of accountability that departs from the following: Who is responsible for protecting women in Juárez from this sordid violence? Regardless of their age or gender, these residents deserve a safe place to live and work. Is the government of Mexico doing all it can to prevent these crimes? Are corporations contributing to the rule of law or distributive justice in Juárez? Should they? Who is liable, and who has an affirmative duty to protect in this situation?

Framework: The Three Dimensions of Justice

In attempting to look at the issue of feminicide in Juárez in a multidimensional way, and in a spirit of not trying to minimize the dilemma, I will use Rama Mani's (2002) framework of the three dimensions of justice. Mani tells us that in post-conflict situations, we must address three dimensions of injustice, which include symptom, consequence, and cause, to rebuild through three dimensions of justice, including legal, rectificatory, and distributive justice. Though the city is not a post-conflict context, I would contend that Mani's approaches to justice are instructive and applicable in a context where massive human rights abuses are seemingly unending and irresolvable. This framework is a useful tool in analyzing what can be done to find justice for the crimes of violence perpetrated against women in Juárez, where an acute division of labor and a severe unequal distribution of wealth are the backdrop of these injustices.

This chapter will focus on two potential strategies for legal justice: through the Inter-American system to enforce state obligations to protect its citizens, and through the U.S. legal system to demand corporate accountability in border industries. These two legal strategies are by no means comprehensive legal justice solutions. They are meant only to be complementary to domestic mechanisms and to be alternatives in the instance where there has been an exhaustion of remedies through national mechanisms or where remedies at the state level are futile because any resolution is unreasonably prolonged within Mexico. The case of futility for the murders in Juárez arguably has been long established. The paper will not explore measures for rectificatory justice, one of the three forms of justice in the framework, which, according to Mani (2002, 87), "contends with the claims for justice arising from violations committed" and is meant to punish the perpetrators and vindicate the victims. To do this kind of exploration, a more complete understanding of who has committed the crimes would be necessary but unavailable in the case of Juárez. In looking toward measures of distributive justice, I will look at possible state-level and community-level interventions calling for a genuine investment in infrastructure by Juárez's resident corporations as well as by the state, both of whom reap the greatest rewards of a cheap gendered labor force. While exploring these issues, those focusing on Juárez must also recognize the many attempts seeking social reconciliation already being undertaken autochthonously, whether through the painting of crosses on lampposts or through songs written by musicians for the recognition of the problem.

Mani (2002, 47) cautions that "justice . . . is not reducible to rights. . . . Rights are a partial but incomplete expression of justice." Strengthening the rights of women in Juárez and implementing measures for the enforcement of these rights are only part of the answer to the dilemma of feminicide. When a community has experienced a loss of trust as a result of a merciless disrespect for each other's right to exist, whether that is the result of war or serial murders, it is difficult to structure solutions that will allow the community to repair itself. According to Mani (2002, 170), part of healing should include approaches that seek "incremental maximalism," which, for Mani, "implies a framework which embeds the rule of law in justice, human rights and values, and which concerns itself with both its form and its substance, with both its institutions and its ethos." It is through a concern for holistic solutions that this chapter looks to the community — its strongest actors and its resources — to identify measures that go beyond the prosecution of the persecutors or repeated talk of reinforcing human rights, particularly when this is not immediately possible.

Strategies for Litigation and Legal Justice

One means for attaining legal justice in the case of Juárez is to bring a claim against the government of Mexico within the regional human rights justice systems.

REGIONAL STRATEGY: THE INTER-AMERICAN SYSTEM

Before filing a case in the Inter-American system, there are a number of limitations and barriers to consider. First, only a state (party to the Inter-American Convention on Human Rights who has accepted jurisdiction of the Inter-American Court of Human Rights) or the Inter-American Commission on Human Rights (IACHR) may bring a claim before the court. Second, a case before the court would be limited against the state as defendant, precluding any litigation against corporate actors or individual perpetrators (non-corporate actors) through this system. However, any person or group can file a petition to the IACHR, the sister body to the court, alleging a violation of the convention or of the American Declaration of the Rights and Duties of Man (Weissbrodt 2001, 598). Thus, the case for victims of Juárez may be sought under the auspices of a nongovernmental organization (NGO) or by the victims, who would have to submit a petition to the commission in the hope that the commission will recommend the claim to the court. Also, the commission "serves as a forum of last resort when national courts do not adequately protect the rights guaranteed under the Inter-American human rights scheme" (Roht-Arriaza 2005, 102).

This course of action has been significantly explored, and attempts to bring claims before the commission by individuals and organizations have been made. These attempts have had some success, as shown in the commission's response to the situation of feminicide in Juárez, but not all results of these various attempts are readily apparent from the published reports by the commission (IACHR 2003b). Nevertheless, it is clear that, "despite local and international pressure, Mexico has failed to adequately investigate the murders and punish the perpetrators, and the murders continue" (Robinson 2005, 167–68). Therefore, holding the Mexican state accountable for its failures to investigate and resolve this situation is an appropriate case to seek before the Inter-American system.

The IACHR has, "upon notice by individuals and organizations about the Juárez murders, carried out an on-site investigation into the murders" (Robinson 2005, 167) and submitted a report entitled "The Situation of the Rights of Women in Ciudad Juárez, Mexico: The Right to Be Free from Violence and Discrimination (IACHR 2003b). As of now, it is not clear whether the commission has declared any individual petitions admissible to the court,[1] though it discusses within its report that it was "processing petitions 104/02, 281/02, 282/02 and 283/02 in accordance with its Rules of Procedure, and evaluating others as they are received" (IACHR 2003b, para. 26, supra note 9). In its report, the commission eloquently explains the failure by the state in its response to the feminicide: "The response of the authorities to these crimes has been markedly deficient. There are two aspects of this response that are especially relevant. On the one hand, the vast majority of the killings remain in impunity; approximately twenty percent have been the subject of prosecution and conviction. On the other hand, almost as soon as the rate of killings began to rise, some of the officials responsible for investigation and prosecution began employing a discourse that in effect blamed the victim for the crime" (IACHR 2003b, para. 4, supra note 9). The issuance of this report should by no means serve as the final measure by the Inter-American system. Where the state has failed to provide sufficient redress to the families of the victims and its measures for prosecuting people have been obviously deficient, the commission to some extent has strengthened the evidence needed to hold the government of Mexico accountable for its failure to protect its citizens before the court.

Four years after the issuance of the commission's report, there is additional reason to consider referring a case to the court to make a finding against Mexico and to push compliance on the state in its investigations and handling of the situation generally. The urgency of the issue continues.[2] In addition to the commission's report on Juárez, a number of reports by human rights organizations now exist to substantiate a claim against Mexico. NGOs such as Amnesty International have issued their own findings that link the case of Juárez to state inaction or inadequate action. In its report "Intolerable Killings," Amnesty International (2003) explains:

> The failure of the competent authorities to take action to investigate these crimes, whether through indifference, lack of will, negligence or inability, has been blatant over the last ten years. Amnesty International has documented unjustifiable delays in the initial investigations, the period when there is a greater chance of finding the woman alive and identifying those responsible, and a failure to follow up evidence and witness statements which could be crucial. In other cases, the forensic examinations carried out have been inadequate, with contradictory and incorrect information being given to families about the identity of bodies, thereby causing further distress to them and disrupting their grieving process. Other irregularities include the falsification of evidence and even the alleged use of torture by officers from the Chihuahua State Judicial Police, in order to obtain information and confessions of guilt.

The incompetence of the state police and legal authorities seems to encourage crime and feminicide on the border. That the continuation of the severity and the number of murders occurring has not abated is in large part due to the impunity now associated with violence against women more generally, not limited to within the borders of Mexico. Esther Chavez, an activist in Juárez, believes the murders are committed not by a "serial killer," but by countless men who rape, torture, and murder because they know they can get away with it (Nathan 2003). There is no fear of being held accountable by law enforcement officials for harming, torturing, or even killing women.

Even Mexican authorities have issued reports citing their own failure in the investigations and protection of women:

> Five years after rights groups started tracking feminicide in Ciudad Juárez, the National Commission for Human Rights issued a report charging gross irregularities and general negligence in state investigations including the mis-identification of corpses, failure to obtain expert tests on forensic evidence, failure to conduct autopsies or obtain semen analysis (the first and only semen analysis was taken in 1999), failure to file written reports, incompetence in keeping records of the rising tide of women murders. As a

result, the newly elected [Institutional Revolutionary Party] governor of Chihuahua appointed Suly Ponce as special prosecutor for crimes against women in the State of Chihuahua to head the investigation. Shortly before she took office, 500 kilos of the victims' clothing were mysteriously incinerated. (Fregoso 2000, 137–38)

With the mounting evidence against Mexico, a case for its inability to prevent the feminicide and its botched investigations seem well grounded.

Since the historic case of *Velásquez-Rodriguez v. Honduras* (1988), the Inter-American Court of Human Rights, using the American Convention on Human Rights, has held governments responsible in instances of disappearance where the government has failed to exercise due diligence to prevent, investigate, and punish those responsible. In the case of Juárez, this same approach has been taken. The argument being that the state is responsible for a failure to resolve these crimes. It is now generally understood that "acts or omissions of non-state actors are themselves generally not attributable (to the state); however, the state may incur responsibility if it fails to exercise due diligence in preventing or reacting to such acts or omissions" (Hessbruegge 2004, 265, 268). According to one analysis of the applicability of the due diligence doctrine in Juárez:

> Under Article 1(1) of the Convention, the Velasquez court found two obligations, the obligation "to respect the rights and freedoms," and the obligation to "ensure" the free and full exercise of rights. . . . In the Juárez murders, while there is evidence of police and official corruption and complicity, and perhaps even participation, the evidence may not be strong enough to hold Mexico accountable under the first obligation of Article 1(1), to "respect the rights" of citizens. Mexico's refusal to prevent hundreds of murders, begin or complete investigations, and punish perpetrators does, however, violate the second obligation of Article 1(1), to "ensure" the rights of its citizens. (Robinson 2005, 185–86)

I would contend that holding Mexico accountable for failure to "respect the rights and freedoms" of the victims and their families has now become a strong claim for the continued failure to provide redress for these violations. Therefore, the court could find the state responsible in a failure of the two obligations espoused by the *Velásquez* court. Decisions by the Inter-American Court of Human Rights since *Velásquez* would seem to support this position. Through these cases, "the Inter-American Court of Human Rights has decided that the Inter-American Convention on Human Rights obliges states to exercise due diligence to prevent attacks on a person's life, physical integrity, or liberty. Moreover, states are required to punish any violation of these rights and must attempt, if possible, to restore the right violated and provide compensation for damages resulting from the violation" (Hessbruegge 2004, 275) The Special Rapporteur on Violence against Women, has explained, "States must promote and protect the human rights of women and exercise *due diligence*: To prevent, investigate and punish acts of all forms of [violence against women] whether in the home, the workplace, the community or society, in custody or in situations of armed conflict" (United Nations 2003b). Due diligence is therefore a substantial argument against the state of Mexico in this case.

One of the greatest obstacles to bringing a successful case before the Inter-American system is a lack of a uniform strategy by the victims of Juárez.[3] It is important for litigators and advocates for the victims to keep in mind that "the Commission will not examine a complaint which essentially duplicates a petition pending or previously settled by itself or by another international governmental organization of a similar nature. Where a case is opened but the basic requisites . . . are not shown to have been met, the Commission will declare the case inadmissible" (Weissbrodt 2001, 594). It would seem that one of the central and most immediate issues for victim's groups to focus on would be to come to an agreement as to how to bring an action on behalf of the victims as a class similarly situated, rather than incrementally through individual petitioners. The case is severely hindered, as it would present the problem of duplication and therefore inadmissibility until consensus can be reached by the victims' representatives.

BUILDING A CASE USING THE ALIEN TORT CLAIMS ACT

Where a case against the state of Mexico is well established and quite acceptable or seen as logical from a human rights perspective, an avenue far less explored is legal justice through litigation against corporations in Juárez. Corporations that run maquiladoras are benefiting from an atmosphere of impunity that exists in Juárez. Maquiladoras employ cheap labor that is readily available in Juárez, partly because of the lack of law and pervasive poverty in the city. Not only do these corporations currently not bear any responsibility for the crimes taking place just outside their factories, but the maquilas themselves are often the site of discrimination and exploitation of labor that goes on unchecked within. While there are rules for conducting business inside the maquila (set by the heads of these corporations and by treaty agreements), the corporations are not generally concerned with complying with international labor standards that are not enforced by the international community or the national governments that host them. Corporations that locate their factories in Mexico go largely unregulated by the state because of negotiated agreements for deregulation of industries, particularly under the North American Free Trade Agreement. Taking advantage of and exploiting cheap labor is now part of global enterprises. In Juárez, "The maquiladoras primarily employ young women. The managers' claim that women are better suited to factory work because of their manual dexterity and their ability to tolerate tedious and repetitive work. . . . In addition to paying the female workers cheaply for long hours . . . the maquiladoras also monitor their female employees more closely than male employees. Before hiring new female employees, managers require medical exams and often inquire about their employees' sexual activities. Pregnancy tests are routinely administered" (Livingston 2004, 62). Where these same policies would be prohibited in the home countries of these corporations, or in the countries where these corporations are incorporated, the unregulated policies that they can promulgate in foreign jurisdictions are often viewed by corporate management as one of the assets to taking their business to places like Juárez,[4] or other places in the world, where governments are willing to sacrifice the rights of their labor force for business.

There is little doubt that corporations located in this border city are in the best position to facilitate the rule of law in Juárez because they are the most powerful actors in this community. They have the resources to potentially empower and strengthen the "tripod or triad of the justice system — the judiciary, the police, and prisons" in the community they inhabit (Mani 2005, 56). They enjoy even more power and wealth than the actual local and statewide authorities. Bringing legal action against these corporations would help prevent these powerful actors from avoiding responsibility, even if indirect, for the crimes committed in their "own backyards."[5] Such litigation would also be one small step toward achieving legal justice in a community whose livelihood is extremely dependent on globalized corporate industry. Placing issues of power aside, there is sufficient room to deduce that the murders and the crimes that proliferate in Juárez are an indirect and (though contested) direct consequence to the business and the exploitation that dominates life in Juárez. Deborah Weissman best explains the direct relationship: "[Ciudad] Juárez has been transformed by economic liberalization policies. Populations have been dislocated; workers, particularly women, have been exploited. A comprehensive explanation for the murders in Cd. Juárez must take into account the demise of organizations that protect workers, the degradation of physical space, the lack of resources for social services, and the conditions that contribute to drug trafficking" (quoted in Weissman 2005, 802). Because of the recent history and impact of these corporations in Juárez, there is a direct responsibility for conditions they have helped create. Corporations have a duty to protect their workers and a lesser, though equally important, responsibility to contribute to the protection of the residents in the sphere these businesses occupy. Where the state has been set aside for the rule of business, it must be asked, why is it not appropriate, both legally and morally, to require that the corporations be accountable for a failure of protection in the community they dominate, in the same manner we would attribute such responsibility to a state?

One potential course of action to demand that corporations help combat these abuses and provide protection is through the Alien Tort Claims Act (ATCA).[6] It states, "The district courts shall have original jurisdiction of any civil action by an alien for a tort only, committed in violation of the law of nations or a treaty of the United States." ATCA is a jurisdictional statute that does not explicitly define the type of claims that may be brought under it within its text. However, there are now cases using ATCA against corporate complicity.[7] In fact, U.S. courts have applied ATCA to non-state actors since 1995.[8] To make a claim based on corporate complicity would require that "a corporation be held accountable for acts committed by its partner in a joint venture, which it knew about, benefited from, abetted and tacitly if not explicitly approved even if they were not directly committed by its employees" (Earth Rights International 2004, 19). The claims that could be brought against these corporations would be based on the concepts and doctrines of tortious negligence, failure to protect, and aiding and abetting. In Juárez, corporations are, at a minimum, benefiting from the unregulated state of affairs around them, and at most contributing directly to the murders by inaction.

Corporations have general knowledge and awareness of the abuses that go on around them in Juárez. Moreover, they are fully aware of the lack of control by authorities over the situation because these cases have been widely reported. It would seem a logical though difficult step to argue that these corporations have an affirmative duty to act, especially when they are partially filling a vacuum of power in this case. A model for an ATCA claim against corporations in Juárez can be found in the case of *Doe v. Unocal* (2005): "The case against [the] California energy company Unocal, brought by villagers from Burma who were enslaved, tortured, and raped by Burmese military forces providing security for Unocal's pipeline in that country, has gone farther than any other corporate case." In that case, "Plaintiffs claimed that Unocal aided and abetted Burma's military regime . . . in the human rights abuses committed to further the joint venture, a natural gas pipeline built through indigenous territory in southern Burma" (Earth Rights International 2004, 18). Similar, though not identical, claims could be made in a case against corporations by victims of feminicide. Litigators must keep in mind that where direct evidence of complicity was available in Unocal, it is not as readily apparent that similar evidence is available in Juárez. This may present a significant obstacle in a potential claim.

To form the foundation for a case, moreover, a violation of the law of nations must be identified to establish a sufficient basis for the claim using ATCA. Framing a crime within this context calls for some creativity and an expanded interpretation of the current framework for claims under corporate accountability cases. One key question to answer is whether negligence to protect their own workers, and the larger community these corporations inhabit, could be classified as a violation of the law of nations sufficient to hold corporate actors responsible? Should it be? In practice, these are separate questions with very different answers. The first question requires that we work within the given structure and interpretations of the law to find claims allowable under ATCA. It is also safe to assume that the answer would be in the negative, *unless* direct links could be made between corporate knowledge and the actual murders. The second question allows some exploration of international instruments to develop these violations.

International instruments are one place to start conceptually developing "the duty to protect" by corporations. The Organization for Economic Cooperation and Development (OECD) has developed a set of recommendations to corporations in its OECD Guidelines for Multinational Enterprises," to which potential litigators can turn to formulate the kinds of duties for which corporations in Juárez should be held accountable.[9] It is important to note that these guidelines are currently not obligations on corporations. However, this kind of litigation could help move these standards toward a direction of transforming these norms into obligations. According to the guidelines' general policies,

> enterprises should take fully into account established policies in the countries in which they operate, and consider the views of other stakeholders. In this regard, enterprises should:
>
> 1. Contribute to economic, social and environmental progress with a view to achieving sustainable development.
>
> 2. Respect the human rights of those affected by their activities consistent with the host government's international obligations and commitments.
>
> 3.Encourage local capacity building through close co-operation with the local community, including business interests, as well as developing the

enterprise's activities in domestic and foreign markets, consistent with the need for sound commercial practice.

4. Encourage human capital formation, in particular by creating employment opportunities and facilitating training opportunities for employees.

5. Refrain from seeking or accepting exemptions not contemplated in the statutory or regulatory framework related to environmental, health, safety, labor, taxation, financial incentives, or other issues.

6. Support and uphold good corporate governance principles and develop and apply good corporate governance practices.

7. Develop and apply effective self-regulatory practices and management systems that foster a relationship of confidence and mutual trust between enterprises and the societies in which they operate. (OECD 2000)

These guidelines provide the concepts and language to begin to formulate a claim. Unfortunately, even these guidelines lack substantive force. They are diluted guidance in situations where the states in which the corporations operate have weak policies for protecting their own citizens from gender-based violence, where these policies merely "guide" corporations to take "account of the policies of the countries in which they work." However, the first three points under the general policies do help bolster a claim that corporations located in Juárez should in fact be responsible for strengthening the community mechanisms of Juárez. Other international instruments, including the Universal Declaration of Human Rights (UDHR) and the International Covenant on Economic and Social and Cultural Rights (ICESCR), provide further assistance in developing a claim. In these documents, a right to work and a right to work in safe conditions are recognized. Article 23(1) of the UDHR provides "the right to work, to free choice of employment, to just and favorable conditions of work and to protection against unemployment." Article 7 of the ICESCR recognizes "the right of everyone to the enjoyment of just and favorable conditions of work," including "safe and healthy working conditions." The difficulty with basing a claim against corporations solely on these instruments is that these are obligations on states and not private parties, such as corporations. However, the UDHR and the ICESCR might provide some conceptual guidance and support in formulating violations in a claim for litigation.

The U.S. Supreme Court recently affirmed that violations of definite, widely accepted international norms are actionable under ATCA (Earth Rights International 2004, 6). The Supreme Court demarcates the limits of ATCA within the decision of *Sosa v. Alvarez-Machain* (2004; see Earth Rights International 2004, 6). Through *Sosa*, "The ruling . . . ensures that there will neither be an explosion of ATCA cases, nor will ATCA become a general corporate accountability measure. Rather, it will serve as a tool for corporate liability — and justice for victims — in a limited set of circumstances. As such, ATCA will continue to deter corporate complicity in severe human rights crimes anywhere in the world" (Earth Rights International 2004, 6). Part of the answer to the question of how to formulate a violation of the law of nations in the context of Juárez will therefore depend heavily on whether these corporations are complicit in violations regarded as "definite and widely accepted" among nations. In practice, negligence for protection of workers may not be definite or widely accepted, particularly within the scope of purely domestic laws. This could be the end of the road to making a claim against corporations; however, there may be room still to argue for a case under ATCA if direct links can be made to the corporations for which so many of the victims of Juárez's ongoing feminicide worked. Finding these links would allow the claims against these corporations to include, in addition to complicity, such violations as knowledge and assistance in disappearances, torture, and even killings, which have been established as definite and widely accepted violations of the law of nations.

To determine the causal link between corporations and the deaths of these young women, some insight into the degree of knowledge and the role that corporations take, directly and indirectly, in encouraging the ongoing abuses in the community is required. Engaging in the actual exploration of this component of the claim is well beyond the reach of this chapter. Determining the actions and inactions of the corporations working out of Juárez requires investigation and discovery mechanisms that are possible only within the context of litigation or criminal investigation, where corporations would be required to provide such information. However, there is room for speculation.

Some have observed that there may be disturbing evidence linking the maquilas to the murders. In the documentary *Señorita Extraviada* (Missing Young Woman), Lourdes Portillo (2001) expounds on the possibility that these corporations, at least at a managerial level, might in fact have more involvement in supporting the possible web of actors at play in these murders than one might assume. Going a step further, Portillo explains that some factories have a policy of taking pictures of their mostly female employees. In at least one case described in Portillo's documentary, a maquila worker went missing soon after this kind of photo was taken at the maquila where she worked. Could the corporations be assisting the murderers in identifying their victims? Figuring out when women go missing and identifying patterns would be part of the process of validating such a claim. There is significant evidence that the victims are targeted on their way to and from the maquiladoras. Many mothers of the victims interviewed link their daughters' disappearance to times when they were either on their way to or from work.[10] Those familiar with Juárez know that "each day factory workers have to walk through unlit dirt roads to company buses that transport them to work" (Livingston 2004, 61). Therefore, determining whether corporations are doing enough to provide adequate resources for their workers to make it to the workplace safely should be part of the inquiry. Investigating all of these possibilities is required. As a place to start, a team of potential litigators, investigators, and community groups already involved in collecting information could map out or create a database of all of the victims and list a number of factors that might shed light on the corporate interconnections between them.[11] These factors could include where the victim worked, the hours during which she went missing, where she lived, and, if possible, routes or places she frequented.

Another possible avenue for evidence in these corporate cases would be to follow the money. Who is benefiting from the presence of these corporations in Juárez? Some observers fear that there might be a more insidious link between clandestine industries such as the drug cartels and the murders. However, this is the most difficult route for investigation, as clandestine activities are such for a reason: They are often outside the spectrum of observation and legal accountability.

In the process of collecting evidence, it is important to keep in mind whether there is any available information to establish evidence of liability. For instance, how many of the women who disappeared or were murdered were in fact maquila workers is a primary question. There are now conflicting narratives on this topic. Assuming that a significant number of victims were workers at particular maquiladoras, one must ask which corporations these women worked for and whether there is a pattern with regard to the maquilas for which they worked. This could potentially provide significant leads to resolve the actual cases — or provide no answers at all if there is no pattern. Either result must be anticipated.

Jurisdictional issues also play a major role in building the case against corporations. First, it must be determined which corporations are potential defendants. The choice of forum would be dependent on the state of incorporation for U.S. corporations or on whether these corporations have sufficient contacts with the forum in which they would be served. This may or may not be difficult depending on the information that is available about the corporations in Juárez. Only U.S. corporations could be sued in U.S. district courts using ATCA. European- and Japanese-owned companies, which are also resident in Juárez, could potentially be sued within the jurisdictions in which they are incorporated, but this is a possibility that this chapter will not explore.

Litigators must be aware and ready to argue against potential barriers to bringing a claim in U.S. district courts, including issues of exhaustion of remedies and forum *non conveniens*. One argument against such litigation in U.S. courts would be that the first logical place to bring a suit would be in Mexico. This is the standard argument for exhaustion of remedies. While this is a compelling argument, there is some significant legal development that would allow plaintiffs in Juárez to sue U.S. corporations in U.S. courts. In the case *Rodriquez-Olvera v. Salant Corporation*, a "district court in Southern Texas has found — and the appellate courts have not yet rejected — [that] a U.S. corporation may be subject to jurisdiction in the U.S. court system and face liability for actions arising in a foreign country, involving foreign residents, and stemming from the actions of the corporation's foreign subsidiary" (Cowman and Rich 2004). The acts for which the suit was brought took place within Mexico but were argued to be most related to corporate acts in Texas. In this case, "Fourteen young workers at Salant Corp[oration]'s Mexican subsidiary were killed when the company's bus, which was taking the workers to the clothing company's maquiladora, overturned and burned in a sewage ditch" (Cowman and Rich 2004). The plaintiffs in this case successfully argued that the claim would be best brought in U.S. courts for a number of reasons. The case included the following arguments:

— Mexico cannot provide an alternative forum for the case because the Mexican government is predisposed toward the case and biased against Plaintiffs.
— There is no inconvenience to Salant Corp. to try the case in Texas because Salant has its principal place of business in Texas.
— Texas, as opposed to Mexico, has the "most significant relationship" with the case, based not "on the number of contacts, but more importantly on the qualitative nature of those contacts as affected by the policy factors."
— As a jurisdiction with laws limiting liability and the recovery of damages, Mexico has no interest in applying such laws, unless a citizen of its own jurisdiction is a defendant in the action, even if the triggering event occurred in Mexico.
— The laws of Texas would have no "substantial adverse effect" on commercial interrelations between Mexico and the United States.
— Mexico's only legitimate interest in the case is to see that its citizens are adequately compensated for their injuries, and this interest is best accomplished by applying Texas law.
— Texas has a strong interest in regulating corporations doing business in Texas, including a policy of deterring and punishing corporations' tortious conduct, thus, Texas's own policies would be thwarted by the application of Mexico's laws to the action. (Cowman and Rich 2004)

This legal reasoning seems to provide a significant means through which victims' families could sue corporations in the case of Juárez because it provides a model for a claim based on negligence. In that case, "The negligence-based complaint set forth allegations that Salant Corp. failed to maintain the bus properly and the bus driver was not adequately trained to drive the vehicle" (Cowman and Rich 2004). This reasoning opens a door to possible litigation for other claims of negligence by corporations in the feminicides of Juarez. According to the attorneys Jordan W. Cowman and Kimberly Rich, "The Rodriguez-Olvera case has put fear into parent companies with overseas operations. . . . Its importance is paramount to alert U.S. employers of the future increment of lawsuits filed by Latin American employees for actions stemming from its operations in Latin America. If there is 'control' over the overseas subsidiary by the U.S. parent, some courts will allow non-U.S. citizens to take advantage of U.S. law and sue in U.S. courts" (quoted in Cowman and Rich 2004).

Another aspect to consider in potential ATCA litigation, which may be determinative of success, is whether to bring the claim for an individual plaintiff versus a class action. Unfortunately, it is very unlikely that all of the victims who were workers at maquiladoras worked for the same subsidiary of the same corporation. The fact that victims would be various claimants against various corporate defendants might in fact preclude a class action in the case of Juárez's using ATCA, unless the claims are for the same alleged violations. Another difficulty in envisioning a class action would be the possible exclusion of victims who were not maquila workers in this kind of a suit.

Despite the difficulties presented, the opportunity to bring forth claims against corporations is ripe and, possibly, nearly over. Partly due to the spotlight phenomenon, when attention is brought to "corporations caught engaging in unfair or abusive practices," which "cast[s] a shadow of scorn," corporations are quickly moving out of Juárez (Nathan 2003). "Lately, maquilas have been moving from Juárez to countries such as China, which offer even cheaper labor. In the past two years, according to the *New York Times*, Juárez has lost some 300,000 maquila jobs. Women's rights activists say that the resulting unemployment is aggravating domestic and sexual violence, yet Juárez has only one battered women's and rape crisis center, Casa Amiga, with an annual budget of just $4,500" (Nathan 2003). The pattern by which corporations reap wealth and move on to places where they have less or no accountability and an even cheaper labor force is one of the most destructive consequences of the global market. This is an even greater reason to hold corporations accountable for failing to take responsibility for the socioeconomic environments that surround them.

Distributive Justice and (Re)Construction

Community perceptions of distributive justice are an added dimension worth exploring and understanding within the context of the feminicide in Juárez and a necessary aspect of justice building. According to Mani (2002, 127), "Often, although by no means always, underlying or proximate causes of conflict appear to centre on contentions about distributive injustice." The undercurrent of distributive *in*justice in Juárez is undeniable. "Until the mid 1990s, [Ciudad] Juárez was considered a reasonably safe place: it is now known as a social disaster and one of the most distressed urban areas in the Western Hemisphere. Rising rates of violence have accompanied environmental degradation and sprawling squatter settlements inhabited by a rapidly increasing migrant population" (Weissman 2005, 824). However, it is difficult to frame the issue of feminicide squarely within Mani's understanding of how injustice serves as a trigger of conflict versus as a trigger of serial murders, in this case. Mainly, how do we explain the gendered nature of the violence being triggered by distributive injustice that an entire community experiences? The resulting conflict is also not of that between groups of equal or even unequal power battling each other, but that of an oppressive targeting of the most vulnerable within the society — poor women of color. Not knowing the character of the people responsible or the motivation of those committing the serial killings hampers the analysis even further. However, Mani's approach becomes valuable in identifying distortions in distribution, including those that have been created in the division of labor on the border, which at the very least contribute to violence against women in Juárez.

The inequities in Juárez are multiple. They range from the hard-felt national inequity with Mexico's wealthier neighbor — the United States; the inequities between the prosperous corporations and the colonias; the wealthy drug cartels and the working poor; and now the working-poor female laborers in the factories and the unemployed, largely male community in Juárez. Some observers have suggested that the feminicide is one way to reveal a "macho backlash" against the maquiladoras for employing so many female workers (Esther Chávez Cano, quoted in Dillon 1998a, A3). This idea cannot be validated; nor can it be invalidated. The danger in viewing the problem in these terms, however, is that it would seem to portray cultural attitudes about gender roles as the culprit of the feminicide, turning the debate to paternalistic views about reforming society. Activists in Juárez "wonder uneasily whether they've opened a Pandora's box of false accusations and sexist moralizing" (Nathan 1997, 22). It is therefore necessary to look at root causes in a much more expansive sense rather than reducing it to a debate about machismo and cultural inferiority.

A fundamental aspect of achieving distributive justice is through community reconstruction and social approaches to healing and reconciliation, what Mani also refers to as social justice. Therefore, what must be placed at the forefront of this discussion is how "mass violence results in the breakdown of societal structures—social and economic institutions, and networks of familial and intimate relationships that provide the foundation for a functioning community. Indiscriminate and episodic violence occurs at random and affects people at a neighborhood level" (Fletcher and Weinstein 2002, 573, 576). Critical to the overall response to feminicide in Juárez is repair at the societal level. Legal justice and rectificatory justice, if achievable, are therefore not the only forms of justice to urgently respond to in this case.

Unique to the case of Juárez is the strong groundswell of movement already taking place. Social mobilization and grassroots community responses to the feminicide are an autochthonous development that has gone from the local to the transnational and the international, as can be seen in ongoing human rights campaigns to bring attention to the feminicide.[12] It is from these community-based responses, or "community-generated responses" (Fletcher and Weinstein 2002, 633), that we can begin to witness and further promote construction and reconstruction of social justice. Within Juárez, community organizing has burgeoned. Groups have coalesced around the issue of feminicide, in part to put pressure on the Mexican government to fulfill its obligations, but also to begin a process of healing and reconstruction. These groups, such as the group Voces sin Eco (Voices without an Echo), have often started with the families of the victims organizing vigils and other activities of remembrance. One group "has organized marches and called for the state police official overseeing the investigations to resign," while another focuses "on prevention programs with families and young women, and on getting criminal sentences increased" (La Franchi 1997, 132). Victims' rights groups paint telephone poles with pink squares and black crosses in a desperate attempt to keep the city's attention focused on the crisis (Nathan 1999). Rosa-Linda Fregoso (2000, 147) explains, "In Ciudad Juárez, the black crosses on pink backgrounds represent the unspeakable

they mark the unrepresentable. The cross marks a class of people targeted. These various community based mechanisms, have served to
further community reconciliation and healing."

Community-generated responses serve as a starting point for thinking
about construction and reconstruction of justice in Juárez, during and
after the feminicide. In post-conflict contexts, Mani (2002, 155) warns,
"National and international actors have often appeared to be driven in
their post-conflict reconstruction efforts by a myopic vision, which is
frequently accompanied by a deficit of commitment. The policies of
national political actors are often demarcated by a specific time horizon
— that of the electoral calendar. . . . The policies of international actors
often reflect the pressure to demonstrate quick and visible results and to
plan a rapid exit strategy." These same warnings apply in the case of
Ciudad Juárez. Former President Vicente Fox exclaimed that a majority
of the more than three hundred cases of killings have been resolved,
although many reports contradict his declaration (Vargas 2005). In early
2005, Mexico unveiled a fund to compensate some of the relatives of the
victims (BBC News 2005). However, this kind of response may be ill-
suited to a situation in which the murders are ongoing and may also be
insufficient in addressing all of the various needs of the victims and those
left behind. For example, a substantial crisis is building around children
of the victims that are now orphaned as a result of feminicide (Cabrera
2004). Therefore, we must ask whether the state's intervention is an
adequate response. Rather than using the issue of feminicide as a platform for political attention and quick solutions, a genuine commitment
to resolving the problem is needed by all authorities involved. Moreover,
genuine commitments and investment in infrastructure development is a
responsibility that must be undertaken by all community members, from
the government and the corporations to the individuals who live in
Juárez. Individual community members are undertaking efforts to meet
this responsibility. Juárez is becoming an example of social mobilization
and social response to tragedy at the community level. What is lacking
currently is a similar showing of commitment from state and corporate
authorities.

Conclusion

In combining community-based responses with Mani's theory of distributive justice, we can advance the idea of a need for investment by the
state and corporations in Juárez. According to Laurel Fletcher and Harvey Weinstein (2002, 637), for any society to reconstitute in a peaceful

fashion, alternative interventions must be considered in synergy with judicial mechanisms for resolution. What must be asked is: What would drive such investment in Juárez? Is the threat of civil suits and prosecution before national and international judicial bodies the appropriate impetus for these actors to act? Rather than completely rest the argument on the moral aspects of the issue, which would posit that it is the role of the government to invest in its communities and infrastructure and that corporations *should* invest as they are benefiting from their presence in the community, the minimization of costs to these actors should be apparent and part of the less emotive impulse for these actors to take action. Economically, it would be to the advantage of the corporations to have a labor force that is empowered, and it would be more efficient for their enterprises. These same corporations would not have to abandon entire cities of industry they build due to unsavory practices they would rather not have publicized. The government should also see this as a significant opportunity to advance its own political interests by responding to calls of the community to investigate and to invest in long-term resolutions. In essence, the question should not be, Why invest? It should be, Why not?

This chapter has explored a "web of possible interventions" in the case of feminicide in Juárez. It is in a combination of these approaches — petitioning the regional system, litigation against corporate complicity, and strengthening community responses and the very infrastructure of Juárez — that true accountability for the victims may be found. To not recognize the complexity of the problem and to fail to demand accountability by everyone involved in the larger picture of the feminicide, whether responsible directly or not, would be to serve a further injustice to the hundreds of women whose lives have been cut short.

Notes

1. In reviewing cases deemed admissible since 2003, I did not find any recommendations to the court.

2. *Editor's note*: As of May 2006, there had been at least fifty-six murders of women in Ciudad Juárez and Chihuahua City since 2004 and far more than four hundred since 1993, according to figures in a U.S. Congressional Resolution passed by the House and received by the Senate (U.S. House of Representatives Concurrent Resolution 90, 109th Congress, 2d Session, 2006, available online at http://thomas.loc.gov/cgi-bin/query/C?c109:./temp/c109Nwe 6kh. Printout on file with the author.

3. Interview with Claudia Martin, professor of law, American University,

and co-director, Academy on Human Rights and Humanitarian Law, October 22, 2005.

4. Multinational enterprises "enjoy a greater flexibility in organization. They may locate production facilities in different countries to take advantage of differences in costs of inputs such as labor and materials. They may organize their operations to minimize tax and regulatory burdens" (Vagts et al. 2003, 201).

5. "Eight bodies were found in a field facing the offices of the city's Maquila Owners Association" (Thompson 2002, as quoted in Weissman 2005, 795).

6. Alien Tort Claims Act, 28 U.S. Code, Section 1350.

7. "By addressing the question of corporate complicity in human rights abuses, the courts have taken on one of globalization's biggest problems: multinational corporations have achieved unprecedented international power without corresponding global accountability. . . . The *Unocal* court, in acknowledging the corporation's true role as a culpable partner in human rights crimes, took an important step in filling this accountability vacuum. The *Sosa* Court affirmed this step by indicating that corporations can, indeed, be held liable for their complicity in the most egregious abuses" (Earth Rights International 2004, 19).

8. "The cases against Radovan Karadzic in 1995 presented the [U.S. Supreme Court] with the novel question of whether a non-state actor could be sued under ATCA. . . . The *Karadzic* case set the stage for victims to end [corporate] impunity by suing corporations in U.S. courts for certain abuses" (Ibid., 17).

9. The OECD *Guidelines for Multinational Enterprises* (OECD 2000) are recommendations addressed by governments to multinational enterprises. They provide voluntary principles and standards for responsible business conduct consistent with applicable laws. The guidelines aim to ensure that the operations of these enterprises are in harmony with government policies, to strengthen the basis of mutual confidence between enterprises and the societies in which they operate, to help improve the foreign-investment climate, and to enhance the contribution to sustainable development made by multinational enterprises.

10. See *Testimony of the Mothers*, video, on the Amnesty International website at http://www.amnestyusa.org/women/juarez (accessed July 21, 2005).

11. For an example of this kind of database, see the *Orange County Register* website, available online at http://www.ocregister.com/multimedia/juarez/index.shtml (accessed October 4, 2009).

12. See, e.g., campaigns by Nuestras Hijas de Regreso a Casa (May Our Daughters Return Home), online at http://www.mujeresdejuarez.org, and Amnesty International's campaign on the issue, online at http://www.amnestyusa.org/women/juarez (accessed October 4, 2009).

Photo Essay

IMAGES FROM THE JUSTICE MOVEMENT

IN CHIHUAHUA, MEXICO

1. Symbol of the justice movement in Chihuahua.
Families paint crosses on telephone poles, defying
the mayor of Ciudad Juárez's orders. Photograph by
Angela Fregoso, 2007.

2. Eva Arce, mother of Silvia Arce. From July 2007 to July 2008 mothers and other relatives/activists gathered on the first Thursday of the month and marched silently in front of government offices in Ciudad Juárez. Photograph by Cynthia Bejarano, 2007.

(below) 3. Poster for monthly protest in Ciudad Juárez. Photograph by Angela Fregoso, 2007.

4. Mother of Elena Guadian at the monthly protest in Ciudad Juárez. Photograph by Angela Fregoso, 2007.

(below) 5. An "altar honoring the murdered and disappeared women" created by mothers for the monthly protests in Ciudad Juárez. Photograph by Angela Fregoso, 2007.

(above) 6. Paula Flores, mother of Sagrario González. Photograph by Angela Fregoso, 2007.

7. Mothers of feminicide victims watch as Guillermina González Flores writes their daughters' names on the cross along with her sister's name, Sagrario. Photograph by Cynthia Bejarano, 2007.

8 and 9. The Redressing Injustice installation by Irene Simmons, Las Cruces, New Mexico. Photographs by Cynthia Bejarano, 2006.

(above) 10. Binational protest led by mothers of feminicide victims in Ciudad Juárez. Photograph by Cynthia Bejarano, 2004.

11. Guadalupe Zavala of Mujeres de Negro (Women Wearing Black), from Chihuahua City, marches for justice for her daughter, Erika Ivonne Ruíz Zavala. V-Day events in Ciudad Juárez. Photograph by Cynthia Bejarano, 2004.

12. Relatives of Silvia Arce (disappeared) lead the International Day of Women march. Photograph by Andrea Trimarco, 2008.

(below) 13. Mothers of the feminicide victims participate in the International Day of Women march, Ciudad Juárez. Photograph by Andrea Trimarco, 2008.

PART III

New Citizenship Practices

Translated by Sara Koopman

Testimonio

ROSA FRANCO, MOTHER OF

MARÍA ISABEL VÉLIZ FRANCO,

DISAPPEARED DECEMBER 16, 2001

My daughter, María Isabel Véliz Franco, disappeared on Sunday, December 16, 2001.[1] They kidnapped her as she was leaving her job at the Taxi Boutique, which sells clothes during the Christmas season. They pushed her inside a car, and her corpse showed up in an empty lot in the city of San Cristóbal, Zone 8 of Mixco, on December 18, 2001. That place is vacant but full of brush. They burned [the area] almost completely, and now evidence can't be collected there. The lot is full of brush again, and all of the traces are gone. The signs, well, she was strangled by hand and with a thick rope. Her body had evidence of being strangled with barbed wire and of having had barbed wire on her wrists and ankles. She had a deep puncture wound made by three or four stabs on the left side of her head—that is, the occipital part of her skull. Her skull was fractured with a short sharp instrument. Her left leg was fractured right at the left femur. She was raped. . . .

The process has been very difficult for me. Since her body showed up at that place, it has not been at all easy to face her death or to obtain justice. In Guatemala I denounced everything and even contributed to investigations done by Office 32 of the prosecutor's office, which had my daughter's file. It should have been handled by Office 5 in Mixco, since that was the prosecutor's office that picked up my daughter's body. I went to the national police to report her disappearance on December 17, 2001, . . . but it did no good because they wouldn't help search for her. They just took down a note about the situation and went so far as to ask me whether she had been with her boyfriend, whether she took drugs, whether she was a prostitute. Just imagine!

I suffered a heart attack nine months after my daughter's assassination. I still suffer from after effects and will have to take many medications for the rest of my life. I suffer from high blood pressure, insomnia, and heart trouble. I decided to report the case to the [Inter-American Commission on Human Rights] because I couldn't handle it anymore, without any support from any public authorities. . . . That's all I can say for now, it's hard for me to talk about this. Thanks.

Note

1. *Editor's note:* María Isabel's case is documented in Amnesty International 2005 report on feminicides in Guatemala.

ALICIA SCHMIDT CAMACHO

Ciudadana X

GENDER VIOLENCE AND THE DENATIONALIZATION

OF WOMEN'S RIGHTS IN CIUDAD JUÁREZ, MEXICO

This chapter examines the troubling status of poor migrant women as political actors in the denationalized space of Ciudad Juárez. Subaltern women's labor has served the state as a stabilizing force amid the economic and political crises of the neoliberal regime in ways that both promote and delimit new forms of female agency in the border region. The acute rise in armed social conflict in Juárez, much of it targeted at young women and girls, requires that we examine how the denationalized subjectivity that has occupied recent scholarship on globalization and citizenship is itself produced through state failure and state violence. The impunity of violent crime necessarily devalues both citizenship and citizens: It produces a climate in which sociality is defined less by national belonging than by the more atomizing force of collective fear (see Rotker 2000). If globalization has in fact encouraged the disarticulation of citizenship rights from membership to a single national community, as many analysts maintain, it is nevertheless unclear whether subaltern Mexican women can make substantive claims to the global civil society that the Juárez industries have helped to produce.

Recent scholarship on citizenship contends that changes in the nation-state that result from several aspects of globalization "significantly alter those conditions that in the past fed the articulation between citizenship and the nation-state" (Sassen 2003, 41).[1] Saskia Sassen (2003, 42) writes that the processes of market integration, coupled with the expansion of the international human rights regime, enabled the "deterritorializing of citizenship practices and identities," just as they "have directly and indirectly altered particular features of the institution of citizenship." Although scholars hold no clear consensus on what constitutes the precise substance of denationalized citizenship, the term enjoys currency both as an expression of an "aspirational claim" to new forms of political engagement and solidarity beyond the nation-state, and as a description of global social movements (Bosniak 2000, 453).[2] In a lucid review of current legal studies, Linda Bosniak demonstrates that citizenship, meaning the subject's capacity to exert political agency as a recognized member of a political community, with entitlements to protections and services, clearly exceeds the territorial bounds of nations (Bosniak 2000, 450). Yasemin Soysal (1994, 164–65) attaches her concept of "postnational citizenship" to the emergence of a global civil society in the postwar period based in a "hegemonic language for formulating claims to rights above and beyond national belonging."[3] For Soysal and others, human rights discourse represents a significant instrument for legitimating the political status and concerns of non-nationals within broader transnational polities.

The Mexico–U.S. border has long functioned as a stopping point for restive populations of non-nationalized subjects, but in the current forms of urban violence linked to paramilitary gangs, political corruption, the drug trade, and human traffic, the specter of a more acute process of state failure looms large. Central to current contests over the governance and governability of the border region is the problem of how neoliberal policy permitted (or necessitated) the conversion of poor migrants into a population with little purchase on rights or representation within either the nation-state or new global polities. Ongoing transformations in border governance suggest that, just as globalization enfranchises a new class of post-national elites, it also fosters the conversion of marginalized people into "disposable non-citizens," whose value to the international system derives from their lack of access to rights (Franco 2002, 13).

The Juárez *Feminicidio*

The feminization of the dispensable non-citizen is perhaps most visible in the ongoing brutalization and murder of subaltern Mexican girls and women in the State of Chihuahua. The evident refusal of the Mexican government and much of civil society to provide even the most minimal protection to victims signifies a collapse of law or its replacement with new forms of social control that render racialized migrant women vulnerable to torture, sexual abuse, murder, and disappearance. The fifteen-year *feminicidio* in Ciudad Juárez and Chihuahua marks a campaign of gender terror that alternately mimics the repressive campaigns of Latin

American "Dirty Wars" and the seemingly irrational codes of urban violence and serial killing (Fregoso 2003; Reguillo 2005). The peculiar features of the Juárez killings correspond to the physical and political geography of the northern city, its shared boundary with the United States, and its importance as a site of Mexican partnership with global capitalist institutions.

The unprecedented forms of gender violence directed against border women demand a reckoning with both state and non-state institutions as guarantors of rights or justice. Because of state reprisals against the subaltern movement for justice, women's movements have had to develop political strategies for taking their demands for rights to international political organizations and human rights agencies. Activists searching for institutions capable of administering political pressure for justice have entered into a complex alliance with European, Canadian, and U.S. social movements, private foundations, nongovernmental agencies, and international human rights organisms linked to the United Nations. Access to international exposure, funding, and expertise has expanded the spaces of opposition for members of the grassroots protest movement. International ties currently represent the most crucial source of support for women's incipient claims to group autonomy and identity apart from the nation-state (Tabuenca Córdoba 2003b). But the contradictory, often conflictual, location of subaltern women of color within this global public sphere sets severe constraints on how the political norms that international social movements and human rights law promote as universal may achieve formalization in the border city.

If, as Soysal and others contend, the destabilization of the nation-state by globalization means that "the logic of personhood supercedes the logic of national citizenship," then we must determine the conditions that permit mere persons to act as subjects of rights (Soysal 1994, 164). For most Juarenses, the detachment of citizenship from the nation-state has entailed less an opening for "new political subjects and new spatialities for politics" than the encounter with new forms of social violence and repression at the hands of both state and non-state actors (Sassen 2003, 42). In this context, transformations within the state have expanded its function for social control while simultaneously weakening those institutions that provide the substance of citizenship: access to goods and services, justice, security, and political representation.

The struggle of the feminicidio's targets to assert "the right to have rights" challenges the current limits of both the international human rights regime and state discourses of democratization (Arendt 1951, 296). It is worth asking how neoliberal state policies and economic globalization have increased Juárez women's susceptibility to gender violence. Transformations in the neoliberal state affect how the grass-roots movement against the feminicidio mobilizes its discourse of female citizenship both within and against the nation-state. So, too, existing global frameworks for articulating women's rights may support or impede the pursuit of justice in the Juárez case. What remains most central, and yet most elusive to analysis in these matters, is the particular nature of the border space as a site of subject formation and political conflict over women's social value and claims to rights.

Women's Citizenship in the Border Space

As a critical site of Mexican integration with the U.S. economy and foreign capital, Juárez has long functioned as a denationalized space where border residents exercise national citizenship under the pressures of tourism, foreign investment, illicit activity and legal commerce, and the U.S. police presence. In Chihuahua, the contradiction between poor women's function in securing the viability of the neoliberal program contrasts even more sharply with their subordination to the patriarchal authority of the northern state. As a critical site for the development of the maquiladora industries, Chihuahua played a prominent role in preparing the nation for its integration with the global free market. The border zone's development is ineluctably tied to the capture of women's labor. Juárez enjoys notoriety for its long history of providing inexpensive sex, drugs, and leisure to international tourists, U.S. soldiers, and working-class migrants. The sale of women's sexual labor represents one of the most stable sources of income for local entrepreneurs and, less visibly, the state.[4]

Border industrialization was built on this cross-border scheme for attracting capital with the promise of cheap, pliant labor and limitless service. The pervasive representation of poor Mexican women as female bodies readily available for appropriation reinforces other cultural narratives that convert poor women into sources of value that can easily be discarded as they are consumed. The denigration of working women is not merely an expression of class hostilities or patriarchal re-entrenchments against women's incursions into the public sphere. The feminization of labor — devalued and detached from any concept of labor power — is just one expression of a project of governance that generated new modes and spaces for income generation through the commodification of poor women's bodies and delimited citizenship. Images of women used to sell tourism, merchandise, labor, and sex saturate the border cities in ways that deliberately eroticize the exercise of dominance.

In this period of transformation and crisis, the Mexican state has sought revenue through schemes that increase its vulnerability to co-optation by organizations that use the border as a base for illicit traffic in goods, arms, drugs, and people. The expansion of the informal economy in response to the contraction of the Mexican political economy involved women in new forms of enterprise at the margins of legality. As prostitution and labor contracting grow internationally, women and young girls are increasingly incorporated, voluntarily and involuntarily, into networks of global sex traffic and human smuggling.[5] This traffic responds to the formal legal structures governing migration, commerce, and labor, just as it feeds off entrenched inequalities between consumer societies and countries in crisis. Studies of human trafficking suggest that criminal operations have significant connections to the states in which they operate (Kyle and Koslowski 2001). The prevalence of market-led development strategies is likely only to encourage the interdependence of legal and illegal forms of commerce and production as developing countries compete for investment and income in the global economy. These processes, already long established in the Mexico–U.S. border region, constitute a substantial breach in the capacity of the Mexican state to act as guarantor of rights for its most vulnerable citizens.

While international observers commonly represent the gender violence in Juárez as a regressive cultural manifestation of masculine aggression, it is perhaps better understood as a *rational* expression of the contradictions arising from the gendered codes of neoliberal governance and development. The crimes of the feminicidio are not confined to Chihuahua: Human rights agencies and scholars have called attention to rising rates of women's murders across the country; not surprisingly, the worst indexes of assault correspond to sites of social conflict, including Chiapas and the southern boundary (Olivera 2006). The combined processes of economic restructuring and political transition have had the perverse effect of increasing the state's stake in the denationalization of poor women's citizenship precisely at the moment of their emergence as new political and economic actors. The global economies that convert subaltern women into commodities interrupt women's purchase on the most basic right to personal security. The feminicidios represent an assault on this bodily agency in the extreme.

Ciudadana X

The tragedy of Chihuahua unfolds as a wholesale inability to imagine a *fronteriza* (border) life free of violence. This points to an even more profound collective failure of border and international civil society to conceptualize these young women as autonomous beings, to recognize their value as subjects, and thus to protect them. The absence or refusal of state and civil institutions to ensure women's entitlements to freedom of movement represents a negation of their political agency at its most basic level. It is wholly unnecessary to construct conspiracy theories to account for the state repression directed at the afflicted communities of the feminicide. The combined pressures of state restructuring and economic collapse evacuate political structures' giving any meaningful association to the social pact and horizontal solidarity that constituted the Latin American ideal of nationhood. An estimated 97 percent of reported crimes in Mexico go unpunished; the high index of criminal impunity signifies not only a malfunction in the state institutions of policing, however.[6] Incompetence or corruption cannot account for police failure at this level; rather, such levels of impunity suggest that the security forces and criminal justice system serve an entirely different function within the state. The government not only tolerates popular mistrust of the police; it also exploits public fear for its own interests. By depicting the marginalized poor as alternatively superfluous and a danger to the state both justifies the state's indifference to urban crime and legitimates its own violent tactics of social control.

The violence in Juárez does not represent the absence of law in the border city. Understanding the situation of impunity that permits the feminicidios and the concurrent massacres linked to the drug trade and human traffic requires a distinct measure of what constitutes the rule of law. The Mexican Constitution is as advanced a democratic instrument as any in the Western Hemisphere; feminist legislators have achieved the incorporation of new gender codes with greater success than their counterparts in the United States. The Mexican government was among the first to sign on to the Convention on the Elimination of All Forms of Discrimination Against Women (CEDAW), ratified by the United Nations General Assembly on December 18, 1979. The state has adopted all major conventions on gender equality and women's rights since then. The elegance of the national legal code, then, marks the persistent space between the legislation of rights and their political exercise.

Violence at the northern frontier, tied to criminal mafias and political corruption, exploits this fissure, challenging the state's monopoly on the tasks of social control and its capacity to define the bounds of sociality and order. A new discourse of security accompanies the language of crisis: Where the state fails to serve, new instruments of social pacification have entered the political sphere, with severe implications for subaltern women. The question of rights collides with the demand for social control: What is it? Who wants it? Poor migrant women have served as the ground for this contest between the state and the various non-state actors that have emerged in Juárez.

While justice remains an unattainable abstraction, the afflicted cannot act as agents of their own narrative of wounding and retribution. In this way, gender terror reinscribes the subaltern status of the border communities: through the violent theft of bodily agency in murder and the simultaneous suppression of victims' political rights at the hands of the state. Of the hundreds of people who suffered the loss of a daughter or partner, only a small minority of victims has been able to sustain the effort of denouncing the crimes. This reflects the precarious situation in which the *colonias* subsist. A *colonia* is a neighborhood that typically lacks adequate infrastructure (drinkable water, electricity, sewage systems, paved roads, and street lighting). Oftentimes the housing is poor and unsafe. In Juárez, some housing is made from wood pellets and hazardous material. Most families in *colonias* cannot sustain the material cost of pursuing justice. After her fourteen-year-old daughter Cecilia Covarrubias Aguilar was killed in 1995, Soledad Aguilar went daily to the police to denounce the crime. She reports walking three hours every morning from her colonia to the urban police station, where she filled out the same forms again and again, with no answer to her complaint. Over the decade of her activism, she and her husband lost their home to the cost of her involvement in the protest movement. She continued, she said, not only out of loyalty to Cecilia, but because she wanted to recover her infant granddaughter, who disappeared at the time of her daughter's abduction.

The material costs of pursuing justice accounts only partially for the absence of a broader social movement against the feminicidios. Aguilar describes her own participation in the mothers' struggle as her *Calvario* (burden) of having chosen to persist *against* her own better interests or the needs of her family. The mothers' movement consists of the small percentage of women who were able to mobilize the material and psychological resources to act publicly as the bearers of injustice. Their incorporation into *asociaciones civiles* (civil associations) threatens their prior social integration as workers, wives, parents, and community members. In the wake of their conversion into public victims, women commonly experience the collapse of marriages, the loss of work, and ostracization from their communities. The viability of the justice movement will depend on how it partners the melancholic work of pursuing redress; of creating a rights apparatus that can support the incipient claims of border women to the abstract construct of human rights. Precisely because the feminicidio entails a social fantasy that certain women are made for killing, the movement for justice entails reversing the interpellation of poor women as subjects ineligible for the protection of the law.

The justice movement in Chihuahua represents the most dynamic mobilization of recent decades for extending new political rights to dispossessed female residents of the industrial city. In challenging the impunity of gender crimes, the coalition of mothers' groups, colonia residents, human rights agencies, and nongovernmental organizations (NGOs) has made visible the ambiguous relationship between subaltern women's bodies and the complex of institutions and values that constitute national citizenship in the denationalized space of the border. The diverse actors in this conflict confront each other in their competing claims to the figure of the dead victim, the cadaver in the desert trash heap that cannot voice her own claim to rights. Voicing the unspeakable in public has been a vital means to interrupt the de-valorization of the dead as disposable bodies. Speaking about her daughter's abduction on her route home from the Maquiladora Lear 173, Josefina González testified, "Sabíamos que la llevaron a fuerza, porque aunque Claudia no era miedosa, sí era muy desconfiada (We knew that they took her by force, because although Claudia wasn't timid, she was very distrustful)" (Justicia 2003b, 35).[7] González's account of her daughter's victimization voices an assertion of her daughter's will in life, a refusal to go quietly. The testimonial marks the incipient assertion of a distinct female agency, recognized in the retrospective gaze of mourning. "Ahora con la ayuda de otras mujeres," says Carmen Villegas, mother of Míriam Gallegos Venegas, "estoy apriendendo que tengo derechos y que puedo luchar (Now, with the help of other women, I am learning that I have rights and that I can fight)" (Justicia 2003b, 1).

This new pedagogy of struggle has unleashed a second wave of gender crimes: Mothers themselves are targets of the state's repressive violence. Police routinely tell mothers that, if they wish to see their daughters alive again, they should refrain from "creating scandal in the streets."[8] Local media, business leaders, and civic organizations in Juárez echo this threat, arguing that the protest movement threatens the economic viability of the city, particularly in its precarious relationship to foreign industry and tourism. The most cynical attacks charge the NGOs representing victims and their families with generating a new industry based in demonizing the city. In an interview with *El Diario*, the president of the Maquiladora Industry Association, Rubén Parga Terrazas, denounced the movement, saying, "La acción de grupos locales y de otros puntos de la República y fuera de ella . . . han hecho un 'modus vivendi' con la explotación de la situación de violencia local (The actions of local groups and other parts of the Republic and abroad . . . have made a living out of exploiting the local violence)" (Orquiz 2004, 1). Precisely because Juárez society is so oriented toward the exterior, the management of its image has been a mechanism for silencing the mothers and their associates.

Because the movement's linkages to the international sphere represent a potential challenge to male dominance and local state power, the perception of women's post-national citizenship has become an incitement to further repression and violence. Nongovernmental agencies have come under assault for their supposed threat to the exercise of state sovereignty. At first glance, this hostility may represent the normal retrenchment of the state against its opposition, as state interests give way to human rights claims. But the fragility of the local mobilization places additional burdens on the global public sphere as a vehicle for attaining justice and political representation for the victims of the feminicidio. The local conflict manifests opposing visions of globalization as a vehicle for advancing Mexican interests, staged in complex relation to the very subjects whose labor provided the international linkages that have brought new capital and values to Juárez. And yet the conflict and repression manifested in the feminicidio may themselves be attributed to the inequalities and violence of the current regime of globalization. If denationalization made state citizenship the unattained prize for subaltern women, it may also close off the global as a sphere of rights.

Confronting the Border as the Space of Death

The charge that the fifteen-year spate of killings and disappearances constitute feminicidio moves the private and unspeakable nature of gender crimes into the public realm, revealing its global implications in ways that threaten the power interests governing the apparently neutral orders of state governance of commerce, development, foreign policy, and, perhaps most critically, security. By invoking and gendering the legal term *genocide*, the protest movement seeks to reconstruct conventional understandings about where personal violence intersects with official terror. The term *feminicidio* has other telling implications within the border space. While the Mexican government may in fact be complicit in the killings, the feminized narrative of genocide seeks to construct an account of armed social conflict in which crimes against humanity may not be the coordinated effect of state policy but the work of numerous state and non-state actors operating within the denationalized space of the international boundary. Within this denationalized space, crimes against women occur as a function of both police and paramilitary border operations in social control. Articulating Mexican women's minimal citizenship to an international sphere emerges as a vital strategy for contesting the ways Mexican women's denationalized subjectivity has been conditioned through the imbrications of sanctioned and unofficial gender violence.

How Mexican women may exert rights in the border space is thus fundamentally an *international*, not a national, problem. By this I mean that the implementation of human rights conventions is a matter not simply of remaking the Mexican state, but of addressing the global processes that make Mexican women convenient targets for discrimination, exploitation, and assault. As I have shown, the concept of postnational citizenship seeks to capture the range of social practices that sustain migrant communities in the transnational circuit. Recent scholarship demonstrates how migrants use their new wage-earning power and location to expand their political networks in ways that alter the traditional relationship between the nation and its subjects. "In this process," writes Sassen (2003, 43), "the global city is reconfigured as a partly denationalized space that enables a partial reinvention of citizenship." At the Mexico–U.S. border, the destabilizing effects of globalization on national citizenship offer a markedly different horizon of possibility. The rapid growth that made the Mexican border an emblem of capitalist globalization has also created institutions within and beyond the state that interpellate poor Mexicans as citizens without rights, without effective state protections.

Mexican women are exposed at the northern border to a violence that is distinctly binational in form. While the Mexican and U.S. governments tend to depict border violence as a matter of insufficient policing, due consideration of women's rights would lead us to ask whether, in fact, border policing incites violence against women. Over the past decade, human rights groups and immigrant advocates have reported a rise in the incidents of rape and sexual assault of migrant women at the hands of border-patrol officers from both countries. Sylvanna M. Falcón (2001) argues that increased militarization of the border represents a state of war. Within this context, law-enforcement officers and armed criminal groups routinely subject Mexican women to deliberate acts of gender terror.

The non-sanctioned violence of feminicidio must be understood in relation to the ongoing, sanctioned assault on the same poor Mexican women and girls as they move through the border space. Gender crimes of this scale emerge not merely as aberrant phenomena, with a unique social pathology, but also as a political symptom of the deliberate and concerted reconstruction of rights within the denationalized space of the border and migration. The feminicidio is the shadow supplement of a binational project to produce a feminized population without rights, readily appropriated for work and service in both legal and illicit labor markets. The cultural production of this subaltern group has entailed the sexualization of poor Mexican women's bodies as a means to sell the bleak and fragile partnership between the two countries. The maquiladoras and the tourist industry, which trade so visibly in Mexican women's physical capacities, are only the most obvious sites that eroticize Mexican women's super-exploitation.

The informal economies of human smuggling, drug trafficking, and pornography service and expand the formal economies in Mexican women's labor in the United States. Rape at the border sets a price on women's labor in the United States, rendering migrant women available as a flexible source of service. Informal — even friendly — transactions over the domestic tasks that other women and men cannot do for themselves are inextricably tied to the impunity of rapists in the desert. The coyotes, small entrepreneurs working the contradictions of U.S. immigration law and its labor demands, know both the value and the availability of the migrant woman's body, and how much of it belongs to them. The coyote, as a sexual threat, is just one link in a chain that converts poor Mexican women into people without rights in their journey north.

To illustrate this point, consider the experience of Susana Torres, who cleans houses in the city where I live: New Haven, Connecticut. Torres reports that she can earn $60 for a day's work, an unimaginable sum for an undocumented migrant from southern Mexico.[9] Her family depends on her meager earnings because factory jobs are scarce. It is just possible to imagine that the wages are fair. At any time, however, an employer can impose new terms for her pay. One woman informed Torres that she was unsatisfied with her cleaning, adding laundry and shopping to her duties. What was a matter of convenience to the employer, perhaps even the only way to meet the demands of her own career and motherhood, had altogether different connotations for Torres. In crossing the desert from Sonora to evade Operation Gatekeeper, she had been raped by her coyote. Torres traveled with her nine-month-old son to meet her husband, who had migrated a few months earlier. On their arrival, her husband blamed her for the assault, and their marriage almost collapsed. She did not leave him, she says, in part because she feared she would only face the same hostility from her next partner.

Although her family has asked her to return to Mexico, Torres argues she could not afford to give up her residence in the United States. She has never received treatment for the rape; nor has she reported the crime. Because of the cultural stigma attached to sexual assault, she has not told friends or family what she suffered. Her nine-day experience of gender terror controls her mobility within the denationalized spaces of undocumented citizenship. Torres has not ceased to act as a political subject, but her experience delimits how she perceives herself as an agent of rights. She speaks of achieving state goods and services for her son and minimizes her own entitlement, admitting that she has little claim on the United States without a visa. In her narrative, she seemed to present me with the same account of bodily dispossession that Rosalba Robles has found among battered women in the *colonias* of Ciudad Juárez — that of occupying a body made for violence (Robles 2003).[10]

Torres reports that the coyote told her not to complain, that she was nothing special and that she was one of a series. That may just be what the perpetrators of *feminicidio* tell their victims in Ciudad Juárez.

It is not enough to claim that governments are merely complicit in this violence. Gender crimes in fact sustain a binational project of governance and growth. The gendered order of the denationalized space serves the interests of global capital, of nation building, certainly, but also ruling ideas of cultural value, standards of living, progress, democracy — in short, all of the narratives of development and civilization that require the idea of a border to mask deep social conflict. These narratives are likewise invested in a hidden and dangerously eroticized commerce in migrant women's laboring, even material being, for others.

Reconstructing Women's Rights

The challenge of defending Mexican women from gender violence has prompted feminist movements in both the United States and Mexico to appeal to international human rights organizations for assistance. International human rights discourse, itself a factor in the reconstruction of state citizenship by globalization, has proved an effective instrument for contesting the gender violence targeting poor Mexican women at the border. And yet the legal framework for conceptualizing women's rights does not necessarily coincide with the organic discourse of rights incipient in the movement of subaltern women from the colonias. Violence against Mexican women has taken new forms, rather than disappeared, as border states have incorporated new codes for women's citizenship. Despite significant increases in penalties for crimes against women, prosecution of such assaults remains negligible throughout Mexico. Current legal frameworks for protecting women's rights commonly fail to address the material logic promoting the use of gender violence as a technique of political repression and economic exploitation. Human rights institutions have limited instruments for addressing the particular problems of migrants within a global division of labor. Denationalization, as I have shown, is a concern not only for transnational migrants, but also for those whom capitalist development and state policy have displaced within countries. In Juárez, the two types of migrants reside together. The lack of a legal framework that recognizes the transnational nature of capital and population flows severely hampers the efforts of human rights advocates working at the Mexico–U.S. border region. Amnesty International and Human Rights Watch publish separate national reports about Mexican corruption in the feminicidio and U.S. abuses of Mexican migrants, neglecting to address that both cases concern the same population and, very often, the same space.

The state-centered nature of current human rights discourse severely curtails the promise of the post-national as a vehicle for transforming Mexican women's citizenship. Although CEDAW has provided a powerful instrument for imagining new forms of women's rights, it has little to offer by way of enforcement. Mexico's ratification of CEDAW may actually serve state interests at the expense of popular protest by extending formal legitimacy to the very government that has refused to enforce the codes of universal equality already enshrined in the national constitution. Finally, the state-centered nature of political thought cannot address the combined *international* forces that may be responsible for the violations of women's rights in the border space. How we understand the nature of the violation the feminicidio represents has profound implications for how we conceptualize justice and restitution for the women and children of Chihuahua.

Stories of captive labor and captured sexuality reverberate throughout the conflictive history of Mexican women's travels in the border space. The abuses Mexican women suffer in the international division of labor entail the decomposition of the integral body into its constituent parts: head, hands, arms, breasts, trunk, and legs. Repetitive labor of assembly and service is itself a form of institutionalized gender violence that seeks to detach women's critical agency from their bodily functions. For women in the border region, the feminicidio distorts and mirrors the sanctioned theft of their bodily integrity in migration and at work.

The demand for a new rule of law in the border region returns us to the nature of the violation so brutally inscribed on the victims of feminicidio. The missing and murdered young women, no longer present, nevertheless occupy a place in this contest. The crosses erected in the desert require us to find new ways to think about rights from the vantage point of young girls and migrant women, whose new mobility and emergent sexuality challenge existing relations between women's bodies, the state, and global capital. Imagining a female life free of violence here demands new narratives of gender power, labor value, and political community, a new culture of citizenship—within and beyond the nation—that can carry young women's aspirations and energies out of the border as a space of death.

Notes

I acknowledge the invaluable work of the following scholars and dedicated activists who shaped my thinking for this article: Sandra C. Alvarez, Cynthia Bejarano, Aurora Camacho de Schmidt, Macrina Cárdenas, Esther Chávez Cano, Michael Denning, Rosa-Linda Fregoso, Melissa García, Alma Gómez, Julia Monárrez, Stephen Pitti, Linabel Sarlat, María Socorro Tabuenca Córdoba, Elvia Villescas, and Melissa W. Wright. My greatest debt is to *las integrantes* of Justicia para Nuestras Hijas, to "Susana Torres," and to Soledad Aguilar. Any errors in interpretation or reporting are entirely my own. I received generous funding from the Yale Center for Latin American and Iberian Studies, the Program in Ethnicity, Race, and Migration, and the Yale Center for International and Area Studies. This chapter was originally published in *New Centennial Review* 5, no. 1 (2005): 255–92.

1. The following works inform my discussion of current analyses of "postnational" citizenship and globalization: Basch et al. 1994; Baubock 1995; Benhabib 2002; Bosniak 2000; Castles and Davidson 2000; Falk 1994; Hedetoft and Hjort 2002; Held 1996; Jacobson 1998; Sassen 2003; Soysal 1994; Werbner and Davis 1999.

2. Most of this literature, written from the United States, Canada, and Europe, does not cite the expansive debates on citizenship written in the postcolonial countries where global migration originates.

3. The full argument reads as follows: "The same human rights that came to be secured over the centuries in national constitutions as the rights and privileges of a proper citizenry have now attained a new meaning and have become globally sanctioned norms and components of a supranational dis-

course. It is within this new universalistic discourse that the individual, as an abstract, human person, supplants the national citizen. And it is within this new universalized scheme of rights that nonnationals participate in a national polity, advance claims, and attain rights in a state not their own. The expanse and intensity of concepts of personhood predicate a broadened, postnational constellation of membership in the postwar era" (Soysal 1994, 164).

4. In a related study, Sassen (2004, 1) describes "cross-border circuits in which the role of women, especially the condition of being a foreign woman, is crucial" to the operation of what she terms "alternative circuits for survival, for profit-making, and for securing government revenue." Because these networks exist at the margins of the official economy, and often include illegal activity, Sassen describes these international linkages as "alternative circuits of globalization." Although I coincide with her assessment of migrant women's status, I prefer not to disarticulate the processes described as "*alternative* circuits*" from the more formal global political economy. The widespread practice of illegal labor recruitment through subcontractors, for example, is so central to the transborder economy linking Mexico and the United States that it is hardly distinguishable from the legal operations of parent companies.

5. My primary source for this information is Deputy Sheriff Rick Castro of the San Diego County Police Department. Castro has been a leading force in drawing attention to sex trafficking between Mexico and the United States and has presented testimony to law-enforcement and government agencies in both countries. His involvement in this issue has an interesting history: As one of the sole Spanish speakers on the San Diego police force, he began interviewing children and women apprehended for prostitution more than twenty years ago. Most of the sex traffic he sees services the migrant male population involved in farm labor. He has been cited for his interventions on behalf of trafficked women for adding a humanitarian response to the otherwise routine criminal-justice policy toward prostitutes and undocumented people. I am extremely thankful to Deputy Sheriff Castro for sharing his expertise with me. Our interview took place on February 26, 2004.

6. This statistic originates in Zepeda Lecuona 2002.

7. Unless noted otherwise, translations from Spanish into English are mine.

8. Testimony of Soledad Aguilar, New Haven, Conn., April 15, 2004.

9. I have changed the name and particulars here to protect the subject of the interview: "Susana Torres," undocumented Mexican migrant, interview by the author, New Haven, Conn., November 20, 2003.

10. Robles's study of domestic violence demonstrates how gender terror alienates women from ownership of their bodies so that they cannot even lodge their consciousness within it (Robles 2003).

Feminicidio

MAKING THE MOST OF

AN "EMPOWERED TERM"

This chapter explores the conceptual and practical difficulties that crop up with the use of the term *feminicidio*, the murder of women due to their gender, across the Latin American region.[1] The regional *feminicidio* campaign highlights basic similarities across cases to support generalized conclusions regarding gender-based violence against women.[2] I argue that the drive toward commonalities gives short shrift to different sociopolitical, legal, and cultural phenomena across cases. Yet the goal of bringing attention and justice to the staggering levels of gender-based violence against women is critically important to ending impunity and saving women's lives. Therefore, I call for careful attention to the utility and limits of the term *feminicidio*. In this chapter, I first sketch the contours of the regional *feminicidio* campaign with a focus on Peru, Guatemala, and Mexico. I then explore the utility and limits of the term *feminicidio* in two ways. Through a case comparison of Guatemala and Peru, I proceed to the simplified conclusion that *feminicidio* appears in post-conflict contexts. Then, by reviewing the current debates regarding the term *feminicidio* in Peru, I assess its effectiveness for addressing gender-based violence against women in that context. Throughout this exposition, I integrate an analysis of ethnicity and class as inextricable components of violence against women.

The political stakes involved in developing effective methods to address gender-based violence against women are immense: conserving women's right to life and bodily integrity and women's right to develop a life project of their choice. Social change requires a politics of seeing, of making connections across different manifestations of misogyny that are tacitly supported through patriarchal legal and social systems. These analytical connections are the basis for constructing public education and legal strategies that center women as rights bearers, recognize women's subjectivity and agency,[3] and end the general impunity that perpetrators of gender violence against women enjoy. Therefore, strategizing by activists and nongovernmental organizations (NGOs) must keep in mind the limits of any given term or campaign to adequately address gender-based violence against women. Such an approach demands careful contextual analysis, realistic comparison with other contexts, and alliance building with clear goals.

My point of departure coincides with the position of the feminist lawyer Gladys Acosta Vargas regarding the use of a gender perspective to work toward justice for women. She calls for an analysis that identifies the ways in which legal systems themselves buttress gender discrimination, marginalization, and violence against women. Such an analysis requires reassessing people's daily lived experiences and their ideas of conflict and reparation, taking distance from the interests of patriarchy, and recognizing the rights of men and women in all of their diversity. This type of analysis provides the basis for legislative proposals that advance new ways of constructing justice (Acosta Vargas 1999, 628).

As Celina Romany (1994, 88) argues, "A feminist perspective assumes law as a 'site of struggle.'" While a feminist perspective does not hold the "key to unlock [the] patriarchy," law does provide the "forum for articulating alternative visions and accounts.'" Furthermore, as Acosta Vargas asserts, legal change also contains a symbolic value that reverberates throughout society and can be a vehicle for education and emancipatory change (Acosta Vargas 1999, 623). In the struggle to find justice for gender-based violence against women, whether in wartime or in peacetime, law is a central pillar of the patriarchal apparatus that must be fundamentally reconfigured to recognize women as subjects and enshrine women's rights.

A very important qualification to this approach: I do not assume that the only respectable decision a victim of gender-based violence against women or the family of a victim of *feminicidio* can make is to publicly denounce the crime and proceed with the case through the judicial system. Such an assumption erases the complicated social, cultural, intrafamilial, communal, psychological, and emotional negotiations the survivor or surviviors must make. Moreover, in an ongoing context of impunity, the survivor or survivors must first consider their immediate safety and security. I agree with Mercedes Crisóstomo Meza (2005, 27) when she writes, "No one decision is better than the other and any possible decision—be it silence, reporting the crime or proceeding through the judicial system with an anxious desire for justice—deserves equal consideration, and above all equal respect."

The respect for survivors' choices must go hand in hand with the guarantee of all women's "right to have rights." Rosa-Linda Fregoso (2006, 27) elucidates this point in her reflection on *feminicidio* in Mexico. "Or are the transnational and grassroots activists alliances mobilized to stop feminicide in Mexico reminding us of something much more basic, an element of rights that Hannah Arendt wrote about many years ago: 'the right to have rights, or the right of every human being to belong to humanity, should be guaranteed by humanity itself' (Arendt 1968, 298)? . . . The rights of a targeted group of racialized, poor women, to belong to 'a community willing and able to guarantee any rights.'" Making connections between different types of gender-based violence against women, and the intersecting vectors of oppression that define them, bring into focus the enormous scope of change necessary in social norms, national penal codes, and judicial systems to create the conditions for justice. The regional *feminicidio* campaign makes these necessary connections across different contexts of gender-based violence against women.

The Regional *Feminicidio* Campaign

As a Peruvian feminist NGO worker asserts, *feminicidio* is an "empowered term."[4] The regional *feminicidio* campaign has achieved the "empowerment" of the term *feminicidio* by bringing a unifying conceptual lens and discursive coherence to multiple national contexts in which women are being murdered due to their gender. This is not to say that *feminicidio* is a necessarily new phenomenon. It simply responds to the need for a conceptual framework that reveals the connections between seemingly separate occurrences of gender-based violence against women. The discursive consistency garnered by the term makes a sociopolitical and cultural impact when mobilized, eroding the norms that allow for the banalization of the murder of women due to their gender. A diversity of projects has sprung up to address *feminicidio*, including local, national, and regional organizing among political activists, policy advocacy, artistic and cultural expressions of protest, and activist-academic-based research.

I start this examination of the strategic uses of the term *feminicidio* by exploring the way it has been taken up in Peru in comparison with Guatemala and Mexico. The term *feminicidio* was first introduced in Peru by the

Por la Vida de las Mujeres, Ni una Muerte (For the Lives of Women, Not One More Death), campaign initiated in June 2001 by Isis International. This campaign has the objective of addressing the assassination of women. The participants have produced reports that for the first time systematically register *feminicidio* and its causes in different parts of Latin America.[5] Estudio para la Defensa de los Derechos de la Mujer (Study for the Defense of the Rights of Women; DEMUS), the Peruvian feminist NGO on which I focus, joined this campaign in 2001. The other two NGOs that are involved in the issue of *feminicidio* in Peru are the Centro de la Mujer Peruana "Flora Tristán" (Flora Tristan Center for Peruvian Women) and Amnesty International's Peru section. Because the concept of *feminicidio* has gained political currency on a regional level, it is used by civil society groups to organize around a broad spectrum of gender-based killing of women. According to DEMUS and the Flora Tristan Center, there were 124 to 143 victims of *feminicidio* in 2003 and 100 in 2004.[6]

Feminicidio has been taken up in Peru as a leveraging tool in the ongoing sociopolitical, legal, and cultural struggles around intrafamilial violence. Drawing from Marcela Lagarde y de los Ríos, DEMUS provides a broad definition for *feminicidio* that can include many other types of gender-based violence against women. "*Feminicidio* is genocide against women and it happens when the historical conditions generate social practices that allow violations against the integrity, health, liberty, and the life of women. All these violations share the assumption that women are usable, abusable, dispensable, and disposable. *Feminicidio* is the last link in a long chain of violence that women all over the world are submitted to on a daily basis."[7] While this definition is expansive, the term serves to mobilize around one of the most extreme outcomes of gender-based violence against women, politicizing the problems of sociopolitical normalization and lack of access to fair and timely state judicial response.

The "Informe sobre *feminicidio* en America Latina." (Report on *Feminicidio* in Peru) (DEMUS 2006) presented to the Inter-American Commission on Human Rights names various impediments to addressing *feminicidio*. There are obstacles to the implementation of international human rights at the national level within the judicial system; institutionalized state human rights entities do not recognize women's human rights; and religious institutions have had a very negative influence. These imbricated factors also include the austerity of neoliberal economics and the crisis of governability and state legitimacy. All of these factors conspire to exacerbate existing social hierarchies and close down the possibility for justice, thereby fostering the ongoing conditions for *feminicidio*. Kent Paterson (2006b, 3) would agree with this, framing this phenomenon within the context of a globalized world: "Femicides flourish in areas experiencing social upheavals marked by previous or current armed conflicts, violent rivalries between internationally organized criminal groups, the displacement of old economies in favor of new — often illicit — ones, and the corruption and weakening of traditional forms of state power."

Although DEMUS joined the Por la Vida de las Mujeres, Ni una Muerte, regional campaign in 2001, the pressing domestic issues superseded its drive to build regional alliances. DEMUS had made several frustrated attempts to be in contact with groups working on *feminicidio* in Mexico and Guatemala, but it was not until 2005 that it made building regional alliances a priority. This shift took place when Womankind, a British funder, urged DEMUS to contact a group in Bolivia, the Red Nacional de Trabajadoras/es de la Información y Comunicación (National Network of Workers in Information and Communications; REDADA), which works on the issue of *feminicidio*. Building on that experience, DEMUS was centrally involved in the production of "Report on *Feminicidio* in Latin America," which was presented to the Inter-American Commission on Human Rights, and sent a representative to the hearing in Washington, D.C., in March 2006.[8]

In each national context, advocates for women's rights have drawn on the concept of *feminicidio* to make visible the ongoing tragedy of the daily murder of women. Fueled by the political currency and moral leverage garnered through a regional campaign, advocates adopted the "empowered term" to address the most urgent aspects of gender-based violence against women. Each advocacy group anchors its usage of *feminicidio* to a strategic universalism that unifies its diverse struggles — the misogynistic and sexist underpinnings of the murder of women in the context of violence in a globalized world. These groups also come together in transnational issue networks "drawing activists with very different stories to tell into alliances to pursue overlapping goals" (Tsing 1997, 267). The "Report on *Feminicidio* in Latin America" is a recent example in which representatives from throughout America presented the problem of *feminicidio* to the Inter-American Commission of Human Rights.[9]

To make regional alliances work, groups must also negotiate the differences in their usage of the term *feminicidio*. The varied relationships between *feminicidio*, ethnicity, and class elucidate the potential confusion that can occur when generalizing on a regional level. In Peru, the Flora Tristan Center and Amnesty International (2005, 14) assert that *feminicidio* "is an act that cannot be uniquely associated with a specific context or actor, it happens in times of war and times of peace and women victims do not have a unifying ethnic or socioeconomic profile." This reflects the reality that intrafamilial violence happens across all social sectors. Peruvian advocates emphasize this fact to combat racist and classist assumptions about who commits intrafamilial violence and who is victimized by it. The use of *feminicidio* in Peru focuses on the murder of women related to intrafamilial violence, purposefully de-emphasizing ethnic and class differences. In Mexico and Guatemala, in contrast, *feminicidio* highlights rape, torture, and murder of racialized women. In Mexico, the torture and murder of women is related to myriad factors, including organized delinquency; the traffic of people, drugs, arms, money, and goods; kidnapping; and police, military, and paramilitary violence that are embedded within an overall misogynistic social fabric. In 2004 alone, 1,205 women and girls were murdered in Mexico (CLADEM 2007). *Feminicidio* in Mexico does have a strongly racialized component, with poor mestizas as targets of disappearance and execution (Fregoso 2006). Similarly, in Guatemala *feminicidio* mainly targets poor *ladinas* in marginalized urban areas.[10] Between January 2001 and July 2005, 1,897 women were murdered in Guatemala (CALDH 2005). The use of *feminicidio* in Guatemala addresses a broad range of factors, including familial violence and gang-related violence of the *maras*, yet it also emphasizes clandestine groups directly or indirectly linked to the state.

To avoid confusion about the varied usage of the term *feminicidio*, each national usage must be mapped relationally. The flexibility of the term allows it to be adapted into each sociopolitical and historic context, thereby highlighting the most critical and relevant expressions of gender-based violence against women. A human rights NGO in Guatemala, the Centro de Acción Legal para Derechos Humanos (Center for Legal Action on Human Rights; CALDH), explains that because the concept of *feminicidio* is still under construction, it intentionally fills it with meaning derived from the specific characteristics of the assassination of women in Guatemala (CALDH 2005, 13).

Post-Conflict Guatemala and Peru Case Comparison

Both Guatemala and Peru have weathered brutal internal armed conflicts with systematic sexual violence, and both countries currently suffer from high levels of murders of women. Furthermore, feminist and human rights workers and activists are currently mobilizing around the term *feminicidio* in both countries to bring attention to the murder of women due to their gender. Yet the similarities end there, giving way to very different sociopolitical phenomena that must be balanced with the push to globalize the *feminicidio* campaign. Here I will explore a case comparison to shed light on the efficacy and limits of the use of the term *feminicidio* across cases.

In Guatemala, links have been established between sexual violence during internal armed conflict and the current trend of the assassination of women; in Peru, by contrast, no efforts have been made to establish these connections. Yet for the purposes of a regional campaign, grouping these two cases together may make sense, since they do share various contextual factors that simultaneously foment *feminicidio* and present obstacles to addressing it. It can be argued that in both Guatemala and Peru, internal armed conflict increases the vulnerability of women due to (1) the climate of impunity among armed actors toward human rights violations and gender violence against women specifically; and (2) the general decline of socioeconomic conditions due to the loss of family, community members, animals, and material belongings and the inability to continue subsistence farming or regular income-generating activities and, in the worst cases, displacement.

Both Peru and Guatemala are in post-conflict periods with neoliberal economic policies that exacerbate poverty, unemployment, and lack of access to education, health care, and other basic social services. These conditions only augment the general sense of desperation and frustration that fuels the use of violence. Furthermore, the lack of political will on the part of the Guatemalan state to follow through with the Peace Accords is now being echoed in Peru.[11] The Alianza Popular Revolucionaria Americana (APRA) administration and its alliance with Alberto Fujimori's Alianza para el Futuro (Alliance for the Future) party lack the political will to implement the recommendations of the Truth and Reconciliation Commission's final report.

When we take a closer look at the two cases, the difference in sociopolitical and historical context of gender-based violence against women is significant. The explanatory power of arguments, such as violence in a globalized world, must not be stretched beyond their relevant level of scale. International and regional levels of analyses must be balanced with equal attention to specific national manifestations of gender-based violence against women. Drawing coherent linkages between different manifestations within one sociopolitical and historical context demands effort and care. When attempting to draw out similarities across different contexts, the demand multiplies. Attention to detail and levels of scale form the basis for durable regional alliances. Therefore, deeper investigation is necessary to reveal how and why sexual violence in internal armed conflict and *feminicidio* are connected in Guatemala and separate in Peru. To capture the specificity of these crimes, this optic reads for intersecting vectors of social oppression, such as ethnicity, language, rural/urban, and class.[12]

The report "Guatemala's Femicides and the Ongoing Struggle for Women's Human Rights" (Center for Gender and Refugee Studies 2006a) asserts deep connections between the sexual violence during internal armed conflict (1960–96) and the current extreme levels of *feminicidio*. "The conflict was marked by pervasive state-sponsored violence, which included the annihilation of over 400 indigenous villages in Guatemala's highlands, and the widespread use of barbaric forms of torture. Women were particularly vulnerable to sexual violence, as rape was commonly utilized as a weapon of war. Numerous investigations have concluded that the vast majority of these human rights violations were conducted by members of the Guatemalan intelligence services, many of whom escaped prosecution and now participate in police activities or are members of private security forces, which have been implicated in the femicides" (Center for Gender and Refugee Studies 2006a). The victims of sexual violence during the Guatemalan internal armed conflict had a specific profile: The majority were rural, indigenous Maya. Sexual violence went hand in hand with massacres and mass violence and was converted into a means to eliminate the seed of the indigenous Maya, to eliminate the possibility of their existence (CALDH 2005, 28). Few women who were raped survived the general strategy of social cleansing that led to genocide.

Within the current context of *feminicidio*, the manner in which the torture takes place and the bodies are displayed in public spaces has the signature of the wartime strategy of demonstrative acts (*hechos demonstrativos*) to deliver a message of fear to the population.[13] The way in which women are being kidnapped, raped, mutilated, and killed demands a very organized group with resources, weapons, and training. Perpetrators function within "parallel powers" and have similar modus operandi of gender-based violence against women found during the internal armed conflict. According to Samantha Sams, director of the Guatemala office of Project Counseling Services, an international cooperation agency that accompanies grassroots women's and human rights groups working on the issue of feminicide, the clandestine structures have entrenched themselves in Guatemalan society, growing deep roots over the thirty-six-year conflict. In addition to clandestine security operations, private security officers and the Policía Nacional Civil (National Civil Police) are involved in the killing of women (Center for Gender and Refugee Studies 2006a, 22). Other factors related to *feminicidio* in

Guatemala include familial violence and gang-related violence of the *maras*. The Procuraduría de Derechos Humanos (Attorney General Office for Human Rights; PDH), in its 2003 report, states that "organized crime and the 'maras' have developed a mode of behavior and thinking that is distinguished by impulsiveness, the constant search for stimulus, a cold and calculating attitude, and the disregard of social norms. These modes of behavior and thinking lead to a disrespect for life and the integrity of others, facilitating criminal acts of extreme cruelty that are similar to acts committed during the internal armed conflict" (CLADEM 2007, 61).

In Guatemala, the level of *feminicidio* increased in 2000–2001, four years after the 1996 Peace Accords. Sams puts forward the hypothesis that, since the state did not hold perpetrators of human rights violations accountable for their acts, the message of impunity gave them free rein in the post-conflict context. The broken peace process leaves the culture of violence intact, exacerbating overall social decomposition and the current high levels of *feminicidio*.[14] Within this culture of violence and impunity, general insecurity has increased, violence against women has increased, and the extreme level of intentional brutality practiced against women has increased. An analysis of these material links is presented succinctly in the following excerpt: "The parallel powers, patterns and modus operandi inherited from the internal armed conflict, in addition to the violent character of the patriarchal system, are factors that combine twofold interests. On the one hand, to maintain ingovernability and the inoperability of a state of law and, on the other, to repress women that participate in spaces or take up tasks that are outside of their traditional roles, thereby continuing gendered discrimination and control over women's bodies, minds and lives."[15]

CALDH, the Guatemalan NGO, uses the elements of analysis included in the concept of *feminicidio* yet prefers naming this violence the assassination of women. Within the Guatemalan penal code, homicide may or may not be intentional murder, while assassination always implies intentionality. Therefore, *assassination of women* is the terminology used to maintain the component of intentionality within the broader analysis of *feminicidio* (CALDH 2005, 13). The type of assassination of women and the excessive and intentional brutality, as well as the general denial of women's rights and the discrimination against the criminal investigation of these cases, are key factors that fit an analysis of *feminicidio* in Guatemala (CALDH 2005, 45).

In Guatemala sexual violence during internal armed conflict and *feminicidio* go hand in hand. The case of Peru stands in stark contrast. Although attention to *feminicidio* and sexual violence during the Peruvian internal armed conflict (1980–2000) has developed in tandem over the past six years 2001–2007,[16] the two types of gender-based violence against women are treated as separate issues. In 2001, President Alejandro Toledo gave the Truth and Reconciliation Commission (TRC) a mandate to investigate the causes and consequences of the internal armed conflict between the Communist Party of Peru–Shining Path, the Túpac Amaru Revolutionary Movement, and the armed forces.[17] The armed conflict started in 1980 in the Andean department of Ayacucho and expanded outward, gravely affecting the neighboring Andean departments of Huancavelica, Junín, and Apurimac and the Amazonian departments of San Martín and Huanuco. The majority of the 69,280 victims were Andean Quechua-speakers or people from the Amuesha, Asháninka, and Nomatsiguenga ethno-linguistic groups of the Amazon (Crisóstomo Meza 2004, 11). The general conclusions of the TRC note that racism and historical devaluation of these populations since the beginning of the Republic of Peru is to blame for the national disregard of this tragedy (Peruvian Truth and Reconciliation Commission 2003).

Due to newly developed international gender norms,[18] international pressure, and internal TRC advocacy, the TRC integrated a gendered perspective belatedly into its research design. Sofia Macher, one of the two female commissioners, advocated for the gender program. Julissa Mantilla (2001), a TRC employee, presented a compelling argument to the commissioners and doggedly promoted the idea. The goal of the gender program was to make visible gender-based violence against women using an international human rights framework. Of the acts of sexual violence reported to the TRC, 83.46 percent were committed against women.[19] Factoring in the ethnic profile of victims, racialized women were the overwhelming targets of sexual violence.

Quechua-speaking *campesinas* find themselves in the crosshairs of many structures of subordination, including gender, ethnicity, rurality, and class. Most are monolingual Quechua-speakers in remote rural areas who make a living through farming and raising a few livestock. Only 58.2 percent of women in the Andes hold a national identity card, a material indicator of a long history of discrimination (Velásquez 2004, 3). Poor, rural Quechua-speaking Andean women are othered and disposable, with even lower than average numbers who exercise the right to a name and identity. These abject subjects of the nation are considered savage, undesirable, and an excess in the national imaginary, yet in the context of the extremely centralized nation-state, they are necessary for the construction of the modern, civilized Limeño.[20] While the process of colonization assumed the feminization of indigenous populations as the basis for patriarchal structures, the inverse — the "Indianization" of women — is the presupposition that undergirds modern patriarchy (De la Cadena 1996, 202).

While the issue of sexual violence during conflict has gained limited attention on the national stage due to the work of the TRC's Gender Program, a handful of NGOs have created programs to investigate, document, and address this crime. During the conflict, feminist NGOs did not address this issue in any sustained manner.[21] To date, the women's movement as a whole has not made the issue of sexual violence during internal armed conflict a priority on its agenda. Only DEMUS has programming that focuses on sexual violence during the conflict, with a branch office in Huancavelica in the community of Manta.[22] I focus on the work of DEMUS because it is the only Peruvian NGO that also has programming on *feminicidio*. Yet even by DEMUS, sexual violence during internal armed conflict and *feminicidio* are addressed separately. María Ysabel Cedano, director of DEMUS, critiques this institutional disconnection. First, the problematic of the assassination of women by their partners due to jealousy lacks an analysis that considers the social impact of the political violence.[23] Simplifying the root cause of *feminicidio* as patriarchy erases its inter-relation with the generalized social trauma that results from state terrorism. Second, DEMUS began working with the concept of *feminicidio* without full consideration of the class and ethnic components. Cedano asserts that "without centering these variables in the analysis of what happens to women, it is impossible to determine if there is a connection to political violence or not."[24]

Within civil society, feminist and human rights NGOs are the only entities that address gender-based violence against women. Only feminist NGOs employ the concept of *feminicidio* to address the issue of familial violence. Sexual violence during the internal armed conflict is addressed more frequently, albeit reluctantly, by human rights NGOs because testimony about human rights violations during the internal armed conflict are overflowing with oblique yet repetitive references to it. Unfortunately, collaboration between human rights and feminist NGOs on the issue is minimal due to mutual distrust and differences in focus and political priorities. A few human rights NGOs are defending cases of sexual violence during the internal armed conflict, yet most have not advanced out of a preliminary investigation stage, and the few that have did not produce a sentence.[25] Human rights NGOs do not address other manifestations of gender-based violence against women, such as *feminicidio*.

While the term *feminicidio* is used to name the murder of women due to their gender in both Guatemala and Peru, a closer look reveals vast differences in what constitutes *feminicidio* in each post-conflict context and its relationship to sexual violence during internal armed conflict. The process of establishing the regional *feminicidio* campaign must not be made at the expense of minimizing different national contexts. On the contrary, the campaign is strengthened by balancing attention to regional analyses, assessment of national manifestations of gender-based violence against women, and careful comparative evaluation. Other aspects to keep in sight are the ways in which feminist and human rights workers and activists address the issue. In the next section, I turn the analysis to the specific challenges faced by feminist NGOs working with the term *feminicidio* in Peru.

Use of *Feminicidio* in Peru

The debate regarding *feminicidio* by NGOs in Peru offers a window into the utility and limits of the term. Peruvian legal advocates are elaborating the ways in which the term can be legally typified or used as an aggravating factor in cases of homicide. Accompanying public-awareness campaigns have the long-term goal of changing social norms, which is necessary to support paradigm shifts in legal discourse and the reconfiguration of judicial frameworks. NGOS' differences on the issue of *feminicidio* echo more historical divergences between feminist and human rights approaches. This notwithstanding, the debates regarding *feminicidio* continue to be central in the process of redefining the way in which each NGO addresses gender-based violence against women. I will explicate three main approaches to the issue: the legal-political approach, the social-impact approach, and the legal-technical approach.

As I mentioned earlier with regard to the regional *feminicidio* campaign, DEMUS was the first Peruvian NGO to take up the concept of *feminicidio* in 2001. The *"feminicidio* frenzy," the impulse to include a broad spectrum of gender-based violence against women under the umbrella term, resonated with DEMUS's long-term advocacy and activist agenda. The *feminicidio* campaign became a useful tool to address familial violence through public-awareness programming. The DEMUS *feminicidio* program survived an institutional restructuring and personnel change, yet the conceptual focus and strategic logic behind the campaign were lost in the transition. According to DEMUS, the use of the concept of *feminicidio* continued as the next step in elaborating the framework for its familial-violence services. *Feminicidio* allows for an analysis of the sociopolitical dynamics of familial violence and a critique of ineffective laws.[26]

On December 24, 1993, the Law against Intrafamilial Violence framed the issue as an interpersonal problem within the language of civil law and the Penal Code. This framework enshrined the issue within the private sphere. As Romany (1994, 90) explains, the private–public dichotomy parcels out legal privilege along gender lines. Verónica Matus elaborates on this line of analysis: Masculine supremacy is established through a gender hierarchy institutionalized by law that privatizes the practices of masculine domination of women, such as sexual and intrafamilial violence. I qualify the concept of masculine supremacy as an institutionalized privileging that permits violence against women as the legitimate expression of hyper-masculinity. Therefore, men enjoy impunity as perpetrators of gender-based violence against women, while women are left with the choice of receiving abuse in silence or with publicity provided through the same masculine logic that will inevitably question, minimize, or ignore women's claims (Matus 1999, 67). Moreover, class and ethnicity further facilitate the access to legal privilege or compound the lack thereof. According to DEMUS, the only positive outcome of the 1993 legislation is that it positioned the issue within the scope of formal political debate.

Feminist legal advocates draw on international human rights to create a framework in which to name the assassination of women *"feminicidio."*[27] DEMUS uses the concept of violence against women from the Convention of Belém do Pará as the basis for identifying intrafamilial violence as violence against women in intimate relations (*violencia contra la mujer en pareja*). In addition to offering new ways to frame violence against women, these international conventions help to reveal women's lack of access to justice and due process and the need to guarantee women's rights at the national level.

Given that Peru ratified the Convention of Belém do Pará in 1996,[28] DEMUS asserts women as bearers of international human rights and subjects of a sociopolitical phenomenon, not depoliticized objects of the private sphere, as the national legal system would have it. Historically, women's voices have been silenced, rendering women simultaneously invisible and objectified in the public political and discursive spaces of law and justice. As Ana Elena Oblando (1999, 140) writes, "Women's voices have not been part of the 'formal discourse of the law' because women's daily experiences have been silenced under a masculine universal paradigm of justice and law." The concept of *feminicidio* fills this absence by offering a sample of what critical women's voices might say. For example, *feminicidio* facilitates an exacting critique of the discourse of romantic love that justifies women's structural dependence on men, the assumption of women's selflessness, and the related emotional and psychic suffering women must endure within this arrangement.[29] Reframing intrafamilial violence in terms of *feminicidio* politicizes the issue and demands analytical links with larger misogynistic ideological and structural factors, such as compulsory heteronormativity and impunity, pushing it back into the public political sphere.

Clearly, *feminicidio* is a very strong tool for public-awareness campaigns, yet on the national juridical level, *feminicidio* is less effective because it is not elaborated within the Penal Code. The gender-based aspect of the murder of women is eclipsed within the Penal Code, which categorizes murder as homicide, parricide, or qualified homicide or as a crime of passion (Dador Tazzini 2006, 5). The current Penal Code leaves the social and cultural assumptions regarding masculine power and control over women's sexuality and bodies unquestioned. The goal of penal codification of *feminicidio* is to identify the social and cultural specificities of the crime, deconstructing the gender hierarchy inherent in the judicial system and exposing the injustice of masculine supremacy. The effectiveness of this goal is highly debatable, as I will illustrate through the different sociopolitical and juridical positions regarding the utility of the term *feminicidio*.

A more technical problem is that the term *feminicidio* has not been defined in a precise manner, making its legal incorporation difficult in typifying crimes. "While the term *feminicidio* politicizes the murder of women due to their gender," says Janet Llaja of DEMUS, "recognizing the power relations that underlie it, in the area of the law, there are rules that one must respect. In the area of penal codes, the rules are even stricter. A crime is exact, and must be to respect the rights of the accused. The murder of women due to their gender is too general to be made a category in penal code."[30] Furthermore, Jennie Dador Tazzini explains the juridical problem of determining the value of proof and the severity of the sentence in cases of *feminicidio* in Peru. The legal and doctrinal criteria for sentencing cases of *feminicidio* are not clear, leaving a large margin of interpretation. Given the cultural context, social representation, and official moral codes that generally work against women's rights, such space for interpretation can be manipulated through the presentation of special circumstances and aggravating factors and will not facilitate justice for women (Dador Tazzini 2006, 12). Therefore, Dador argues that the root issue is that the judicial system does not function properly. If it did, one could correct some aspects of the Penal Code and use aggravating factors to make visible the gender-based aspect of the murder of women. Therefore, it would not be necessary to create a new Penal Code category of *feminicidio*.

Representing a less legal-technical critique of *feminicidio* and echoing Gladys Acosta Vargas's assertion regarding the symbolic value of legal change, María Ysabel Cedano argues for a formal political debate about *feminicidio* as a category to be included in the Penal Code. While the possibility of altering the Penal Code is remote, the symbolic value of such a debate is to situate the theme in public discussion, thereby forcing public recognition of the *gendered* nature of violence against women. In general, women are marginalized as subjects under the law. The term *feminicidio* recognizes women as subjects and, more important, reveals them as subjects with the right to freely exercise their sexuality. This free expression of women's sexuality is exactly what the murder of women due to their gender extinguishes in order to maintain patriarchal power and control. Therefore, the debate is important for the public political process that it generates and its potential to shift political morals. As Cedano explicates, "Public debate regarding the law precedes changes in legal norms. Public debate has the potential of instilling new political morals. In relation to *feminicidio*, it is a discursive strategy for feminist criticism of legal codes, the administration of justice, and cultural norms. It is necessary to create a new language of law on the national level that interprets crimes against women within the framework of constitutional and international human rights that can comprehend, sanction, and repair violence against women as a collective phenomenon in its magnitude and systematic nature."[31] In contrast to Dador's legal-technical assessment of the juridical utility of the term *feminicidio*, Cedano presents a legal-political envisioning of its utility to promote sociopolitical change.

Given these various positions regarding the use of *feminicidio* and the lack of consensus within DEMUS regarding the juridical utility of the term, in 2007 DEMUS decided to withdraw from the regional Por la Vida de las Mujeres, Ni una Muerte, *feminicidio* campaign. Cedano's assessment is that it has accomplished the goal of making visible that women are dying; it has broken the banalization of violence against women. Furthermore, the public-awareness campaign lacked a well-thought-out message to give it longevity and coherence. *Feminicidio* was an entry point; now DEMUS is shifting toward an evaluation of the justice system and a potential campaign about the administration of justice and its inability to protect against, sanction, and repair violence against women. In addition, DEMUS is shifting its focus to a perspective of sexual and reproductive rights, in which violence against women is understood as a mechanism to control women's sexuality. The right to free expression of one's sexuality reinforces women's liberties from an affirmative approach. Cedano states that if we constantly focus on the negative and the trauma of violence against women, we cannot center women as active subjects and construct a vision of change for a different future.

The work on *feminicidio* done by the other two NGOs, the Flora Tristan Center and Amnesty International's Peru section, is interlinked and further elucidates the different approaches that fuel ongoing debates. In 2004, the Flora Tristan Center agreed to work with AI's Peru Section on the *feminicidio* campaign Por la no Violencia contra la Mujer (No Violence against Women). The goals of the campaign were to (1) situate the concept in the discourse of criminology; and (2) make visible the systematic and silent violence against women that is due to indifference and social tolerance. *Feminicidio* is "a crime against women, an extreme expression of the violence based in gender inequality, exercised by men toward women with the intention of gaining domination and control" (Centro de la Mujer Peruana "Flora Tristan" and Amnesty International 2005, 14). By using the term *feminicidio*, one exposes the backdrop of misogyny behind the daily murder of women, a specifically gendered crime.

As the two NGOs got more deeply involved in the issue, differences started to arise. From the perspective of the Flora Tristan Center, *feminicidio* is a term that facilitates political struggle and cultural transformation. Change starts with social impact and then reverberates out accordingly as changes in laws and culture. *Feminicidio* makes visible the fact that "this culture maintains patriarchal values that limit the self-determination of women and convert women into persons not equal to men. It makes evident the fact that men see women as something they can use, throw away, and disappear from this world without any problem. The mechanisms to negotiate agreements between men and women do not work, the state does not guarantee women's rights and the culture does not provide useful tools."[32] DEMUS and the Flora Tristan Center coincide in calling for attention to sexual rights and a need to change the focus to fully understand the phenomenon of violence against women. Overall, the center calls for the continued use of this "empowered term" for social impact because it has become a global category.

The social approach that the Flora Tristan Center advocates began to create friction with the more legalistic approach of Amnesty International's Peru section based on international human rights. As the Amnesty International's Peru section began to fully assess the legal implications of the use of the term *feminicidio*, it came to see the complications and difficulties that surround it, especially since there is no international legal consensus on the meaning of the term. The preliminary assessment of Amnesty International's Peru section is that *feminicidio* does not have juridical utility, and it is more effective to work with *homicide of women for reasons of gender*.[33] Yet at the same time, opinions are diverse, and no position has been formally adopted. There is also mixed support for using the term for social impact. Amnesty International's Peru section jumped into the *feminicidio* frenzy too early, without the backing of a formal decision on the topic from Amnesty International or sufficient internal debate within the section.

Jessica Estrada explains her version of the critique by Amnesty International's Peru section: "We cannot use a term only for social impact if it does not have legal evidence or proof to back it up. In contrast to the feminist NGOs, since [Amnesty International] only works with international conventions, it does not draw from the Convention of Belém do Pará. The [Amnesty International] framework is more rigid in that its goal is for governmental authorities to take responsibility. Therefore, the parameters of action are limited by what the state is willing to hear. Strong legal argumentation and backing is required, and this has yet to be constructed for the use of *feminicidio*."[34] Estrada adds that it is necessary to understand and respect the legal margins for change and work to make the maximum change within those margins.[35] In contrast, feminists are not only focused on what the state is willing to hear, but their strategies tend to be much more transgressive, with a focus on the society in general. Amnesty International's Peru section demands a higher level of coherence between the legal, political, and social aspects of the campaign. These differences in approach ultimately caused the dissolution of the agreement between Amnesty International's Peru section and the Flora Tristan Center.

DEMUS, the Flora Tristan Center, and Amnesty International's Peru section each stress different approaches in their *feminicidio* programming: the legal-political approach, the social impact approach, and the legal-technical approach, respectively. DEMUS is most concerned with the legal-political implications of its use of the term *feminicidio*, emphasizing the need for a formal public political debate on the issue to generate a shift in political morals and sociocultural norms. After initiating work on *feminicidio* in Peru and establishing it within the feminist agenda, DEMUS is now withdrawing from the regional campaign and shifting the focus of its work on violence against women to sexual and reproductive rights. The Flora Tristan Center emphasizes the need for continued use of *feminicidio* as a globalized "empowered term" that politicizes the murder of women due to their gender and heightens social impact. Amnesty International's Peru section began working with the Flora Tristan Center and then withdrew after struggling with the questionable juridical utility and international legal legitimacy of the term.

These variations in approach also reflect historical trends within the feminist and human rights movements. Feminists prioritize justice for women and the generalized social change necessary to create conditions for justice, supporting public political impact through social and discursive intervention that highlights structural inequalities. The human rights movement is more bound by legal norms in its scope of work and strategy building. The international human rights agenda of Amnesty International is strongly oriented toward juridical utility, ultimately emphasizing individual responsibility. The crux of the conflict in the use of the term *feminicide* is embedded in the divergence between the drive to generalize for social impact and the push to specify for juridical utility.

As each NGO is in the process of defining its relationship to the term *feminicidio*, one can look back and assert that the rush to fit into the regional *feminicidio* campaign led to conceptually muddled arguments and confused legal and social strategies on the part of feminist and human rights workers. A more positive read would be that the *"feminicidio* frenzy"* opened a rich debate on the approaches to addressing gender-based violence against women, creating the need for a more precise focus and careful strategizing. All of the groups called for a national meeting to debate the various positions and develop a common conceptual, analytical, and theoretical basis of understanding. Such a meeting happened in part in 2005 with Amnesty International's Peru section, DEMUS, and Asociación de Comunicadores Sociales Calandria (Association of Social Communicators Calandria), another NGO that had collected media information on gender-based violence against women. They initiated discussions regarding the relevance of the term *feminicidio* in Peru and the appropriate legal strategy to create a new category in the Penal Code or to use the term as an aggravating factor.[36] Further discussion is necessary to clarify the different approaches to *feminicidio* and gender-based violence against women in general. As both Liz Menendez of the Flora Tristan Center and Jessica Estrada of Amnesty International's Peru section assert in relation to past differences, we should value the interdisciplinarity of the discussions and look for complementarity of approaches instead of adopting oppositional positions.

Conclusion

The regional campaign developed around *feminicidio* has propelled it to the status of an "empowered term." This analysis calls for a careful assessment of the utility and relevance of the term both for naming gender-based violence against women in national contexts and for making connections across multiple contexts. Clearly, it is critically important to make visible the links between gender-based violence against women to defend women's rights and to open the possibility of envisioning alternative realities that value women's lives, bodies, and sexualities in all of their diversity.

The regional *feminicidio* campaign packs a strong punch on international, regional, and national levels by highlighting the most extreme result of gender-based violence: the murder of women. Yet looking for quick generalizations — such as that post-conflict contexts experience an increase in *feminicidio* — tends to gloss over complex details, weakening the internal coherence of the campaign. To avoid "prostituting the term" and thereby losing the political leverage of the campaign, it is necessary to ground its usage at every analytical level, from international to regional to national. In this sense, a recent study by the Comité de América Latina y el Caribe para la Defensa de los Derechos de la Mujer (Latin American and Caribbean Committee for the Defense of Women's Rights; CLADEM) calls for increased support and spaces to discuss the use of the term and the methodologies used to research it (CLADEM 2007, 32).

By exploring the current *feminicidio* debates in Peru, what comes to light is a critical rethinking of how to apply existing legal frameworks. This is a very important discussion for the advancement of women's rights, yet it may not be reflected in the use of the term *feminicidio*. If the long-term goal is to create the conditions for justice for women, the name is not as important as the content and analysis. After all, *feminicidio* has played an important part in a national process of redefining the movement's focus and strategy. The *feminicidio* debates continue on every level, from national contexts such as Peru, Guatemala, and Mexico, to regional networks such as CLADEM, to international organizations such as Amnesty International. Since the current utility of *feminicidio* cannot be denied, each group must conscientiously determine how and why they are using the term.

Notes

1. To date, the concept of femicide as developed by Jill Radford and Diana Russell (1992) has been translated in Latin America as *femicidio*, *feminicidio*, and *violencia femicida* (CLADEM 2007, 32).

2. Isis International initiated the Por la Vida de las Mujeres, Ni una Muerte, campaign in June 2001. A variety of formal and informal regional networks organize around the concept.

3. Saba Mahmood (2001) proposes a way to think about agency that breaks out of its liberal humanist parameters. Although this is beyond the

scope of this chapter, I develop this concept of agency in relation to Quechua-speaking Andean women in my dissertation, "Use and Abuse of Human Rights" (2009).

4. *Un termino empoderado.* Interview with Liz Menendez, Centro de la Mujer Peruana "Flora Tristan," January 3, 2007.

5. For more details, see the Isis International website at http://www.isis.cl.

6. M. Rodríguez 2005, 12–13. Both NGOs conducted studies on feminicide in 2003 and 2004. The resources to conduct studies and the data are both limited.

7. See the DEMUS website at http://www.demus.org.pe.

8. Interview with María Ysabel Cedano, director, DEMUS, November 12, 2006.

9. The report was elaborated with contributions from the following groups: Comisión Mexicana de Defensa y Promoción de los Derechos Humanos; CLADEM; Federación Internacional de Derechos Humanos; Centro por la Justicia y el Derecho Internacional; Kuña Aty (Paraguay); DEMUS (Peru), Católicas por el Derecho a Decidir (México); Grupo de Mujeres de San Cristóbal de las Casas (Mexico), Centro de Promoción de la Mujer, Gregoria Apaza (Bolivia); REDADA (Bolivia); Centro par la Acción Legal en Derechos Humanos (Guatemala); Sisma Mujer (Colombia), Red de la No Violencia contra las Mujeres de Guatemala; and Washington Office on Latin America.

10. Due to the sociopolitical insecurity, thorough research has not been possible. Therefore, accurate and reliable demographic data regarding the ethnic and class backgrounds of feminicide victims does not yet exist. For this reason, I use *ladinas* in its broadest interpretation to encompass both women of mixed indigenous and European descent and indigenous women displaced to urban centers who have adopted urban ways.

11. "El incumplimiento de los Acuerdos de Paz, en especial el de Forteci-miento del Poder Civil y el Papel del Ejército en una Sociedad Democrática, ha favorecido el desborde de la problemática de seguridad por la negativa a aplicar las medidas acordadas para favorecer un ambiente de libertad y democ-racia para la realización plena de la población. De particular incidencia en el repunte de la criminalidad y la violencia, fue la negativa a investigar y desar-ticular los cuerpos ilegales y aparatos clandestinos de seguridad por una comi-sión especifica . . . surgidos durante el conflicto armado interno al amparo y aquiescencia del Estado y cuya vinculación con las actuales organizaciones del crimen ha sido señalada reiteradamente por entidades nacionales e interna-cionales. De mucha importancia en esta problemática es también la negativa a cumplir con el traslado al Ministerio de Gobernación del control de armas y municiones que sigue en manos del ejército, cuya falta de transparencia es un caldo de cultivo para el tráfico, portación y uso indiscriminado de armas de fuego. El Estado se ha negado también a crear y fortalecer los mecanismos civiles de investigación e inteligencia que continúan militarizandos y entor-pecen, debilitan y neutralizan la actuación de las instituciones de seguridad y

justicia" (see Unidad Revolucionaria Nacional Guatemaleteca at http:// www.terrelibere.org (accessed August 10, 2005).

12. As Tina Sideris argues, this type of approach is especially important for understanding the conditions of subordination that facilitate the perpetration of gender-based violence against women. "Yet subordination is neither static nor uncontested. It is elaborated in different ways by class, race, ethnicity, and culture within and across time and space. In this sense, then, context shapes gender-specific violence, the forms it takes, the way women and men experience and understand it, and the possibilities for resisting it" (Sideris 2002, 157).

13. Interview with Samantha Sams, director, Guatemala office, Consejería en Proyectos, November 21, 2006.

14. El informe de la PDH "Muertes violentas de mujeres durante el 2003," señala que este problema es "parte de un proceso acumulativo de descomposición social, que se fundamenta en la cultura de la violencia" y establece que las practices de salvajismo y repression contra las mujeres durante la Guerra interna son antecedentes de la situación actual ("Violent Deaths of Women during 2003" dictates that the problem is "part of a cumulative process of social decomposition founded in a culture of violence" and establishes that savage and repressive practices against women during internal war are antecedents to the contemporary situation). http://www.terrelibere.org/counter .php?riga=208 (printout on file with the author).

15. Ibid.

16. According to the final report of the Peruvian Truth and Reconciliation Commission, sexual violence includes forced prostitution, forced marriage, sexual slavery, forced abortion, forced pregnancy, sexual assault, forced nudity, and rape, among other crimes that have yet to be researched (see APRODEH 2005). I would also add unwanted pregnancy and the psychological, material, and emotional costs of bringing up an unwanted child, not to mention legal problems and social condemnation for the child when he or she is not recognized legally by his or her biological father. Internal armed conflict refers to the armed conflict internal to the nation-state. "Armed conflict is a narrow category of the general term 'conflict,' denoting conflicts where one or both sides resort to the use of force" (Moser 2001, 6). In the case of the Peruvian internal armed conflict, all sides resorted to violence, including the armed forces, the Communist Party of Peru–Shining Path, and the Túpac Amaru Revolutionary Movement.

17. President Alejandro Toledo, Decreto Supremo no. 065–2001-PCM, *El Peruano*, June 4, 2001.

18. The Declaration and Program of Action of the 1993 United Nations Human Rights Conference in Vienna, the Declaration and Platform of Action of the 1995 United Nations Women's Conference in Beijing, the Convention on the Elimination of all Forms of Discrimination against Women (CEDAW), and the Inter-American Convention on the Prevention, Punishment, and Eradication of Violence against Women (the Convention of Belém do Pará), the

jurisprudence of the International Criminal Tribunal for Rwanda and International Criminal Tribunal for the Former Yugoslavia, and the Rome Statute.

19. See vol. 6, chap. 1.5 of the final report (Peruvian Truth and Reconciliation Commission 2003).

20. For the concept of abject subject, see Fregoso 2006. See also Kristeva 1982.

21. Many feminists were active in individual or small-group initiatives that were not institutionally adopted by any feminist NGO.

22. This program started in December 2004. The district of Manta, in the northern part of the Department of Huancavelica, suffered an incursion by Sendero Luminoso (Shining Path) in 1980. In 1983, the armed forces occupied the community, established a base, and imposed its presence for sixteen years. The TRC documented a collective case of twenty-six rapes by military officers during that time. Experts assert that the majority of women in Manta were victims of sexual violence during the fourteen-year period of occupation, yet silence dominates among the survivors. This is one of two cases of sexual violence documented by the TRC and passed to the Defensoria del Pueblo (Peruvian National Ombudsman's Office) ready for prosecution, out of a total of forty-seven cases of human rights violations. The other sexual violence case involves a woman in Lima.

23. *El asesinato de las mujeres por parte de sus parejas por causa de celos.* Cedano used this terminology to specify exactly what kind of gender-based violence against women she was referring to, beyond the term *feminicidio.* Also, Cedano inherited the feminicide project when she took the position of director of DEMUS. Political violence refers to the violence that occurred during the internal armed conflict.

24. Interview with María Ysabel Cedano, March 11, 2007.

25. These NGOs are the Instituto de Defensa Legal and the Comisión por los Derechos Humanos and Asociación Pro.

26. Interview with Janet Llaja, DEMUS, February 27, 2007.

27. CEDAW and the Convention of Belém do Pará.

28. Resolución legislativa no. 26583, March 25, 1996.

29. Interview with María Ysabel Cedano, November 12, 2006. Liz Kelly (2000) argues this point in more depth.

30. Interview with Janet Llaja, DEMUS, February 27, 2007.

31. Interview with María Ysabel Cedano, November 3, 2007.

32. Interview with Liz Menendez, Centro de la Mujer Peruana "Flora Tristan," March 1, 2007.

33. Interview with Jessica Estrada, legal consultant, Amnesty International's Peru section, March 14, 2007.

34. Ibid.

35. Ibid.

36. Interview with Maria Jennie Dador Tazzini, DEMUS, February 28, 2007.

Paradoxes, Protests, and the Mujeres de Negro of Northern Mexico

On November 25, 2002, thousands of people marched through the streets of Mexico City and demanded, in the name of social justice, an end to the violence against women in northern Mexico. "Ni una Más (Not One More)" was their chant and the name of their social justice campaign. Their words referred to the hundreds of women and girls who have died violent and brutal deaths in northern Mexico and to the several hundreds more who have disappeared over the past ten years. Many of the victims reveal patterns of ritualistic torture and serial murder. Others appear to be victims of domestic violence, drug-related violence, random sexual violence, and the like.[1] The Ni una Más marchers, many working with human rights and feminist organizations in Mexico, are protesting against the political disregard and lack of accountability at all levels of government in relation to this surging violence against women. The symbolic leaders of their movement are the Mujeres de Negro (Women Dressed in Black), a group of women from the northern capital city of Chihuahua, where some of the murders have occurred and about 360 kilometers south of Ciudad Juárez, the border city where the vast majority have taken place.

Over the past decade, as international coverage of the violence has grown, various new organizations have emerged to lead the protests and to provide structure for people who want to express their outrage over the crimes and the lack of governmental response to them.[2] As is so often the case in social justice causes, the various organizations that constitute the Ni una Más campaign stake out different areas of expertise and terrain, and tensions often run high among them over the controversial issues of religion, feminism, abortion, and definitions of family. Particularly in Ciudad Juárez, such tensions have contributed to the proliferation of distinct organizations, as opposed to the formation of a consolidated umbrella group, and disputes among them often play out publicly in the local newspapers.[3] While these organizations do sometimes work together in the border city on major events, their mutual antagonisms are widely known and often interfere with the coordination of activities. Yet in contrast to the Ciudad Juárez organizations, Mujeres de Negro has succeeded in pulling together a wide and diverse coalition of groups located primarily in Chihuahua City and who, despite internal political and other differences, have established an umbrella organization to serve as a base for their activities.

To understand how the group has succeeded in forming such alliances, I chose to focus on Mujeres de Negro in my research into the new civic networks that have grown through the formation of the Ni una Más campaign. From January 2003 through July 2004, I interviewed Mujeres de Negro members and other participants in the Ni una Más campaign. I participated in coordinated events, and I followed the constantly changing dynamic of the social networks that constitute the campaign. This research on Mujeres de Negro represents one piece of a larger ethnographic project on the Ni una Más campaign, more generally, and its impact on changing notions of transnational citizenship. To do this work, I lived in Ciudad Juárez for more than a year, traveled regularly to Chihuahua City, and became integrated with the participants in the movement. My research was an ethnography not of any particular organization but of the movement as it unfolded through the social networks of its participants, some of whom worked directly with specific organizations and others who merely attended the activist and academic events that keep the movement going. Like any social movement, the structure of this phenomenon lies in these networks that are constantly transforming via the formation and disappearance of organizations, the making and breaking of alliances, the shifts in strategies, and the other mundane activities that generate social ties. This chapter represents one attempt to present how some of these dynamics form, change, and contribute to a larger social movement.

In the course of this research, I relied heavily on Rosalba Robles, an instructor at the Universidad Autónoma de Ciudad Juárez, who helped me set up interviews and whose own work on domestic violence directly informs my analysis (Robles 2004). I conducted archival research that consisted primarily of searching all of the regional dailies (in northern Mexico and in El Paso, Texas) for coverage, since the mid-1990s, of the protests surrounding the violence against women and the incipient formation of Mujeres de Negro and the other organizations within the campaign. In addition, I conducted interviews with civic and business leaders in Ciudad Juárez, Chihuahua City, Mexico City, and El Paso for their perspectives on the movement and its impact on the economic development of the border region.

Early in this research, I realized that Mujeres de Negro confronts a powerful paradox in its efforts to form a public coalition to advocate for the rights of women to be safe on the street and to demand government accountability in relation to these rights. The paradox is this: In taking their protests to the public sphere and exercising their democratic rights as Mexican citizens, the participants in Mujeres de Negro are publicly declaring the right of women to exist in the public sphere both as citizens and as people who deserve to be free from violence and fear. Yet as they take to the streets, they are vulnerable to attacks that they are "public women" in a discursive context in which that label continues to be used effectively to dismiss and devalue women for "prostituting" themselves by venturing beyond the domestic sphere, that traditional domain of female purity and obligation (see Castillo 1999; Wright 2004). Therefore, the participants in Mujeres de Negro face the paradox that by exercising their democratic voices through public protest, they are dismissed, by their detractors, as "unfit" citizens based on their contamination as "public women" whose causes are equally contaminated by their public presence. This gendering of space and of the democratic process, a process that by definition requires the active public participation of the citizenry, and the dismissal of women's democratic voices based on their exercise of democratic rights creates a powerful conundrum that Mujeres de Negro cannot ignore.

One of my aims in this article is to demonstrate that even as Mujeres de Negro challenges the twisted logic that dismisses its public protests due to its public nature, it cannot fully escape its implications. For as Michel Foucault (1995) well illustrated, there is no total escape from the discursive context in which this paradox makes sense. Like women activists through time and space, the participants in Mujeres de Negro do not have the luxury of ignoring or escaping the contradictions of modern democracies that, while proclaiming equality and liberty, have been founded around the exclusion of women from the democratic process (see Landes 1998; Scott 1997). They must, as the geographer Lynn Staeheli (1996) has shown, constantly reconfigure the boundary between public and private as they confront the tautological argument that women are not fit for the public sphere because their proper place is in the private sphere, and thus their trespassing beyond the private sphere represents a degradation of the public sphere. Consequently, women who dare to question such exclusions encounter the vexing tautology that their future exclusion from the public sphere — the domain of modern democracy — is justified by their past exclusion from this sphere.

Likewise, Mujeres de Negro has to engage constantly with the discourses by which "public women" come to represent social and human contamination and, as a result, are not suitable citizens or democratic participants (see also Castillo 1988; Hershatter 1999). Its participants do not have the option of broadly declaring that such assertions are "nonsense" or "ludicrous" in an environment in which this discourse is commonly used to blame women for the violence they suffer, to deny them access to public protections, and to enforce a patriarchal concept of the domestic domain as the proper place for women (see Wright 2001a). And, as I endeavor to show here, while they take on the discourse that dismisses their public protests on the basis that they are "public women," they do indeed open up new spaces for women's civic activism in Mexico, even as they paradoxically reinforce many of the traditional prohibitions against women's access to politics and to the public sphere.

Public–Private Women

The leaders of Mujeres de Negro are primarily middle-class women with experience in activist organizations and nongovernmental organizations (NGOS), and its members include anyone who is willing to put on a black tunic and pink hat and carry a sign as a Mujer de Negro in protest over the crimes against women and the political incompetence surrounding them.[4] Their public protests and events usually incorporate dramatic gestures. In addition to their own stark clothing, they often march with crosses, which they sometimes adorn with dismembered mannequin parts to evoke images of the suffering endured by the victims. They have walked hundreds of miles across Mexico and left crosses with victims' names throughout the Chihuahuan desert. They have led marches in numerous Mexican cities. They have orchestrated funerary processions into public offices. They have interrupted military parades; held up traffic at the international bridges spanning the Mexico–U.S. divide; held silent vigils in city plazas; yelled at government officials during public events; and lain down in front of cars on busy avenues. Through such activities, these women have directed international attention to the impunity enjoyed by the criminals, to the political disregard for the crimes, and to the suffering of the victims and their families.

According to several of its members, Mujeres de Negro drew its inspiration for its public image from the many other women, around the world, who have used the black clothing of mourning, domesticity, and female modesty to express their identities as social justice and human rights activists. Particularly throughout the Americas of the twentieth century, the black-dressed woman activist has played a high-profile role in challenging repressive governments, neoliberal politics, and state-sanctioned violence (Bouvard 1994; Del Olmo 1986; Friedman 1998; Stephen 1995). Probably the most internationally famous of such activists are the Madres de la Plaza de Mayo, in Buenos Aires, whose question, "Where is my child?" provoked a crisis of legitimacy for the brutal military dictatorship that terrorized Argentina from 1977 to 1982. The group's self-portrayal as mothers provided legitimacy for them as women who were on the street not as political subversives or as "women of the street" but, rather, as women doing what women are publicly sanctioned to do. They were looking for their children.

As Joan Scott (2002) has written, the woman-in-black activist is paradoxical because she "signifies powerlessness" while simultaneously posing a powerful challenge to governing elites in the name of social justice. For the rage of the woman-in-black activist is born of sorrow, grief, a mother's worry, and beneath her black cape and pink hat we expect to find a soft, feminine body — no weapons, no muscles, no phallus. Hers is a politics of emasculation. In this way, Mujeres de Negro of northern Mexico, like women/activists in black around the world, take to the streets neither as aggressive youth nor as politicians but as women whose provenance from the private sphere legitimates their public activities. In other words, their legitimacy as public agents derives from their self-portrayal as women bound by the private domain (see also Martin 1990).

This paradox is particularly salient in the case of Mujeres de Negro because this group is composed principally of women who are well known for their participation in other activist and political organizations. The most prominent spokespeople of the Mujeres de Negro group have experience with or make a living in legal-aid, feminist, and political organizations; some have served in statewide political offices; some have organized radical activist operations, particularly against the privatization of public utilities in the mid-1990s. Therefore, to portray themselves as women whose motivations derive from the domestic, rather than the public, sphere, many of these women have had to change from women known for their public convictions into women known for their private ones. This transformation takes place in public space, since it is there — on the streets, in the plazas, and in public offices — that the Mujeres de Negro come to life as a group of women who stand in the public sphere to represent the private sphere. As such, Mujeres de Negro illustrates, as many feminist geographies have shown, how women activists often resort to paradoxical spatial strategies to navigate the myth of the private–public divide and the gendered hierarchies it supports (see Desbiens 1999; Mahtani 2001; Rose 1993). Mujeres de Negro deploys this spatial strategy to reinvent its participants publicly as private women as a way to neutralize accusations by regional elites that women on the street, no matter their purpose, represent the source of social trouble rather than its resolution. As "family-minded" women, the participants in Mujeres de Negro are able to deflect such accusations and claim, as many black-dressed women activists have before them, that they have taken to the street to protect their families and cultural traditions. And they emerge as "public–private women," women whose domestic allegiances are publicly performed.

In addition to justifying their presence on the street, this strategy of publicly defining themselves as family women also allows the activists to define the victims as fundamentally "family girls" or "daughters" (*hijas*). This strategy has arisen in direct response to the allegations of regional elites that the victims had, through their own illicit behavior, invited the violence that ended their lives. This age-old "blame the victim" strategy is a transparent effort on the part of regional elites and the police to deflect criticism of their responsibility vis-à-vis the violence as they, instead, blame the women who attracted trouble by venturing into the street, by wearing short skirts, by dancing, by not being at home.

This discourse of blaming the victim gains its footing in the story of the woman on the street who signifies "the whore," who is, in turn, the woman whose embodiment of contamination extends to the cultural spaces she inhabits. The women of Ciudad Juárez have gained particular prominence over the past half century as emblematic of this cultural contamination as they have made the city infamous as a place where they, in contrast to traditional Mexican women, are easily found on the street, either as women walking the street for a living or as women who walk the street en route to their factory jobs.[5] This presence of women on the streets of Juárez has contributed to the city's ignominy, throughout Mexico, as the place where Mexican culture has been corroded by the perverse influences of globalization and the cultural intrusions of its northern neighbor (see Tabuenca Córdoba 1996–97). And as Mujeres de Negro takes to the street under the Ni una Más campaign, it constantly encounters the accusation that it is violating the boundaries separating pure family women from those sullied by public ambitions as its participants "prostitute" themselves and victims' families for personal political gain.

Mujeres de Negro is thus in a difficult position of having to navigate this Janus-headed discourse of "the whore" that binds women's presence on the street to all sorts of cultural problems, ranging from the violence that stalks women to the erosion of Mexican culture, while it actively takes on a multilevel system of government in which corruption, torture, and lack of accountability are still common. These activists have taken on two different political parties, two different gubernatorial administrations, several mayors, and resistant police officers who have all tried, at one point or another, to downplay the significance of the murders and kidnappings and to dismiss the activists as "misplaced" women-as-women who should be at home. They have, however, finally provoked a response from the former president, Vicente Fox, who at International Women's Day celebrations in Mexico City on March 8, 2004, declared that he would use all of the power of his office to punish the criminals while calling on the governor of Chihuahua State to correct the incompetence of the state's juridical system (R. E. Vargas 2004). They are also taking on the systemic problem of violence against women, whose roots in domestic violence (which, according to domestic abuse facilities in Ciudad Juárez, afflicts 70 percent of women in the State of Chihuahua),[6] challenge the myth of the home as the sanctity of Mexico's daughters, sisters, wives, and mothers (see also Robles 2004).

While their activist strategy—based on their own reinvention as public–private women—has proved effective for galvanizing an international movement around the issues of political accountability, misogyny, and human rights abuses, this approach is not without pitfalls. In re-creating the dichotomy that distinguishes the "public" woman from the "private" one, and by basing their own authenticity as activists on this difference, they reproduce the very prohibitions that so often limit women's access to the public sphere. As they justify their public movement on the strength of their private convictions, the participants in Mujeres de Negro are vulnerable to their exposure as women with political careers and public professions. Such exposure takes direct aim at their authenticity as traditional Mexican women who represent the honest convictions of the traditional Mexican family, since any evidence of their public lives links them to the notion of the "public woman," who is always suspected of some form of "prostitution." Consequently, Mujeres de Negro activists must navigate the paradox that their presence in public space undermines their legitimacy as public agents in an environment where a woman's legitimacy in the public sphere depends on the strength of her domesticity.

In the following, I begin with a brief discussion of how the Mujeres de Negro activists have effectively deployed their contradictory positioning as public–private women as a means for inspiring an international human rights campaign. I then examine how this strategy coincides with that used by the movement's antagonists, who seek to expose the public source of the Mujeres de Negro activism and, in the process, discredit the Ni una Más campaign.

Paradoxes and Protests

The group of women now officially known as Mujeres de Negro originated in November 2001 in Chihuahua City, when a handful of civic organizations rallied in response to the discovery of eight young women's corpses in Ciudad Juárez. The bodies, showing signs of prolonged torture and sexual assault, had been found in an empty lot that sits at a highly trafficked intersection in southeastern Ciudad Juárez, across the street from the Maquiladora Industry Association (AMAC) offices, about two kilometers from Wal-Mart and down the street from a prestigious country club. This shocking discovery exposed the impunity of the murderers and the undeniable danger that young women face in Ciudad Juárez daily. On November 15, Alma Gómez, a former state legislator and schoolteacher and current director of Mujeres Barzonistas, a rural legal-aid organization, announced to the press that there would be a protest in Chihuahua City during the November 20 celebration of the Mexican Revolution. Other participants in the protest included women who had worked with Mujeres por Mexico (Women for Mexico), an organization that works for women's civil rights; the Comisión de Solidaridad y Defensa de los Derechos Humanos (Commission for the Solidarity and Defense of Human Rights); the Circulo de Estudios de Genero (Gender Studies Reading Group), an organization of women who read feminist scholarship; 8 de Marzo (Eighth of March), an organization formed in the early 1990s to support women's reproductive rights and to make domestic violence a crime under Mexican law; the Red Nacional de Abogadas Feministas (National Network of Feminist Lawyers); and the Fondo Nacional de Mujeres (National Organization of Women), among others. On November 20, Mujeres de Negro made its debut when some three hundred women dressed in black interrupted the parade in Chihuahua City, declared a moment of silence in what is usually a festive event, and publicly admonished the governor for his negligence concerning the murders. Journalists referred to this diverse assemblage of women as Mujeres de Negro. As one member told me: "They called us Mujeres de Negro out of laziness (*por flojera*). So now it's our name."

A few months later, the activists' identity as Mujeres de Negro was firmly established when some one hundred women walked the 360 kilometers across the desert, from Chihuahua City to Ciudad Juárez, to join with the hundreds who protested the violence against women as part of the International Women's Day celebration on March 8. The Chihuahua group called its march Exodo por la Vida (Exodus for Life). For this event, Mujeres de Negro had coordinated the uniforms of a black tunic and pink hat, which it handed out to anyone who would join the event. Mujeres de Negro designed a large black cloth that could be worn simultaneously by some twenty women, as if they were wearing the same dress, with their pink-covered heads poking through holes in the fabric, which they wore as they marched down the 16 de Septiembre, a principal avenue in Ciudad Juárez. Mujeres de Negro's use of crosses and black clothing had antecedents in the victims' family organization Voces sin Eco (Voices without an Echo), established in 1998, which had organized the painting of pink crosses on black telephone poles throughout Ciudad Juárez. The symbol of the cross, along with the wearing of black mourning clothing, was calculated, as one of the Mujeres de Negro leaders told me, to let the public know that "our movement is about family." The march's culminating moment occurred when, flanked by the other protestors, Mujeres de Negro erected a large wooden cross at the international bridge (Santa Fe) in downtown Ciudad Juárez. The cross was decorated with torn clothing, photographs, and 268 nails to represent each woman murdered in Ciudad Juárez since 1993. Since that time, Mujeres de Negro has participated in marches and events throughout northern Mexico and in Mexico City.

Mujeres de Negro does not represent an official organization. It is not a registered civil association; it has neither an organizational charter nor office space. In other words, Mujeres de Negro exists only when these women get together, put on their tunics and pink hats, and stand in the street. Some participants in Mujeres de Negro do not like each other; some, even, are publicly known to have deep political differences. For instance, one Mujer de Negro activist explained, "We are not all friends. Some of us fight politically with each other. Serious fights. I mean '*hasta la muerte* (to the death)? But we come together when it is important. And this is important." As another explained, "The Mujeres de Negro are a strategy for political activism. It doesn't exist for any other reason." In short, the women who constitute Mujeres de Negro are creating a public identity that does not exist privately. This space of this identity is on the street. As Irma Campos, one of the leaders of Mujeres de Negro, put it: "If we didn't put on black clothing and stand in the street, then there would not be the Mujeres de Negro."

Yet, ironically, this public identity of the Mujer de Negro hinges directly on the public performance of the private woman, which the women who constitute Mujeres de Negro achieve by subsuming their public identities as politicians and activists to a private identity as family women. As Alma Gómez explained, "People know who I am. I was a state legislator. I have been active in politics with the Barzon. But when I am part of Mujeres de Negro, I am not acting on behalf of any political party. I am a woman concerned about what is happening." As Campos said, "When we dress in black, we are identifying ourselves as women who want a response. We are women concerned about our city and our community." Isabel, a Mujeres de Negro activist who works with a political party, explained this combination of symbols: "We are not about political campaigns. We are women who want this violence to stop." Or, as another member told me at a protest in Ciudad Juárez in February 2003, "Some of us have political experience. But right now we are here as women, as mothers, and we are concerned for our daughters and the young women of Juárez and Chihuahua."

This strategy for reinventing themselves as a public group organized by private, rather than politically seasoned, women ties directly into the discourse, used by numerous activist groups, to portray the victims as "innocent daughters." This discourse of victims as daughters speaks directly to the accusation, launched by political and corporate elites since the mid-1990s, that the victims provoke this violence by being on the street, by dancing in cantinas, and by being sexually provocative (Tabuenca Córdoba 2003b). This accusation effectively declares that these victims, and future victims, are not worth worrying about, investigating, or even protecting (Wright 1999). According to this logic, a prostitute, or anyone suspected of being one, is still a woman who is understandably violated and murdered in public space. As Debbie Nathan (2002, 6) has noted, "Between a rock and a hard place, families are thus loath to deal with the fact that many beloved daughters do go to cantinas, and many do communicate sexuality through their clothing. Yet to acknowledge this is to imply that one's child is a slut undeserving of redress. It's a cruel conundrum that has forced activists in Juárez to use a public rhetoric in which victims are all church-going, girlish innocents."

But first, before declaring the innocence of the daughter, the victim has to be recognized as a "daughter" above other possible identifiers, such as woman, girl, friend, worker, lover, and so forth. Mujeres de Negro, as well as several other activist organizations such as Nuestras Hijas de Regreso a Casa (Bring Our Daughters Home) and Justicia para Nuestras Hijas (Justice for Our Daughters), constantly reiterate the familial condition of the victim as daughter. In this way, they have a response to the question asked by two governors and by corporate leaders: Why wasn't she at home in the first place? The answer from these organizations is that this daughter was on the street, just like the Mujeres de Negro, for a legitimate family reason, and this reason makes her a legitimate victim.

This strategy for legitimating the public presence of women, both as activists and as victims, around their private identities has succeeded in intensifying international pressure on the Mexican government to take action. International human rights organizations; representatives of the United Nations; and legislators from the United States, Brazil, and Spain, among others, have criticized the Chihuahua State government for incompetence and harassment of activists. Heated attention has also turned to the responsibility of the maquiladora industry, which continues to rely on low-wage female workers who live in impoverished neighborhoods that lack many basic services, such as drainage, potable water, and electricity. Visual artists, filmmakers, playwrights, and poets, among others, have turned a critical eye toward the role of international companies, Mexican politicians, and corrupt police forces in the perpetuation of the violence and the lack of convictions.

As a result of its efficacy in generating international pressure on state and federal officials, Mujeres de Negro has increasingly been a target of public hostility. The governor's office under the administration of Patricio Martínez had been particularly aggressive in its efforts to diffuse the group's impact, and it has organized counter-protests that sometimes resorted to violence to intimidate the activists. For instance, in June 2002, after the cross was stolen from the plaza in front of the governor's office, Mujeres de Negro marched to the governor's office while carrying a banner that declared, "Se Busca una Cruz (A Cross at Large)." The group was met in front of the governor's office by women wearing white who were flanked by men holding baseball bats. When the men started pounding the pavement with their bats, the Mujeres de Negro participants sat on the street, and some made phone calls to the press to alert it to the events. Despite the fact that they were sitting directly in front of the governor's office, no police officers could be found. As one of the Mujeres de Negro explained, "I'm sure if the press hadn't arrived, there would have been violence." When, a few months later, the new cross that Mujeres de Negro had commissioned from a local blacksmith's shop was stolen at gunpoint by eight heavily armed men who tied up the workers and threatened to kill them, Mujeres de Negro commissioned yet another cross. The second cross is also still at large.

Like many participants in the Ni una Más movement, those in Mujeres de Negro have reported anonymous threats, phone taps, unknown vehicles parked outside their homes, and intimidating men following them on foot or in cars, in addition to physical abuse. "There are a lot of people who are scared, but we can't let that stop us," said Alma. "This is a bad time in Chihuahua."

While these forms of intimidation do frighten many of the activists, they have not been largely effective in stopping their activities. However, one strategy used by the governor's office has proved somewhat successful in, at least, causing Mujeres de Negro to pause and regroup. The governor's office has forced Mujeres de Negro into a defensive position by extending the "prostitution" and "bad mother" accusation to include the allegation that the group's members are prostituting themselves by benefiting financially and politically from the "pain of the mothers." This accusation revolves around the concept that Mujeres de Negro is accepting "dirty money" or "filthy lucre," which represents how the activists contaminate motherhood and Mexican cultural tradition when they take to the streets.

Filthy Lucre

This allegation made the headlines in Chihuahua City on February 23, 2003, when the state's attorney general announced that Mujeres de Negro was taking money from the families of the victims to launch a political campaign against the governor's Institutional Revolutionary Party (PRI). The headline of the *Heraldo de Chihuahua*, based on the state attorney general's allegation that Mujeres de Negro and other activist groups were embezzling money from victims' families, declared: "Lucran ONGs con Muertas (NGOs Profiting from Deaths)" (see Piñon Balderrama 2003). The allegation also implied that many of the Mujeres de Negro activists were personally fortifying their own coffers and political futures by peddling the sorrow and pain of families to international organizations, which provided donations, and to sensationalist reporters who made them famous. The charge carried extra weight given that many participants in Mujeres de Negro live in middle-class circumstances while the victims' families are usually economically impoverished. This accusation pointed to a most terrible distortion of motherhood as Mujeres de Negro was accused of feigning grief and making a mockery of the victims' mothers for their own political ambition and greed.

On February 24, Mujeres de Negro met in the office of the Mujeres Barzonistas (Women of the Barzon) to discuss its response. "This accusation is very serious," explained Alma, "because many people are ready to believe it, mainly because we are women, and women who are not in the home, taking care of their families, are suspicious." She added that the class differences between the middle-class Mujeres de Negro and the economically poor families made the accusation even worse. As Irma Campos put it, "These families don't have any money to steal. How can we steal what they don't have?"

In the ensuing days, the governor declared that activists such as Mujeres de Negro, through their public rabble-rousing, were impeding the judicial process and presenting obstacles to the investigations. He reproached Mujeres de Negro for contributing to the social decomposition of northern Mexico, which the activists were fostering by forsaking their private duties in the interest of their public ambitions. He declared that the crimes originated not with government negligence but with a "series of social problems, of a weakening of the family" (Barrientos Márquez 2003, 3–9). Campos responded in the press by stating that the governor and his attorney general had "declared war" on civil organizations instead of declaring war against the criminals (Perea Quintanilla 2003). Graciela, another of the Mujeres de Negro, elaborated: "All of us here [in the room where they were discussing their response] work with organizations. We are women who work outside of the home. This makes us an easy target." She continued, "It is easy for him to blame us. That's what he is good at."

"The problem," explained Alma, "is that we need to discuss what we mean by this word *lucrar*. If *lucrar* means that some of us work with organizations that have budgets, well, yes, then we are *lucrando*. We have to support our activities. But if it means that we are getting personally rich, no, that is not happening. There is just a general ignorance over the meaning of *lucrar*."

"One of the problems," explained Campos, "is that this kind of accusation can create tensions between us and the victims' families. Most of the families are poor. They live in very humble circumstances. When they hear that we are making money, even though this is a lie, it creates problems." Another of the Mujeres de Negro elaborated: "The families sometimes feel used by Mujeres de Negro. The idea that people are earning a living from this movement when they are poor and suffering a terrible trauma is very difficult for them. It is difficult for everyone."

Julia Monárrez Fragoso, who has studied the violence against women in Ciudad Juárez, explained that this government's strategy for dismissing Mujeres de Negro had a corrosive effect on the relationship between victims' families and non-family activist organizations. "A lot of families feel that they are being used by political organizations and by individuals for their own reasons. It creates an impossible situation," she said.[7]

Alma summarized the problem this way: "We have to have a political strategy. You cannot organize for social justice without a political strategy. And we have to support ourselves. This takes time and resources. The government uses this fact against us."

This government campaign has also fostered divisions among the many organizations run by women that participate in the Ni una Más campaign, which want to distance themselves from the groups charged with prostituting themselves to remain in good public standing as organizations motivated by "clean" intentions. For instance, Astrid Gonzalez of Lucha contra Violencia announced in an article in the *Heraldo de Chihuahua* on February 25 (two days after the lucre accusation) that, in an echo of the governor's words, the "social decomposition of Ciudad Juárez" had penetrated the NGOs. She said, "There are pseudo-organizations and pseudo-leaders who benefit (*lucran*) not only politically, but also with the donations that they receive in bank accounts in the name of women assassinated in Ciudad Juárez" (quoted in Meza Rivera 2003, 2–25). She continued: "The time has come to identify a difference, in order to clean up the image of the NGOs." Meanwhile, more articles appeared in which Mujeres de Negro was linked with delinquency, graffiti, familial distress, and the general destruction of society (see Luruena Caballero 2003, 3–4).

Another issue used to "out" Mujeres de Negro as composed of inherently public rather than private women has been the affiliation of some of its members with political organizations, particularly the Partido Revolucionario Democratico (Revolutionary Democratic Party; PRD). The PRD traditionally has a stronger presence in the central part of the country than in the north, where it represents an alternative to the other two major parties, PRI and the Partido Acción Nacional (National Action Party; PAN), which have dominated local and state offices. The PRD represents "the left" in contrast to the PRI, which formerly governed the entire country under an autocratic system, and the socially conservative and pro-business PAN. Several of the Mujeres de Negro participants have been active in the PRD, with some running and serving in public office and with some having familial relations to PRD members. Because at that time their activism had politicized the issue of violence against women, the governor's office, under the PRI banner, accused Mujeres de Negro of using the murders as a means to gain ground in statewide elections. The previous governor, Martínez, who at one point was considered a possible favorite for the PRI's presidential nomination, came under attack for his failure to live up to his campaign promise to resolve the murders. The response from his office was to charge that Mujeres de Negro members were hiding their PRD affiliations and bald political ambition behind a cloak of domesticity and mourning. The women have also been accused of being "feminists," "lesbians," and women who cater to the lust of an American audience always hungry for a tasty story about sex and violence.

This strategy for "outing" Mujeres de Negro activists as public women has fed into another strategy for dismissing victims who do not have real mothers to protest on their behalf. While, of course, all women are "daughters," even if they do not have parents, the discourse that narrows the legitimacy of daughter status to only those victims who have mothers actively searching for them represents one more tactic for ignoring the severity of the violence against women in general. Those victims who do not emerge as daughters disappear from public discourse concerning the crimes. These victims include women and girls who could be identified as workers, neighbors, friends, mothers, or prostitutes or simply as people in general whose lives were brutally ended. And these women represent the large majority of those murdered in northern Mexico over the past decade. For instance, even though domestic violence is widely recognized as a serious problem throughout the region (Robles 2004), the connections between that crime and the murders is rarely broached. Instead, the discourse of victim-daughters re-creates the myth that the family is the haven of women's honor and safety, even though recent studies reveal that most women are murdered or raped by their current or former husbands or lovers. As a result, this discourse that stakes the authenticity of the victim on her filial status contributes to the trivialization of the gendered violence that is pandemic in northern Mexico.

Moreover, when Mujeres de Negro and other activists try to include the murders of other, non-daughter women in the discussion, they are accused of "inflating" the numbers and fanning the sensationalist fires of an international press that is damaging northern Mexico's reputation among businesses and tourists (Guerrero and Minjares 2004). This accusation, again, leads to another, in which the governor's office has maintained that Mujeres de Negro and other activist groups are the reason that northern Mexico's economy is faltering. This charge holds a great deal of weight at this time, particularly in Ciudad Juárez, which has lost a quarter of its manufacturing jobs in the maquiladora sector since 2000. Unemployment rates are rising, and regional elites are visibly panicked about the possibility that more maquiladoras will shut their doors and move to China. Several business organizations and the governor's office have claimed that part of the problem is the negative reputation of Ciudad Juárez that is being perpetuated by the activists who call international attention to the crimes against women. As one business leader exclaimed in 2003 during a public forum in Ciudad

Juárez organized around the economic crisis: "The news media just covers the women who talk about murders. They just cover trash. That's all it is, . . . trash. And that's what everyone thinks of now when they think of Juárez. They don't know that this is a good place for families. Where traditional families are strong. All they know is that we've got murders, and dead girls and all the trouble."[8]

Similar statements have surfaced from the governor's office, which has reiterated that Mujeres de Negro contributes to the "social disintegration" of Ciudad Juárez and Chihuahua by "manipulating information" and creating the idea that Ciudad Juárez is the "murder capital of the world," which scares off business and tourist dollars (Prado Calahorra 2003a, 5A). As a result, according to the governor's office, it is this social disintegration and the bad reputation generated by these public women that is destroying both Mexican tradition and the Mexican economy (Prado Calahorra 2003b; Martínez Coronado 2003).

Shortly after these statements were made, Mujeres de Negro vowed to renew its Ni una Más campaign. Irma Campos put it this way: "It scares them to see women taking charge, being political. And it is easy to criticize us for not being at home. It makes things hard for us. We have to create a certain image. But we don't have a choice. We have to do something. We can't just sit at home while women are being murdered and kidnapped all around us."

The paradoxes that Mujeres de Negro both confronts and perpetuates with its activist strategy again surfaced when the group dramatically interrupted the International Conference of Forensic Sciences, which was being held in Chihuahua City in August 2003. As a result of the disruptions to the otherwise orderly meetings, Mujeres de Negro succeeded in extracting a public promise from the federal attorney general to pay attention to the crimes. Yet his carefully worded statement revealed the caveat surrounding his promise: "We want to strengthen families, to strength people, and I am not going to hide [in the face of activists' accusations over incompetence], and all of the public officials have to respond to those people who *legitimately demand attention, because of the pain they have suffered.* You have to attend to them" (quoted in Prado Calahorra 2003a; emphasis added). Of course, the attorney general and much of the public realize that the Mujeres de Negro activists have not suffered the pain of the mothers who have lost daughters to the violence. His statement therefore leaves open the possibility that these activists are not legitimate.

Conclusion

Mujeres de Negro, like activist groups around the world, does not have the luxury of choosing the circumstances for its battles. It does not create the discourse that aligns public women with public trouble. Nor does it write the story that women in the home are the keepers of tradition and cultural authenticity. Especially in Ciudad Juárez, a city plagued with social problems, the meaning of the public woman has been bandied about as political incumbents try to evade culpability over the city's ills and turn the blame, instead, on the young women who commute at all hours of the day and who go dancing at all hours of night. The old story of the whore — as the consummate public woman — who contaminates the cultural space she inhabits is having new applications in Ciudad Juárez today as Mujeres de Negro must navigate its spatial implications.

The group's success in organizing an international human rights movement speaks to its determination not to be fully defined by this discourse of the public woman as whore and cultural contaminant. Its participants, through their activism, have created a new social identity in northern Mexico — the Mujer de Negro, the private woman who exists only in the public domain. The fact that people throughout the world know about the murders in Ciudad Juárez, that films and plays and articles are written about these murders, owes everything to the women activists who brave vicious criticism, threats, and harassment as they take to the streets.

Again, to invoke Joan Scott (1997), Mujeres de Negro's activities illustrate how feminist politics has only paradoxes to offer, since the productive effects of Mujeres de Negro's contradictory positioning are not contained within a single dialectical continuity. In other words, its activities do not surface strictly as "resistance" against a strictly "hegemonic" power structure. By binding their legitimacy as social activists to their private concerns as women and as mothers, rather than as politicians, feminists, or human rights activists, the Mujeres de Negro activists re-create the dialectic by which a private woman has more legitimacy in the public sphere than a self-avowed public one. Within the discursive climate whereby the private woman gains her legitimacy as activist in contrast to the public one, such claims effectively peel back the layers of black clothing and reveal the naked ambition of political women. Consequently, their activities illustrate how women activists are constantly caught within the following contradiction: While they are asserting their rights as citizens and their concerns as people who care about family, politics, community, and their country, their location on the street threatens the very basis on which they can make such claims, since public women, according to the familiar refrain of the story of the contaminated whore, represent threats to all of the above.

As long as the discourse of the whore — of the woman whose embodied contamination oozes from her onto the sidewalk, into the air, into the culture, and into the family — continues to be told and believed, women activists around the world will continually face the sorts of paradoxes confronting Mujeres de Negro in northern Mexico. This old story, whose roots extend far beyond the here and now of northern Mexico, is a most versatile and contemporary technology for justifying the many forms that violence against women takes in the modern world. As such, this story has directly contributed to what Amnesty International has labeled "intolerable negligence" on the part of the Mexican government in regard to these most "intolerable murders" (Amnesty International 2003, 65). Without the discourse of the whore — of the culturally contaminating contaminated woman — the strategy used by the Mujeres de Negro activists to turn themselves into publicly known private women would not make sense. The victims would not need to be daughters, and the activists would not need to be mothers, to count as valuable members of their cities, their families, their communities, their countries, their regions, their neighborhoods, their workplaces. It is even plausible to imagine that without the discourse of the whore, the Mujer de Negro might be able to take to the street as the "Mujer de Rojo" — as the woman in red.

As their words and deeds indicate, the fact that Mujeres de Negro cannot resolve the paradoxes of its activism, and that it even contributes to them, does not dampen the group's dynamism. It has added many more nails representing the murdered women to the cross that stands yet again in front of the governor's office in Chihuahua City. Given the way things are going in northern Mexico, it appears that these women, and the other activists of the Ni una Más movement, will be navigating the many paradoxes of their protests into the foreseeable future.

Notes

I thank Rosalba Robles, Guadalupe de Anda, Armine Arjuna, and Anu Sabhlok for their invaluable assistance on this project. I also thank Alicia Schmidt Camacho, Lorraine Dowler, and the anonymous reviewers for their helpful comments on various drafts of this chapter. I am especially indebted to the many informants, including activists and civic officials, who allowed me time for interviews, and I thank the library staff at the Instituto Municipal de Investigación y Planeación in Ciudad Juárez for their assistance with archival research. This material is based on work supported by the National Science Foundation under Grant No. 0215522. All opinions, findings, conclusions, and recommendations expressed in this material are those of the author and do not necessarily reflect the views of the National Science Foundation. This chapter originally appeared in *Gender, Place and Culture* 12, no. 3 (2005): 277–92 (available online at http://www.tandf.co.uk/journals).

1. The actual numbers of murders and kidnappings are not known. Official government figures are much lower than researchers' figures, which are also lower than activists' figures (Monárrez Fragoso 2001; Nathan 2002). Official statistics do reveal, however, that the homicide rate for women in Chihuahua quadrupled during the 1990s.

2. For a discussion of the coverage of the V-Day events in February 2004, see Rojas Blanco 2005.

3. For an example of how the local press presents antagonism among organizations and participants in the Ni una Más campaign, see Guerrero and Minjares 2004.

4. Women and men participate as part of the activities, but men do not wear the black tunics and pink hats. They appear in supporting rather than leading roles in the protests.

5. In Mexico, this intimacy binding the whore — as contaminated woman — to the cultural contamination of the nation is most famously captured in the myth of La Malinche, the Azteca who prostituted herself to Hernán Cortéz and betrayed her own people.

6. This figure is that used by Esther Chávez, director of Casa Amiga, a sexual-assault and rape crisis center in Ciudad Juárez that treats victims of domestic violence. She is referring to a study conducted since 2000 estimating that at least 70 percent of adult women in the State of Chihuahua have experienced domestic violence. I was unable to obtain a copy of this study.

7. Julia Monárrez Fragoso, personal communication.

8. Anonymous by request, personal communication.

Translated by Sara Koopman

Testimonio

NORMA LEDEZMA ORTEGA, MOTHER OF

PALOMA ANGELICA ESCOBAR LEDEZMA,

DISAPPEARED MARCH 2, 2002

My name is Norma Ledezma, and six years ago my life changed with the disappearance and death of my daughter Paloma Angelica Escobar Ledezma. Paloma worked in a maquiladora from 6 a.m. to 3:30 p.m., Monday through Friday; in the afternoon she went to high school; and on Saturdays she took computer classes at a school located downtown. . . . On Saturday, March 2, 2002, Paloma left her house at 3:15 p.m. to go to her computer class. She should have returned home at about 8:30 p.m. or 9 p.m., but she didn't come home. She never came home.

We started searching for her immediately, that same night, with family and friends, but it was useless. The next day we filed the appropriate criminal complaint, but the police did not search for her right away. The whole family started looking. We put up flyers with her photo all over the city, but it was useless. We looked for her, without stopping, for twenty-seven days. During that time the assistant deputy district attorney, the district attorney, and the governor of the State of Chihuahua, Patricio Martínez, met with us. They assigned several commanders and agents to search for her (that was what the governor promised me), but it was all useless. They didn't find her.

The only clue was testimony from a young woman who said that she had seen Paloma on March 2 in a black car very close to the school, and that outside the car was a man named Francisco who worked at that [computer] school, and that she [Paloma] looked half asleep, as if she were drugged. That's what the young woman who supposedly saw her said. That was the only clue. Days later, they called saying that she was in the southern part of the city. The police told us that she was fine, that they had found her, and that she wouldn't get away from them. Lies, it was all lies.

For twenty-seven days, from March 2 to March 29, 2002, the inquiry into Paloma's case was in the media — on television and in newspapers — and I started getting phone calls from women whose daughters had been disappeared for some time. We met with the governor and during the meeting he committed to helping us find them [our daughters]. On March 29, after twenty-seven days of searching for Paloma, I received a call from the Prior Investigations Unit informing me that they had found the body of a young woman who appeared to be Paloma. If in fact this was Paloma's body, she was found at the 4.5-km marker on the road to Ciudad Aldama. A couple who was passing by a ditch in that area found her body.

My girl was thrown there, in that dry ditch, completely clothed. I never saw her body. I never saw her again, but I did recognize and identify her clothes. There is no doubt it was Paloma. I confronted the authorities. I yelled at them that it was their fault for not having searched for her, and that was why she was dead now. It has been more than seven years, and they still haven't found the murderer.

That March 29, Good Friday, we founded Justicia para Nuestras Hijas (Justice for Our Daughters) to confront government authorities and demand transparency in the investigation process. That is how we started Justicia para Nuestras Hijas. We all united under the one cause of seeking justice for our daughters.

Throughout this journey of pain we've learned to love each other, since now Justicia para Nuestras Hijas has twenty-six cases of disappeared and murdered women. We, the families of all of these young women, are united. It is not a struggle of hate or vengeance. It is a struggle of love, of our love for them. Human rights workers, people who have always struggled for women, accompany us. Today we have attorneys and consultants; we also have a special prosecutor who works only on the association's cases. Along with other organizations, we have managed to get the Argentine Forensic Anthropology Team to come to Chihuahua. They have identified some of the bones of disappeared and dead young women whose families are part of our organization.

This event changed the path of my life. I've traveled unknown paths, ones that I never thought I would walk down. I keep on struggling; I'm still on the front lines of this exhausting war — sometimes with rage, sometimes with sadness, but always with the hope of finding justice for our daughters. One day my father urged me to never stop struggling to find justice for Paloma. Whatever happens, he said, for a child you give your very life without even stopping to think about it.

A few days ago my son Fabian, who is eighteen, also told me, "Mom, don't wait for an angel to come down from the sky to tell the authorities what they have to do. You are the hands of god, his feet, his voice. You and your *compañeras* are the conduit that God uses to do justice for the young women who were so cruelly murdered."

So when I feel tired and don't have the strength to go on, I remember that I have a debt to my Paloma, and I remember my son's words, and my father's, and, well, I keep going. I don't know if one day I will find justice for her, but I do know that I will keep struggling and that, even if everyone forsakes me, God will never leave me, and he will sustain me, as he has up to now. Because if the desert of Chihuahua was irrigated with innocent blood, from there the blood of our daughters clamors for justice. We, the overwhelmed and tired parents, are here struggling. We, the exhausted mothers, sisters, and brothers of the young women — our daughters who are no longer physically with us — will keep their names alive until we find justice here on Earth. We hope to see one day, with our own eyes, the light of justice that we so yearn for.

References

Court Cases

Adeniyi v. Bureau of Immigration. 2005. 157 Fed. Appx. 461, 465 (2d Cir.).

Ali v. Reno. 2001. 237 F.3d 591, 598 (6th Cir.).

Aumeervddy-Cziffra et al. v. Mauritius. 1990. Communication no. 35/1978, U.N. doc. CCPR/C/OP/2 at 226.

Aydin v. Turkey. 1998. European Human Rights Tribunal 57/1996/676/866. International Criminal Court for the Former Yugoslavia. It-96–4-t, ICTR Chamber I, sentence of September 2, para. 597.

Azanor v. Ashcroft. 2004. 364 F.3d 1013, 1019 (9th Cir.).

Chuidian v. Philippine National Bank. 1990. 912 F.Supp 1095 (9th Cir.).

Delgado Paez v. Columbia. 1990. Communication no. 195/1985, U.N. doc. CCPR/C./39/D/195/1985.

Doe v. Qi. 2004. 349 F.Supp 2d 1258 (N.D. Cal.).

Doe v. Unocal. 2005. 403 F.3d 708 (9th Cir. 2005).

Elcida Arévalo Perez et al. v. Colombia. 1989. Communication no. 181/1984, U.N. doc. CCPR/C/37/D/181/1984.

Filártiga v. Peña-Irala. 1980. 630 F.2d 876 (2d Cir).

Forti v. Suarez-Mason (Forti I). 1987. 672 F.Supp 1531 (N.D. Cal.).

Lovelace v. Canada. 1981. Communication no. R.6/24, U.N. doc. supp. no. 40 (A/36/40) at 166.

Lukwago v. Ashcroft. 2003. 329 F.3d 157, 183 (3d Cir.).

Mack v. Guatemala. 2003. Judgment of November 25, Inter-Am. C.H.R., OEA/ser. C.

Martí de Mejía v. Peru. 1996. Case 10.970, report no. 5/96, Inter-Am. C.H.R., OEA/ser. L/V/II.91, doc. 7, 157.

Mwani et al. v. Bin Laden. 2005. 417 F.3d 1. (D.C. Cir.).

Ontunez-Tursios v. Ashcroft. 2002. 303 F.3d 341, 355.

Reyes v. Ashcroft. 2004. 384 F.3d 782, 787 (9th Cir.).

Rodríquez-Olvera v. Salant Corp. 1999. No. 97–07–14605-CV (365th Dis. Ct., Maverick County, Tex.).

Sosa v. Alvarez-Madarin. 2004. 542 U.S. 692.

Velásquez Rodriguez v. Honduras. 1988. Judgment of July 29, Inter-Am. C.H.R., OEA/ser. C. 172.

Vos v. the Netherlands. 1999. Communication no. 786/1997, U.N. doc. *CCPR/C/66/D/786/1997.*

Other Sources

Acosta Vargas, Gladys. 1999. "La Mujer en los códigos penales de América Latina y el caribe hispano." In *Género y derecho*, ed. Alda Facio and Lorena Fries, 621–85. Santiago, Chile: Lom Ediciones.

Agamben, Giorgio. 1998. *Homo Sacer: Sovereign Power and Bare Life.* Stanford, Calif.: Stanford University Press.

———. 2005. *Estado de excepção.* São Paulo: Boitempo Editorial.

"Agudizan abusos contra mujeres transgénero en Ciudad Juárez." 2008. Centro Independiente de Noticias. October 31. Available online at http://cinoticias.com (accessed October 6, 2009). Printout on file with volume editors.

Aguilar, Sonia Isabel. 2007. "Desaparecen 124 personas en tres meses: Reportan mil 190 extravíos; la mayoría son mujeres." *Norte de Ciudad Juárez.* February 23, 1, sec. B.

Altolaguirre, Martha. 2003. *Situación de los derechos de la mujer en Ciudad Juárez, México: El derecho a no ser objeto de violencia y discriminación.* Inter-American Commission on Human Rights, March.

Alvarez Asencio, Jeannette Esmeralda. 2004. *Informe de crímenes contra mujeres en Guatemala*, ed. Amnesty International. Santiago, August. Available online at http://www.isis.org (accessed May 4, 2004).

Améry, Jean. 1980 (1977). *At the Mind's Limits: Contemplations by a Survivor of Auschwitz and Its Realities.* Bloomington: Indiana University Press.

Amir, Menacher. 1971. *Patterns in Forcible Rape.* Chicago: University of Chicago Press.

Amnesty International. 2002. "Guatemala: The Civil Defence Patrols Re-Emerge." September 4. Available online at http://www.amnesty.org. Printout on file with volume editors.

———. 2003. "Intolerable Killings: Ten Years of Abductions and Murders in Ciudad Juárez, Summary Report and Appeal Cases" ("Muertes Intolerables: Diez años de desapareciones y asesinatos de mujeres en Ciudad Juárez y Chihuahua"). August 11. Both versions available online at http://

www.amnesty.org (accessed November 1, 2006). Printouts on file with volume editors.

———. 2005. "No Justice: Killings of Women in Guatemala." June 12. Available online at http://web.amnesty.org. Printout on file with volume editors.

———. 2006. "Guatemala: No Protection, No Justice: Killings of Women (an Update)." July. Available online at http://www.amnestyusa.org. Printout on file with volume editors.

———. 2007. "Maze of Injustice: The Failure to Protect Indigenous Women from Sexual Violence in the USA." April 24. Available online at http://www.amnesty.org. Printout on file with volume editors.

Amorós, Celia. 1990. "Violencia y pactos patriarcales." In *Violencia y sociedad patriarcal*, ed. Virginia Maquieira and Cristina Sánchez, 39–53. Madrid: Pablo Iglesias.

Andersen, Margaret. 1988. *Thinking about Women*. New York: Macmillan.

Appadurai, Arjun. 1996. *Modernity at Large: Cultural Dimensions of Globalization*. Minneapolis: University of Minnesota Press.

———. 2006. *Fear of Small Numbers*. Durham: Duke University Press.

APRODEH (Asociación pro Derechos Humanos/Association for Human Rights). 2005. "Violencia contra la mujer durante el conflicto armado interno Warmikuna Yuyuriniku lecciones para no repetir la historia, selección de textos del Informe Final de la Comisión de la Verdad y Reconciliación." Lima: APRODEH.

Arendt, Hannah. 1951. *The Origins of Totalitarianism*. New York: Harcourt.

———. 1968. *The Origins of Totalitarianism*. San Diego, Calif.: Harcourt.

———. 1998 (1949). *Origens do totalitarismo*. São Paulo: Complain das Letras.

Asamblea de la Organización de Estados Americanos. 1994. *Convención interamericana para prevenir, sancionar y erradicar la violencia contra la mujer*. Belém do Pará, Brazil.

Atencio, Graciela. 2003. "El circuito de la muerte." *Triple Jornada* (monthly feminist supplement to *La Jornada*). September, 61.

Balderas Domínguez, Jorge. 2002. *Mujeres, antros y estigmas en la noche juarense*. Chihuahua: Instituto Chihuahuense de la Cultura.

Barkin, David. 2006. "Building a Future for Rural Mexico." *Latin American Perspectives* 33, no. 2: 132–40.

Barria, Lilian A., and Steven D. Roper. 2004. "Economic Transition in Latin American and Post-Communist Countries: A Comparison of Multilateral Development Banks." *International Journal of Politics, Culture and Society* 17: 619–38.

Barrientos Márquez, Heriberto. 2003. "En 10 anos la PGR no ha detenido ni un homicida: Patricio." *El Heraldo de Chihuahua*, March 13, 3A.

Bartra, Armando. 2005. "Cuando los hijos se van: Dilapidando el 'bono demográfico.'" *Masiosare* (supplement to *La Jornada*), August 4, 42.

Basch, Linda, Nina Glick Schiller, and Cristina Szanton Blanc, eds. 1994. *Nations Unbound: Transnational Projects, Postcolonial Predicaments, and Deterritorialized Nation-States*. Langhorne, Penn.: Gordon and Breach.

Baubock, Rainer. 1995. *Transnational Citizenship: Membership and Rights in International Migration*. Cheltenham: Edward Elgar.

Baxi, Upendra. 2006. *The Future of Human Rights*, 2d ed. New York: Oxford University Press.

BBC News. 2005. "Fund Unveiled for Mexican Murders." March 3. Available online at http://news.bbc.co.uk. Printout on file with volume editors.

———. 2006. "'Vigilante Killings' in Guatemala." February 10. Available online at http://news.bbc.co.uk. Printout on file with volume editors.

Beauvoir, Simone de. 1999. *El segundo sexo*, trans. Juan García Puente. Buenos Aires: Editorial Sudamericana.

Bejarano, Cynthia L. 2002. "Las Super Madres de Latino America: Transforming Motherhood and Contesting State Violence through Subversive Icons." *Frontiers* 23, no. 1: 126–50.

Benhabib, Seyla. 2002. *The Claims of Culture: Equality and Diversity in the Global Era*. Princeton: Princeton University Press.

Benítez, Rohry, Adriana Candia, Patricia Cabrera, Guadalupe de la Mora, Josefina Martínez, Isabel Velásquez, and Ramona Ortiz. 1999. *El silencio que la voz de todos quiebra: Mujeres y victimas de Ciudad Juárez. S. Taller de Narrativa*. Chihuahua: Ediciones del Azar.

Berkins, Lohana, ed. 2007. *Cumbia, copeteo y lágrimas*. Buenos Aires: Asociación de Lucha por la Identidad Travesti–Transexual.

Biebesheimer, Christina. 2005. "The Impact of Human Rights Principles on Justice Reform in the Inter-American Development Bank." In *Human Rights and Development: Towards Mutual Reinforcement*, ed. Philip Alston and Mary Robinson, 269–96. Oxford: Oxford University Press.

Binion, Gayle. 1995. "Human Rights: A Feminist Perspective." *Human Rights Quarterly* 17, no. 3: 509–26.

Boltvinik, Julio. 2000. "Aumento la pobreza en la actual administración." *La Jornada*, September 18.

———. 2005. "Debate, desigualdad y pobreza." *La Jornada*, April 28.

Boltvinik, Julio, and E. Hernández Laos. 2000. *Pobreza y distribución del ingreso en México*. Mexico City: Siglo XXI.

Bonilla, Rafael, and Patricia Ravelo Blancas, dir. 2005. *La batalla de las cruces. Una década de impunidad y violencia contra las mujeres*. DVD. Mexico City: Rafael Bonilla y Ascouados.

Borer, Tristan Ann. 2006. "Truth-telling as Peace-building Activity: A Theoretical Overview." In *Telling the Truth: Truth Telling and Peace Building in*

Post-Conflict Societies, ed. Tristan Ann Borer, 1–57. Notre Dame, Ind.: University of Notre Dame Press.

Bosniak, Linda. 2000. "The State of Citizenship: Citizenship Denationalized." *Indiana Journal of Legal Studies* 7, no. 2: 447–510.

Bourdieu, Pierre. 1999. *Razones prácticas: Sobre la teoría de la acción*. Barcelona: Editorial Anagrama.

Bourdreaux, Richard. 2003. "Mexico Sends 300 Agents to Probe Killings." *Los Angeles Times*, July 24, A3.

Bouvard, Marguerite. 1994. *Revolutionizing Motherhood: The Mothers of the Plaza de Mayo*. Wilmington, Del.: Scholarly Resources.

Brems, Eva 2003. "Protecting the Human Rights of Women." In *International Human Rights in the 21st Century*, ed. Gene Martin Lyons and James Mayall, 100–139. Lanham, Md.: Rowman and Littlefield.

Brown, Wendy. 2004. "The Most We Can Hope for . . . : Human Rights and the Politics of Fatalism." *South Atlantic Quarterly* 103, nos. 2–3 (Spring–Summer): 451–63.

Brysk, Alison. 1999. "Recovering from State Terror: The Morning after in Latin America." In *Societies of Fear*, ed. K. and D. K. Koonings, 249–44. London: Zed Books.

Bueno-Hansen, Pascha. 2009. "The Use and Abuse of Human Rights: Women and the International Armed Conflict in Peru." Ph.D. diss., University of California, Santa Cruz.

Bunster-Burotto, Ximena. 1993. "Surviving beyond Fear: Women and Torture in Latin America." In *Feminist Frameworks*, ed. Alison M. Jagger and Paula S. Rothenberg, 252–70. Boulder, Colo.: McGraw-Hill.

Buscaglia, Edgardo. 2005. "Eslabones del sistema de administración de justicia de Chihuahua y mejores prácticas internacionales relevantes" (Links in the Chihuahua justice system and relevant international best practices). In *Feminicidio, justicia y derecho*, ed. Comisión para Conocer y Dar Seguimiento a las Investigaciones Relacionadas con los Feminicidios en la República Mexicana y a la Procuración de Justicia Vinculada, Cámara de Diputados, LIX Legislatura, Mexico City, 105–18.

Cabrera, Yvette. 2004. "The Orphans: Young Life Thrown Off Course." *Orange County Register*, June 13–20. Available online at http://www.ocregister.com. Printout on file with volume editors.

CALDH (Centro de Acción Legal en Derechos Humanos/Center for Legal Action for Human Rights). 2005. *Asesinatos de mujeres. Expresión del feminicidio en Guatemala*. Guatemala City: SERVINSA. Available online at http://genero.bvsalud.org/lildbi/docsonline/get.php?id=247 (accessed October 6, 2009).

Cámara de Diputados del H. Congreso de la Unión. 2006. *Violencia feminicida en 10 entidades de la República Mexicana*. Mexico City: LIX Legislatura

Comisión Especial para Conocer y Dar Seguimiento a las Investigaciones Relacionadas con los Feminicidios en la República Mexicana y a la Procuración de Justicia Vinculada.

Cameron, Deborah, and Elizabeth Frazer. 1987. *The Lust to Kill: Feminist Investigation of Sexual Murder*. New York: New York University Press.

Campbell, Federico. 2004 (1989). *La memoria de Sciascia*. Mexico City: Fondo de Cultura Económico.

Cançado Trindade, Antonio A. 2002. "Presentation of the Annual Report to the Committee on Judicial and Political Affairs." Permanent Council of the Organization of American States, OEA/ser. G., CP/CAJP-1932/02.

Caputi, Jane, and Diana E. H. Russell. 1992. "Femicide: Sexist Terrorism against Women." In *Femicide: The Politics of Woman Killing*, ed. Jill Radford and Diana E. H. Russell, 13–26. New York: Twayne.

Carcedo, Ana. 1994. *Mujer no estás sola. Cinco mil mujeres deteniendo el maltrato*. San José, Costa Rica: Centra Feminista de Información y Acción.

Carcedo, Ana, and Montserrat Sagot. 2002. *Femicidio en Costa Rica, 1990–1999*. San José, Costa Rica: Organización Panamericana de la Salud.

Carcedo, Ana, and Alida Zamora. 1999. *Ruta critica de las mujeres Afectadas por la violencia intrafamiliar en Costa Rica*. San José, Costa Rica: Organización Panamericana de la Salud.

Castillo, Debra A. 1988. *Easy Women: Sex and Gender in Modern Mexican Fiction*. Minneapolis: University of Minnesota Press.

———. 1999. "Border Lives: Prostitute Women in Tijuana." *Signs* 24: 387–433.

CEDAW (Convention on the Elimination of All Forms of Discrimination against Women). 2005. "Informe de Mexico." United Nations, New York. Available online at http://www.un.org. Printout on file with volume editors.

CEH (Comisión para el Esclarecimiento Histórico/Historical Clarification Commission). 1998. *Memory of Silence: Report of the Historical Clarification Commission*. Guatemala City: Comisión para el Esclarecimiento Histórico.

Center for Gender and Refugee Studies. 2005. "Getting away with Murder: Guatemala's Failure to Protect Women and Rodi Alvarado's Quest for Safety." November. Available online at http://cgrs.uchastings.edu. Printout on file with volume editors.

———. 2006a. "Executive Summary of Update to 2006 Report 'Guatemala's Femicides and the Ongoing Struggle for Women's Human Rights.'" Available online at http://cgrs.uchastings.edu. Printout on file with volume editors.

———. 2006b. "Guatemala's Femicides and the Ongoing Struggle for Women's Human Rights: Update to CGRS's 2005 Report 'Getting away with

Murder.'" September. Available online at http://cgrs.uchastings.edu. Printout on file with volume editors.

Centro Centroamericano de Población. 2001. *Datos demográficos de Costa Rica*. San José: Universidad de Costa Rica.

Centro de la Mujer Peruana "Flora Tristán" and Amnesty International. 2005. *La violencia contra la mujer: Feminicidio en el Perú*. Lima: Centro de la Mujer Peruana "Flora Tristán."

CERIGUA (Centro de Reportes Informativos sobre Guatemala/Center for Informative Reports on Guatemala). 2005a. "Gobierno crea comisión para abordar el femicidio." December 20. Available online at http://www.cerigua.org. Printout on file with volume editors.

———. 2005b. "Un avance en la búsqueda de la justicia a favor de las mujeres." December 6. Available online at http://www.cerigua.org. Printout on file with volume editors.

———. 2006a. "Violencia intrafamiliar. Antesala del femicidio." March 17. Available online at http://www.cerigua.org. Printout on file with volume editors.

———. 2006b. "Presidente Óscar Berger acepta que hay femicidio en Guatemala." March 9. Available online at http://www.cerigua.org. Printout on file with volume editors.

———. 2006c. "Seprem presentó comisión que abordará el femicidio en Guatemala." March 9. Available online at http://www.cerigua.org. Printout on file with volume editors.

———. 2006d. "Informe sobre crímenes de mujeres en Guatemala." Available online at http://cerigua.info (accessed May 28, 2008).

———. 2009. "Instan a Denunciar la Violencia contra las Mujeres." May 16. Available online at http://cerigua.info (accessed August 15, 2009).

Cerna, Christina M. 2004. "The Inter-American System for the Protection of Human Rights." *Florida Journal of International Law* 16: 195–212.

Chafetz, Janet S. 1988. *Sex and Advantage: A Comparative Macrostructural Theory of Sex Stratification*. Totowa, N.J.: Rowman and Allanhel.

CHANGE (Center for Health and Gender Equity). 1999. *Ending Violence against Women*. Baltimore: School of Public Health, Johns Hopkins University.

Charlesworth, Hillary. 1999. "Feminist Methods in International Law." *American Journal of International Law* 93: 386–94.

Chow, Esther N., and Catherine W. Berheide. 1994. *Women, the Family and Policy: A Global Perspective*. New York: State University of New York Press.

CLADEM (Comitê Latino-americano e do Caribe para a Defesa dos Direitos da Mulher/Latin American and Caribbean Committee for the Defense of Women's Rights). 2007. *Investigación feminicidio. Monitoreo sobre femicidio/feminicidio en El Salvador, Guatemala, Honduras, México, Nicaragua y*

Panama. Available online at http://www.cladem.org. Printout on file with volume editors.

Clark, Ann Marie. 2001. *Diplomacy of Conscience: Amnesty International and Changing Human Rights Norms*. Princeton: Princeton University Press.

Comaroff, Jean, and John L. Comaroff. 1999. "Occult Economies and the Violence of Abstraction: Notes from the South African Postcolony." *American Ethnologist* 26, no. 3 (May): 279–301.

Comisión Especial para Conocer y Dar Seguimiento a las Investigaciones Relacionadas con los Feminicidios en la República Mexicana y a la Procuración de Justicia Vinculada. 2005a. *Por la vida y la libertad de las mujeres*. Primer Informe Sustantivo de Actividades 14 de abril 2004 al 14 de abril 2005. Cámara de Diputados, H. Congreso de la Unión, LIX Legislatura, Mexico City.

———. 2005b. *Violencia feminicida en 10 entidades de la República Mexicana*. Cámara de Diputados, H. Congreso de la Unión, LIX Legislatura, Mexico City.

———. 2006a. *Geografía de la violencia feminicida*, vol. 1. Cámara de Diputados, H. Congreso de la Unión, LIX Legislatura, Mexico City.

———. 2006b. *Investigación diagnóstica sobre violencia feminicida en la República Mexicana*, 13 vols. Cámara de Diputados, H. Congreso de la Unión, LIX Legislatura, Mexico City.

———. 2006c. *Recommendations Made to the Government of Mexico by National and International Organizations Regarding Feminicide*. DVD. Cámara de Diputados, H. Congreso de la Unión, LIX Legislatura, Mexico City.

———. 2006d. *Violencia feminicida en Chihuahua*. Cámara de Diputados, H. Congreso de la Unión, LIX Legislatura, Mexico City.

———. 2006e. *La Ley de Acceso de las Mujeres a Una Vida Libre de Violencia y tipificación del feminicidio como delito de lesa humanidad: Iniciativas aprobadas para la H. Cámara de Disputados*, Cámara de Diputados, H. Congreso de la Unión, LIX Legislatura, Mexico City.

Comisión Especial sobre los Feminicidios en la República Mexicana. 2005. *Documentos para la investigación, elaborados por el Comité Científico, Congreso de la Unión. Mexico City*.

Comisión para Prevenir y Erradicar la Violencia contra las Mujeres en Ciudad Juárez y El Colegio de la Frontera Norte. 2005. *Sistema socioeconómico y georeferencial sobre la violencia de género en Ciudad Juárez. Análisis de la violencia de género en Ciudad Juárez, Chihuahua: Propuestas para su prevención*. Ciudad Juárez.

Communities against Rape and Abuse. 2006. "Taking Risks: Implementing Grassroots Community Accountability." In *Color of Violence: The Incite! Anthology*, ed. Incite! Women of Color against Violence. Cambridge, Mass.: South End Press.

Comunicación e Información de la Mujer (CIMAC). 2008. Available online at http://www.cimac.org.mx (accessed January 20, 2009).

Congreso de la Republica de Guatemala. 1992. *Codigo Procesal Penal de Guatemala*. September 28. Centro Nacional de Análisis y Documentación Judicial, Guatemala City. Available online at http://www.oj.gob.gt. Printout on file with volume editors.

———. 1996. "Law to Prevent, Punish, and Eradicate Intrafamily Violence." November 28. Available online at http://www.acnur.org. Printout on file with volume editors.

———. 2005. *Feminicide in Guatemala: Crimes against Humanity*. Bench of the Guatemalan National Revolutionary Unity, preliminary research, photocopies, Guatemala City.

Coordinadora Departamental de Defensorías Comunitarias del Cusco. 2005. *Hablan las defensoras comunitarias: Una justicia distincta para las mujeres*. Lima: Instituto de Defensa Legal.

Copelon, Rhonda. 1995. "Gendered War Crimes: Conceptualizing Rape in Time of War." In *Women's Rights, Human Rights: International Feminist Perspectives*, ed. Julie Peters and Andrea Wolper, 197–214. New York: Routledge.

Corchado, Alfredo, and Ricardo Sandoval. 2004a. "Inquiry Indicates Police, Drug Ties." *Dallas Morning News*, February 28.

———. 2004b. "Juárez Police Leaving Force in Droves." *Dallas Morning News*, May 1.

Cowman, Jordan W., and Kimberly Rich. 2004. "Liability Concerns When Operating a Maquiladora." *Society for Human Resource Management*, May 5. Available online at http://www.shrm.org. Printout on file with volume editors.

Crisóstomo Meza, Mercedes. 2004. *Memorias de mujer (en el conflicto armado interno)*. Lima: Consejería en Proyectos.

———. 2005. "Las mujeres y la violencia sexual." In *Violencia contra la mujer durante el conflicto armado interno Warmikuna Yuyuriniku lecciones para no repetir la historia. Selección de textos del informe final de la Comisión de la Verdad y Reconciliación*, ed. Asociación pro Derechos Humanos, 11–30. Lima: APRODEH.

Cubilié, Anne. 2005. *Women Witnessing Terror*. New York: Fordham University Press.

Dador Tazzini, Maria Jennie. 2006. "Feminicidio en el Perú." Unpublished internal document, DEMUS.

Dakolis, Maria. 1996. "The Judicial Sector in Latin America and the Caribbean: Elements of Reform 3." Technical paper no. 319. World Bank, Washington, D.C.

Davis, Diane E. 2004. "State Implosion, Social Fragmentation, and the Dark

Side of Police Reform: Lessons from Mexico 5." Paper presented at the Security and Democracy in the Americas Conference, New York, April 4. Available online at http://www.newschool.edu (accessed April 6, 2005).

Deans, Gary, dir. 2004. *Toni Morrison Uncensored*. Films for the Humanities and Social Sciences, Princeton, N.J.

De la Cadena, Marisol. 1996. "Las mujeres son mas indias." In *Detrás de la Puerta: Hombres y mujeres en el Perú de hoy*, ed. Patricia Ruiz-Bravo, 11–30. Lima: Pontífica Universidad Católica de Perú.

DeLaet, Debra L. 2006. "Gender Justice: A Gendered Assessment of Truth-Telling Mechanisms." In *Telling the Truths: Truth Telling and Peace Building in Post-Conflict Societies*, ed. Tristan Anne Borer, 151–79. Notre Dame, Ind.: University of Notre Dame Press.

De la O Martínez, María Eugenia. 2001. "Ciudad Juárez: A Center of Industrial Growth." In *Globalization, Work and Maquilas: The New and Old Borders in Mexico*, ed. María Eugenia de la O Martínez and Cirila Quintero, 25–71. Mexico City: Plaza y Valdés.

Delgado Wise, Raúl. 2006. "Migration and Imperialism: The Mexican Workforce in the Context of NAFTA." *Latin American Perspectives* 33, no. 2: 33–45.

Del Olmo, Rosa. 1986. "Women and the Search for the Detained/Disappeared Persons of Latin America." *Resources for Feminist Research* 15: 42–43.

DEMUS (Estudio para la Defensa de los Derechos de la Mujer/Studies for the Defense of the Rights of Women). 2006. "Informe sobre feminicidio en America Latina." Report presented to the Inter-American Commission on Human Rights, Lima.

Derrida, Jacques. 1972. *Marges de la philosophie*. Paris: Minuit.

Desbiens, Carolyn. 1999. "Feminism 'in' Geography: Elsewhere, Beyond and the Politics of Paradoxical Space." *Gender, Place, and Culture* 6: 179–85.

de Sousa Santos, Boaventura. 2002. "Nuestra America: Reinventing a Subaltern Paradigm of Recognition and Redistribution." *Rutgers Law Review* 54: 1049–86.

Dillon, Sam. 1998a. "Rape and Murder Stalk Women in Northern Mexico." *New York Times*, April 18, A3.

———. 1998b. "What Went Wrong? Mexico Can't Fathom Its Rising Crime." *New York Times*, June 28, A1.

Dobash, Rebecca, and Russell Dobash. 1979. *Violence against Wives*. New York: Free Press.

Domínguez-Ruvalcaba, Héctor. 2007. *Modernity and the Nation in Mexican Representations of Masculinity*. New York: Palgrave Macmillan.

Domínguez-Ruvalcaba, Héctor, and Patricia Ravelo. 2006. "Los cuerpos de la violencia fronteriza." *Nómadas* 24 (April): 142–51.

Donaldson, Laura E. 1999. "On Medicine Women and White Shame-ans: New Age Native Americanism and Commodity Fetishism as Pop Culture Feminism." *Signs* 24, no. 3: 677.

Earth Rights International. 2004. "In Our Court: ATCA, *Sosa* and the Triumph of Human Rights." Washington, D.C., July.

Eckstein, Susan. 1998. "Women in Latin America." *DCRLA News*, Winter, 1–2.

Elson, Diane. 2002. "Gender Justice, Human Rights, and Neo-liberal Economic Policies." In *Gender Justice, Development and Rights*, ed. Maxine Molyneux and Shahra Razavi, 78–114. Oxford: Oxford University Press.

Ensalaco, Mark. 2006. "Murder in Ciudad Juárez: A Parable of Women's Struggle for Human Rights." *Violence against Women* 12: 417–40.

Erb, Nicole Eva. 1998. "Gender-Based Crimes under the Draft Statute for the Permanent International Criminal Court." *Columbia Human Rights Law Review* 29: 401–35.

Ertürk, Yakin. 2004. "Informe especial de crímenes contra Mujeres en Guatemala." Amnesy International, Chile.

Ertürk, Yakin, and Commission on Human Rights. 2005. "Integration of the Human Rights of Woman and the Gender Perspective: Violence against Women, Report of the Special Rapporteur on Violence against Women, Its Causes and Consequences." United Nations Economic and Social Council, doc. E/CN.4/2005/72/Add.3, February 10. Available online at http://daccessdds.un.org. Printout on file with volume editors.

Esquivel, Jesús, and Marco Appel. 2006. "Narcoterrorismo." *Proceso*. Available online at http://www.proceso.com.mx (accessed October 29, 2006).

European Commission. 2008. *Gendering Human Rights Violations: The Case of Interpersonal Violence*. Final report of the Coordinated Action on Human Rights Violations. Luxembourg: Office for Official Publications of the European Communities.

Ewelukwa, Uché U. 2002. "Women and International Economic Law: An Annotated Bibliography." *Law and Business Review of the Americas* 8: 603–32.

Falcón, Sylvanna. 2001. "Rape as a Weapon of War: Advancing Human Rights for Women at the U.S.–Mexico Border." *Social Justice* 28, no. 2: 31–50.

Falk, Richard. 1994. "The Making of Global Citizenship." In *The Condition of Citizenship*, ed. Bart Van Steenbergen, 127–40. London: Sage.

Federación Internacional de Derechos Humanos (International Federation of Human Rights). 2006. *Misión Internacional de Investigación: El femicidio en México y Guatemala*. Report no. 31, 446/3 (April). Available online at http://www.fidh.org. Printout on file with volume editors.

"Femicides on the Rise: Governments of Both Countries Demonstrate the Incapacity and Lack of Interest in Preventing Female Genocide." 2006. *Latin American Press*, Peru, May 10.

Feminicidio en América Latina. 2006. "Report Presented to the Inter-American Human Rights Commission." March. Available online at http://www.isis.cl. Printout on file with volume editors.

Feministas de Chiapas. 2004. *Posicionamiento contra la violencia en SCLC*. San Cristóbal: Centro de Derechos de la Mujer, Mujer Centroamericana, Kinal, and Mujeres Independientes.

Fitzpatrick, Joan. 1994. "The Use of International Human Rights Norms to Combat Violence against Women." In *Human Rights of Women: National and International Perspectives*, ed. Rebecca J. Cook, 532–71. Philadelphia: University of Pennsylvania Press.

Fletcher, Laurel E., and Harvey M. Weinstein. 2002. "Violence and Social Repair: Rethinking the Contribution of Justice to Reconciliation." *Human Rights Quarterly* 24: 573–639.

Forché, Carolyn. 1993. *Against Forgetting: Twentieth Century Poetry of Witness*. New York: W. W. Norton.

Foucault, Michel. 1995. *Discipline and Punish: The Birth of the Prison*. New York: Vintage Books.

———. 1999. "Lecture of March 17, 1976." In *Em defesa da sociedad: Curso no College de France (1975–1976)*, 239–64. São Paulo: Martins Fontes.

Fox, Jonathan. 2005. "Unpacking 'Transnational Citizenship.'" *Annual Review of Political Sciences* 8: 171–201.

Franco, Jean. 2002. *The Decline and Fall of the Lettered City: Latin America in the Cold War*. Cambridge, Mass.: Harvard University Press.

Franke, Katherine M. 2006. "Gendered Subjects of Transitional Justice." *Colombia Journal of Gender and the Law* 15, no. 3: 813–29.

Fregoso, Rosa-Linda. 2000. "Voices without Echo: The Global Gendered Apartheid." *Emergences* 10, no. 1: 137–55.

———. 2003. *Mexicana Encounters: The Making of Social Identities on the Borderlands*. Los Angeles: University of California Press.

———. 2006. "We Want Them Alive! The Politics and Culture of Human Rights." *Social Identities* 12, no. 2: 109–38.

Frenkiel, Olenka. 2006. "Murder Mystery in Guatemala." BBC *This World* (television broadcast), May 3. Available online at http://news.bbc.co.uk. Printout on file with volume editors.

Freshwater, Patricia J. 2005. "The Obligation of Non-Refoulement under the Convention against Torture: When Has a Government Acquiesced in the Torture of Its Citizens?" *Georgetown Immigration Law Journal* 19: 585–610.

Friedman, Emil. 1998. "Paradoxes of Gendered Political Opportunity in the Venezuelan Transition to Democracy." *Latin America Research Review* 33: 87–135.

Gardam, Judith. 2001. *Women, Armed Conflict and International Law*. New York: Springer Press.

Ghandi, P. R. 1998. *The Human Rights Committee and the Rights of Individual Communication: Law and Practice*. Aldershot.: Ashgate.

Gilman, Alexis James. 2003. "Making Amends with the Mexican Constitution: Reassessing the 1995 Judicial Reforms and Considering Prospects for Further Reform." *George Washington International Law Review* 35: 947–76.

Goldblatt, Beth, and Sheila Meintjes. 1998. "South African Women Demand the Truth." In *What Women Do in Wartime: Gender and Conflict in Africa*, ed. Meredeth Turshen and Clotilde Twagiramariya, 27–61. London: Zed Books.

Golub, Stephen. 2003. *Beyond Rule of Law Orthodoxy: The Legal Empowerment Alternative*. Carnegie Empowerment for International Peace, no. 41. Available online at http://www.carnegieendowment.org. Printout on file with volume editors.

Gonzáles, A. 2006. "La Plaza de Hidalgo se viste de negro." *El Diario de Ciudad Juarez*, March 9, 3A.

Gonzáles, Roberto, and Rosa Vargas. 2005. "Baja pobreza rural, pero crece la desigualdad." *La Jornada*, August 25.

González, Rosa Maria, and Patricia Ravelo. 2006. "La violencia en el arte. Dos hipótesis recurrentes." Paper presented at the Border Social Forum, Ciudad Juárez, Mexico, October 13–15.

Gonzalez de la Rocha, Mercedes. 2001. "From the Resources of Poverty to the Poverty of Resources?" *Latin American Perspectives* 28, 4: 72–100.

González Rodríguez, Sergio. 2002. *Huesos en el desierto* (Bones in the desert). Barcelona: Anagrama.

Grandin, Greg. 2004. *The Last Colonial Massacre: Latin America in the Cold War*. Chicago.: University of Chicago Press.

Guatemalan Human Rights Commission. 2006. *Guatemalan Human Rights Update*, vol. 18, no. 9, May 16–31.

Guerrero, Cecilia, and Gabriela Minjares. 2004. "Hacen mito y lucro de los femincidios." *El Diario de Ciudad Juárez*, July 22, 1A.

Gunew, Sneja. 2002. "Feminist Cultural Literacy: Translating Difference, Cannibal Options." In *Women's Studies on Its Own: A Next Wave Reader in Institutional Change*, ed. Robyn Wiegman, 47–65. Durham: Duke University Press.

Gutiérrez, Alejandro. 2004. "Un guión para adentrarse a la interpretación del fenómeno Juárez." In *Violencia sexista, algunas claves para la comprensión del feminicidio en Ciudad Juárez*, ed. Griselda Gutiérrez Castañeda, 63–74. Mexico City: Universidad Nacional Autónoma de México.

Hakki, Murat Metin. 2002. "The Silver Anniversary of the United Nations Human Rights Committee: Anything to Celebrate?" *International Journal of Human Rights* 6: 85–102.

Hammergren, Linn. 2006. "Rebuilding Nation Building: Latin American Experience with Rule of Law Reforms and Its Applicability to Nation Building Efforts." *Case Western Reserve Journal of International Law* 38: 63–93.

Hardt, Michael, and Antonio Negri. 2000. *Empire*. Cambridge, Mass.: Harvard University Press.

Harrington, Joanna. 2003. "Punting Terrorists, Assassins and Other Undesirables: Canada, the Human Rights Committee and Requests for Interim Measures of Protection." *McGill Law Journal* 48: 55–87.

Harvey, David. 2000. *Spaces of Hope*. Los Angeles: University of California Press.

———. 2003. *Espacios de esperanza*. Madrid: Ediciones Akal.

Hayner, Priscilla B. 2001. *Unspeakable Truths: Confronting State Terror and Atrocity*. New York: Routledge.

Hedetoft, Ulf, and Mette Hjort, eds. 2002. *The Postnational Self: Belonging and Identity*. Minneapolis: University of Minnesota Press.

Heise, Lorie, J. Pitanguy, and A. Germain. 1994. *Violencia contra la mujer. La carga oculta sobre la salud*. Washington, D.C.: World Bank.

Held, David. 1996. *Democracy and the Global Order: From the Modern State to Cosmopolitan Governance*. Palo Alto, Calif.: Stanford University Press.

Helfer, Laurence R. 2002. "Overlegalizing Human Rights: International Relations Theory and the Commonwealth Caribbean Backlash against Human Rights Regimes." *Columbia Law Review* 102: 1832–1911.

Hernandez, Idulvina. 2005. *A Long Road: Progress and Challenges in Guatemala's Intelligence Reform.* October. Washington, D.C.: Washington Office on Latin America. Available online at http://www.wola.org. Printout on file with volume editors.

Hershatter, Gail. 1999. *Dangerous Pleasures: Prostitution and Modernity in Twentieth-century Shanghai*. Berkeley: University of California Press.

Hessbruegge, Jan Arno. 2004. "The Historical Development of the Doctrines of Attribution and Due Diligence in International Law." *New York University Journal of International Law and Practice* 36 (Spring): 265–306.

Holland, Max. 2005. "Private Sources of U.S. Foreign Policy: William Pawley and the 1954 Coup d'État in Guatemala." *Journal of Cold War Studies* 7: 36–73.

Hollander, Nancy Caro. 1996. "The Gendering of Human Rights and the Latin American Terrorist State." *Feminist Studies* 22, no. 1: 41–80.

Holt, Benjamin, and Michael Waller. 2004. "International Trade and Workers' Rights: Practical Tools for Reading Labor Rights Provisions of Free Trade Agreements." *Human Rights Brief* 11: 42–44.

Human Rights Watch. 2001. "Canada/Mexico/United States: Trading away Rights, the Unfulfilled Promise of NAFTA's Labor Side Agreement." April. Available online at http://www.hrw.org. Printout on file with volume editors.

———. 2002. "From the Household to the Factory: Sex Discrimination in the Guatemalan Labor Force." Available online at http://hrw.org. Printout on file with volume editors.

———. 2004. "Mexico: Workers' Rights at Risk under Fox Plan." December 9. Available online at http://hrw.org. Printout on file with volume editors.

———. 2006. "Guatemala: Transgender People Face Deadly Attacks. "February 20. Available online at http://www.hrw.org (accessed January 20, 2009).

———. 2008. "Americas: Women's Rights Defenders Seek Protection." October 29. Available online at http://www.hrw.org. Printout on file with volume editors.

Hunter, Davis. 2003. "Using the World Bank Inspection Panel to Defend the Interests of Project-Affected People." *Chicago Journal of International Law* 4: 201–11.

IACHR (Inter-American Commission on Human Rights). 2001. "Report on Ciudad Juárez." Informe 54/01, Case of Maria da Penha. Brasila, April 16.

———. 2003a. "Justicia e inclusión social. Los desafíos de la democrácia en Guatemala." December 29. Available online at http://www.cidh.oas.org. Printout on file with volume editors.

———. 2003b. "The Situation of the Rights of Women in Ciudad Juárez, Mexico: The Right to Be Free from Violence and Discrimination." March 7. Available online at http://www.cidh.org (accssed October 6, 2009). Printout on file with volume editors.

INEGI (Instituto Nacional de Estadística, Geografía e Informática/National Institute for Statistics and Geography). 2001. "Propiedades sociales y ejidatarios, según disposición de parcelas y sexo: VIII Censo Ejidal, Resumen Nacional por Entidad." Aguascalientes, Mexico.

———. 2005. "Encuesta nacional de ocupación y empleo 2005." Aguascalientes, Mexico.

Instituto Chihuahuense de la Mujer. 2003. "Homicidios de mujeres. Auditoría periodística." Research carried out by Montañez and Associates, Chihuahua City, January 1993–July 2003.

Inter-American Development Bank. 1959. "Agreement Establishing the Inter-American Development Bank." Available online at http://www.iadb.org (accessed August 23, 2009).

———. 1999. "Violence as an Obstacle to Development." Technical note 4. Available online at http://www.iadb.org (accessed August 21, 2009).

———. 2006. "Social Sector." Available online at http://www.iadb.org (accessed August 21, 2009).

———. 2007. "Violence Prevention." Available online at http://www.iadb.org (accessed August 21, 2009).

Jacobson, David. 1998. *Rights across Borders: Immigration and the Decline of Citizenship.* Baltimore: Johns Hopkins University Press.

Jhally, Sut. 1990. *The Codes of Advertising*. New York: Routledge.

Johnson, H. 2000. "Enhancing Knowledge on Violence against Women." Paper presented at the 10th United Nations Congress on the Prevention of Crime and the Treatment of Offenders, Vienna, April 10–17, 2000.

Justicia para Nuestras Hijas. 2003a. *Informe sobre Feminicidios*. Available online at http://espanol.geocites.com/justhijas (accessed April 7, 2008).

———. 2003b. *Nunca las han buscado. Testimonios leídos ante el relator del Alto Comisionado para los Derechos Humanos de la Organización de Naciones Unidas, Ciudad Juárez, Chihuahua, 31, Julio, 2003*. Chihuahua: Editorial La Gota.

Keesing, Roger M., Malcolm Crick, Barbara Frankel, Jonathan Friedman, Elvin Hatch, J. G. Oosten, Rik Pinxten, Jerome Rousseau, and Marilyn Strathern. 1987. "Anthropology as an Interpretative Quest: Comments and Reply." *Current Anthropology* 28, no. 2 (April): 161–76.

Kelly, Liz. 2000. "Wars against Women: Sexual Violence, Sexual Politics and the Militarized State." In *States of Conflict: Gender, Violence and Resistance*, ed. Susie Jacobs, Ruth Jacobson, and Jennifer Marchbank, 45–65. New York: Zed Books.

Koonings, Kees, and Dirk Kruijt. 1999. *Societies of Fear: The Legacy of Civil War, Violence and Terror in Latin America*. New York: Zed Books.

Koyre, Alexandre. 1945. "The Political Function of the Modern Lie." *Contemporary Jewish Record*, June.

Kristeva, Julia. 1982. *Powers of Horror: An Essay on Abjection*. New York: Columbia University Press.

Kyle, David, and Rey Koslowski, eds. 2001. *Global Human Smuggling: Comparative Perspectives*. Baltimore: Johns Hopkins University Press.

La Capital. 2003. "Rastreo de llamadas telefónicas implican a militares en Resonantes secuestros." November 23. Available online at http://archives.lacapital.com.ar (accessed August 23, 2009).

La Franchi, Howard. 1997. "Girls Who Find New Roles in Mexico also Face Danger." *Christian Science Monitor*, June, 1.

Lagarde y de los Ríos, Marcela 1994. *Democracia Genérica*. Mexico City: Red de Educación Popular Entre Mujeres de America Latina y el Caribe and Mujeres para el Dialogo.

———. 1996. *Género y feminismo. Desarrollo humano y democracia*. Madrid: Horas y Horas.

———. 1999. *Una mirada feminista en el umbral del milenio*. San José, Costa Rica: Instituto de Estudios de la Mujer, Universidad Nacional.

———. 2004. Presentation given at an event organized by the Interparliamentary Network of Women (Mexico, Guatemala, and Spain) in the Congress of Guatemala. September.

———. 2005. *Por la vida y la libertad de las mujeres. Primer informe sustantivo de las actividades de la Comisión Especial para Conocer y Dar Seguimiento a las Investigaciones Relacionadas con los Feminicidios en la República Mexicana y a la Procuración de Justicia Vinculada*. Cámara de Diputados, H. Congreso de la Unión, LIX Legislatura, Mexico City.

———. 2006. "Introduccíon: Por la vida y la libertad de las mujeres." In *Feminicidio: Una perspectiva global*, ed. Diana E. H. Russell and Roberta A. Harmes, 15–42. Mexico City: Centro de Investigaciones Interdisciplinarias en Ciencias y Humanidades and Universidad Autónoma de Mexico.

Lakshmanan, Indira A. R. 2006. "Unsolved Killings Terrorize Women in Guatemala." *Boston Globe*. March 30. Available online at http://www.boston.com. Printout on file with volume editors.

Lalvani, Suren. 1995. "Consuming the Exotic Other." *Critical Studies in Mass Communication* 12, no. 3 (September): 263–86.

Landes, Joan. 1998. *Feminism, the Public and the Private*. Oxford: Oxford University Press.

Latin American Weekly Report. 2003. "Mexico: Juarez Murder Cases 'Mishandled.'" *Latin American Newsletters*, November 25: 5.

La Voz del Interior. 2004. "Detienen a un policía acusado de matar a una prostituta." May 20. Available online at http://buscador.lavoz.com.ar (accessed August 23, 2009).

Law Commission of Canada. 1999. *From Restorative Justice to Transformative Justice*. Ottawa, Canada.

"Ley General de Acceso de las Mujeres a una Vida Libre de Violencia y tipificación del feminicidio como delito de lesa humanidad." 2006. Initiative approved by the Comisión Especial para Conocer y Dar Seguimiento a las Investigaciones Relacionadas con los Feminicidios en la República Mexicana y a la Procuración de Justicia Vinculada, Cámara de Diputados, H. Congreso de la Unión. LIX Legislatura, Mexico City.

"Ley para Prevenir, Sancionar y Erradicar la Violencia Intrafamiliar." 1996. Congreso de la República, October.

Livingston, Jessica. 2004. "Murder in Juárez: Gender, Sexual Violence, and the Global Assembly Line." *Frontiers* 25, no. 1: 59–76.

López-Montiel, Angel Gustavo. 2000. "The Military, Political Power, and Police Relations in México City." *Latin American Perspectives* 27, no. 2: 79–94.

López Urbina, María. 2006. *Informe final sobre los homicidios de mujeres en Ciudad Juárez*. Procuraduría General de la Republica, Fiscal Especial para la Atención de Delitos Relacionadas con los Homicidios de Mujeres en el Municipio de Juarez, Chihuahua, February.

Luruena Caballero, Manuel. 2003. "Mujeres de Negro." *El Heraldo de Chihuahua*, March 4.

Lutz, Ellen L., and Kathryn Sikkink. 2000. "International Human Rights Law and Practice in Latin America." *International Organizations* 54, no. 3 (Summer): 633–59.

Lynch, Michael J., Raymond J. Michalowski, and W. Bryon Groves. 2000. *Critical Perspectives on Crime, Power, and Identity*. Monsey, N.Y.: Criminal Justice Press.

MacKinnon, Catherine. 1998. "Rape, Genocide, and Women's Human Rights." In *Violence against Women: Philosophical Perspectives*, ed. Stanley G. French, 43–56. Ithaca: New York: Cornell University Press.

Mahmood, Saba. 2001. "Feminist Theory, Embodiment, and the Docile Agent: Some Reflections on the Egyptian Islamic Revival." *Cultural Anthropology* 16, no. 2: 202–36.

Mahtani, Minelle. 2001. "Racial Remappings: The Potential of Paradoxical Space." *Gender, Place, and Culture* 8: 299–305.

Maldonado, Alba Estela. 2005. *Feminicidio en Guatemala: Crímenes contra la humanidad*. November. Available online at http://www.congreso.gob.gt. Printout on file with volume editors.

Mani, Rama. 2002. *Beyond Retribution: Seeking Justice in the Shadows of War*. Malden, Mass.: Blackwell.

Mantilla, Julissa Falcon. 2001. "La Comisión de la Verdad en el Perú: El inciso que faltaba." Unpublished report on file with author.

Martin, JoAnn. 1990. "Motherhood and Power: The Production of a Woman's Culture of Politics in a Mexican Community." *American Ethnologist* 17: 470–90.

Martínez Coronado, Benjamin. 2003. "Desintegración sociofamiliar, germen de crímenes: Patricio." *El Heraldo de Chihuahua*, February 20, 1A.

Marx, Karl. 1977. *Manuscritos económico-filosóficos de 1844*. Mexico City: Ediciones de Cultura Popular.

———. 1979. *El Capital* (Capital). Vol. 1, 1–3. Mexico City: Siglos XXI Editores.

Matus, Veronica. 1999. "Lo privado y lo público, una dicotomía fatal." In *Genero y derecho*, ed. Alda Facio and Lorena Fries, 61–74. Santiago, Chile: Lom Ediciones.

McGoldrick, Dominic. 2001. *The Human Rights Committee: Its Role in the Development of the International Covenant on Civil and Political Rights*. Oxford: Oxford University Press.

McWilliams, Monica. 1999. "Violence against Women in Societies under Stress." In *Rethinking Violence against Women*, ed. R. Emerson Dobash, 111–140. Thousand Oaks, Calif.: Sage Publications.

Meares, Tracey L. 2002. "Praying for Community Policing." *California Law Review* 90: 1593–1634.

Medina, Cecilia. 1985. "Women's Rights as Human Rights: Latin American Countries and the Organization of American States." In *Women, Feminist Identity, and Society in the 1980s*, ed. Myriam Diaz-Diocaretz and Iris Zavala, 63–80. Amsterdam: John Benjamins.

Méndez, Juan E. 2006. "The Human Right to Truth: Lessons Learned from Latin American Experiences with Truth Telling." In *Telling the Truths: Truth Telling and Peace Building in Post-Conflict Societies*, ed. Tristan Anne Borer, 115–50. South Bend, Ind.: University of Notre Dame Press.

Méndez, Juan E., and Javier Mariezcurrena. 1999. "Accountability for Past Human Rights Violations: Contributions of the Inter-American Organs of Protection." *Social Justice* 26, no. 4 (Winter): 84–98.

Meyer, Mary K. 1999. "Negotiating International Norms: The Inter-American Commission of Women and the Convention on Violence against Women." In *Gender Politics in Global Convergence*, ed. Mary K. Meyer and Elisabeth Prügl, 58–71. Lanham, Md.: Rowman and Littlefield.

Meza Rivera, Froilan. 2003. "Si reciben donativos los ONGS." *El Heraldo de Chihuahua*, February 25, 2, 25.

Mignolo, Walter. 2000. *Local Histories/Global Designs*. New Haven, Conn.: Princeton University Press.

Minjares, Gabriela, and Sandra Rodríguez. 2006. "Usaron a muertas para crear 'leyenda negra.' 'Aprovecharon' tragedia autores, partidos, medios de comunicación, ONGS y gobiernos." June 5. Available online at http://www3.inpro.com.mx (accessed June 5, 2006).

Mohammed, Patricia. 2006. "The Plasticity of Gender in Social Policy Formation." In *Engendering Human Security: Feminist Perspectives*, ed. T. Thanh-Dam Truong, Saskia Wieringa, and Amrita Chhachhi, 277–96. New York: Zed Books.

Mohanty, Chandra Talpade. 1997. "Women Workers and Capitalist Scripts: Ideologies of Domination, Common Interests, and the Politics of Solidarity." In *Feminist Genealogies, Colonial Legacies, Democratic Futures*, ed. M. Jacqui Alexander and Chandra Talpade Mohanty, 3–29. New York: Routledge.

Monárrez Fragoso, Julia. 1999. "La cultura del feminicidio en Ciudad Juárez. 1993–1999." *Frontera Norte* 12, no. 23: 87–111.

———. 2000. "La cultura del feminicidio en Juárez, 1993–1999." *Frontera Norte* 12, no. 23: 87–118.

———. 2002. "Feminicidio sexual serial en Ciudad Juárez: 1993–2001." *Debate Feminista* 25: 279–308.

———. 2005a. "Elementos de análisis del feminicidio sexual sistémico en Ciudad Juárez para su viabilidad jurídica." In *Feminicidio, justicia y derecho*, ed. Comisión Especial para Conocer y Dar Seguimiento a las Investigaciones Relacionadas con los Feminicidios en la República Mexicana y a la Procuración de Justicia Vinculada, Cámara de Diputados, H. Congreso de la Unión, LIX Legislatura, Mexico City, 4–18.

———. 2005b. *Feminicidio sexual sistémico: víctimas y familiares, Ciudad Juárez, 1993–2004*. Mexico City: Universidad Autónoma Metropolitana.

———. 2005c. "Las diversas representaciones del feminicidio y los asesinatos de mujeras en Ciudad Juárez." In *Comisión para Prevenir y Eradicar Violencia en Ciudad Juárez*, 186–231. Ciudad Juárez.

———. 2006a. "No es un mito." Available online at http://www.colef.mx (accessed May 26, 2008.)

———. 2006b. "The Victims of the Ciudad Juárez Feminicide: Commodities." *Fermentum* (Mérida, Venezuela) 16, no. 46 (May–August): 429–45.

Monárrez Fragoso, Julia, and César M. Fuentes. 2004. "Feminicidio y marginalidad urbana en Ciudad Juárez en la década de los noventa." In *Violencia contra las mujeres en contextos urbanos y rurales*, ed. Torres Falcón Marta, 43–70. Mexico City: El Colegio de México.

Monárrez Fragoso, Julia, Pedro Diaz de la Vega Garcia, and Patricia Morales Castro. 2006. *Sistema socioeconómico y geo-referencial sobre la violencia de género en Ciudad Juárez. Análisis de la violencia de género en Ciudad Juárez, Chihuahua: Propuestas para su prevención*. Comisión para Prevenir y Eradicar la Violencia contra las Mujeres en Ciudad Juárez, El Colegio de la Frontera Norte, and Instituto Nacional de Estadistica, Geografia e Informática, Ciudad Juárez, July.

Morais, Herbert V. 2000. "The Globalization of Human Rights Law and the Role of International Financial Institutions in Promoting Human Rights?" *George Washington International Law Review* 33: 71–96.

Morales Trujillo, Hilda. 2002. *Traduciendo en Acciones la CEDAW en Guatemala: El caso de María Eugenia Morales de Sierra*. Guatemala City: United Nations Development Fund for Women.

Morgan, Robin. 1989. *The Demon Lover: On the Sexuality of Terrorism*. New York: W. W. Norton.

Moser, Caroline. 2001. *Violence in a Post-Conflict Context: Urban Poor Perceptions from Guatemala*. Washington, D.C.: World Bank.

Moshan, Brook Sari. 1998. "Women, War and Words: The Gender Component in the Permanent International Criminal Court's Definition of Crimes against Humanity." *Fordham International Law Journal* 22:154–184.

Musalo, Karen, and Stephen Knight. 2002. "Unequal Protection." *Bulletin of Atomic Scientists* (November–December). Available online at http://www.thebulletin.org. Printout on file with volume editors.

Nathan, Debbie. 1997. "Death Comes to the Maquilas: A Border Story." *Nation*, January 13, 18–22.

———. 1999. "Work, Sex and Danger in Ciudad Juárez." *North American Congress on Latin America Report on the Americas* 33 (November): 24–30.

———. 2002. "The Missing Elements." *Texas Observer*. August 30, 1–9. Available online at http://www.womenontheborder.org. Printout on file with volume editors.

———. 2003. "The Juárez Murders." *Amnesty Magazine*. Spring. Available online at http://www.amnestyusa.org. Printout on file with volume editors.

———. 2004. "The Face Maker." *Texas Observer*, February 13. Available online at http://www.texasobserver.org/showArticle.asp?ArticleID=1565. Printout on file with volume editors.

Neild, Rachel. 2002. *Sustaining Reform: Democratic Policing in Central America*. October 3. Washington, D.C.: Washington Office on Latin America. Available online at http://www.wola.org. Printout on file with volume editors.

Nesiah, Vasuki. 2006. "Discussion Lines on Gender and Transitional Justice: An Introductory Essay Reflecting on the ICTJ Bellagio Workshop on Gender and Transitional Justice." *Colombia Journal of Gender and the Law* 15, no. 3: 799–813.

Nessel, Lori. 2004. "Willful Blindness to Gender-Based Violence Abroad: United States' Implementation of Article Three of the United Nations Convention against Torture." *Minnesota Law Review* 89: 71–162.

Neumayer, Eric. 2003. "The Determinants of Aid Allocation by Regional Multilateral Development Banks and United Nations Agencies." *International Studies Quarterly* 47: 101–22.

Ní Aoláin, Fionnuala, and Eilish Rooney. 2007. "Underenforcement and Intersectionality: Gendered Aspects of Transition for Women." *International Journal of Transitional Justice* 1: 338–54.

Nowak, Manfred. 2005. *United Nations Covenant on Civil and Political Rights: CCPR Commentary*. Kehl, Germany: N. P. Engel.

Nuestras Hijas de Regreso a Casa. 2003. "Por Nuestras Hijas." Available online at http://www.geocities.com/pornuestrashijas (accessed July 18, 2003).

Oblando, Ana Elena. 1999. "Feminismo, género y patriarcado." In *Género y derecho*, ed. Alda Facio and Lorena Fries, 139–42. Santiago, Chile: Lom Ediciones.

Ochoa, Enrique C., and Tamar Diana Wilson. 2001. "Introduction." *Latin American Perspectives* 28, no. 3: 3–10.

OECD (Organization for Economic Cooperation and Development). 2000. *Guidelines for Multinational Enterprises*. Available online at http://www.oecd.org. Printout on file with volume editors.

Olivares, Emir, and Rubén Villalpando. 2007. "Ante la creciente violencia, presentan el Observatorio Ciudadano del Feminicidio" *La Jornada*. August 3. Available online at http://www.jornada.unam.mx (accessed March 17, 2008).

Olivera, Mercedes. 2006. "Violencia Femicida: Violence against Women and Mexico's Structural Crisis." *Latin American Perspectives* 33, no. 2: 104–14.

Olivera, Mercedes, and Guadalupe Cárdenas. 1998. "Violencia estructural hacia las mujeres." In *Reclamo de las mujeres ante la violencia, la impunidad y la guerra*, ed. *La Correa Feminista*, 15–24. Mexico City: San Cristóbal.

Oosterveld, Valerie. 2005. "The Definition of 'Gender' in the Rome Statute of the International Criminal Court: A Step Forward or Back for International Justice?" *Harvard Human Rights Journal* 18:55–84.

Organization of American States. 2005. *Objetivos del desarrollo del milenio. Una mirada desde America Latina y el Caribe*. Mexico City: Comisión Económica para America y el Caribe.

Orihuela, Sandra, and Abigail Montjoy. 2000. "The Evolution of Latin America's Sexual Harassment Law: A Look at Mini-Skirts and Multinationals in Peru." *California Western International Law Journal* 30 (Spring): 323–43.

Orquiz, M. 2004. "Basta de denigrar a Juárez: Sectores." *El Diario de Ciudad Juárez*, April 22, A1.

Ortiz, Fernando. 1975 (1940). *Del fenómeno social de la tranculturación*. In *Fernando Ortiz y la Cubanidad*, ed. N. Suarez. Havana: Ediciones Union.

Otero, Joaquin F. 1995. "The North American Agreement on Labor Cooperation: An Assessment of Its First Year's Implementation." *Columbia Journal of Transnational Law* 33: 637–62.

Paterson, Kent. 2006a. *Americas Program Report: Femicide on the Rise in Latin America*. March 8. Available online at http://americas.irc-online.org (accessed March 28, 2006).

———. 2006b. *Femicide on the Rise in Latin America*. Silver City, N.M.: International Relations Center.

———. 2008. "Juarez Mothers Demand Justice for Their Murdered Daughters." Americas Policy Program report, Center for International Policy. Washington, D.C., May 9. Available online at http://americas.irc-online.org. Printout on file with volume editors.

Patterson, David. 1988. *Literature and Spirit: Essays on Bakhtin and His Contemporaries*. Lexington: University Press of Kentucky.

Paz, Octavio. 1982. *Sor Juana Inés de la Cruz o las trampas de la fe*. Mexico City: Fondo de Cultura Económica.

PDH (Procurador de los Derechos Humanos de Guatemala/Attorney General for Human Rights for Guatemala). 2005. *Muertes violentas de mujeres durante el 2004*. Available online at http://www.wola.org. Printout on file with volume editors.

Peker, Luciana. 2003. "Crímenes con Marca." *Página/12*. June 27. Available online at http://www.pagina12.com.ar (accessed August 23, 2009).

Perea Quintanilla, Enrique. 2003. "Declaro PGJE la Guerra Sociedad Civil." *El Heraldo de Chihuahua*, 1A.

Periera, Anthony W., and Diane E. Davis. 2000. "New Patterns of Militarized Violence and Coercion in the Americas." *Latin American Perspectives* 27, no. 2: 3–17.

Peruvian Truth and Reconciliation Commission 2003. *Final Report*. Available at http://www.cverdad.org.pe/ingles/ifinal/conclusiones.php (accessed November 6, 2006).

Pincikowski, Scott E. 2002. *Bodies of Pain: Suffering in the Works of Hartmann von Aue*. New York: Routledge.

Piñon Balderrama, David. 2003. "Lucran ONGs con muertas." *El Heraldo de Chihuahua*, February 25, 1A.

Pogge, Thomas W. 2005. "Human Rights and Human Responsibilities" In *Global Responsibilities: Who Must Deliver on Human Rights?* ed. Andrew Kuper, 3–36. New York: Routledge.

Portenier, Giselle, dir. 2006. "Killer's Paradise." BBC *This World*, television broadcast, May 4.

Portillo, Lourdes, dir. 2001. *Señorita Extraviada*. Independent Television Service. Xochitl Films.

Prado Calahorra, Edgar. 2003a. "Protestan mujeres ante procurador." *El Norte de Ciudad Juarez*, August 14, 5A.

——. 2003b. "'Acachan' a madres desapariciones." *El Norte de Ciudad Juarez*, June 3, 8A.

Preston, Julia. 2009. "New Policy Permits Asylum for Battered Women." *New York Times*. July 16. Available online at http://newyorktimes.com (accessed July 27, 2009).

Proyecto Estado de la Nación. 2000. "VI Informe del estado de la nación en desarrollo humano sostenible" (Report VI on the state of the nation in the development of human sustainability). Programa de Naciones Unidas para el Desarrollo, San José, Costa Rica.

Radford, Jill. 1992. "Introduction." In *Femicide: The Politics of Woman Killing*, ed. Jill Radford and Diana E. H. Russell, 3–12. New York: Twayne.

Radford, Jill, and Diana E. H. Russell, eds. 1992. *Femicide: The Politics of Woman Killing*. New York: Twayne.

Ravelo, Patricia. 2005a. "La costumbre de matar: Proliferación de la violencia en Ciudad Juárez, Chihuahua, México." *Nueva Antropología* 65 (May–August): 149–66.

——. 2005b. "Violencia feminicida en Chihuahua." In *Violencia feminicida en 10 entidades de la República Mexicana. Comisión Especial para Conocer y Dar Seguimiento a las Investigaciones Relacionadas con los Feminicidios en la República Mexicana y a la procuración de Justicia Vinculada*. Cámara de Diputados, H. Congreso de la Unión, LIX Legislatura, Mexico City.

Ravelo, Patricia, and Sergio Sánchez. 2005. "Identidad y cultura en torno de las condiciones de vida y de trabajo del sector obrero de las maquiladoras de Ciudad Juárez." In *Chihuahua hoy 2005: Visiones de su historia, economía, política y cultura*, 3:97–148, ed. Victor Orozco. Ciudad Juárez: Instituto Chihuahuense de la Cultura and Universidad Autónoma de Ciudad Juárez.

Ravelo, Ricardo. 2006. "En crisis el cártel del Golfo, la segunda organización criminal más poderosa de México." *Proceso*, November 6. Available online at http//:www.proceso.com.mx (accessed November 6, 2006).

Recovery of Historical Memory Project. 1999. *Guatemala Never Again: The Official Report of the Human Rights Office, Archdiocese of Guatemala*. Maryknoll, N.Y.: Orbis Books.

Red de Salud de las Mujeres Latinoamericanas y del Caribe. 2008. "Declaración: Exigimos respetar la vida de defensoras de derechos humanos en Nicaragua." October 8. Available online at http://www.reddesalud.org (accessed March 17, 2009).

Registro Agrario Nacional. 2005. *Documentos y superficie certificada y/o titulada de 01/01/05 al 18/05/05*. Tuxtla Gutiérrez.

Reguillo, Rossana. 2005. "Ciudades y violencias: Un mapa contra los diagnósticos fatales." *Ciudades Translocales: Espacios, Flujo, Representación: Perspectivas desde las Americas*, ed. Rossana Reguillo y Macial Godoy Anativia, 393–412. Tlaquepaque, Jalisco: Instituto Tecnológico y de Estudios Superiores de Occidente (ITESO); New York: Social Science Research Council.

Reproductive Health Response in Conflict Consortium. 2002. *If Not Now, When? Addressing Gender-based Violence in Refugee, Internally Displaced and Post-Conflict Settings*. New York: Reproductive Health Response in Conflict Consortium. Available online at http://www.rhrc.org (accessed August 9, 2003).

Rieff, David. 2007. "After the Caudillo." *New York Times*, November 18, 1.

Robinson, Joan H. 2005. "Another Woman's Body Found Outside Juarez.: Applying Velasquez Rodriguez for Women's Human Rights." *Wisconsin Women's Law Journal* 20: 167–88.

Robles, Rosalba. 2003. "La violencia doméstica, un estar y no estar." Paper presented at the Primer Encuentro Sobre Estudios de la Mujer en la Región Paso del Norte: Retos Frente al Siglo XXI, sponsored by Colegio del la Frontera Norte, Ciudad Juárez, Chihuahua, November 14.

——. 2004. "La violencia contra la mujer." In *Violencia contra la mujer*, ed. Teresa Fernández de Juan, 157–74. Mexico City: Comisión Nacional de los Derechos Humanos. Available online at http://www.cndh.org.mx (accessed August 14, 2005).

Rodley, Nigel. 2001. "Civil and Political Rights, Including the Questions of Torture and Detention: Report of the Special Rapporteur." Submitted pursuant to Inter-American Commission on Human Rights Resolution 2000/43, Visit to Azerbaijan, United Nations doc. E/CN.4/2001/66/Add.1.

Rodríguez, Miguel. 2005. *Informe sobre feminicidio en el Perú*. Lima: Asociación Aurora Vivar, A.C.S. Calandnia y DEMUS-Estudio para la Defensa de los Derechos de la Mujer.

Rodríguez-Garavito, Cesar A. 2005. "Global Governance and Labor Rights: Codes of Conduct and Anti-Sweatshop Struggles in Global Apparel Factories in Mexico and Guatemala." *Politics and Society* 33: 203–33.

Roht-Arriaza, Naomi. 2005. *The Pinochet Effect*. Philadelphia: University of Pennsylvania Press.

Rojas Blanco, Clara E. 2005. "The V-Day March in Mexico: Appropriation and (Mis)Use of Local Women's Activism." *National Women's Studies Association Journal* 17: 217–27.

Romany, Celina. 1994. "State Responsibility Goes Private: A Feminist Critique of the Public/Private Distinction in International Human Rights Law." In *Human Rights of Women: National and International Perspectives*, ed. Rebecca Cook, 85–115. Philadelphia: Univerisity of Pennsylvania Press.

———. 2000. "Themes for a Conversation on Race and Gender in International Human Rights Law." In *Global Critical Race Feminism*, ed. Adrien Katherine Wing, 53–66. New York: New York University Press.

Rose, Gillian. 1993. *Feminism and Geography: The Limits of Geographical Knowledge*. Minneapolis: University of Minnesota Press.

Ruíz, Olivia. 2006. "Migration and Borders: Present and Future Challenges." *Latin American Perspectives* 33, no. 2: 46–55.

Russell, Diana E. H. 1977. "Report on the International Tribunal on Crimes against Women." *Frontiers* 2, no. 1: 1–6.

———. 2001a. "Defining Femicide and Related Concepts." In *Femicide in Global Perspective*, ed. Diana E. H. Russell and Roberta A. Harmes, 12–28. New York: Teachers College Press.

———. 2001b. "Introduction: The Politics of Femicide." In *Femicide in Global Perspective*, ed. Diana E. H. Russell and Roberta A. Harmes, 3–11. New York: Teachers College Press.

Russell, Diana E. H., and Roberta A. Harmes, eds. 2001. *Femicide in Global Perspective*. New York: Teachers College Press.

Russell, Diana E. H., and Jill Radford. 1992. *Femicide: The Politics of Woman Killing*. New York: Twayne.

Sagot, Montserrat. 1994. "Marxismo, interaccionismo simbólico y la opresión de la mujer" (Marxism, Symbolic Interaction, and Women's Oppression"). *Revista de Ciencias Sociales* 63 (March): 88–108.

———. 2004. *Resultados de la Encuesta Nacional de Violencia contra las Mujeres*. San José: Universidad de Costa Rica.

Saiz, Ignacio. 2004. "Bracketing Sexuality: Human Rights and Sexual Orientation: A Decade of Development and Denial at the UN." *Health and Human Rights* 7, no. 2: 48–80.

Sandá, Roxana. 2005. "El tráfico sexual de mujeres en Argentina." *Página 12*, February 4.

Sanford, Victoria. 2008. "From Genocide to Feminicide: Impunity and Human Rights in Twenty-First Century Guatemala." *Journal of Human Rights* 7, no. 2: 104–22.

Santillán, Jorge Regalado. 2002. "Public Security versus Private Security." In *Transnational Crime and Public Security*, ed. John Bailey and Jorge Chabat, 181–91. San Diego: Center for U.S.–Mexican Studies and University of Southern California.

Sassen, Saskia. 2000. "The State and Economic Globalization: Any Implications for International Law?" *Chicago Journal of International Law* 1: 109–16.

———. 2003. "The Repositioning of Citizenship: Emergent Subjects and Spaces for Politics." *New Centennial Review* 3, no. 2: 41–66.

———. 2004. "Strategic Instantiations of Gendering in the Global Economy." Unpublished ms. on file with author, 1–21.

Saul, Ben. 2004. "Compensation for Unlawful Death in International Law: A Focus on the Inter-American Court of Human Rights." *American University International Law Review* 19: 523–85.

Scheman, L. Ronald. 1997. "Banking on Growth: The Role of the Inter-American Development Bank." *Journal of Interamerican Studies and World Affairs* 39: 85–100.

Schirmer, Jennifer. 1998. *The Guatemalan Military Project: A Violence Called Democracy*. Philadelphia: University of Pennsylvania Press.

Schlesinger, Stephen, and Stephen Kizer. 1999. *Bitter Fruit: The Story of the American Coup in Guatemala*. Boston: Harvard University Press.

Schmidt, A. 2000. "Migrant Subjects: Race, Labor and Insurgency in the Mexico–U.S. Borderlands." Ph.D. thesis, Stanford University, Stanford, Calif.

Schmidt Camacho, Alicia. 2004. "Body Counts on the Mexico–U.S. Border: Feminicidio, Reification, and the Theft of Mexican Subjectivity." *Chicana/Latina Studies* 4: 22–61.

Schmitt, Carl. 2006 (1922). *Political Theology*. Chicago: University of Chicago Press.

Scott, Joan W. 1997. *Only Paradoxes to Offer*. Cambridge, Mass.: Harvard University Press.

———. 2002. "Feminist Reverberations." *Differences* 13: 1–23.

Segato, Rita. 2003a. "La estructura de género y el mandato de violación." In *Las estructuras elementales de la violencia. Ensayos sobre género entre la antropología, el psicoanálisis y los derechos humanos*, 21–54. Buenos Aires: Universidad Nacional de Quilmes/Prometeo.

———. 2003b. "La célula violenta que Lacan no vio." In *Las estructuras elementales de la violencia: Ensayos sobre género entre la antropología, el psicoanálisis y los derechos humanos*, 85–107. Buenos Aires: Universidad Nacional de Quilmes/Prometeo.

———. 2003c. "Las estructuras elementales de la violencia." *Prometeo/3010*, Universidad Nacional Quilmes, Buenos Aires.

———. 2004. "Territorio, soberanía y crímenes de segundo estado: La escritura en el cuerpo de las mujeres asesinadas en Ciudad Juárez." In *Ciudad Juárez: De Este Lado del Puente*, ed. Isabel Vericat, 75–93. Mexico City: Epikeia.

———. 2006. *La escritura en el cuerpo de las mujeres asesinadas en Ciudad Juárez.* Mexico City: Universidad del Claustro de Sor Juana.

———. 2007. "Qué es un feminicidio. Notas para un debate emergente." In *Fronteras, violencia, justicia. Nuevos discursos*, ed. Marisa Belausteguigoitia and Lucía Melgar, 35–48. México: Programa Universitario de Estudios de Género, Universidad Nacional Autónoma de México, and United Nations Development Fund for Women.

Sellers, Patricia Viseur. 2002. "Sexual Violence and Peremptory Norms: The Legal Value of Rape." *Case Western Reserve Journal of International Law* 34, no. 3: 287–303.

Servicio Internacional para la Paz. 2005. "Guerrero. Un mosaico de esperanza sobre un muro de impunidad." *Informe 10*, 2.

Sharp, Lesley A. 2000. "The Commodification of the Body and Its Parts." *Annual Review of Anthropology* 29: 287–328.

Shaw, Clifford R., and Henry D. McKay. 1969. *Juvenile Delinquency and Urban Areas: A Study of Rates of Delinquency in Relation to Differential Characteristics of Local Communities in American Cities.* Chicago: University of Chicago Press.

Sideris, Tina. 2002. "Rape in War and Peace." In *The Aftermath: Women in Post-Conflict Transformation*, ed. Sheila Meintjes, Meredith Turshen, and Anu Pillay, 46–62. New York: Zed Books.

Simmons, William Paul. 2006. "Remedies for the Women of Ciudad Juárez through the Inter-American Court of Human Rights." *Northwestern University Journal of International Human Rights* 4: 492–517.

———. 2007. "Liability of Secondary Actors under the Alien Tort Statute: Abiding and Abetting and Acquiescence to Torture in the Context of the Femicides of Ciudad Juárez." *Yale Human Rights and Development Law Journal* 10: 88–140.

Slover, Thomas W. 1999. "Tequila Sunrise: Has Mexico Emerged from the Darkness of Financial Crisis?" *Law and Business Review of the Americas* 5: 91–135.

Smith, Andrea. 2006. "Heteropatriarchy and the Three Pillars of White Supremacy: Rethinking Women of Color Organizing." In *Color of Violence: The Incite! Anthology.* Cambridge, Mass.: South End Press.

Soysal, Yasemin Nuhoolu. 1994. *Limits of Citizenship: Migrants and Postnational Membership in Europe.* Chicago: University of Chicago Press.

Speed, Shannon. 2000. "Mujeres indígenas y resistencia de género a raíz de Acteal: Las acciones dicen mas que las palabras." In *Identidades indígenas y genero*, ed. Mercedes Olivera, 110–29. Tuxtla Gutiérrez: Facultad de Ciencias, Universidad Autónoma de Chiapas.

Spencer, Grace C. 2004–2005. "Her Body Is a Battlefield: The Applicability of the Alien Tort Statute to Corporate Human Rights Abuses in Juárez, Mexico." *Gonzaga Law Review* 40: 503–33.

Staeheli, Lynn. 1996. "Publicity, Privacy and Women's Political Action." *Environment and Planning D: Society and Space* 14: 601–19.

Statistics Canada. 1993. "Violence against Women: Survey Highlights and Questionnaire Package." Canadian Centre for Justice Statistic, Ottawa.

Stephen, Lynn. 1995. "Women's Rights Are Human Rights: The Merging of Feminine and Feminist Interests among El Salvador's Mothers of the Disappeared (CO-MADRE)." *American Ethnologist* 22: 807–27.

Stern, Steven J. 1995. *Women, Men and Power in Late Colonial Mexico: The Secret History of Gender*. Chapel Hill: University of North Carolina Press.

———. 1998. "What Comes after Patriarchy? Reflections from Mexico." *Radical Historical Review* 71: 54–62.

Stevens, Evelyn P. 1971. "Mexican Machismo: Politics and Value Orientations." In *Conflict and Violence in Latin American Politics*, ed. Francisco Jose Moreno and Barbara Mitrani, 80–92. New York: Thomas Y. Cromwell.

Strauss, Murray A., Richard J. Gelles and Suzanne K. Steinmetz. 1980. *Behind Closed Doors: Violence in the American Family*. Garden City, N.Y.: Anchor Books.

Sullivan, Donna. 1995. "The Public/Private Distinction in International Law." In *Women's Rights Human Rights*, ed. Julie Stone Peters and Andrea Wolper, 126–34. New York: Routledge.

"Sumán 43 homicidios desde el viernes hasta esta tarde." 2009. *El Diario*, August 17. Available online at http://www.diario.com.mx (accessed August 23, 2009).

Tabuenca Córdoba, María Socorro. 1996–97. "Viewing the Border: Perspectives from the 'Open Wound.'" *Discourse* 18: 146–95.

———. 2003a. "Baile de fantasmas en Ciudad Juárez al final/principio del milenio." In *Mas allá de la ciudad letrada. Crónicas y espacios urbanos*, ed. Boris Muñoz and Silvia Spitta, 411–37. Pittsburgh: Biblioteca de America, Instituto Internacional de Literatura Iberoamericana, University of Pittsburgh.

———. 2003b. "Día-V Permanente en Ciudad Juárez." *El Diario de Ciudad Juárez*, March 2, 21A.

Taussig, Michael. 1980. *The Devil and Commodity Fetishism in South America*. Chapel Hill: University of North Carolina Press.

Theidon, Kimberley. 2007. "Gender in Transition: Common Sense, Women, and War." *Journal of Human Rights* 6: 453–78.

Thompson, Ginger. 2001. "Chasing Mexico's Dream into Squalor." *New York Times*, February 11, A1.

———. 2002. "Wave of Women's Killings Confounds Juarez." *New York Times*, December 10, A1.

Truong, Thanh-Dam, Saskia Wieringa, and Amrita Chhachhi. 2006. "Introduction: Gender Questions in the Human Security Framework." In *Engendering Human Security: Feminist Perspectives*, ed. Thanh-Dam Truong, Saskia Wieringa, and Amrita Chhachhi, ix–xxx. New York: Zed Books.

Tsing, Anna. 1997. "Transitions and Translations." In *Transitions, Environments, Translations: Feminisms in International Politics*, ed. Joan Scott, Cora Kaplan, and Debra Keates, 253–72. New York: Routledge.

Unga, Mark. 2006. "Crime and Citizen Security in Latin America." In *Latin America after Neoliberalism*, ed. Eric H. and Fred Rosen. New York: New Press and North American Congress on Latin America.

Unidad Revolucionaria Nacional Guatemalteca. 2005. *El feminicidio en Guatemala*. August 10. Available online at http://terrelibere.org (accessed October 6, 2009). Printout on file with volume editors.

United Nations. 1979. "Declaration on the Elimination of Violence against Women." General Assembly Resolution no. 48/104, Geneva.

———. 1991. *The World's Women 1970–1980: Trends and Statistics*. New York: United Nations.

———. 2000. *The World's Women.: Trends and Statistics*. New York: United Nations.

———. 2003a. *Diagnóstico sobre la situación de los derechos humanos en México*. Mexico City. Available online at http://www.cinu.org.mx (accessed August 13, 2009).

———. 2003b. "Report of the Special Rapporteur on Violence against Women: Developments in the Area of Violence against Women (1994–2002)." E/CN.4/2003/75 and Corr.1, January 6.

United Nations Committee against Torture. 2006. *Exámen de los informes presentados por los estados partes en virtud del Artículo 19 de la Convención*. United Nations doc. CAT/C/GTM/CO/4, May 18. Available online at http://www.unhchr.ch (accessed November 26, 2007)

United Nations Development Program. 2005. *Informe sobre el desarrollo humano*. New York.

United Nations General Assembly. 2006. "Guatemala's Many Laws, Programs Need to Be Harmonized to Effectively Address Violence, Trafficking, Women's Anti-Discrimination Committee Told." Press Release, United Nations doc. WOM/1559, May 18.

Urias, Tania. 2005. "El Salvador: Las mujeres también son victimas." Available online at http://www.elsalvador.com.Printout on file with volume editors.

U.S. Department of Justice. 1999. "Board of Immigration Appeals Interim Decision, in re R-A-, 22 I&N Dec. 906." Available online at http://www .usdoj.gov (accessed December 12, 2005).

———. 2000. *Questions and Answers on the R-A- Rule*. December 7. Available online at http://www.ailc.com (accessed March 21, 2005).

U.S. Department of State. 2005. *Guatemala: Country Reports on Human Rights Practices, 2004*. February 28. Washington, D.C.: U.S. Department of State. Available online at http://www.state.gov. Printout on file with volume editors.

———. 2006. *Guatemala: Country Reports on Human Rights Practices, 2005*. March. Washington, D.C.: U.S. Department of State. Available online at http://www.state.gov. Printout on file with volume editors.

Vagts, Detlev F., William S. Dodge and Harold Hongju Koh. 2003. *Transnational Business Problems*. New York: Foundation Press.

Valenzuela, Maria Elena. 1999. "Gender, Democracy and Peace: The Role of the Women's Movement in Latin America." In *Towards a Women's Agenda for a Culture of Peace*, ed. Ingeborg Breines, Dorota Gierycz, and Betty Reardon, 157–79. Paris: United Nations Educational, Scientific, and Cultural Organization.

Van Schaack, Beth. 2004. "With All Deliberate Speed: Civil Human Rights Litigation as a Tool for Social Change." *Vanderbilt Law Review* 57: 2305–48.

Vargas, Jorge A. 2004. "An Introductory Lesson to Mexican Law: From Constitutions and Codes to Legal Culture and NAFTA." *San Diego Law Review* 41: 1337–72.

Vargas, Rosa E. 2004. "Toda la fuerza del estado para aclarar los crímenes de Juárez." *La Jornada*, March 9. Available online at http://www.jornada .unam.mx. Printout on file with volume editors.

———. 2005. "Fox: Resueltas, las dos terceras partes de los feminicidios." *La Jornada*, November 6. Available online at http://www.jornada.unam.mx. Printout on file with volume editors.

Vásquez, Norma. 1997. "Motherhood and Sexuality in Times of War: The Case of Women Militants of the FMLN in El Salvador." *Reproductive Health Matters* 15, no. 9:139–46.

Vela, Manolo, Alexander Sequén-Mónchez, and Hugo Antonio. 2001. *El lado oscuro de la eterna primavera violencia. Criminalidad y delincuencia en la Guatemala de pós-guerra*. Guatemala City: Facultad Latinoamérica de Ciencias Sociales.

Velásquez, Tesania. 2004. *Vivencias deferentes. La indocumentación entre las mu-*

jeres rurales del Perú. Lima: DEMUS, Oxfam International, and Department of International Development (U.K.).

Vesa, Andreea. 2004. "International and Regional Standards for Protecting Victims of Domestic Violence." *American University Journal of Gender, Social Policy and Law* 12: 309–60.

Villaseñor Velardi, Maria Eugenia. 1996. *Violencia domestica y agresión social en Guatemala*. Guatemala City: Fundación Fredrich Ebert.

Vincentini, Ana. 1999. "Entre 'tyche' e automaton. O propio nombre de Edipo." *Percurso* 23, no. 2: 59–67.

Wahi, Namita. 2006. "Human Rights Accountability of the IMF and the World Bank: A Critique of Existing Mechanisms and Articulation of a Theory of Horizontal Accountability." *University of California, Davis, Journal of International Law and Policy* 12: 331–407.

Washington Valdez, Diana. 2005. *Cosecha de mujeres: Safari en el desierto mexicano*. Mexico City: Océano.

Watts, Simon. 2005. "Guatemala Secret Files Uncovered." BBC, December 5. Available online at http://news.bbc.co.uk (accessed January 5, 2006).

Weissbrodt, David, ed. 2001. *International Human Rights: Law, Policy and Process*, 2d ed. Cincinnati, Ohio: Anderson Publishing.

Weissman, Deborah. 2005. "The Political Economy of Violence: Toward an Understanding of the Gender-Based Violence in Ciudad Juárez." *North Carolina Journal of International Law and Commercial Regulation* 30: 795–867.

Werbner, Pnina, and Nira Yuval Davis, eds. 1999. *Women, Citizenship and Difference*. London: Zed Books.

Williams, Patricia J. 2001. "On Being the Object of Property." In *Theorizing Feminism: Parallel Trends in the Humanities and Social Sciences*, ed. Anne C. Herrmann and Abigail J. Stewart, 276–94. Boulder, Colo.: Westview Press.

Wilson, Ara. 2002. "The Transnational Geography of Sexual Rights." In *Truth Claims: Representation and Human Rights*, ed. Mark P. Bradley and Patrice Petro, 251–66. New Brunswick, N.J.: Rutgers University Press.

Wilson, Richard. 2001. *The Politics of Truth and Reconciliation in South Africa: Legitimising the Post-Apartheid State*. Cambridge: Cambridge University Press.

WOLA (Washington Office on Latin America). 2002. "Rescuing Police Reform: A Challenge for the New Guatemalan Government." Executive summary, Washington, D.C., January. Available online at http://www .wola.org. Printout on file with volume editors.

———. 2007. "México: Proyecto de Ley Conjunto de la Cámara de Diputados y el Senado sobre los asesinatos de mujeres en Ciudad Juárez y Chihuahua." Available online at http://www.wola.org (accessed May 2, 2008)

Wright, Melissa W. 1999. "The Dialectics of Still Life: Murder, Women and the Maquiladoras." *Public Culture* 29, no. 3: 453–73.

———. 2001a. "Feminine Villains, Masculine Heroes, and the Reproduction of Ciudad Juarez." *Social Text* 19: 93–113.

———. 2001b. "A Manifesto against Femicide." *Antipode* 33, no. 3: 550–66.

———. 2004. "From Protests to Politics: Sex Work, Women's Worth and Ciudad Juárez Modernity." *Annals of the Association of American Geographers* 94: 369–86.

———. 2005. "Paradoxes, Protests and the Mujeres de Negro of Northern Mexico." *Gender, Place, and Culture* 12: 277–92.

Wyschogrod, Edith. 1985. *Spirit in Ashes: Hegel, Heidegger and Mass Death*. New Haven, Conn.: Yale University Press.

Young, Iris Marion. 2003. "The Logic of Masculinist Protection: Reflections on the Current Security State." *Signs* 29, no. 1: 1–25.

———. 2005. *On Female Body Experience: "Throwing Like a Girl" and Other Essays*. New York: Oxford University Press.

Zamora, Stephen. 1995. "NAFTA and the Harmonization of Domestic Legal Systems: The Side Effects of Free Trade." *Arizona Journal of International and Comparative Literature* 12: 401–28.

Zepeda Lecuona, Ernesto. 2002. "Inefficiency in the Service of Impunity: Criminal Justice Organization in Mexico." In *Transnational Crime and Public Security: Challenges to Mexico and the United States*, ed. John Bailey and Jorge Chabat, 71–107. La Jolla, Calif.: Center for U.S.–Mexican Studies, University of California, San Diego.

Contributors

PASCHA BUENO-HANSEN is an assistant professor in women's studies at the University of Delaware. She is the author of *Queertrafficking through Feminist Movements in the Americas* (forthcoming).

ANA CARCEDO CABAÑAS is a feminist activist and co-founder and president of the Centro Feminista de Información y Acción. She holds a master's in women's studies and teaches and conducts research at the Universidad de Costa Rica. She has published widely in the area of women's human rights, violence against women, and femicide.

ADRIANA CARMONA LÓPEZ is the general director of Attention to Victims of Crimes in Mexico City and the external legal adviser for the Centro de Derechos Humanos de las Mujeres and Justicia para Nuestras Hijas, both in Chihuahua, Mexico, where she helped represent feminicide cases in Ciudad Juárez and Chihuahua and before the Inter-American Commission on Human Rights.

JENNIFER CASEY holds a juris doctorate from the Hastings College of Law, University of California. She practices immigration law in the Boston area.

LUCHA CASTRO RODRÍGUEZ is the coordinator of the Centro de Derechos Humanos de las Mujeres and legal representative for mothers of disappeared and assassinated young women of Ciudad Juárez and Chihuahua, including Justicia para Nuestras Hijas. She has worked as a consultant for nongovernmental organizations and as a mediator in conflict resolution and has instructed workshops on gender, human rights, civil resistance, and Mexican law.

ANGÉLICA CHÁZARO is an attorney with the Northwest Immigrant Rights Project in Seattle. She is the co-author (with Jennifer Casey) of *Getting Away with Murder: Guatemala's Failure to Protect Women and Rodi Alvarado's Quest for Safety* (2006) and "Witnessing Memory and Surviving Domestic Violence: The Case of Rodi Alvarado Peña," in *Passing Lines: Immigration and Sexuality* (2007).

REBECCA COPLAN is pursuing a master's degree in interdisciplinary studies at Arizona State University, with an emphasis on gender in global development. She also co-chairs the Corporate Health and Safety Committee at UPS.

HÉCTOR DOMÍNGUEZ-RUVALCABA is an associate professor in the department of Spanish and Portuguese, University of Texas, Austin. He is the author of *La modernidad abyecta. Formacion del discurso homosexual en Hispanoamérica* (2001); and *Donde las voces fecundan* (2001); *Modernity and the Nation in Mexican Representations of Masculinity: From Sensuality to Bloodshed* (2007). He is the co-editor (with Patricia Ravelo Blancas) of *Entre las duras aristas de las armas. Violencia y victimización en Ciudad Juárez* (2006).

MARTA FONTENLA is an attorney and graduate of Universidad Nacional de Buenos Aires. She has been a feminist activist with the organization Asociación de Trabajo y Estudio de la Mujer "25 de Noviembre" since 1982, working on issues of prostitution and the human trafficking of women and girls, and has published in journals in Argentina and Spain.

ALMA GÓMEZ CABALLERO is a former political prisoner. She has been the director and founder of several organizations working with colonias, teachers, debtors, and women. She is also a former state senator for Chihuahua, Mexico, and a consultant for the Argentine Anthropological Forensic Team. Further, she co-founded Justice for Our Daughters and the Center for Women's Human Rights.

CHRISTINA ITURRALDE is a legal fellow at the Puerto Rican Legal Defense and Education Fund. She is a graduate of the Hastings College of Law, University of California, where she interned with the Center for Gender and Refugee Studies (2004); with Human Rights First, Washington, D.C. (2004); and with the Department of Justice, Executive Office of Immigration Review, San Francisco (2005).

MARCELA LAGARDE Y DE LOS RÍOS has a doctorate in anthropology from the Universidad Nacional Autónoma de México (UNAM) and is a professor of graduate students in anthropology and sociology at the School of Philosophy and Letters and the School of Political and Social Sciences, UNAM; in the Diplomado in Feminist Studies Program, Center for Interdisciplinary Research in Sciences and Humanities; and in the Diplomado in Gender, Democracy, and Development Program, Fundación Guatemala and Center on Sciences and Humanities, UNAM. She served as president of the Comisión Especial para Conocer y Dar Seguimiento a las Investigaciones Relacionadas con los Feminicidios en la República Mexicana y a la Procuración de Justicia Vinculada, Chamber of Deputies, 59th Legislature, in 2003–2006.

JULIA ESTELA MONÁRREZ FRAGOSO is a professor and researcher at El Colegio de la Frontera Norte, Ciudad Juárez, Chihuahua, Mexico. She received her doctorate in social sciences with a specialty in women's studies and gender relations from the Universidad Autónoma Metropolitana and conducts research in gender and violence studies.

HILDA MORALES TRUJILLO is an attorney and holds a master's degree in human rights from the Universidad de San Carlos de Guatemala.She is a member of the Red de la No Violencia contra las Mujeres (Network of Nonviolence against Women). She is the author of *Traduciendo en acciones la* CEDAW *en Guatemala, el caso María Eugenia Morales de Sierra* (2002); *Violencia y legislación. Manual para Administradores de Justicia* (2003); *Derechos humanos de las mujeres en la legislación guatemalteca* (2004); and *Impunidad y violencia contra las mujeres en Guatemala. Conflicto y post conflicto* (2005).

MERCEDES OLIVERA is a researcher at the Center for Higher Studies of Mexico and Central America, Universidad de Ciencias y Artes de Chiapas. She is also a member of the Center for Women's Rights and the Independent Women's Movement, the author of *De cambios, sumisiones y rebeldías: Mujeres indígenas de Chiapas* (2004), and the co-editor (with María Benitez Maldonado) of *Violencia Feminicida en Chiapas* (2008).

PATRICIA RAVELO BLANCAS received her doctorate in Sociology at the Universidad Nacional Autónoma de México (UNAM) and is affiliated with the Centro de Investigaciones y Estudios Superiores en Antropología Social, Mexico City. She is the co-editor (with Sara Elena Pérez-Gil Romo) of *Voces disidentes: Debates contemporáneos en los estudios de género en México* (2004) and the author of "Estrategias y acciones de resistencia en torno de la violencia sexual," *El Cotidiano* (2002), among others.

KATHERINE RUHL is a staff attorney with the Florence Immigrant and Refugee Rights Project. She received her juris doctorate from the University of California, Davis, where she was an active member of the Immigration Law Clinic.

MONTSERRAT SAGOTIS is a professor of sociology and women's studies at the University of Costa Rica; is a founding member of the anti-violence against women movement in Central America; and was the facilitator of some of the first support groups for abused women in Costa Rica in the 1980s. She is the author of *The Critical Path of Women Affected by Family Violence in Latin America: Case Studies from Ten Countries* (2000).

ALICIA SCHMIDT CAMACHO is an assistant professor of American studies at Yale University. She has published articles about gender violence, migration, labor, and human rights in the Mexico–U.S. border region and is the author of *Migrant Imaginaries: Cultural Politics in the Mexico–U.S. Border-*

lands (2007) and *The Carceral Border: Social Violence and Governmentality at the U.S.–Mexican Frontier* (forthcoming).

RITA LAURA SEGATO is a professor in the department of anthropology at the Universidad de Brasilia, senior researcher at the Consejo Nacional de Investigaciones Científicas, and project director with the NGO Ações em Gênero Cidadania e Desenvolvimento (Actions in Gender Citizenship and Development). She is the author of *Santos e daimones. O politeísmo afro-brasileiro ea tradição arquetipal* (2005) and *Las estructuras elementales de la violencia* (2003).

WILLIAM PAUL SIMMONS is an associate professor of political science at Arizona State University. His articles exploring transnational remedies for the femicides in Ciudad Juárez have been published in the *Journal of International Human Rights* and the *Yale Human Rights and Development Law Journal*. He is currently working on a book titled *Human Rights of the Marginalized Other: Toward a Deconstruction and Reinvigoration of Human Rights Law* and has served as a consultant on democracy and human rights issues in the United States, China, and West Africa.

DEBORAH M. WEISSMAN is a professor of law and director of clinical programs at the University of North Carolina School of Law. Her research, teaching, and practice interests include local and international gender-based violence law, civil rights, immigration law, and human rights. She is the author of "The Personal Is Political and Economic: Rethinking Domestic Violence," *Brigham Young University Law Review* (2007); "Un proyecto de derechos humanos: Una perspectiva critica," *TEMAS* (2006); and "The Political Economy of Violence: Toward an Understanding of the Gender-Based Murders of Ciudad Juárez," *North Carolina Journal of International Law and Commercial Regulation* (2005).

MELISSA W. WRIGHT is an associate professor of geography in the department of women's studies at Pennsylvania State University. She is the author of *Disposable Women and Other Myths of Global Capitalism* (2006), as well as many articles on capitalism, gender, power and nationality in Mexico and China.

Index

Page numbers in *italics* refer to illustrations.

National Human Rights Commission
(Mexico), 188, 190, 200, 204
National Statistics Institute, 137
Nayarit, Mexico, xx
Nazar, Leyla, 120
Neoliberal capitalism: female agency
and, 275; feminicidal violence and,
31, 50–55, 277–78, 293; greed and,
70, 72, 84; hypermasculinity and,
159; impact of, 296; power and,
191; social polarization and, 52
Network of Non-violence against
Women, 98, 106, 135
"Ni una Más" campaign, 267–68, 312,
322–23, 325, 327, 329
Nongovernmental organizations
(NGOS): *feminicidio* and, 300, 301;
gender violence and, 291; globalization and, 194; governmental actions and, 190–91; grassroots, 27–
29; mobilization by, xiii; reports to,
xi
Non-nationals, 276
Nores, Ana María, 117, 118, 120, 122
North American Agreement on Labor
Cooperation (NAALC), 238–39
North American Free Trade Agree-
ment (NAFTA): deregulation and,
250; impact of, xiii, 33, 72; rule of
law and, 238–39
Nuestras Hijas de Regreso a Casa, 26,
27–28, 70, 321

OAS (Organization of American
States), 52, 130, 219
Observatorio Ciudadano del Femini-
cidio, 26
Observatorio Ciudadano de los De-
rechos de las Mujeres, 26–27
Observatorios Comunitarios, 26–27
OECD (Organization for Economic
Cooperation and Development),
252–53
Office on Drugs and Crime (U.N.),
171

Optional Protocol 1, 205, 208
Organización Panamericana de la Sa-
lud, 149
Organization for Economic Coopera-
tion and Development (OECD),
252–53
Organization of American States
(OAS), 52, 130, 219
Organized crime: as alternative state,
236; feminicide and, xiv, 192; law
enforcement complicit with, 98;
Mexican government and, 182–85;
state complicit with, 32
Osario, Francisco, 94
Otherness, xiv, 67, 74, 87, 158

"Pacto de sangre" (music video), 186
PAN (Partido Acción Nacional), 325
Panamerican Health Organization,
149
Parga Terrazas, Rubén, 284
Parricide, 129, 130
Partido Acción Nacional (PAN), 325
Partido de la Revolución Democrática
(PRD), xvi, 325–26
Partido Revolucionario Institucional
(PRI), 325
Patriarchy: Civil Code and, 101–2;
feminicidal violence and, xxi, 124,
300; gender relations and, 61; kill-
ing and, 65; law and, 291; misog-
yny and, 13–14; power and, xiv
Pavluczkl, Diego, 120
Peace Accords (1996), 100, 127, 134,
298
Peace and justice, 91
Pelliza, Carlos Alberto, 122
Peña-Irala, Américo Norberto, 210
Pérez, Dinora, 135
Pérez Duarte y Noroña, Alicia Elena,
131
Pérez Mendoza, Jaime, 71
Peru, 293, 295, 298–307
Peruvian Truth and Reconciliation
Commission (TRC), 29, 296, 299

ROSA-LINDA FREGOSO is a professor of Latin American
and Latino studies at the University of California, Santa
Cruz. She is the author of *MeXicana Encounters: The Making
of Social Identities on the Borderlands* (2003) and *Bronze Screen:
Chicana and Chicano Film Culture* (1993). She is the editor of
Lourdes Portillo: The Devil Never Sleeps *and Other Films* (2001)
and (with Norma Iglesias) *Miradas de mujer: Encuentro de
cineastas y videoastas mexicanas y chicanas* (1998).

CYNTHIA BEJARANO is an associate professor of criminal
justice at New Mexico State University. She is the author of
Que Onda? Urban Youth Culture and Border Identity (2005)
and a co-founder of Amigos de las mujeres de Juárez.

Library of Congress Cataloging-in-Publication Data
Terrorizing women : feminicide in the Américas /
Rosa-Linda Fregoso and Cynthia Bejarano, eds.
p. cm.
Includes bibliographical references and index.
ISBN 978-0-8223-4669-2 (cloth : alk. paper)
ISBN 978-0-8223-4681-4 (pbk. : alk. paper)
1. Women — Crimes against — Latin America. 2. Women —
Violence against — Latin America. 3. Murder — Latin
America. I. Fregoso, Rosa Linda. II. Bejarano, Cynthia L.,
1973—
HV6250.4.W65T47 2010
362.83 — dc22   2009047827